Jossey-Bass Teacher

Jossey-Bass Teacher provides educators with practical knowledge and tools to create a positive and lifelong impact on student learning. We offer classroom-tested and research-based teaching resources for a variety of grade levels and subject areas. Whether you are an aspiring, new, or veteran teacher, we want to help you make every teaching day your best.

From ready-to-use classroom activities to the latest teaching framework, our value-packed books provide insightful, practical, and comprehensive materials on the topics that matter most to K–12 teachers. We hope to become your trusted source for the best ideas from the most experienced and respected experts in the field.

The School Counselor's Guide to Helping Students with Disabilities

Laura E. Marshak

Claire J. Dandeneau

Fran P. Prezant

and Nadene A. L'Amoreaux

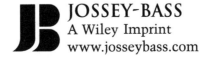

JOSSEY-BASS
A Wiley Imprint
www.josseybass.com

Published by Jossey-Bass
A Wiley Imprint
989 Market Street, San Francisco, CA 94103-1741   www.josseybass.com

Library of Congress Cataloging-in-Publication Data

The school counselor's guide to helping students with disabilities / Laura Marshak . . . [et al.].
    p. cm.   (Jossey-Bass teacher)
   Includes bibliographical references and index.
   ISBN 978-0-470-17579-8 (pbk.)
     1. Students with disabilities—Counseling of—United States.   2. Students with disabilities—Education—United States.   3. Educational counseling—United States.   I. Marshak, Laura E.
   LC4031.S365 2010
   371.91—dc22

2009031945

Printed in the United States of America
FIRST EDITION
PB Printing   10 9 8 7 6 5 4 3 2 1

Contents

PART TWO
MEETING THE NEEDS OF STUDENTS WITH DISABILITIES:
ADDRESSING THE AMPLIFIED ASCA DOMAINS

PART THREE

DISABILITY-SPECIFIC INFORMATION:

IMPLICATIONS AND PRACTICAL APPLICATIONS

Contents

Acknowledgments

This book represents the effort, voice, talents, and wisdom of so many. We thank all who contributed their thoughts, ideas, feelings, and energy. This includes many practicing school counselors, students, parents, and teachers who helped shape our understanding. We can acknowledge only some by name. Others, such as the school counselors who responded to our survey, we thank anonymously.

We are grateful to Kari Hoffman, Josie Badger, Lauren C. Ostrowski, Alice Jacoby, Tina Calabro, Cynthia Rossi, school counselors at Carle Place School District in New York, and Lynn Drucker for their invaluable input. We also wish to note the contributions of Carolyn Grawi, the director of education and advocacy at the Ann Arbor Center for Independent Living, and Gena Clowes, the author of *One of the Gang: Nurturing the Souls of Children with Food Allergies*.

We are indebted to Danielle Wolfe for creating original artwork for the book, copyediting, and endless hours of manuscript preparation. We also could not have done it without the efforts and computer savvy of Jason Mangold, who worked tirelessly to ensure the accuracy of thousands of citations. Our graduate assistants, Melissa Lynch and Kelly Webb, were a great help in researching material for this book. We also appreciated the efforts of Todd Van Wieren for his valuable contributions to Chapter Nine and the Appendixes. Special thanks to Susan J. Glor-Scheib for her valuable consultation on Chapter Four.

We thank Susan Fridie, the clinical director of the Nathaniel Kornreich Technology Center at Abilities! for providing information on assistive technology considerations. We appreciated the candor of the high school students at the Henry Viscardi School who participated in a focus group on plans for the future, obstacles they faced, and their career aspirations. Thanks go to Armand Duerr and Jill Caroll at the Henry Viscardi School for their insights. We also appreciated Marjorie S. McAneny, senior editor at Jossey-Bass, for understanding that life does not always go according to plan.

About the Authors

Laura E. Marshak is a professor in the Department of Counseling at Indiana University of Pennsylvania (IUP). She has a doctorate in rehabilitation counseling and was a professor of rehabilitation in the Department of Special Education for many years at IUP. This is her sixth book that addresses disability-related topics. These include being a coauthor of *Married with Special Needs Children (2007), Disability and the Family Life Cycle (1999),* and *Counseling Persons with Physical Disabilities* (1993). She has spoken at many national and international conferences on related topics. She has a particular interest in the impact of disability on marriages and families. Marshak is a cofounder of North Hills Psychological Services in Pittsburgh, Pennsylvania, where she specializes in working with parents of children with disabilities and adjustment issues for adolescents and adults with disabilities.

Claire J. Dandeneau is a professor and chairperson of the Department of Counseling at Indiana University of Pennsylvania, where she has also served as interim dean of the graduate school and research. She has a doctorate in counselor education. Dandeneau is a Licensed Professional Counselor and an Approved Clinical Supervisor. She has coauthored two other books: *Elementary School Counseling: A Commitment to Caring and Community Building* (2nd edition, 2003) and *Working with Adolescents: Building Effective Communication and Choice-Making Skills* (1994). In 2005, she received the Pennsylvania Counselor Educator of the Year award. She is a former director of residential and treatment services for John de la Howe School in South Carolina. She also worked for the Texas Youth Commission at its Fairfield Wilderness Camp as a group work supervisor and counselor in a therapeutic wilderness camping program.

Fran P. Prezant is a senior vice president and director of Research and Evaluation at Abilities! (National Center for Disability Services) in New York. She has a master's degree in speech and language pathology and is certified by the American Speech Language and Hearing Association. Prezant was a therapist in public and private settings and in 1986 joined the faculty at Indiana University of Pennsylvania where she taught in the Department of Special Education and developed and administered the Parent Information Project, a program for parents of children with disabilities. In 1999, she joined Abilities!, a nonprofit organization dedicated to enhancing self-sufficiency, independence, and participation by people with disabilities. Through her work there, she has directed innovative programs; written employment, training, and educational grants; and presented nationally and internationally. She has been actively involved in increasing access for people with disabilities in the New York City area through her representation on the Steering Committee of the New York Museum Access Consortium. Prezant has coauthored *Married with Special Needs Children* (2007) and *Disability and the Family Life Cycle* (1999) as well as numerous journal articles on disability issues.

Nadene A. L'Amoreaux is an associate professor in the Department of Counseling at Indiana University of Pennsylvania, where she teaches courses relevant to working with children in community and school settings. She received her doctorate from Kent State University, is a licensed professional counselor, and works part time as a counselor with children, adolescents, adults, couples, and families. Her previous work experience includes working in community mental health settings with injured workers as a rehabilitation counselor and in higher education in student services.

Preface

This book grew out of a spirited debate between two of the authors. One of us expressed surprise at learning that graduate students preparing to be school counselors did not have a requirement to learn to work with students who have disabilities. For her, having been a professor of rehabilitation in a special education department before transferring to a counseling department, this seemed inconceivable. The other one of us, a professor of counselor education, said that school counseling students were being prepared since they were learning to work developmentally with all students and viewed disability as a multicultural issue. Furthermore, she thought that it was unnecessary to view the needs of students with disabilities as somehow different from others.

We realized quickly that the dichotomy of our views was not unique. In fact, a search of school counseling textbooks verified that very little attention (sometimes as little as a paragraph) was given to working with children and youth with disabilities. We surmised that school counseling students might be getting this knowledge in other academic departments, like special education, school psychology, or rehabilitation. We also speculated to the compartmentalized nature of higher education where each discipline can be seen as a silo, and though we teach collaboration, very little true collaboration exists in higher education. We decided to write a book for school counselors that circumvented the inadvertent barrier between the knowledge of disability specialists (in rehabilitation and special education) from that knowledge generally provided to school counselors in their own discipline.

Our goal was to develop this book to serve as a resource for practicing school counselors and counselor educators, to provide them the insight, knowledge, and strategies to work more effectively to meet the needs of students with disabilities. Toward this end, we formed a collaboration with other professionals who brought a depth of knowledge about working with students with disabilities and their parents, educational advocacy, vocational rehabilitation, child counseling, and school counseling. Two of the authors are professionals in the disability field and also have raised their own children with disabilities.

In addition to our combined and varied areas of expertise, different vantage points, and years of experience, we sought the input of others: practicing school counselors, other school personnel, and students with different types of disabilities. We elicited their thoughts and feelings through focus groups, questionnaires, and interviews in our attempt to fully understand the nature of many of their challenges and the approaches most commonly used to address them. Our desire was to have each chapter permeated by multiple professional perspectives as well as the candid reflections of students and their parents.

This book is divided into three parts.

The five chapters in Part One are designed to provide a general foundation of knowledge for school counselors so that they can more comprehensively integrate disability into their counseling programs. Chapter One outlines the expanded role of the school counselor. We present the specialized developmental needs of students with disabilities, which we identify as "amplified" as compared to their typical peers. In addition, Chapter One applies this concept to the American School Counselor Association (ASCA) Domains and Standards.

A major obstacle for students with disabilities is that professionals, as well as the public, often do not see their potential or the ways in which effective, appropriate help can be provided. Therefore, Chapter Two focuses on some common assumptions that may interfere with understanding the needs of students with disabilities. It also provides basic and practical information to enable counselors to be more comfortable interacting with students and their parents. Chapter Three details how to transform a school counseling program so that it facilitates competency development for students with disabilities. It also explores the key concepts related to the inclusion of students with disabilities into school counseling programs and how school counselors can provide the critical leadership and advocacy to make effective inclusion happen. Chapter Four provides an essential understanding of the letter and the spirit of the federal legislation related to students with disabilities, helping readers appreciate the historical context that led to this landmark legislation. In addition, this chapter includes an understanding of the role of the school counselor in Individualized Education Program (IEP) meetings, Section 504 plans, and transition plans.

Chapter Five examines ways for school counselors to form more effective partnerships with parents and sensitizes readers to some of the frequent experiences, feelings, and realities for the parents of children with disabilities.

The focus of Part Two is the ASCA domains: academic, personal/social, and career. The amplified developmental needs identified in Chapter One are explored in depth for each domain. Chapter Six discusses ways in which school counselors can be instrumental in addressing the academic needs of students with disabilities. It explores a range of potential strategies that school counselors should be familiar with, such as instructional adaptations, classroom accommodations, and assistive technologies. Ways the school counselor's role can help teachers create a positive learning environment are also discussed. Chapter Seven addresses the personal and social needs of young children with disabilities, with special attention to the effects of peers and peer relationships. It includes strategies for promoting resilience and social integration in school settings beyond the classroom. Chapter Eight is devoted to the personal and social needs of secondary students with disabilities.

These needs often intensify during adolescence because key aspects of development become more complex for these youth. There are often disability-related considerations regarding identity, sexuality, and separation and individuation. In addition, social rejection often peaks, and the school day becomes quite difficult. Ways that counselors can help are presented.

Chapter Nine focuses on the important domain of career education and development. Although school counselors are trained in career counseling, the issues surrounding the career needs of children with disabilities are rarely addressed. This chapter seeks to bridge that knowledge gap by presenting the career needs of children with disabilities and the unique challenges they face. It also addresses how to help prepare students for the transition to work, training, or higher education.

Part Three provides practical information about disabilities that fall under each of the thirteen categories of the Individuals with Disabilities Act (IDEA). For each disability we provide the following:

- General background information about the disability

- What students and parents wish that teachers and school counselors knew about their disability

- Practical applications in the personal, social, academic, and career areas for school counseling and consulting with teachers and IEP, Section 504, and transition teams

- Resources to acquire more detailed information about the specific disability

As we reflect on the journey of writing this book, we are acutely aware of how much we have learned. We have affirmed our collective belief in cross-disciplinary synergy. This book is so much richer than any one of us could have written alone. We see the outcome of our efforts as a true representation of the ASCA qualities of leadership, collaboration, and advocacy. Our hope is that in some small measure, we are contributing to a broad systemic change in how school counseling programs respond to the needs of students with disabilities.

Part One

Counseling Students with Disabilities

The Basics

Chapter 1

Possibilities and Practicalities

Many students with disabilities who are now grown have been in our thoughts while writing this book. One of them is a man, now a research scientist, whose attention deficit hyperactivity disorder resulted in his being described as "absolutely unmanageable and unwilling to listen." We are also thinking about the man with Down syndrome who is an integral part of his community and a highly valued employee. Then there is the master's-level therapist whose dyslexia posed major problems throughout her school years. All of these former students surprised many people. But it is very hard to predict outcomes when it comes to students with disabilities. What we can predict is that they will run into obstacles that hinder their possibilities and that this will usually occur far more often than for typical students. We can also predict that their capabilities often exceed what people commonly assume.

The title of this chapter embodies our overriding goal for this book. Our purpose for this book is to provide a resource that helps counselors understand what students with disabilities can achieve—their possibilities—and how school counselors can be a critical part of the team that helps this happen by understanding the realities and the challenges that these young people face—the practicalities. This book arose from the recognition that only a minority of school counselors receive course work in the area of disability in their graduate education, yet they are faced with great responsibility for these students. The issue of lack of training yet much professional involvement with students with disabilities is confirmed by the research study conducted by Milsom in 2002.[1] Anecdotally, a counselor we interviewed was pulled aside in her first week on the job and told that she would be handling all of the students with disabilities in the school. She had never taken one disability-related class and had never worked with a student with a disability up to that point.

Given this reality, we have worked to create a user-friendly resource that reflects the realities of the working roles of school counselors, which includes many more students with disability as part of their already large student caseloads. One school counselor remarked to us, "It seems as if 20 percent of my caseload are classified [with disabilities] and consume 80 percent of my time. There is never enough time to attend to everyone's needs." This reality is very consistent with the national data. Estimates are that approximately 7 million students in schools have disabilities. These students represent nearly 14 percent of all students in school.[2] The national average ratio, as reported by ASCA, is 479 students per 1 school counselor (the recommended ASCA ratio is 250:1 students per counselor).[3] When these data are extrapolated, this means that each school counselor will have at least 67 students with disability on his or her caseload. We know that this figure is actually a low estimate because the figure is higher in the general or adult population: estimates are that 1 in 5 adults, or 20 percent, for a total of 59 million individuals, have been identified with disabilities in the United States.[4] This makes the number of students with disabilities served by a school counselor much higher. Using these estimates, school counselors would serve nearly a hundred students with disabilities on their already extremely high caseloads.

Despite these pressures and constraints, the potential of school counselors to make a real difference in the lives of students with disabilities is far greater than is often realized. Not only can school counselors help individual students in meaningful ways, but they can have an impact on programming that can affect the millions of students with disabilities.

Putting this information in a historical context is important. It is easy to assume that students with disabilities have always been a part of our educational system. But this is not true. We have come a long way from the time in which children with disabilities had no right to an education. Before the Americans with Disabilities Act (ADA) was implemented in 1990, the civil rights of children (and adults) with disabilities were not protected in general. For example, in 1988, Senator Lowell Weicker made the following statement when he introduced the ADA before Congress:

> People with cerebral palsy are turned away from restaurants because proprietors say their appearance will upset other patrons. People who use wheelchairs are blocked by curbs, steps and narrow doorways from getting into many arenas, stadiums, theatres and other public buildings; many facilities have no provisions for people with hearing and visual impairments. It has been over 30 years since the zoos and parks were closed to keep blacks from visiting them at the height of the civil rights demonstrations and boycotts. Yet it was only last month that *The Washington Post* reported the story of a New Jersey zookeeper who refused to admit children with Down's syndrome because he feared they would upset the chimpanzees.[5]

Before the passage of PL-142, Education for All Handicapped Children Act (later renamed IDEA), in 1975, all children with disabilities were placed in the same classroom despite their abilities or at times totally excluded or denied entrance to school. For example, "A 1989 Commission on Disability report from the California Attorney General noted that 'In one town, all disabled children are grouped into a single classroom regardless of individual ability.' A bright child with cerebral palsy was assigned to a class with mentally retarded and other developmentally disabled children solely because of her physical disability."[6] This actually occurred more than eight years after states were required to comply with the federal mandate to provide a free, appropriate public education, consistent with the student's individual needs and provided in the least restrictive setting.

Although such blatant examples of discrimination do not occur as routinely today, students with disabilities are still sometimes seen as less important than other children. This shows up in many ways. One mother recently mentioned that in her school, "The special education students were all grouped together at the end of our graduation ceremony. It was like they were the caboose on a train." Examples abound. These include the report of a teacher in Florida who allowed the classmates of a five year old, who was being evaluated for Asperger's syndrome, to vote him out of class after he had been sent to the principal's office twice for discipline problems.[7] To a large extent, what these situations have in common is an "us" and "them" mind-set—a dividing line between children and children with disabilities.

Students with disabilities have a right to a school environment in which "disabilities are viewed as neither bizarre nor embarrassing, nor unduly burdensome, but rather as natural expected and even welcomed."[8] School counselors have an important role in realizing this ideal.

The Role of the School Counselor

The role of the school counselor in the lives of students with disabilities is often not clearly understood, and this ambiguity can lead to role confusion for practicing school counselors. We believe that it is important to address this issue and clarify the school counselor's role in helping the student with disabilities.

Before we look at some of the specifics, we present two common and problematic viewpoints that frequently define the role of the school counselor:

- Problematic view 1: Students with disabilities are not the school counselor's responsibility.

- Problematic view 2: School counselors work with all children. In so doing, they are responding to the needs of children with disabilities.

These outdated viewpoints limit school counselors' contact with students with disabilities and decrease the potential effectiveness of their place in those students' lives.

The first problematic view is that the responsibility for addressing the needs of students with disabilities is a matter for the special education department, not the school counselor or school counseling program. One mother of two children with disabilities spoke of this reality:

> Our school district had a policy that if you were a student with a disability that had an IEP [individualized educational program] attached, you didn't really work with the school counselors at all. . . . If you tried to talk to the school counselors, they would always say, "I'm sorry, you have to go through the office of special education." I tried to tell them that the counseling department needed to be heavily involved with all students who had disabilities. . . . I tried to let them know that it was a really important issue, especially for career counseling [when it came to that point], but it just did not change.

The widespread belief that students with disabilities belong to the special education department further marginalizes them and does not allow them to benefit from the school counselor's expertise or the school counseling programs. This is just one of many ways in which the false dichotomy between children and children with disabilities results in separate services that diminish their potential.[9] It is easy to see how this resulting marginalization is the antithesis of the philosophy of school counseling. However, this often represents the day-to-day reality of many school counselors. Given this reality, it is helpful and important that special education is considered a service, not a place.[10] Viewed as a service, it is much easier to see how it can and should dovetail with the school counseling programs. This collaborative mind-set fosters a tremendous synergy in meeting the needs of children with disabilities. According to Snow, "It's [special education] supposed to be a method of helping a child become successful in the same world the rest of us are in."[11] Undoubtedly school counseling personnel, programs, and services are an essential part of that process.

The second role viewpoint that undercuts the potential of school counselors to make a difference for these students is the belief that students with disabilities are just like all the other students in a school. School counselors with this mind-set believe that their role is to serve the developmental needs of all children. Subsumed within this role is the mistaken belief that the developmental needs of students with disabilities are the same as those of their peers who do not have disabilities. Thus, they mistakenly believe that they are indeed serving the students with disabilities. Despite the good intentions of school counselors with this view, this strategy has not worked because the lives of students with disabilities in the school setting are not like those of the other children, and their developmental needs are often amplified and distinctive. They face very different obstacles, and often their developmental transitions are more complicated for logistical and personal reasons.

Throughout this book, we present the developmental reality of students with disabilities and seek to inspire school counselors to do right by these students by recognizing them and addressing those amplified needs. We present these amplified developmental differences within the context of the ASCA National Standards for academic, personal/social, and career development.

The best starting point for gaining clarity and understanding the role of school counselors with students with disabilities is ASCA's position statement, *The Professional School Counselor and Students with Special Needs.* The foundational belief on which the school-stated role is based reads, "Professional school counselors are committed to helping all students realize their potential and make adequate yearly progress despite challenges that may result from identified disabilities and other special needs."[12] Specifically, this commitment to students with disabilities translates to the actual role that ASCA defines for them as follows:

When appropriate, interventions in which the professional school counselor participates may include but are not limited to:

- Leading school counseling activities as a part of the comprehensive school counseling program
- Providing collaborative services consistent with those services provided to students through the comprehensive school counseling program
- Serving on the school's multidisciplinary team that identifies students who may need assessments to determine special needs within the scope and practice of the professional school counselor
- Collaborating with other student support specialists in the delivery of the services

- Providing group and individual counseling
- Advocating for students with special needs in the school and in the community
- Assisting with the establishment and implementation of plans for accommodations and modifications
- Providing assistance with transitions from grade to grade as well as post-secondary options
- Consulting and collaborating with staff and parents to understand the special needs of those students
- Making referrals to appropriate specialist within the school system and the community

The professional school counselor advocates for students with special needs and is one of many school staff members who may be responsible for providing information as written plans are prepared for students with special needs.[13]

This position statement is an important starting point. We believe that school counselors need to play many additional instrumental roles. They are critical school professionals who can have a tremendous impact on the quality of school life for students with disabilities by facilitating their academic, personal and social, and career achievement and success.

Promoting Genuine Inclusion

One of these vital roles is to help students with disabilities to be genuinely included. Despite the passage of valuable federal legislation, students with disabilities often do not experience genuine inclusion. There is a difference between presence and participation in educational opportunities. Murray described the common occurrence of "exclusion wearing the face of inclusion . . . of being there without in any real sense belonging."[14] Illustrations of this phenomenon are all too plentiful, like the example taken from the recent experience of a mother of a young daughter with Down syndrome. She was very happy that her daughter was included in a regular kindergarten and met with the teacher before the school year began. She found her to be warm and welcoming. However, when she attended the first parents' night, her daughter's artwork was not displayed on the wall with the other children's and her daughter did not appear in the videotaped class performance of a dance routine. This dramatic exclusion was done by a kind-hearted, well-intentioned teacher. The teacher thought that somehow masking this little girl's differences was better for everyone. Done under the guise of inclusion, such exclusion can be the most harmful for the child and, as in this case, for the parent as well. School counselors must take a leadership role and work to ensure that professional educators fully embrace inclusion. More important, schools must strive to create an overall, genuine inclusive attitude. "Inclusion," however, "requires more than allowing the other in."[15]

School counselors play a critical role in advocating for genuine inclusion and finding ways to help this happen. They consult with teachers, help create welcoming social environments, and solve logistical problems that present barriers to inclusion. There is an exception that is important to note: occasionally parents do not want inclusion because it is not in the best interests of their child. An example might be when a child's autism is so severe that his needs cannot be met in a public school setting that can offer only an approximation of the intense specialized educational and therapeutic interventions that are needed throughout the day. The best interest of the child always supersedes the emphasis on inclusion.

Looking Out for Students

Protecting the rights of children with disabilities in the school environment is another key aspect of the school counselor's role. Parette and Hourcade identify one important role as addressing the many instances of intentional and unintentional discrimination against students with disabilities that occur in the school environment.[16]

In addition to fostering more genuine inclusion and protecting these students' rights, school counselors can help students with disabilities manage the complexities of school that are introduced by virtue of having a disability. There is no doubt that school is harder for those with a disability; in addition, others are not always aware of some of these difficulties. For instance, we may not be aware of the fears of some students with physical disabilities of being knocked down in crowded halls filled with students changing classes or the unusual levels of fatigue that accompany some disorders. Other difficulties for those with physical or nonvisible disabilities such as learning disabilities include embarrassment, being accused of not trying hard enough, not fitting in, needing help but being embarrassed to ask, being bullied, and falling behind due to illnesses or learning difficulties despite trying hard to keep up. In different ways, many view the role of the school counselor as making school easier and safer. For example, one principal described how she views the role of school counselors: "We need to help children with disabilities navigate through the mainstream. They tend to fall through the cracks."

Along similar lines, Milsom sees school counselors as needing to play a role in helping other educators "create more positive school experiences that promote their academic, career, and personal/social growth."[17] Rutter (1985) underscored the importance of positive school experiences: "The long-term educational benefits from positive school experiences probably stem less from what children are specifically taught than from effects on children's attitude to learning, on their self-esteem, and on their task orientation and work strategies."[18]

Addressing the Needs of Stakeholders: Parents, Teachers, and Students

Many school counselors view their role as being in a unique position to assist students with disabilities, their parents, and teachers. School counselors work collaboratively with parents and school professionals to provide meaningful and appropriate opportunities for each child's academic, personal and social, and career development needs. It is highly important that school counselors stand as strong advocates for these needs. A counselor who responded to our survey exemplified this advocacy: "I'm passionate about getting everything for my children and their families but I've been criticized by upper-level administration for going the extra mile for them. I've dared to tell their parents about their rights and to ask hard questions even when I get into trouble for mentioning things like 504, ADHD, etc. If I'm going to get in trouble, I want it to be because I've stretched the rules to help a child."

Deck, Scarborough, Sferrazza, and Estill emphasize the role of the school counselor with other stakeholders: "When planning school counseling programs, school counselors need to identify the specific guidance and counseling needs of students with disabilities, as well as the related needs of these students' parents and teachers."[19] Another school counselor elaborates on this multifaceted role:

> I believe that school counselors' skills in empathy and communication put them in the natural position of being able to empathize with all stakeholders involved in the inclusion process. As a school counselor, I see my role as the professional who looks out for the social and emotional health of the school community. You are not a special education specialist. But you are a specialist in dealing with the emotions of children and adults. As school counselors, we can help schools hear what parents' hopes and dreams are for their child and we can facilitate communication between the school and the parents. We are also in a position to empathize with and support teachers. We need to be able to imagine what it is like to be in someone else's shoes. For the student: "What is it like to be in this environment? What is it like to be in the hallways?" We also need to understand what it feels like to be the teacher in a classroom with challenging students.

This counselor's view of her role and her guiding philosophy is clearly reflected in her work. Once a school counselor has walked in the shoes of everyone involved, he or she can assimilate all of those needs into a plan that will bring everyone together and meet the needs of the identified child. An example is shown pictorially in Figure 1.1 and as a narrative in "My Role as a Counselor in Eliza's World."

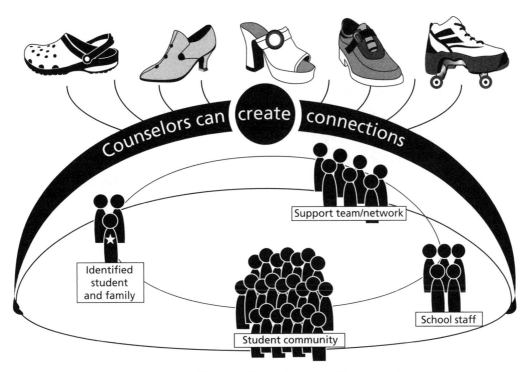

Figure 1.1 Counselors Create Connections

My Role as a Counselor in Eliza's World

Even before I transferred to my new job as the school counselor in an elementary school across town, I was a part of the team. A first-grade student, previously placed in an out-of-district classroom for children with hearing impairments, would be starting in our school in the fall. We needed to prepare. Our team consisted of the school principal, special education team chair, school nurse, special education teacher, speech and language pathologist, classroom teacher, classroom aide, and the school counselor. We met with our new educational audiologist. We trained, discussed, negotiated, brainstormed, and unified as a support network for this young girl—I'll call her Eliza—who has a cochlear implant.

The classroom teacher, as well as all staff, would need to use an FM system to directly connect to Eliza's cochlear implant. She would also need to be pretaught all instruction and vocabulary before school each day so she would be able to access the curriculum in the

(Continued)

My Role as a Counselor in Eliza's World (Continued)

regular classroom. Her classroom was carpeted, and sound-reducing feet were placed on chairs in the resource room. We were taught that when communicating with Eliza, we needed to get her attention and talk face-to-face so she could speech-read [read our lips]. As we discussed these needs, my thoughts began to center on how to widen Eliza's world. We should not be the only ones in the school to get this training. Playground aides, lunch staff, custodians, secretaries—all needed this information. What about her future friends? How could we help all of our student population to understand how to be friends with this sparkling, vibrant, eager first grader?

As a school counselor, I see my role as the professional who looks out for the social and emotional health of the school community. Eliza needed the road to relationships paved with the education of her peers. We needed to teach her typically developing peers and their parents about her learning differences. In my counseling program, I provide biweekly lessons in all of our classrooms. Every time I visit a classroom, I send home a brief newsletter to parents outlining my lesson for that day. This lesson would be called "Hearing in a Different Way." I felt the best method of instruction would be to use a story for young children that would spark discussion, allow modeling, and eliminate barriers to friendships. After researching many Web sites and libraries, I discovered that there was nothing available that met my needs. So I wrote Eliza's story. The book speaks directly to the audience about Eliza's life story in a nontechnical, down-to-earth, kid-to-kid manner.

It addresses the skills peers need to get a friend's attention, talk face-to-face, speak slowly and clearly, and keep trying to get a friend's attention even if they don't hear the first time. It goes on to describe how the teacher uses an FM system and what students can do in situations where it may be more difficult to understand spoken language: in cafeterias, playgrounds, assemblies, and so forth.

I needed to be sensitive to Eliza and her family, so they were my first audience to read and hear the book. Through our tears, I realized the parents were put at ease, and Eliza was thrilled to have her story told in such a developmentally appropriate manner. Eliza even agreed that when I shared the story with the other classes, she would like to help to teach that lesson! Eliza trusted her new school and felt safe enough to not only share her story but demonstrate how her implant worked, show what face-to-face discussion looks like, and teach others how to get her attention.

At school, our ongoing struggles include how to make sure all of the students know how to use the microphone to the FM system throughout the school day. Our team must ensure safety protocols that consider Eliza's needs in an evacuation drill, bus drill, or lockdown drill. My recent discussions with Eliza have been about meeting other students who use special technology to hear, see, or even touch (one of our students uses a prosthesis on her arm). Now Eliza and I can help other students to understand if they have questions or point and whisper, wondering, "What is *that* on her ear?"

Eliza is now viewed as a happy first-grade student, running on the playground with her friends, talking and laughing at lunch, and learning reading, writing, and math. More important, she has taught me that school counselors can truly make a difference.

Kari S. Hoffmann, elementary school counselor (November 2007).

Fostering Resilience

School counselors can also play a critical role in fostering resilience. As Werner stated, "Resilient children have at least one person who accepts them unconditionally, regardless of temperamental idiosyncrasies, physical attractiveness or intelligence."[20] School counselors are often in a better position than some other educators to be that person. Segal described the importance in the school environment of a "person with whom they identify *and from whom they gather strength.*"[21] One example of why this is so important can be found in the comments of a student with a learning disability who reflected back on her childhood school memories: "I was constantly told to sit down, to stop talking; if the teacher gave instructions, I was always one step behind everyone; if we were supposed to hang up our coats, I would be easily distracted by something else. I was constantly yelled at for being disruptive, and I remember feeling guilty, but also confused: I did not mean to disrupt my class, and I often didn't even realize I was doing anything wrong."[22]

Resiliency development helps foster the persistence and hope that all students need to achieve and succeed in school and in life. As important as this is for all students, we believe students with disabilities have a heightened need for resiliency. Werner described resilient individuals as having a "a feeling of confidence that odds can be surmounted."[23] They can often bounce back from difficulties and retain a hope for the future in the face of problems. They face rather than avoid problems and appreciate their personal strengths. Hope is also an important component of resiliency that enables students with disabilities to persist even when they are feeling worn down by obstacles. The concept of fostering resilience encapsulates much of our approach to working with students with disabilities. It provides some of the scaffolding that undergirds their success in achieving academic, career and personal and social competencies.

Neill offers a basic formula for thinking about fostering resilience:[24]

Growth = challenge and support.

We build on this basic approach to fostering resilience, and readers will find discussions of resilience throughout the book, especially as it pertains to the different domains of functioning. In short, we believe that school counselors should help students with disabilities:

- Acquire the resiliency attitudes, knowledge, and skills that will help them deal with life's challenges

- Understand that positive growth in all areas of life comes from being challenged

- Learn to appreciate the value of support and assistance and use it to enhance their growth

Amplified Needs

The overall purpose of the school counseling program is to help student achieve the personal and social, career, and academic competencies defined in the ASCA standards.

As we discuss throughout this book, students with disabilities generally have amplified needs in each of the three domains. We use the term *amplified* to denote needs that are intensified or more complex (although not necessarily unique). We are only introducing this concept at this point. Each of the remaining chapters contributes to understanding what is meant by these amplified needs and how to address them productively. It is important to clarify that many of these amplified needs are due to the circumstances surrounding living with a disability and do not reflect inherent limitations. Examples include higher rates of sexual abuse, restricted opportunities to develop interests and hobbies, and heightened needs for self-advocacy due to environmental and social barriers. Certainly some disabilities also directly have an impact on these competencies apart from any environmental considerations. For example, children and youth with disorders such as Asperger's syndrome have a harder time acquiring competencies in the personal and social domain, yet these are critical. Therefore, we believe one of the most important roles of school counselors as they work with students who have disabilities is to address these amplified developmental needs in a manner that helps these young people achieve the possibilities in their lives.

Blum's discussion of the transition of adolescents with disabilities into adulthood reflects our concern: "There is substantial evidence that young adults with disabilities are less likely than their peers to realize their future. They are less likely to marry—though their marital aspirations are not different from their peers—and they are less likely to be employed. They are less likely to achieve higher education and independent living."[25] When we address the needs of students with disabilities in this deliberate and purposeful fashion, we are realizing our mission to fully serve all children and doing so without losing sight of their amplified needs.

The ASCA National Standards Amplification of the Needs of Students with Disabilities

Exhibits 1.1, 1.2, and 1.3 present an overview of the amplified developmental needs within the context of the ASCA standards. In-depth information about these needs is provided in Chapters Six through Nine.

Exhibit 1.1 Amplified Academic Domain

Academic Domain

Amplified: Academic developmental needs are particularly amplified for students whose disabilities interfere with the many aspects of learning. This includes students with attention deficit disorder/attention deficit hyperactivity disorder, learning disabilities, mental health disorders and cognitive disabilities (mental retardation), and traumatic brain injuries.

Standard A

Students will acquire the attitudes, knowledge, and skills that contribute to effective learning in school and across the life span.

(Continued)

Exhibit 1.1 Amplified Academic Domain (Continued)

A: A1—Improve Academic Self-Concept

Amplified: For many students, academic struggles can result in a domino effect in which difficulties affect academic self-efficacy and academic self-esteem. This becomes manifest in the mind-set, "Other kids can do it, and I can't." Simply being placed in "special education" can be internalized as being "less than" and deficient. These students need to be able to retain a sense of academic self-esteem even if their learning styles differ from more typical classmates.

A: A2—Acquire Skills for Improving Learning

Amplified: Students who frequently face academic disappointments need additional skills to bounce back and persist.

A: A3—Achieve School Success

Amplified: Students with disabilities often face an uphill battle because they are dealing with unremitting challenges throughout school. Some of the challenges stem directly from disabilities, and many others stem from physical, social, and attitudinal barriers in school environments. In order to achieve school success, students need to manage potential problems ranging from academic accommodations to social exclusion.

Standard B

Students will complete school with the academic preparation essential to choose from a wide range of substantial postsecondary options, including college.

A: B1—Improve Learning

Amplified: For students with disorders that affect learning, academic standards are often lowered. These students have a need for educators to accept their differences and find the best instructional strategies to help them improve their learning.

A: B2—Plan to Achieve Goals

This is not an amplified need due to the fact that federal regulations mandate academic planning with Individualized Educational

Programs (IEP) or 504 plans. (IEP and 504 plans are defined and detailed in Chapter Four.)

Standard C

Students will understand the relationship of academics to the world of work and to life at home and in the community.

A: C1—Relate School to Life Experiences

Amplified: Some students with disabilities have limited exposure to a broader range of life experiences. There is a need to be proactive in making sure school-based after-school activities are accessible to them. Students with disabilities have a much higher dropout rate than typical students. Therefore, they have an amplified need to connect academics to the real world. This provides them with a reason to persist.

Exhibit 1.2 Amplified Personal and Social Domain

Personal and Social Domain

Amplified: Personal and social developmental needs are particularly amplified for students whose disabilities interfere with their acquisition of interpersonal skills. This includes students with attention deficit disorder/attention deficit hyperactivity disorder, learning disabilities, mental health disorders, cognitive disabilities (mental retardation), and brain injuries.

Standard A

Students will acquire the knowledge, attitudes, and interpersonal skills to help them understand and respect self and others.

PS: A1—Acquire Self-Knowledge

Amplified: Students with disabilities are often prone to internalizing societal stereotypes and being devalued, resulting in a negative

(Continued)

Exhibit 1.2 Amplified Personal and Social Domain (Continued)

self-image. Students need to recognize their many attributes along with understanding their disability.

PS: A2—Acquire Interpersonal Skills

Amplified: Some disabilities have a direct impact on the acquisition of interpersonal skills. Social skills deficiencies can often jeopardize their ability to be an included member of the classroom and the school community. Some students with disabilities need intentional fostering of social skills as part of their general education. In addition, students with disabilities have a higher need for self-advocacy skills.

Standard B

Students will make decisions, set goals, and take necessary action to achieve goals. This standard is particularly amplified for students who have grown accustomed to high levels of assistance and direction. These students need educators to provide opportunities for self-determination so that they may take a more active role in formulating and achieving their goals.

PS: B1—Self-Knowledge Application

Amplified: Students with disabilities generally have experienced relatively fewer opportunities to make their own decisions. This is a consequence of being the recipients of high levels of professional and parental help. They often have an amplified need to practice making decisions, setting personal goals, and acting on their own behalf.

Standard C

Students will understand safety and survival skills.
Amplified: Students with disabilities experience shockingly high rates of sexual and other forms of abuse, including drug abuse. This creates many amplified needs for safety. Also, certain medical disabilities carry an inherent survival risk.

PS: C1—Relate School to Life Experiences

Amplified: Some students with disabilities have limited exposure to a broader range of life experiences. There is a need to be proactive in making sure school based after-school activities are accessible to them.

Exhibit 1.3 Amplified Career Development Domain

Career Development Domain

Amplified: Of the three domains, career development needs are amplified for the majority of students with disabilities. The context in which career development occurs is different from that of many other students. There is simply more to figure out about how one fits into the world of work. Students with disabilities face formidable attitudinal and logistical barriers that result in a high unemployment rate nationwide for this population. These students have more to consider and explore, such as the potential impact of accommodations and technology, logistical concerns, and handling the doubts of others who do not have insight into how disability-related obstacles can be surmounted.

Standard A

Students will acquire the skills to investigate the world of work in relation to knowledge of self and to make informed career decisions.

C: A1—Develop Career Awareness

Amplified: Students with disabilities often lack readily accessible role models of successfully employed adults with similar disabilities. There are fewer opportunities to develop interests and hobbies because of competing medical or therapeutic activities or other obstacles. Also, standardized career assessments that are used for self-awareness often provide a skewed picture of self.

(Continued)

Exhibit 1.3 Amplified Career Development Domain (Continued)

C: A2—Develop Employment Readiness

Amplified: Student with disabilities experience employment readiness needs that are complex and include being knowledgeable about legal protections such as the Americans with Disabilities Act and handling financial disincentives that result in a perspective that they might be "better off not working." Even interviewing is more complex because they are faced with having to decide whether to disclose a nonvisible disability.

Standard B

Students will employ strategies to achieve future career goals with success and satisfaction.

C: B1—Acquire Career Information

Amplified: Access to career information is readily available. However, career materials rarely depict individuals working in a wide variety of occupations. Students may need to see how career information is pertinent to their career planning.

C: B2—Identify Career Goals

Amplified: Students with disabilities have a high risk of early career foreclosure due to lowered career expectations they and others hold. Lowered expectations can be exacerbated by inappropriate use of standardized testing or assessments and poor school performance.

Standard C

Students will understand the relationship of personal qualities, education, training, and the world of work.

C: C1—Acquire Knowledge to Achieve Career Goals

Amplified: The success of students with disabilities in achieving career goals is contingent on understanding the laws and rights related to their disability and knowledge of resources, such as state-federal vocational rehabilitation services.

C: C2—Apply Skills to Achieve Career Goals

Amplified: In order to navigate the post-K–12 experience, students with disabilities need to learn self-advocacy skills. Services that were readily available before now need to be procured through independent efforts.

We highlighted the roles that school counselors need to play with respect to students with disabilities because it is through their efforts that school counseling programs will be modified to fully include students with disabilities. These program modifications can happen only if school counselors are the advocates, leaders, and collaborators who make the systemic change happen.

Chapter 2

The Art of Helping Students with Disabilities

School counselors who work well with students in general are not necessarily effective with students with disabilities. The helping process can go awry in more ways. For example, it is harder to perceive students with disabilities accurately because we often see them through the lens of stereotypes about disabilities. Naturally this distorted perception can undermine effective helping. Firsthand accounts as well as the professional literature indicate that many people with disabilities find relationships with counselors to be disempowering.

This chapter focuses on information that should help counselors avoid stereotypical thinking and problematic forms of helping. In addition to these fundamental issues, this chapter sets out the essentials of disability etiquette and person-first language so that counselors can be more comfortable in interactions with students and their parents. Although we begin by looking at distorted perceptions of students with physical disabilities, we certainly will be addressing those of students with invisible disabilities because these are every bit as problematic.

Everyday Distortions of People with Physical Disabilities

"How easy it is to romanticize the lives of people who are disabled, to make of them heroes or tragic victims, larger or smaller than life. How easy it is to think of them as quite unlike ourselves."[1] Although this quote was made twenty years ago, this phenomenon persists. For example, an excellent elementary school teacher recently said, "All those little kids in wheelchairs are always so happy. There is something special about them." Even positive stereotypes are ultimately detrimental because they obscure individuals and people become what Pippa described as "cardboard cutouts lacking psychological depth."[2] This was reflected in the comments of one student we know who said, "I'm tired of having to educate people that I am as much of a human being as they are!"

A combination of factors challenges the ability of most to perceive people with disabilities in nondistorted ways. These include perceptual processes pertaining to impression formation, as well as deeply entrenched cultural stereotypes. An understanding of the most common of these factors is important for three reasons: to avoid them, to better understand the social world in which students with disabilities must operate, and to be able "to detect, reflect, and clarify erroneous beliefs of teachers, parents and students."[3] The last of these enables us to contribute to realistic and positive (rather than negative) self-fulfilling prophecies.

Spread and Global Evaluations

Spread, one of the most common perceptual traps, is the tendency to perceive one impairment (or disability) and automatically assume others are present.[4] As one mother told us, "People look at my daughter in a wheelchair and don't realize she is a person with some degree of intelligence. They look at people in a wheelchair and think that person can't talk, is stupid, or whatever."

Spread routinely has an impact on judgments and decisions about students with disabilities. We can see how common the phenomenon of spread is simply by thinking about how often people automatically talk loudly to people who have blindness. Another example of spread can be found in the experiences of a college student we know who had difficulty with articulation due to cerebral palsy, but had a good vocabulary and was very bright. When he went to the local emergency room, one of the attending medical professionals turned to a colleague and said, "We have a possible MR [mentally retarded patient] here."

Through spread, disability becomes a central defining characteristic. It becomes the largest factor in the process of impression formation and results in *global evaluations*. A clear illustration of this perceptual process follows: "Micheline Mason, who, like many people who generally get about on crutches occasionally has recourse to a wheelchair, draws attention to the marked change in attitudes she encounters when using the chair: 'One stereotype is that you're either in a wheelchair and helpless or on your own two feet and capable. A total change of attitude happens when you can stand up.'"[5]

Typecasting

Professionals do not differ much from the general public in terms of holding stereotypes of people with disabilities. Olkin summarizes this research: "The bottom line is that those helping professionals who children and adults with disabilities are likely to encounter most frequently are teachers, medical personnel, and employers, whose attitudes are no better than those held by the general public, and in many cases worse."[6] For this reason, it is useful to become familiar with four common forms of typecasting: tragic figures, "super-crips," mascots, and eternal children. "The only choices we have are extreme. We are seen as either victims or supercrips," said a young adult with a physical disability.

Tragic Figures

One of the most ubiquitous stereotypes is viewing students with physical disabilities as tragic figures. People with physical disabilities commonly have strangers walk up to them and express sympathy or offer a prayer. Sometimes they are faced with a hug and the reassurance that "everything will be all right." This is one way that students with physical disabilities experience a different social context than other students do. As one student told us, "It is not unusual for me to be minding my business only to have a stranger walk up and either give me money or say a prayer for me. It has happened in parking lots, bathrooms, and shopping malls."

Few school counselors pass out unsolicited charity or prayers in public places when spotting someone with a severe disability, but many of us do look at a student with a severe disability and assume his or her life will be a tragedy. This perception has the power to reverberate with the student, peers, parents, and teachers.

There is no doubt that tragic things do happen to some of the students we help. For example, if a student returns to school after a major car accident that left him with quadriplegia, it would be hard not to see that as a tragic event. However, that is different from regarding that student's life as a tragedy. Viewing the lives of students with severe disabilities as fundamentally tragic is problematic for several reasons. First, it is generally not accurate. Research studies over the past thirty years conclude that adults with disabilities regard their lives very similarly to the general population in terms of life satisfaction.[7] People with disabilities or illness generally rate their lives as more satisfying than others imagine. Gilbert writes, "Whatever a blind person's life is like, it is about much more than blindness. And yet, when sighted people imagine being blind, they fail to imagine all the other things that such a life might be about, hence they mispredict how satisfying such a life can be."[8] Second, it is often lack of accommodations, blocked opportunities, and financial problems that are more problematic than the direct effects of a disability. This is what is tragic.

Why does any of this matter? Primarily because when school counselors see these students as tragic figures, they often respond with pity. This resulting pity does not help. As long as they pity the individual, they lose sight of how diminishing barriers will improve their life. Pity is humiliating and engenders social distance and professional passivity.[9] Clearly this is different from empathizing with a student.

Inspirations and Supercrips

The word *supercrip* is used in the context of portraying a person with a physical disability as exceptionally strong or inspirational for his or her accomplishments. At first glance, it may be hard to understand why this portrayal is problematic. Haller described it well as the "the back side of pity."

> "People with disabilities are put on pedestals because of their inspirational quality in doing ordinary things, which is actually a patronizing way to laud people, imbued with charity. Presenting someone as inspirational is just another way of pitying them for the 'tragedy of their fate.' These beliefs tie into societal attitudes. Society holds few expectations for people with disabilities—so anything they do becomes 'amazing.' Any disabled person who does any basic task of living becomes 'inspirational.'"[10]

Overpraise is part of typecasting someone as a supercrip. "Many people with disabilities don't know how to react when you praise us about things that are just normal to us. What are we supposed to say? Thank you for telling me that doing the ordinary is some kind of superhuman feat?"[11] It is also problematic because of the social role expectations that it may unintentionally convey. "But it's become a media-hyped cliché 'the brave crip kid who's overcoming everything with a big grin.' It's a lot to live up to, and they have just as much right to slump around grumpy as any other teenager."[12]

Eternal Child

Adolescents, young adults, and adults with disabilities are often treated as if they are children. This can be seen in the ways people frequently speak to them, for example. Researchers have found that people are more likely to use child-like speech, diminutive names, repetitive explanations, shorter sentences, and exaggerated inflections when speaking to people sitting in wheelchairs.[13] Seeing youth and adults with disabilities as eternally childlike leads many professionals (and parents) to be overly protective, directive, and controlling as one would be with a child. As an extension of this form of typecasting, school counselors often become parental in their actions. In addition, sexuality is often not acknowledged as it needs to be. As one student said, "They assume you are a eunuch and don't prepare you for the rest of life."

Mascot

Another closely related stereotype is the common tendency to treat youth, and sometimes adults, with prominent disabilities as if they are mascots. People feel they are being friendly, but they are actually patronizing. One mother described this common occurrence particularly well: "We have those people that [since he uses a wheelchair] just feel compelled to pat him on the head! My four-year-old daughter summed it up one day when a stranger 'petted him.' She looked at this person like they just fell from the atmosphere of another planet and sweetly said, 'Please do not pet my brother. He is not a pet, just shake his hand.'"[14] This characterization often has an impact on the student's social role in the classroom or school environment.

It is easy to understand why school counselors tend to share the attitudes of the general public toward people with physical disabilities. Most of us grew up immersed in a culture that shaped the very attitudes we have been discussing. Growing up as natural helpers, we were often drawn to charitable events such as Jerry Lewis's Labor Day Telethon, which is notable for raising enormous amounts of money for muscular dystrophy. The telethon was a product of an earlier social era that regarded helping children with disabilities as charity rather than seeing them as individuals with equal rights. The process of soliciting money required tugging on the heartstrings of the public, and pity was an inextricable part of the process. In the process, persons with disabilities were portrayed in ways that emphasized their lack of potential. For example, reflecting on what life would be like as a child with muscular dystrophy in a wheelchair, Jerry Lewis stated, "I realize my life is half, so I must learn to do things halfway. I just have to learn to try to be good at being a half a person."[15] On another occasion he stated, "My kids cannot go into the workplace. There's nothing they can do."[16]

Some persons with disabilities have protested that their portrayal in the media sensationalizes their "suffering" and does more harm than good.[17] The debate over Jerry Lewis's impact arouses strong feelings on both sides and does not belong here. Nevertheless, it is necessary to recognize how these underpinnings of pity and charity can shape perception and an overall orientation toward helping and disability.

Distorted Perceptions of Students with Nonvisible Disabilities

Distorted perceptions of students with nonvisible disabilities, such as learning disabilities, attention deficit disorders, or neurobehavioral disabilities, tend to take a different trajectory that includes relatively more stigma. "In ascending order, this is the hierarchy of stigma [Figure 2.1]. Individuals with physical disabilities have the least amount of stigma directed toward them, individuals with cognitive disabilities have more stigma, individuals with intellectual disabilities experience even more stigma, and finally, those with psychiatric disabilities experience the greatest amount of stigma."[18]

Stigma results in a discredited social identity. This includes skepticism about the veracity of these individuals' needs and the genuineness of their disorders.[19] Miller and Sammons describe the common assumption: "If you *look* okay, then you must *be* okay." Elaborating they write, "In the absence of visible evidence otherwise, a person is expected to be 'normal' or 'average.' Because non-visible disabilities give no real evidence of impairment, some people think they aren't real disabilities."[20]

Students with invisible disabilities (as well as their parents) are used to the tendency of educators to infer that a student's behavior reflects something other than the identified (nonvisible) disability. Even casual discussions about school with parents of children with invisible disorders elicit many examples:

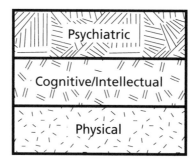

Figure 2.1 Hierarchy of Stigma

The School Counselor's Guide to Helping Students with Disabilities

"When my son was absent from class for twenty minutes [having a seizure in the boys' room], I was told that he had been avoiding class."

"The teacher told me that my child refused to color in the lines. He couldn't SEE the lines because of his vision problems! It didn't matter that this was documented in his IEP [individualized educational program] or that the vision problems were apparent if she ever really looked at my child."

"I couldn't believe it! When we got to the IEP, the principal said she doubted whether our son actually had obsessive compulsive disorder because she saw him lying on the floor. With her limited knowledge, she assumed he couldn't do this due to a fear of germs. What did she think? That all these years of treatment and educational interventions were simply irrelevant and our child was merely stubborn? If only it had been that simple of a problem."

The refrain is generally that a student is not trying hard enough and could do whatever was asked if only he or she would try.

People also often assume that those with invisible disabilities frequently use them to their own advantage.[21] Does this mean that students with disabilities never use their disorders to their advantages? Sometimes they do. But the assumption that an individual is taking advantage of his or her disorder occurs often as a knee-jerk reaction. This assumption leads to many actions such as not providing the kinds of accommodations that the student needs for overall better functioning. The accuracy of our judgments can never be 100 percent, and error is always involved. We need to wisely choose the type of errors we are more willing to accept. It is always better to err in the direction of believing a child.

Miller and Sammons suggest that it is relatively harder for people to imagine what it feels like to have an invisible disorder, such as a specific learning disability (in contrast to having a physical disability). They also offer two useful insights, based on first-person accounts they obtained, into what it can feel like to have a specific learning disability:

Did you ever misunderstand the words on an airport loudspeaker when static alternated with recognizable words such as "delayed" or "gate change"? Try to recall your frantic behavior as you strained to get a handle on which flight and which gate was announced and your panic at the thought of missing your flight. This is similar to the challenges that people with auditory processing problems face many times a day.[22]

Miller and Sammons continue:

As I write, reversals appear almost one per sentence. It is as though that part of my brain controlling letter order and spelling stalls momentarily or short-circuits, and during that instant I write "whis" instead of "wish." . . . The severity of all my symptoms can vary from day to day, from hour to hour. It feels like a tide that rises and falls, even like waves that wash in, sweep over me and then recede. Unlike the tide, however, I cannot predict the rising and subsiding of my symptoms. . . . For most of my life I had no idea why this happened to me. The experience of it has ranged from frustrating to embarrassing to devastating.[23]

Not understanding the experiences of students with disabilities can also lead to lack of empathy. A mother of a child with social phobia recently shared that on disclosing her son's disorder, she was told by a school counselor, "I don't deal with mental diseases!"

Global Evaluation and Invisible Disabilities

The tendency toward global evaluation of students with invisible disabilities is as problematic as it is with those who have physical disabilities. We assume if they have difficulty in one area, they must not have much potential in others. Educators often have a hard time with the concept that someone can have both a learning disability and be gifted, and they often regard these students as simply underachievers or lazy: "Educators often assume that gifted students do not require any special intervention—they will make it on their own."[24] One school counselor put it this way:

Another area that is hard to deal with as a counselor is convincing regular education teachers that the child in their class, who shows no *obvious* disabilities either physically or mentally, is really disabled and in need of modifications or accommodations. Perhaps the hardest are those students that should be twice labeled, for example, gifted with a learning disability. I feel like I beat my head against the wall when trying to convince a regular education teacher (and sometimes special education teachers) that the gifted student that can talk a good game is really working from a writing disability and is not just lazy!

Clearly people are prone to dichotomous thinking when it comes to disability. To avoid this:

- Develop the habit of routinely double-checking perceptions due to the almost ever-present nature of spread.

- Look for assets that are overshadowed in global evaluation.

- Think about disability as existing on a continuum and in different domains of functioning rather than a dichotomy.[25]

Not only do global evaluations keep a child's potential from being seen, but the harm can also extend to the core of the child. One woman, looking back on her life with a learning disability, underscored this well: "Can we not focus on my strengths or positive attributes? As a child, my foundation for hating myself grew out of my much noted shortcomings *and a lack of any abilities deemed positive* [italics added]."[26]

Diagnosis and Perception

Diagnostic labels have a powerful impact on perception, especially if the diagnosis is a particularly stigmatizing one. As professionals, we need to use discretion and remember that a diagnosis can alternately be helpful or harmful. Snow advises that the number one reason to use a diagnosis is to obtain necessary services. She describes medical diagnoses as "socio-political passports to services." A diagnosis should be used to obtain services, not to define possibilities or describe personalities, needs, and abilities.[27]

Kathie Snow wisely admonishes professionals and parents alike to strictly limit their use of a child's diagnosis: "When we routinely use a person's label, we frequently do so with the intention of communicating what the person's needs are. But this effort can backfire in a big way! A label can be the genesis of a range of unintended and unfortunate reactions—including but not limited to pity, prejudice, misinformation, and/or confusion. . . . *A description of the person's actual and individual needs is far more important, more accurate, and more respectful than a label.*"[28]

Diagnostic labels have a particularly powerful impact on the perception of students with relatively stigmatizing disorders and can skew counseling interactions. For example, shortly into a discussion of their problems, many students with psychiatric disorders are asked, "Are you taking your meds?" In effect, they are seen only through the lens of their diagnosis. The use of the diagnosis is problematic because it negates the total life experiences of the individual. When this lens is used, the counseling interaction becomes very limited, with the emphasis solely on the disability. This limited counseling interaction produces an unintended response reaction: the student with a disability also begins to see everything through the lens of his or her disability. This is problematic when the perception is continuously reinforced by the use of the label. Similarly, when students with significant cognitive disabilities approach school personnel with problems, what they are discussing is often seen through the lens of their low IQ scores, a numeric label. This leads to inferences about attention seeking. In these instances, the labels lead counselors to be inadvertently dismissive of genuine concerns.

A closer look at the issue of diagnosis and its impact on the counseling relationship and process reveals that often the well-intended school counselor hears the student's concern and immediately filters it through the context of the student's disability. For example, an elementary school counselor is approached by a young boy who complains that other children will not play with him. The school counselor is aware of the boy's diagnosis of attention deficient hyperactivity disorder (ADHD) and uses this information to respond to the boy, basically reminding him that *he* must be patient and learn to play with others more appropriately and that the other children see *his* impatience as troublesome and as a result do not want to play with him. Here, the school counselor is using the diagnosis in a problematic fashion by not seeking to fully understand the young boy's situation and using the label only to shape the counseling response. The response is that the child hears the counselor say, "You are the problem."

Given that situation, an elementary school counselor can use the diagnosis in a more helpful manner. First, the counselor can work to understand the situation, take it at face value, and not make any assumptions. While listening, the counselor understands that the boy is asking to be included in a game of tag on the playground. The situation is that there are only four children playing this game, and they have sought to exclude all others from it. The other children on the playground have dismissed the exclusion and have moved on to other activities, but this boy is unable to do so and, in reaction to his exclusion, persists with his desire to join them. A counselor who takes this more expansive look understands that the issue is more complex than simply the child's ADHD diagnosis. Here, the counselor understands the needs of the others to bond with their friends as well as the friendship needs of the young boy and can work with him on his friendship skills so that he sees many options for friends, not just the group playing tag. With assistance, the boy is able to reach out to play with many others. The counselor also understands how exclusivity on the playground can be a troublesome norm and plan to do some classroom guidance lessons on inclusion.

This preferred use of diagnosis can lead to a more comprehensive understanding of the student's issue and result in a more effective and helpful intervention (Table 2.1). A student should never be reduced to the disability. Given the power of diagnostic labels, we need to take steps to diminish the impact of them. Consciously set aside the diagnosis when you listen to the personal concerns of the student with a disability. Listen as you would to any other student. Later, a disorder can be factored in as one aspect of the student's life but not the first and foremost one. "It is patently unfair," writes Snow, "to let a diagnosis determine a child's future: how he will spend his time, where he'll be educated, what he may do as an adult, and so forth."[29]

Table 2.1 Proper Use of Diagnosis

Problematic Use of Diagnosis	Preferred Use of Diagnosis
Presenting concerns: Seen in context of diagnosis	Presenting concerns: • Taken at face value • Factor in developmental issues • Personal characteristics including disability and cultural considerations

Possibilities: Seeing What Cannot Easily Be Seen

The perception of possibilities is at the heart of effective helping. This involves seeing beyond a disability. Perhaps the most important and compelling illustration of this can be found in the work of Marc Gold, whose work spanned from the 1960s through his death in the 1980s. His name is associated with his Try Another Way approach, which he developed to teach complex work skills to individuals with measured IQs as low as 10.[30] "Using positive behavioral approaches," wrote Cohen, "his simple training techniques enabled individuals who had been highly devalued to assemble items as complex as 18-piece bicycle brakes and electronic circuit boards, all in accordance to industry quality and time standards."[31] What is remarkable about Gold's work is that these accomplishments did not require highly educated trainers or advanced degrees. As he stated, "At one of our research stations, we trained a moderately retarded man as the trainer, and within basically the same periods of time that we usually do, he brought the other mentally retarded, severely retarded, individuals to criterion on the bicycle brakes."[32]

One of the most important lessons of his work is to beware of negative self-fulfilling prophecies about students with disabilities (Figure 2.2). The way that one thinks about students with disabilities, particularly those that affect cognition, can result in self-fulfilling prophecies. Expecting less often generates lower results because less is given or offered as a result of the disability. Objective, educational options provide the opportunity for possibilities and results without preconceived limitations.

Gold asserted that when someone fails to learn something, our reflexive reaction as professionals is to assume the problem is inherent in the learner. He argues that the failure is not in the individual but in our approach to teaching. So an individual's "failure to learn" something becomes reframed as a clue that it is our responsibility to find a better way to teach it.[33]

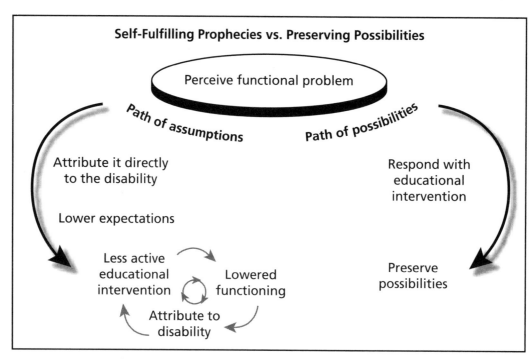

Figure 2.2 Self-Fulfilling Prophecies Versus Preserving Possibilities

Possibilities: Predicting the Future

We need to be humble in recognizing that we do not really know what a student is ultimately capable of. Following are comments from a man with ADHD that illustrate this point.

> Lines. I'm almost incapable of waiting in lines. I just can't wait, you see. That's the hell of it. Impulse leads to action. I'm very short on what you might call the intermediate reflective step between impulse and action. That's why I, like so many people with ADD, lack tact. Tact is entirely dependent on the ability to consider one's words before uttering them. We ADD types don't do this so well. I remember in the fifth grade I noticed my math teacher's hair in a new style and blurted out, "Mr. Cook, is that a toupee you're wearing?" I got kicked out of class. I've since learned how to say these inappropriate things in such a way or at such a time that they can in fact be helpful. But it has taken time. That's the thing about ADD. It takes a lot of adapting to get on in life. But it certainly can be done, and be done very well.[34]

The chances are that Mr. Cook, who had kicked this fifth grader out of class, did not predict that the student would one day become a physician. This individual, as well as many others, grew and changed in ways that others would not have predicted.

That is also why we need to be careful not to make predictions about what is possible. One mother illustrated this: "My son graduated college with honors, a fact that would shock people who knew him in high school. During those years, he often alienated people because he was just so irritable. Medication side effects worsened all of this. At best, he squeaked by. Only a few people looked beyond his disorder and understood there was a great kid somewhere in there who was struggling."

We also cannot often predict how supports and accommodations can enable people to work in professions that exceed most people's expectations.

Seeing the Student in the Environment

Another aspect of perception that we need to think about consciously is what in our perception emerges and what recedes. The image in Figure 2.3 is a classic one for demonstrating the manner in which either the figure (chalice) or the ground (profiles) emerges in our visual perception. It takes deliberate intent to see both. When working with students with disabilities, we need to do just that.

The equation B = P + E is derived from the work of Kurt Lewin and states that behavior (B) is a function of the person (P) and the environment (E).[35] The impact of the environment is often ignored when evaluating a person's capabilities. For example, we often hear of the high unemployment rate for persons with disabilities. Many people ignore the environment and interpret this figure as reflective of the capabilities of persons with disabilities. They do not take into account the environment: the impact of stereotypes on employer attitudes, architectural barriers, lack of accessible transportation, and the like. Understanding the impact of environment on student functioning cannot be overestimated.

We need to remember that we are seeing behavior (or performance) in the context of a particular environment. Changing the (educational) environment often

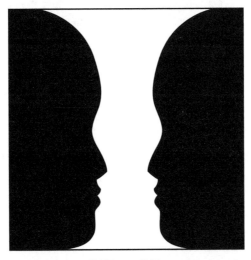

Figure 2.3 Visual Perception

changes the behavior. This principle is illustrated throughout this book in examples that show how changing the environment through accommodations and classroom climate, among others, makes a great difference to students with disabilities.

One of the main barriers when working with students with disabilities has to do with the lenses through which we often look at these students (Figure 2.4). Many introduce distortions into the process, and together they result in caricatures and missed opportunities. Lenses can magnify deficits, shrink attributes, and darken the view of the future. Lenses can paint too rosy a picture and ignore a child's struggles. What we need are good, clear, wide-angle lenses that can also diminish environmental obstacles.

With all this discussion of mistakes in perception, how should we look at students with disabilities? Simply as the individuals they are:

- They are children and adolescents first.

- They are students who have disabilities as one part of them.

- They are students who experience a greater frequency of negative reactions.

- They are students whose assets may be overshadowed by awareness of their disability.

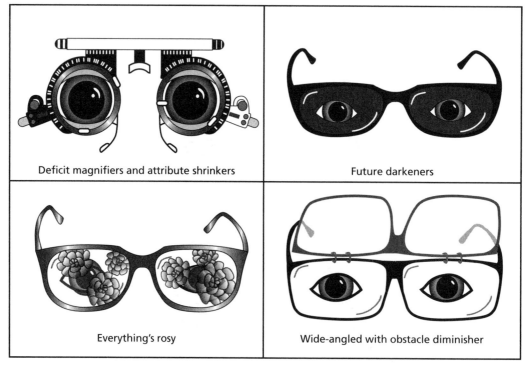

| Deficit magnifiers and attribute shrinkers | Future darkeners |
| Everything's rosy | Wide-angled with obstacle diminisher |

Figure 2.4 Looking Through Lenses

The School Counselor's Guide to Helping Students with Disabilities

Effective Helping Orientations:
Social-Minority Versus Medical Models

The model we use to conceptualize the source and solutions of problems of persons with disabilities has a far-reaching impact on how we approach the needs of students with disabilities within schools. Historically, there have been three main ways in which the problems of persons with disabilities have been conceptualized; each posited contrasting perspectives on what constitutes the "problem" of disability, who is responsible for it, and what potential solutions are. The oldest one, the *moral model*, regarded disability as punishment for sin. In the case of children, disability was seen as either retribution or a test of faith.[36] Manifestations of the moral model are still evident, but the medical model currently predominates in the general culture. All too often, it also guides educational practice.

The *medical model* regards the problem of disability as residing solely in the individual and due to the presence of a defect in functioning. The solution to problems is helping the individual become as close to the norm as possible. In essence, the belief is that the individual is broken and needs to be fixed in order to have access to life's opportunities. "Traditional explanations of the disadvantage experienced by disabled children rest on the medical model of disability which holds that the trauma of impairment is in itself an explanation for the individual's failure to achieve a reasonable quality of life. The 'social model' shifts this emphasis away from pathologizing the individual and stresses restrictive environments and attitudes."[37]

The *social model*, also known as the *minority model*, contends that disability is essentially a social construct that is reinforced by negative societal attitudes and lack of access to many domains of life. Society defines who is "normal" and who is not. Those considered normal are entitled to a fuller range of "rights." There are many illustrations of the often arbitrary nature of who we label as disabled and the related social ramifications of being defined in this manner.

Smart refers to Sobsey in order to provide a compelling illustration of the subjective nature of how we judge the capabilities of people who have been labeled as disabled: many men left institutions during World War I and World War II to fight in the U.S. military. Sobsey told of thirteen men from an institution in Connecticut who, in spite of being labeled as having mental retardation, enlisted to fight in World War II. Four of these men were promoted to higher ranks, and seven were wounded in action. In spite of their war records, most of these men returned to institutions after the war.[38]

Although disability is a natural part of the human experience, pervasive societal attitudes often resist this. Rather than accepting that we are all part of one large group that is inherently diverse, societal attitudes promote separating those with disabilities out and it becomes *us* and *them*. All too often we direct all our efforts to "fixing them" to be like us rather than recognizing the need to change the environment to accommodate expected differences. Does this mean we should no longer help a child with a specific learning disability learn to read better? Of course not. But it does mean that we need to embrace the removal of barriers that keep students from being full participants in all aspects of the school and learning opportunities.

Snow is one of many who point out the ramifications of adhering to a medical model as the main way to conceptualize the needs of people with disabilities:

> The lives of many children and adults are aberrant, but not because of the disability. Their lives are abnormal because of all the "help" they receive when client-hood replaces citizenship. Many individuals with disabilities do not experience the ordinary (but precious) activities of being children, brothers or sisters, employees, friends, volunteers, or the many other typical roles and opportunities taken for granted by most Americans. The disability has defined who they are, and treatments and services to address the "problems" of the disability become the focus of their lives.[39]

A key point of the minority model is that it emphasizes that the problems of persons with disabilities are often not due to the direct effects of the disability itself. The problem is no longer viewed as a deficit that resides within the individual. "The *minority* model," writes Olkin, "takes the problem out of the realm of the person with a disability and places it in the social, political and economic world. Solutions are universal design, education of those without disabilities about persons with disabilities, laws ensuring equal access and protection, and better enforcement of such laws."[40] The impact of restricted opportunities causes more personal difficulty than the presence of the disability itself:

> We all have our own ideas about what human condition is best, based on our own assumptions about other people's lives. These assumptions don't always jibe with reality. People who assume that I live for the day when a cure is found, when I (or future generations) can live disability-free, simply don't understand my reality. It is a question of priorities. On the list of things I want, a cure for my disability is pretty low. Higher up on the list would be achievement of my personal, professional and social goals, and these are not in any way dependent on a cure.[41]

An understanding of the social minority model provides a way for school counselors to think about the needs of their students from a more accurate and useful perspective. It brings the environment into clearer perspective as a major cause of functional limitations and lack of opportunities. In doing this, it clarifies that a lower quality of life is not inevitable since it is not generally a direct correlate of the disability itself.

Help That Is Helpful

*Help is not a simple common sense phenomenon
rooted in the good intentions of the helper.*

NANCY KERR (1984)

A number of factors complicate the establishment of genuine helping relationships. These include the ease with which distorted perceptions of persons with disabilities and stereotypical beliefs slip into our mind-sets. How to help is not always intuitive. Robert Nathanson has written about seven syndromes that are common but problematic in terms of helping students with disabilities, reprinted with permission from the American Counseling Association:

Syndrome 1. All that matters is your label. At the beginning of the school year, a new student enrolled in the ninth grade at a high school acclaimed throughout the state for its pioneering efforts in mainstreaming students with disabilities into regular classes. The student, who had had an arm amputated above the elbow as the result of an accident at the age of 10, was particularly strong and well-coordinated, and expressed an avid interest in athletics. When the student attended her first physical education class and realized the class was solely for the school's students with disabilities, she protested.

The student was referred to one of the school's guidance counselors to discuss the matter. The counselor listened, nodding with every few sentences and grinning cynically, as the student made a case for participating in a regular physical education class with students without disabilities. The counselor responded that the student was "not the first amputee we've had here—we've had at least a dozen over the years." Without further exploration of possibilities for the student's participation in the regular class, the counselor talked about the school's "wonderful adaptive physical education class," and concluded that the student's request could not be honored.

Syndrome 2. I feel sorry for you. A fifth-grader, who had lost both legs in an accident three years before, excitedly wheeled his chair into the school counselor's guidance office to tell his counselor that he had very recently joined a troop of Boy Scouts in a neighboring town and would soon be going on an overnight camping trip. As the student expressed his joy, the counselor seemed proud of the student's accomplishments. Speaking in an uncommonly slow, gentle fashion, the counselor then asked the student how he was feeling. The student responded that he was feeling fine, noting that the counselor wore a pained facial expression and appeared to be staring at the stumps of his amputated legs. The student said goodbye and departed. As the student briskly wheeled down the hall to class, the counselor's head shook slowly, the pained expression still evident. Joined in the hallway by a colleague, the counselor reminisced about "how active that boy used to be; it's such a pity."

Syndrome 3. Don't worry, I'll save you. A high school student, wheel-chair bound because of paralysis below the waist, complained to his counselor of "too much work" in an American History class. The counselor listened intently as the student talked about having a particularly difficult time completing a required term paper. The counselor expressed an understanding of the student's difficulty and promised, "I'll see what I can do for you."

Later that day, the counselor caught up with the history teacher in the school's parking area and asked the teacher to "go easy on T. He has had enough problems already, the poor kid." After discussing the matter for a few minutes the teacher agreed to "forget about" the term paper, promising that the student would receive a good grade in the class because "the kid tries so hard."

Syndrome 4. I know what's best for you. A student with a hearing impairment and characteristically impaired speech was invited to meet with his school's new tenth-grade guidance counselor. After exchanging pleasantries the counselor asked if the student had begun thinking about a career. The student responded by talking about a long-standing interest in mathematics, and a desire to someday become an accountant. The student began to mention a neighbor who was an accountant, whereupon the student counselor interrupted, asking whether the student was aware that a college degree was a prerequisite for such a job.

As the student indicated such an understanding, the counselor glanced down at his academic record. Overlooking the student's fine mathematics grades, the counselor remarked that he had done very well in woodworking and metal shop classes in the ninth grade. The student nodded in agreement and smiled proudly. The counselor asked whether the student was presently enrolled in shop class, and the student responded that he was studying printing. They continued their session discussing the printing trade as a profession. The counselor did most of the talking, several times mentioning the deaf printer in the next town who "makes a decent living."

Syndrome 5. If I'm lucky, you'll miss today's appointment. Two months into the school year, a fourth-grade teacher referred a student to the school's guidance counselor to discuss difficulties the student was having in getting along with classmates. Although the counselor had never worked with the student, the counselor had observed the student on several occasions and was aware of the student's congenital deformities of face and head. Eleven days after the referral was made, the counselor met with the student. The counselor greeted the student somewhat abruptly, seemed impatient, talked with the student in an uncommonly clinical manner, and spent less time with the student than usually spent with other students. The counselor tended to fidget with a pencil and to focus on the pencil for extended periods, seldom making eye contact with the student. After the initial session, the counselor suggested to the student's teacher that another appointment be made "in a week or two."

Syndrome 6. I'm amazed by your courage. At the conclusion of the spring semester, before summer vacation, two college freshman, one of whom was blind, stopped in at their college counselor's office to say they had passed their courses. The counselor responding with great emotion, remarked how "competent" the blind student was and how the student "never ceases to amaze." The counselor lavished particular praise on the blind student for completing the requirements of an English composition course, exclaiming, "that's really great!" Almost as an after-thought, the counselor urged the other student to "keep up the good work, too," and wished both students an enjoyable vacation.

Syndrome 7. Who's more anxious, you or I? On numerous occasions a college junior with cerebral palsy, which resulted in lack of muscle control and severely impaired speech, was encouraged by a counselor in the college's office of career planning to "stop into the office whenever you want to see me." Although outwardly very friendly and solicitous, the counselor was either "seeing someone" or "not in the office at the moment" each time the student showed up at the office. On two occasions specific appointments had been made, but they were broken by the counselor for one reason or another, each time apologetically.

At the counseling sessions when the student and counselor did meet, the counselor tended to do most of the talking. Often, as the student began to speak, the counselor cut short her sentence with a raised voice, completing the sentence by trying to anticipate what the student was going to say. Although several inappropriate responses by the counselor made it obvious to the student that the counselor was having a difficult time understanding her speech, a nervous nod of agreement accompanied each statement the student made. At no time did the counselor overtly indicate a lack of understanding, nor was the student ever asked to clarify or repeat what she had said.[42]

These seven syndromes illustrate problems with pity, stereotyping, discomfort, and paternalism. It is important for school counselors to appreciate the difficulties of students with disabilities, especially those navigating an environment where they are very much in the minority. Help is quite different from pity and has its roots in empathy rather than sympathy: appreciate difficulties; do not lower expectations, but add supports; listen to what the person thinks will help; empower rather than pity; and remove barriers.

Middleton compiled the following useful list of what students with disabilities viewed as helpful:

Young people want adults who stick up for them; see them as individuals; have a sense of humor; are good listeners; are not embarrassed by their disability; will talk to them about being disabled; talk about their abilities, rather than make assumptions about what they can or can't do; support and encourage achievements; do not take control away; do not impose religious or ideological beliefs; help them develop social and relationship skills; help them meet other children, both disabled and non-disabled; do not trivialize their concerns; are honest and straightforward; make them feel safe in the sense of being trustworthy; do not gossip about them; do not smother them; notice when they are unhappy; do not act on information without consulting them; do not pity, humiliate or abuse them; and do not make promises they can't keep.[43]

Getting Comfortable

People without disabilities often experience anxiety when interacting with people who have physical disabilities, and often the result is increased social distance. Two major factors contribute to this distancing. Siller wrote that the anxiety is due to the fact that we are reminded of our own physical vulnerability to disability; this is heightened when the disability results from disease or accident. Second, researchers have noted a process called "interactional strain." Because of misconceptions and perceptual distortions, we tend to assume the person with the disability is more dissimilar to ourselves than he or she is.[44] Davis notes that conversation becomes unnecessarily "sticky."[45] This has been attributed to fumbling around for a topic in common and fearing unintentional offense. People also often become anxious about the logistics of interacting and anticipate doing or saying the wrong thing. Should you ask someone whose speech you cannot understand to repeat something, or does that make matters worse? Do you ask a student directly about his or her disability?

And then there are the words. What words do I use that won't mistakenly offend a parent? When in doubt, people tend to avoid, and social distance increases. Choose to be involved rather than distant (for fear of making a mistake). We will discuss language first and then provide guidelines for handling logistics when interacting with people with disabilities.

The words we use related to disability matter for several reasons. They shape perception by painting mental images for others. Consider the difference between saying, "that epileptic student" and "that boy with a seizure disorder." The first conjures up more of an image in which the seizure disorder becomes the most important characteristic of the child; the second acknowledges the individual first and then refers to the disability. This is the essence of person-first language: it puts the individual first and foremost. It is also important to be aware of what terms are currently used to describe disorders and what terms have taken on highly stigmatized and offensive connotations. Some people find the term *handicap* offensive, so the term *disability* is generally preferred. The term *handicap* has been seen as derived from the image of people with disabilities begging with "cap in hand." The use of the term *handicapped* is appropriate when describing an environmental barrier or obstacle (for example, "The inaccessible playground is a handicap to Sue's social integration"). Naturally the words we use have some impact on rapport with others. Mistakes are inevitable but are preferable to being uptight, awkward, or avoidant.

It is important to become familiar with preferred language and disability etiquette:

- *Put people first rather than their disability*. People should not be defined by their disabilities. A disability is simply one characteristic.

  For example:

Try saying:	She acquired quadriplegia.	Avoid saying:	She *is* a quad.
Try saying:	He has autism.	Avoid saying:	He *is* an autistic boy.

- *Avoid words that emphasize pity*. These include phrases such as *victim of* or *suffers from*.

Try saying:	He uses a wheelchair.	Avoid saying:	He is *wheelchair bound*.
Try saying:	She has cerebral palsy.	Avoid saying:	She is *afflicted* with cerebral palsy.

- *Be thoughtful about the use of the words* normal *and* defect.

- *Use the words* typical *or* atypical *when relevant*. For example:

Try saying:	You did that like most other people.	Avoid saying:	You did that as if you were *normal*.
Try saying:	She has a congenital disability.	Avoid saying:	She has a birth *defect*.

- *Avoid euphemisms*. These terms tend to be condescending. For example, avoid *handicapable, differently abled, physically challenged*, or *special*.

- *Be careful about language that groups people on the basis of whether they have a disability*. For example, avoid *the disabled* or *able-bodied people*.

Nevertheless, your intentions supersede perfection. It is more important to want to interact even if you say or do the wrong thing. Social distance is far worse.

Logistics

In a similar vein, we offer the following general disability etiquette guidelines:

- Respect all assistive devices such as communication boards, canes, and wheelchairs as the personal property that they are.

- Speak directly to the student with a disability even if he or she is accompanied by a paraprofessional or parent.

- As needed, ask someone if he or she needs assistance, wait for a response, and then follow the student's directions.

- Understand that companion dogs are working. Do not distract them.

- Sit down if you are going to have more than a very brief conversation with a person using a wheelchair.

- Take the initiative to greet and orient a person with blindness or visual impairment.

- When speaking with someone with deafness or hearing impairment, make sure this person can see your facial expression, and position yourself for best illumination.

- If you can't understand someone's speech, do not hesitate to ask the person to repeat what he or she said. This is better than pretending to understand.

- Provide time for people with communication disorders of any type to express themselves at their own pace.

Talking About a Student's Disability

It is important not to overfocus on a student's disability as if that was the student's main characteristic, but it also is not useful to ignore it as a taboo topic. Many individuals express relief when disability can be discussed in this manner. One young man underscored how rare it was to have someone approach the topic of his disability in such a manner: "I worked at McDonald's, and they're very image conscious. I was a bit concerned, but they were fine. They were fantastic about it, you know. They spoke to me about my disability, and that was the first time anyone had done that, which I appreciated."[46] The reluctance to talk about disability, even when it is apparent, creates significant social barriers. "I think the biggest obstacle I face is people's unwillingness to talk about the disability, to ask about it, to want to know about it, get beyond their fear and realize this is ok.

This is not something I hide. This is not something that is hurtful to me; this is part of my identity. I'm comfortable with it. So I want you all to be comfortable with it."[47]

One mother of young adults with cerebral palsy provided cogent advice based on her years of experiences with educators:

> I think a lot of times educators come to the table with preconceived knowledge or ideas about how a student is going to be; we found that a lot of times they had ideas in their head about how they were going to interact with our daughter, or made plans, even though they didn't know her. I think, as educators, you should simply set up a meeting to sit down and speak to each student and ask them questions, get to know them. You could say, "I want to know you, and I want you to tell me your concerns as a student." If you have questions, ask them, such as why a student may need an aide. Then you can integrate this information into your classroom teaching and your interaction with the student, as well as helping that student to socialize in your classroom in order to be a part of the whole classroom environment.

Her opinion is echoed by the advice of one principal: "Take the time to get to know each student. Give them ample time to express their needs. They may not be used to expressing themselves, since often, people have not seen them as real people."

Chapter 3

School Counseling Programs

Genuine Inclusion

We need to be the change we want to see happen.
We are the leaders we have been waiting for.

MAHATMA GANDHI

This quotation from an American School Counselor Association (ASCA) presentation (n.d.-b, slide 6), "School Counselors: Partners in Achievement," represents our guiding belief that school counselors, now and in the future, will adapt school counseling programs so that there is genuine inclusion of students with disabilities.[1]

The most effective way that school counselors can serve the needs of students with disabilities is to apply the concept of genuine inclusion (see Chapter One) and infuse it throughout all school counseling programs. Applied this way, genuine inclusion ensures that students with disabilities and the culture of disability are present in all aspects of school counseling programs and that these programs are purposefully and deliberately designed with them in mind. In this chapter, we explore the key concepts of this application of inclusion of students

47

with disabilities into school counseling programs and how school counselors can provide critical leadership and advocacy.

There are two key levels to consider with respect to incorporation of inclusion. The first is a philosophical and theoretical one. We must first ensure that the culture of disability and the needs of students with disabilities are fully integrated into the discipline of professional school counseling. More specifically, the philosophy and theory that underpin the national model for school counseling programs and the ASCA standards for school counseling programs must be examined. This philosophical and theoretical integration of disabilities and inclusion is critical because the national model and its subsequent standards are the ideal on which state models and local school programs are based. The second level for integration of inclusion of disability is a programmatic and implementation one. At this level, school programs are designed and implemented such that students with disabilities are fully recognized and genuinely included, and their amplified needs are addressed. In these programs, school counselors are conversant in disabilities, are knowledgeable about legal mandates and guidelines, understand the importance of parental collaboration, and recognize that students with disabilities have amplified developmental needs.

The ASCA national model encompasses four quadrants: the foundation (including the three domains of academic, personal/social, and career) and their related standards and competencies, the delivery systems, management support, and accountability. In the following sections we illustrate how easy it is to integrate disabilities into the philosophical and theoretical levels. We also provide examples of how this inclusion can be addressed in implementing a school counseling program. It is not our intent to review every aspect of the ASCA national model; we address those that are most relevant for the purpose of creating a genuinely inclusive program.

The Foundation

This area is perhaps the most important aspect of integration of inclusion into the national model. It is here that we find the core beliefs and philosophies that lead to the school counseling program's mission. These beliefs and philosophy reflect the values on which the program rests. At the local school counseling program level, sometimes these beliefs and philosophy go unstated and are not articulated in a formal way. Nevertheless, articulated or not, these beliefs and mission statements define the attitude and culture surrounding the school counseling program's relation to students with disabilities. If disability is integrated and inclusion is valued in more than a token manner, there should be an overall school philosophy consistent with this. A disability-integrated school counseling program must have these foundational beliefs:

- The school and all its citizens acknowledge that all belong and all are valued.

- The school counselor's role includes working with students with disabilities.

- Resilience, persistence, and hope are at the core of all student success.

- The school's physical and learning environment is welcoming and does not present barriers.

- Students with disabilities are a shared responsibility of everyone in the school.

- Students with disabilities are fully involved and integrated into the school. There is an honest representation of the sentiment, "Nothing about me without me," a disabilities rights slogan that arose in reaction to the fact that too often, others paternalistically make plans for people with disabilities.

- There is an appreciation that sameness is not fairness: accommodations for students with disabilities are natural and "different" can be just.

- Ableism, which refers to a set of practices and beliefs that assign inferior value and worth to people who have disabilities, is not tolerated.

Some of these disability concepts are new and unfamiliar to school counselors and warrant further explanation.

Inclusion

The Ontario Canada Peel District School Board's expressed philosophy is an excellent example that embraces and illustrates this inclusive philosophy. Its credo is, "I belong, you belong, we belong."[2] School counseling programs would do well to embody such inclusive language. The language promises that no matter what their inner or outward differences might be, all students are important and valued.

Too often, others paternalistically make plans for people with disabilities. This is especially evident in the lives of young people with disabilities. They are surrounded by well-intentioned adults who have their own notions about what is in these young people's best interests. This is disempowering. Students with disabilities need to be able to participate in meaningful ways in the decisions that have an impact on their lives. This is in keeping with the emphasis placed on helping them develop the skills for self-advocacy and self-determination.

Sameness Is Not Fairness

Some educators resist the concept of providing accommodations because they have the perception that accommodations are unfair to and discriminate against students who do not need them. We, however, emphasize that sameness is not fairness.

The reality for students who have disabilities is that they are not the same as their typical peers, and often they have to overcome significant physical, social, or emotional challenges that their more typical peers do not, and they are expected to meet the same learning goals as their typical peers. Accommodations acknowledge these challenges and provide a context in which to take these differences into account. For example, a child with an anxiety disorder may spend four hours on a homework assignment and not get any further than writing the first sentence due to the effects of his disability. To require this student to complete the same amount of homework as all other students significantly disadvantages him or her.

Ableism

Ableism is the societal prejudice against individuals with disabilities that often passes unnoticed because we are accustomed to it. It is the expectation that people with disabilities should and must strive to live as those in the majority—those who are able-bodied. The disability is seen as inherently something "bad" that needs to be surmounted in order to have access to the opportunities others enjoy. It is the antithesis of the premise that disability is a natural element of human diversity.[3]

Hehir, writing about confronting ableism in schools, suggests that "minimizing the impact of disability does not mean making misguided attempts to 'cure' disability but rather giving students the supports, skills, and opportunities needed to live as full a life as possible with their disability. Maximizing access requires that school practices recognize the right of students with disabilities to participate fully in the school community—not only in academic programs, but also in sports teams, choruses, clubs, and field trips."[4]

These beliefs and philosophy lead to the school counseling program's mission statement. Typically these mission statements are brief and clearly articulate the purpose of the school counseling program. Following is an example of a mission statement that draws on Hehir's inclusive language and addresses the amplified developmental needs of students with disabilities:

> The mission of our school counseling program is to foster an inclusive and welcoming environment where differences are valued and honored; facilitate

students' development of their unique or amplified academic, personal/social, and career competencies; and to give students, with or without a disability, the supports, skills, and opportunities needed to live as full a life as possible.

Since these foundational beliefs, philosophy, and mission statement related to inclusion are the bedrock on which the rest of the program is built, we recommend that school counselors conduct an informal audit of their program's foundation—its beliefs, philosophy, and mission statements—to assess its measure of inclusion. Our hope is that they will find tangible evidence of inclusion of students with disabilities. If there is not a written statement of these foundation beliefs, it is not easy to assess if and how students with disabilities are integrated into the school counseling program. One quick way to get a gauge is to engage colleagues and others, including students with disabilities, in discussions about disability-related issues. Their responses will provide anecdotal evidence of their beliefs and attitudes about how integrated the school counseling program is. It is relatively easy to modify, in writing, foundational beliefs and philosophies of a school counseling program so that they include disability. We encourage school counselors to advocate for this and work with their local advisory boards to do so.

Although programs can incorporate these revised beliefs and philosophy in their words, there is a need to do more than just give lip-service to these revised beliefs. Incorporating disability into school counseling programs requires that these beliefs permeate the school culture and are part of the lived experience for everyone in the school.

The last foundational area to consider is the ASCA academic, personal/social, and career domains and their subsequent standards and competencies. As we noted in Chapter One, integrating disabilities into these is complex and requires the acknowledgment that the developmental needs of students with disabilities in these areas are similar to those of their peers without disabilities but they can be more complex and multifaceted. In fact, they are amplified. For many school counselors and other professionals, this information about amplified development needs for students with disabilities is new and unfamiliar. One way to integrate disability and transform school counseling programs is to provide education about amplified needs to all stakeholders. Once they truly grasp the different issues and needs of students with disabilities and have a baseline understanding of the need for change, the school counselor may find it easier to marshal support and resources for program modifications or changes. This educational outreach should include school board members, administrators, all school staff, teachers, parents, and students. In addition, school counselors must help all stakeholders have a clear understanding about disabilities and students with disabilities and get comfortable with disabilities. The information that we set out for school counselors in Chapter Two needs to be provided for the stakeholders as well.

Delivery System

The delivery system is the program area where the attention to the issues of disability and inclusion can have the most profound and dramatic effect. It provides the vehicle whereby all students interface with the school counseling program and where competency attainment across all domains is fostered and, it is hoped, achieved. Through classroom guidance lessons, individual planning, individual and group counseling, consultation, and referral, students are assisted to attain the prescribed competencies in all ASCA domains. All of these delivery system areas should also be used as options for addressing the competency needs of students with disabilities. It is essential that school counselors provide the leadership and advocacy to make this happen.

The delivery system should be adapted so that students with disabilities can receive the same benefits from the school counseling program as their typical peers. So as the school counseling guidance curriculum and subsequent lessons are being planned, armed with a greater appreciation and understanding of disability, school counselors can ensure that modifications are made so that the curriculum and lesson plans are relevant and inclusive for students with disabilities. When needed, they can also create specific curricula units designed to meet the amplified needs of students with disabilities. In addition, disability-integrated school counseling programs incorporate students' individualized educational programs (IEPs), 504 implementation plans, and transition plans as part of the program's individual planning efforts of the school counseling program and see the role of the school counselor in that planning as critical. Readers unfamiliar with these terms can find a full explanation in Chapter Four.

As detailed in Chapter Four and emphasized here, we believe all these plans should address the academic, personal/social, and career needs of students. We believe that school counselors are responsible for ensuring that this happens and, most important, that these needs are not overlooked. Also, inclusive school counseling programs seek to engage students with disabilities and respond to their specialized needs and their propensity for high at-risk behaviors through both individual and group counseling and make referrals to outside agencies when necessary.

Management

The management of the school counseling program is essential and critical to its success. There must be clearly negotiated agreements with the administration that define the responsibilities and tasks of the school counselor. For disability-integrated school counseling programs, these responsibilities must include an understanding of the school counselor's role with students with disabilities. Chapter One details these roles; we recommend that the information presented there be used as a resource for developing management agreements.

School counselors play an active role in various student-centered meetings. Formally defining that role increases the collaboration with other school professionals and ensures that school counselors work in collaboration with teachers and parents. We advocate that the roles and duties related to working with students with disabilities be incorporated into the school counselor's position description. In addition, the school counseling advisory council that helps to oversee the counseling program needs to have ample representation of individuals who understand students with disabilities and can help ensure that the needs of those students are addressed within the counseling program. We recommend that a teacher with a special education background, a parent of a child with special needs, and a student with disability be considered as members.

Accountability

As we adapt the school counseling program and integrate a focus on disabilities, it is vital to give active consideration to data collection that validates the efficacy of services to and for students with disability. We believe that these data will validate in tangible ways that students with disabilities benefit significantly from efforts to attend to their amplified needs. Also, in an inclusive school counseling program, the school counselor's efforts, as measured in time devoted to working with students, will verify that he or she is actively engaged in providing services to students with meet their special needs.

From Theory to Practice

ASCA stresses that three key qualities should permeate the successful school counseling program: "Infused throughout the [school counseling] program are the qualities of leadership, advocacy and collaboration, which lead to systemic change."[5] In the previous section, we presented a rationale for systemic change that transforms the school counseling program in detail. A simple review of that section shows how pervasive and important these qualities are and how they are integral to school counseling program success.

We suggest that when disabilities are being integrated into the school counseling program, the quality of advocacy is a first among equals. At the heart of advocacy are the school counseling core values of caring and helping all children achieve to their highest potential. These values need to be combined with a deep compassion for the needs of children with disabilities that is grounded in a strong sense of social justice: in equity, fairness, accessibility, safety, and developing caring inclusive communities.

There are key dispositions, knowledge, skills, and competencies that all school counselors should have so that they can function as effective professional advocates.[6] The essential characteristics that school counselors must possess are a strong commitment to disability advocacy in general and a sincere desire to help those who are different, a belief that family support and empowerment are crucial, a true understanding of the need for advocacy for disabilities that extends beyond the individual student to all his or her social systems, and a strong professional ethical commitment to advocacy. In order to assess these advocacy dispositions, a school counselor must ask:

- Is advocacy for students with disabilities important to me? Do I see a wrong and want to make it right?

- Am I willing to join with and support parents or guardians and work to empower them as they seek to care for their children with disabilities? Am I willing to hear and give voice to their needs and concerns?

- Am I willing to take risks, both personally and professionally, to help my students with disabilities meet their needs?

- Am I willing to work to challenge and remove barriers and inequities for all students, especially those with disabilities?

- Do I possess a personal ethic of caring for individuals with disabilities that dictates that I demonstrate that caring through my actions?

This school counselor advocacy can occur on an individual or a wide systemic level. The wide systemic level refers to advocacy that leads to change from the level of the school district up to the global level. Change through advocacy can also be much more targeted to individual entities such as a school, a classroom, a teacher, a family, a student, or a group of students. In the following sections, we provide an example of both targeted and systemic advocacy.

Targeted Advocacy

Individual advocacy is perhaps the most common form of school counselor advocacy. For example, the school counselor recognizes that an individual student with a disability is being treated poorly by his or her peers (the current situation) and acknowledges that through the counselor's action, this

The School Counselor's Guide to Helping Students with Disabilities

could be rectified (preferred situation). The school counselor could intervene in many ways:

- A classroom guidance unit or lesson on respecting individual differences

- A small group counseling session that deals with conflict resolution strategies

- Consultation with the classroom teacher to institute classroom norms that are respectful of individual differences

Systemic Advocacy

Often school counselors see a common need that transcends the individual. They might realize that many teachers are having difficulty working with students with learning disabilities (the current situation). Since the teachers are having this concern, it is easy to assume that the collective needs of students with disabilities in the school are not being met. The goal of this systemic advocacy is to enhance the teachers' understanding of the needs of students with learning disabilities (the preferred situation).

This scenario was addressed by a group of school counselors and took the form of a teacher in-service. The story is told from the school counselor's view and provides an excellent example of advocacy for a group of students with learning disabilities:

> I enlisted the help and expertise of the special education teacher, who concurred that an in-service would be beneficial and agreed to be involved. After receiving support from the principal, I developed a proposal for a 2-hour in-service based on Richard D. Lavoie's (1990) *How Difficult Can This Be? The F.A.T. City Learning Disability Workshop*, which the special education teacher and I had seen at a conference. Our principal agreed to purchase the video based on my recommendation. The 2-hour in-service became a part of a five-session series focusing on the definition and causes of attention deficit disorder (ADD), special considerations for students with learning disabilities, organizational strategies for children affected by learning disabilities or ADD, and classroom strategies for helping students with special needs. The five-session in-service was coordinated by the special education teacher and the other school counselor. The goal of the in-service was to sensitize the staff to the social, emotional, and cognitive needs of students with learning disabilities and to provide specific interventions that could be used in the classroom. I assumed responsibility for leading the in-service, using Lavoie's (1990) program with its discussion guide

and video. I also addressed possible emotional and self-esteem issues of children with special needs. The special education teacher answered specific questions the teachers raised, added rationale and further explanations for academic interventions, and contributed her ideas for further interventions.[7]

In conclusion, the advocacy efforts of school counselors:

- Offer a voice of hope and empowerment so that tangible support is felt.

- Challenge existing barriers so that the practicalities can be overcome.

- Provide energy and effort toward change so that possibilities can be conceived.

- Recognize amplified developmental needs so that competencies can be obtained and dreams can be realized.

Chapter 4

Protective Legislation and the School Counselor Role

This chapter provides essential information to help school counselors understand the legislation that has been put in place to safeguard the rights of students with disabilities and guarantee them a free and appropriate public education. The objective is to provide useful insight into both the letter and spirit of the law. By understanding both aspects, school counselors can better serve students with disabilities and appropriately advocate for them within the broader school context.

Many readers are too young to remember what the educational system looked like before passage in 1990 of both the Individuals with Disabilities Act (IDEA) and the Americans with Disabilities Act (ADA). It is not unusual today to see users of wheelchairs in public venues or children with significant disabilities in regular education classrooms using augmentative communication devices, adapted keyboards, or other accommodations. This has not always been the case.

President George H. W. Bush compared passage of the ADA, which made such sights commonplace, to "the freeing of the slaves."[1] The history of discrimination of persons with disabilities that led to this remark is beyond the confines of this book; nevertheless, the history of educational discrimination needs to be appreciated.

Those who have been in the disability field for several decades may remember many instances of profound discrimination. One example I (F. Prezant) encountered involved an elementary-aged, nonverbal child with autism in a state institution during the early 1970s. He had been there for several years because his mother was advised that he had little future, and the situation for all would only be worse if he lived at home. His days were spent in a group ward where bigger children stole his lunch from him. His evenings were spent in a locked single room with only a bed, much like a jail cell. Interns applying newly learned therapeutic skills were among the individual contacts Johnnie (a pseudonym) had. This was prior to special education laws. As a child with autism today, Johnnie would probably be in a typical school receiving special education and speech and language therapy, and living at home with his family in his community. Plans would probably also have been made to help him with the transition beyond school to vocational training, employment, and independent living. In actuality, though, Johnnie may never have left that institution.

Being warehoused instead of educated was not a direct result of the severity of a disability. It is very likely that Johnnie could have functioned far better elsewhere, but the assumption was that he had no future and that society would be better off if he were not a part of it. Until a few decades ago, this assumption was the rule, not the exception, and few questioned it. Educational history is replete with examples of discrimination against students with disabilities that deprived children of their educations and futures, and in good part it was the result of our own ignorance. Another example (from cases of parents for whom I have advocated) includes the student with spina bifida who was accompanied by her mother to school every day because the school would permit her attendance only if a family member escorted her to attend to her toileting needs. The mother quit her job to do this for most of a school year before finding out that existing legal precedents identified this practice as a violation of rights.

Over the past several decades, the inclusion movement has brought increasing numbers of children with disabilities into the public school setting due to changes in social attitudes, advocacy, medical advances, and research on best practices in education. Legislation was enacted that supports the concept that children with disabilities should be educated with their nondisabled peers to the greatest degree possible and that all children are entitled to a free and appropriate public education. Today's education for children with disabilities also includes planning for life after school to ensure independence and self-sufficiency in society.

The role of school counselors has also changed. They now play a critical role in seeing to it that the needs of students with disabilities are being met in the school setting. This chapter focuses on how school counselors need to approach the process of being part of the team that creates individualized educational programs (IEPs), transition plans, and 504 plans. In addition to a historical perspective and framework, this chapter provides examples of landmark cases, highlights of legislation that counselors should be familiar with, and examples using student scenarios.

Perhaps one of the best ways to illustrate the importance of legislative changes and the related ways that a school counselor can help a student is by taking a look at one student we refer to as Claudia, a student with a seizure disorder and learning disabilities. (Her full story is provided at the end of this chapter.) Had Claudia entered school in 1970, her story might well have been very different. At that time, a school district had the right to exclude a child from becoming a student in the school based on the opinion of one specialist. There were no multidisciplinary teams, no process of evaluating students or providing special education or accommodations for them in public schools. Schools did not have the specialty staff that exist now: special educators, speech therapists, occupational therapists, and others. Parents at that time might have been asked to pay for a nurse or to come to school with the child. The term *learning disability* was not in use yet, and there were no IDEA categories because there was no legislation and no rights to a free and appropriate, public education. Many people would have equated seizure disorders with low intellectual potential. Claudia would not have received extra time and probably would have been retained at least once. She might have been placed in a special segregated class. The chances are great that she would have dropped out or completed school with only a certificate of attendance.

The current profile and its comparison to what might have happened in 1970 to the same child represent growth resulting from progressive legislation and changing attitudes about disability. Despite these critical changes, children with disabilities continue to experience discrimination routinely. In the early 1900s, students with disabilities did not go to school. Today most finish high school, and many go on to postsecondary education, employment, and independent lives. Statistics reveal, however, that still too many may not meet their potential because possibilities are summarily dismissed, and negative, limiting societal systems, attitudes, and practices still exist that create a variety of barriers.

How We Got Here: A Glimpse Back in Time

In order to understand how the role of different professions has evolved to include students with disabilities, it is important to examine changes in the context of landmark legislation. In the era of growth in the rehabilitation field following World War II and dovetailing with the civil rights movement, changes in attitude led to major legislation specific to education. *Brown* v. *Board of Education*, stimulated by racial inequities in education rather than disparities based on disability, was a major impetus in future court cases that sought to establish the rights to equal opportunities. The two decades after racial desegregation rulings saw many state court cases challenging education inequities for children with disabilities. A few of these landmark cases and laws are listed in Table 4.1.

Table 4.1 Landmark Legislation for Individuals with Disabilities

Year	Court Case or Legislation	Impact for Individuals with Disabilities
1954	*Brown* v. *Board of Education of Topeka*	Established right to equal opportunity for education for all children
1965	Elementary and Secondary Education Act	State and district funding to provide programs for economically disadvantaged children and students with disabilities
1972	*PARC* v. *Pennsylvania*	A class action suit that guaranteed free public education to children with mental retardation
1972	*Mills* v. *Board of Education*	Established equal right to education: lack of funds cannot be used as an excuse for not providing services
1973	Section 504 of the Rehabilitation Act (P.L. 93–112)	Person cannot be excluded on basis of disability from any activity or program that receives federal funding
1975, 1990, 1997, 2004	Individuals with Disabilities Education Act	Originating in 1975 as the Education for All Handicapped Children Act (P.L. 94–142), landmark legislation that guarantees free and appropriate public education in the least restrictive environment to students with disabilities; includes parent rights, development of IEPs, and transition plans and services for students by age sixteen; became law in 1975, with significant amendments in 1990, 1997 and 2004
1990	Americans with Disabilities Act (P.L. 101–336)	Civil rights legislation barring discrimination against persons with disabilities in employment, transportation access, and telecommunications
2002	No Child Left Behind Act	Increased accountability to demonstrate adequate yearly progress through annual assessments that must include students with disabilities; by 2013–2014, all students are expected to be proficient in instructional areas assessed in each state

PARC (Pennsylvania Association for Retarded Citizens) v. *Pennsylvania*, the case that mandated education for children with mental retardation and ordered the reevaluation and education of every child with mental retardation, opened the floodgates that eventually resulted in a more comprehensive federal mandate that superseded all state rulings. In good part, it was due to the efforts of concerned parents that this case even came to court. Parents of children with disabilities would learn from this case that when they were informed, organized, and tactical, they could be change makers who would increase future opportunities for their children and alter societal attitudes. Parents today work with school teams to empower their children and increase inclusion in society. School counselors should see them as allies who are knowledgeable, dedicated, and tireless in their efforts.

IDEA is perhaps the most significant of the landmark laws with regard to education of children with disabilities. First passed in 1975 as the Education for All Handicapped Children Act, this revolutionary legislation mandated the right to a free and appropriate public education for students with disabilities. For the first time, students with disabilities were provided an education; sometimes it was in segregated schools, but it was the beginning of an era in which they were guaranteed an education. This legislation was the federal culmination of court cases fought in individual states and whose rulings pertained only to education in those states. IDEA had national implications for educating students with disabilities in the United States regardless of individual state policies and procedures. Each state was required to comply.

Later revisions and reauthorizations of this act through 2004 were renamed variations of the Individuals with Disabilities Education Act (IDEA). They required that children with disabilities are entitled to a free and appropriate public education; in the least restrictive environment; with needed supports and special education services; with parent rights to consent; and parent rights to be part of the process. IDEA also mandated nondiscriminatory assessment in determining eligibility for special education. Later changes to the act introduced the concept of transition, which focused on outcomes beyond school completion for students with disabilities and mandated that formal planning be put in place by the time a child reaches the age of sixteen. The Division of Career Development and Transition (DCDT) of the Council for Exceptional Children (CEC) suggests that as best practice, consideration of student needs, interests, and preferences in relation to transition should start no later than age fourteen.

Response to intervention (RTI) was also added to IDEA in 2004. Stecker, Fuchs, and Fuchs provide an excellent explanation of RTI:

In 2004, the reauthorization of the Individuals with Disabilities Education Improvement Act (IDEIA; P.L. 108–446) allowed for a student's response to research-based intervention [RTI] to be part of the process for identifying students with specific learning disabilities (SLD). Rather than requiring the traditional aptitude-achievement discrepancy approach to identification, which sometimes necessitated years of poor academic achievement before a student might qualify for special education services (i.e., a wait-to-fail model), IDEIA allows for continued poor response to validated instruction as a means for documenting that a student's disability may require specialized services to produce appropriate learning outcomes. *In other words, if a student continues to perform poorly despite the implementation of scientifically validated instruction, then inadequate instruction is eliminated as a cause for the student's insufficient learning. Instead, the student's lack of appropriate* response *to otherwise generally effective instruction is, in part, evidence for the presence of a disability.*[2]

RTI is thus "both an early intervention strategy within general education and one part in the process by which a student may be identified to receive special education."[3] It is beyond the scope of this book to detail all the nuances of RTI, especially since there is no recognized definition and each individual state can use its own model for RTI. In 2008, the American School Counselor Association adopted a position relative to RTI that "school counselors are stakeholders in the development and implementation" and "align with the RTI process through the implementation of a comprehensive school counseling program designed to improve student achievement and behavior."[4]

Schools today increasingly educate more children with disabilities in regular classrooms with their peers without disabilities, sometimes referred to as *inclusion.* Inclusion as a concept grew out of the observed need for students to be included and integrated into typical settings with typical peers, preferably from the beginning of their schooling, rather than being pulled out, placed in segregated settings, and perhaps being mainstreamed back into the typical classroom some day. Rather than students being removed for services, the intention was that services and supports would be brought to them in general education.

At the time of the original P.L. 94–142, disorders such as Tourette's syndrome, pervasive developmental disorder, autism, and learning disabilities did not even exist in terms of accurate definition. Updated definitions of disability now identify thirteen categories.

The Spirit of the Law Versus the Letter of the Law

In litigious times such as these, we sometimes tend to get caught up in what we have to do legally rather than getting to the heart of why something has became a law and the spirit of its intention. Sometimes the two seem to clash. For example, if a business constructs a curb cut into the sidewalk that meets code and then beautifies the area by planting rose bushes directly behind it, thereby making the sidewalk unusable to pedestrians, it is meeting the letter but not the spirit of the law. Similarly, the counselor who automatically advises all students with learning disabilities to consider something more realistic than a college education without understanding each student's potential may not be working in the spirit of legislation designed to guarantee equal opportunities to appropriate education and promote empowerment and self sufficiency in society. Usually these violations of the spirit are not intentional but a result of:

- Doing what has always been done
- Not being mindful while rushing to handle the demands of many responsibilities
- Trying to balance the needs of the school district and the students served
- The stress of having to do what is required without considering the reason
- Functioning under misconceptions that may still exist due to lack of information
- Not being proactive enough

The information provided about legislation should begin to explain why the landscape has changed over time to include students with disabilities who in the past were the educational responsibility of someone—or no one—else. This also explains why the counselor role has dramatically increased in complexity and why school counseling programs and services must include students with disabilities.

Legislation and the School Counselor's Responsibilities

The Individuals with Disabilities Education Act as reauthorized in 2004 guarantees children with disabilities a free and appropriate public education in the least restrictive environment designed to meet their unique needs. The concept of least restrictive is based on the idea that government intrusion on individual rights should be minimized and that children ideally should be educated, to the greatest degree possible, with peers who do not have disabilities. This legislation provides the blueprint for the school's actions to meet the needs of children with disabilities. Based on ASCA's model, school counselors are integral to this process. Although each state may have different regulations, all states must comply with the federal standard. A school counselor's responsibilities may vary by district, but all should serve on the school team advocating for and educating a child.

Students Who Qualify for Special Education

Special education is specially designed instruction intended to meet the unique needs of a student with a disability. The instruction should be provided at no cost as part of the child's educational program, and it can include instruction in the classroom or, if necessary, in homes, hospitals, institutions, or other settings. Special education may also include instruction in physical education, art, and music; it is not limited to reading, writing, and mathematics.

For example, a child with a learning disability in mathematical reasoning who requires more individualized assistance in order to keep up with the curriculum may work with a resource room specialist teacher several times a week in order to understand the material. Or perhaps the classroom teacher can provide the instruction in a different way that would enable the student to understand, such as simplifying the task, presenting it at a different rate, giving more examples, or providing visuals instead of just auditory information.

Special education also includes the concept of *related services*, which are the transportation and developmental, corrective, and supportive services that a child may need in order to benefit from the education—for example, a bus so the child can get to the educational program or the occupational therapy the child needs in order to use the computer to access the curriculum. Individual or group counseling, peer tutoring programs, and specialized classroom guidance lessons are among the services provided by a school counselor or psychologist that might also be a related service that can help the child.

Disability Labels and Definitions

A child who has a disability does not necessarily need special education. One of the complications in understanding the disabilities that require special education services is that this is not a cut-and-dried issue. It is the educational need created by a specific child's disability that must be considered rather than the label. Nevertheless, that need must fall into one of IDEA's thirteen disability categories:

- Autism
- Deafness
- Hearing impairment
- Deaf-blind
- Emotional disturbance
- Mental retardation
- Multiple disabilities

- Orthopedic impairment

- Other health impairment

- Specific learning disability

- Speech or language impairment

- Traumatic brain injury

- Visual impairment

Descriptions of and resources for these disabilities can be found in Part Three.

Special Education Settings

Special education does not automatically place a child in a separate classroom. If specially designed instruction can be provided in the regular classroom, that is the preferred route. This relates to the concept of the least restrictive environment, which means the student is placed in the setting most like the typical classroom in which he or she can appropriately learn. For some, this is the regular classroom, and for others, it is a separate classroom. The needs of some students are so great that they may require a specialized school (for example, students who are deaf-blind and require specialized services and supports difficult to provide in an integrated regular classroom). The important concept here is that no student is automatically placed in the most restrictive setting if not warranted, and these decisions should be made on the basis of what is most appropriate for the student rather than what is easier for the school. The unique needs of the child and the specially designed instruction are identified first.

Related Services

The following example illustrates the difference between specially designed instruction and related services and how they complement each other to provide an appropriate program for the child.

Jill is a seven year old with a severe hearing loss. It was not diagnosed until after she was four years old, and she had missed critical developmental stages. She has delayed language skills, difficulty with speech, reading comprehension issues, and difficulty keeping up with all academic areas. Jill needs special education to help with her reading comprehension and expression so that she can participate in the curriculum, and she receives specialized instruction. Her teacher and reading specialist work collaboratively with the speech language pathologist who provides related services that are necessary for Jill to benefit from any of the specialized educational services (language therapy three times per week). Since the speech language pathologist is the expert in Jill's language disorder, her services and work or co-teaching with the other educators is critical to Jill's academic success.

Every school counselor and any other school-related professional who has a role on the multidisciplinary team involved in planning for this student should have a good understanding of these components, which are listed in the Code of Federal Regulations 34 (CFR300):

- A free and appropriate public education
- An appropriate evaluation (one that that is nondiscriminatory)
- An individualized educational program
- The least restrictive environment
- Guarantee of procedural safeguards including confidentiality

The following sections explain these concepts and, where appropriate, highlight possible school counselor involvement.

A Free and Appropriate Public Education   Every student, even those with the most severe and profound disabilities, is entitled to an education that is publicly supported through their twenty-first year (unless they graduate before then). This is called the *zero reject policy*. Children who have terminal illnesses or children who are in mental institutions, are hospitalized, or are home bound are eligible to an education at public expense. In certain instances, the district must send a child to a specialized program or school or send a teacher to the child who is outside the school setting.

An Appropriate Evaluation   A school must first conduct an evaluation (with appropriate parental consent) to determine if the student has a disability, if the disability inhibits progress in the general curriculum, and if special education is needed to meet the student's individual needs. The evaluation must use a variety of reliable assessment tools and strategies to gather relevant, functional developmental and academic information; be administered in the language of the child; be culturally unbiased (nondiscriminatory); and assess the areas in which a disability is suspected. These measures could include an intellectual assessment using IQ tests and other psychological measures, hearing tests, speech and language evaluations, occupational therapy assessments, behavior profiles, and parent interviews, for example. Standardized instruments that are considered valid and reliable for the evaluation of typical students may not be valid and reliable for the evaluation of students with a particular disability (see Chapter Nine).

For example, seven-year-old John who was hit by a car and as a result has quadriplegia, does not speak, and can move only his eyes, is entitled to an appropriate education based on an appropriate evaluation. The standard IQ test that is administered for most students would not work in this situation since John is nonverbal and has quadriplegia and could not verbalize responses, point, or write. It seems to be common sense that the traditional measures would not be valid in this case, but reports using such tests have been made and show such erroneous results as severe retardation. This student's situation may require a nonverbal evaluation of his intellectual functioning by someone trained in this area and identification of appropriate assistive technology and computer adaptations that will allow him to communicate. The school team would have to determine how to evaluate John's needs and meet them. If the school has no assistive technology expertise or specialist, this may involve interaction with outside agencies and specialists in order to complete the evaluation process. The evaluation would look at other areas of functioning to fully determine John's skills and needs. Once an accurate evaluation is conducted, there are many ways the school counselor could assist John that include addressing his personal and social developmental needs.

Individualized Education Program   An IEP must be developed if the result of an evaluation finds that the student needs special education. The IEP is a written document with these components:

- A statement of the student's current levels of academic achievement and functional performance, including how the disability affects the student's involvement and progress in the general education curriculum

- A statement of measurable annual goals, including academic and functional goals, designed to meet student needs that result from the disability, enabling the student to be involved in and make progress from the general curriculum, and to meet each of the other educational needs that result from the disability

- A description of how the student's progress will be measured and when periodic reports on the student's progress will be provided

- A statement of the special education, related services, supplementary aids, and services necessary to advance toward attaining the annual goals, to be involved in and make progress in the general education curriculum, and to participate in extracurricular and other nonacademic activities

- An explanation of the degree to which the student will not participate with students without disabilities in the regular class and in extracurricular and other nonacademic activities

- A statement of accommodations necessary to measure the academic achievement and functional performance of the student on state and district assessments, and if the IEP team determines that the student shall take an alternate assessment, explanations of why the student cannot participate in the regular assessments, as well as which alternate assessment has been selected as appropriate for the student

- Projected dates for the beginning of the IEP and the anticipated frequency, location, and duration of the services and modifications

- Beginning not later than the first IEP, to be in effect when the student is sixteen years old and to be updated annually thereafter: (1) appropriate, measurable postsecondary goals based on age-appropriate transition assessments related to training, education, employment, and, where appropriate, independent living skills; transition services including courses of study needed to assist the student in reaching those goals; and beginning not later that one year before the student reaches the age of majority under state law, a statement that the student has been informed of the rights that will transfer to him or her on reaching the age of majority[5]

Least Restrictive Environment   The concept of the least restrictive environment relates to the intent to minimize any restrictions on the student's educational environment that remove him or her from the typical setting. The student should be placed in a setting as close to normal as possible in which he or she can make appropriate progress with the educational services and supports needed. Automatic placement of a student with a disability in a segregated classroom violates the concept of least restrictive environment.

Procedural Safeguards   Procedural safeguards are designed to protect the rights of students and their parents as they proceed through the process of identification and placement. These procedures, which follow, ensure that parents understand their rights to consent and participate in the process:

- Written notice of these protections is provided in the parents' native language.

- Written parental consent must be given before any testing or other action occurs regarding their child's education.

- Parents can present information from independent educational evaluations in considering the presence of a disability or determining IEP content.

- Parents have the right to be part of the team.

- Parents have access to their child's educational records.

- Parents have the right to disagree and request mediation or due process hearings.[6]

A student's parents must receive notice of the planned evaluation with reasons explained, and they must provide consent before testing occurs. Parents are viewed as integral to the team and can introduce information from outside evaluations, bring advocates to the meeting, and have full access to information on their child. They also have a right to disagree with team decisions and can ask for mediation or request a due process hearing to settle the disagreement.

The Meaning of It All

The IEP is a document that drives the educational program of a student with a disability (Figure 4.1). After a school team reviews the results of the assessments completed in the evaluation, reviews the information from the teacher and the family, and determines that the child has a disability that has a significant impact on his or her ability to progress in the general education curriculum, an IEP is developed and reviewed annually.

The IEP team must include at a minimum the parents of the student, a regular education teacher, a special education teacher, a representative of the local education agency, and someone who is trained to interpret evaluation results. The team can also include advocates, other specialists, and the child who must, at least by the age of sixteen, be invited to attend. The team can (but does not always) include many other individuals, such as experts in the field, school counselors, psychologists, the principal, occupational or physical therapists, speech and language pathologists, and assistive technology specialists. These participants can come from the school staff itself or by invitation of the parents. The parents may also request permission to record the meeting for future reference. There is no substitute for the parents at the IEP meeting. They must be notified of a meeting and invited to attend, and the meeting must be scheduled at a mutually convenient time rather than solely for the convenience of the school.

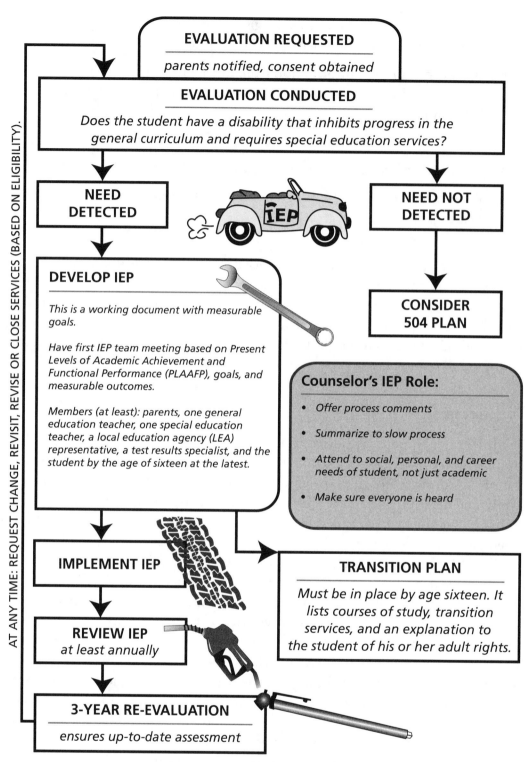

EVALUATION REQUESTED

parents notified, consent obtained

EVALUATION CONDUCTED

Does the student have a disability that inhibits progress in the general curriculum and requires special education services?

NEED DETECTED

NEED NOT DETECTED

CONSIDER 504 PLAN

DEVELOP IEP

This is a working document with measurable goals.

Have first IEP team meeting based on Present Levels of Academic Achievement and Functional Performance (PLAAFP), goals, and measurable outcomes.

Members (at least): parents, one general education teacher, one special education teacher, a local education agency (LEA) representative, a test results specialist, and the student by the age of sixteen at the latest.

Counselor's IEP Role:

- *Offer process comments*

- *Summarize to slow process*

- *Attend to social, personal, and career needs of student, not just academic*

- *Make sure everyone is heard*

IMPLEMENT IEP

REVIEW IEP
at least annually

TRANSITION PLAN

Must be in place by age sixteen. It lists courses of study, transition services, and an explanation to the student of his or her adult rights.

3-YEAR RE-EVALUATION

ensures up-to-date assessment

AT ANY TIME: REQUEST CHANGE, REVISIT, REVISE OR CLOSE SERVICES (BASED ON ELIGIBILITY).

Figure 4.1 The IEP Process

Review of the Process That Culminates in the IEP Meeting

The process begins when the teacher or parent requests an evaluation because the student is having difficulty in school. Actually it is likely that the teacher will first detect the student who is having difficulty and is likely to contact the family for further consultation if the student requires more intensive interventions. The teacher first implements different techniques in the classroom for a period of time and might modify methods or materials used to see if this makes a difference in the student's success. This is referred to as the student's *response to intervention* (RTI). When teachers are developing these strategies, they may consult with the school counselor to explore ways to facilitate the student's learning. In addition to altering the way instruction is delivered, the school counselor may intervene by involving the student in the school's counseling programs.

If none of the interventions makes a difference, then, with the consent of the parents, a formal evaluation is conducted. The evaluation can include psycho-educational batteries, speech and language testing, perceptual motor evaluations, social-behavioral inventories, and observations, as well as detailed parent interviews, a history, and any related medical information. As part of this process, diagnosis in some categories requires outside evaluation by medical or related specialists. If it is determined that the disability has an impact on the child's ability to learn without additional services, aids and strategies, or accommodations in the classroom or school setting, an IEP is developed.

The process was designed so that the IEP development is dynamic. It is not a static document that is prepared, finalized, and presented to the parents as set in stone. The draft IEP at the meeting should be viewed as a working document that can be discussed, amended, changed, and added to during the group meeting. This also guarantees that parents have an active role in the process.

Team members convene at the initial IEP meeting and discuss the student's current levels of academic achievement and functional performance, which is documented in the IEP description. This is part of the documentation of his or her unique needs, on which the rest of the IEP should be based, and describes the child's strengths and needs. The team determines what goals should be developed in the coming year, as well as what services will be provided, by whom, how often, and for what percentage of the school day. The goals are based on an estimate of progress the student can make in the next year, and they must relate to the way in which his or her disability interferes with progress in the general education curriculum. The goals are revisited each year and must be measurable. There should also be discussion of how the team will know that the student has met the goals and objectives and what measures will be used to assess growth. Related services and supplementary supports and accommodations should also be listed.

School counselors are valuable members of the IEP team who can contribute in these ways:

- They can offer process comments: "I am aware this is a lot of information for Susie's parents to take in. Let's stop to check with them to see if they have any questions."
- They can slow the process down by summarizing what they have heard.
- They can ensure that in addition to the academic needs of the student, attention is given to the impact of the student's personal, social, and career development on academic achievement and success.
- They can be advocates for the student.
- They can ensure that all voices at the table are heard.

Importance of the IEP

The IEP serves as the written documentation that delineates the student's current functioning, strengths, needs, and measurable goals for the next year, as well as the programs and services designed to help the child make progress. This document is reviewed annually to discuss progress and determine new goals. It is also a developmental tool that accompanies the student in moving from grade to grade and provides a historical record of what has happened since the student was identified as having disabilities. A reevaluation every three years ensures that assessments are current. There is no rule that says that an IEP cannot be revisited or revised if that is necessary. Parents can seek legal solutions if schools do not provide the services and supports it has agreed to in the IEP (changes in school infrastructure, staffing, or budget are not excuses).

Defining the Least Restrictive Environment

The least restrictive environment means that to the maximum extent appropriate, students with disabilities are educated alongside students who do not have disabilities and that separate class placement or separate school placements occur only when the student's disability is so severe that education in the regular class with supplementary aids and services cannot be achieved in a satisfactory way.[7] This means that placing a student in a special education class solely because he or she has been labeled with a disability may not be appropriate or that putting all students with mental retardation in the same class because they share a similar diagnosis and it is convenient is not appropriate.

Many students with mild, moderate, or severe disabilities may be able to receive their education in the regular classroom with the appropriate supports and increased awareness and accommodations by the teacher and school staff. For example, the student with a visual learning disability that requires additional support for reading may be fine with learning support from the resource teacher and software programs that verbalize the written text. A student with auditory processing problems who requires more visual supports may succeed in the class if the teacher repeats information or provides more handout materials.

School counselors should note special factors that must be addressed and actively responded to for each child when creating the IEP:

- If a behavior program currently is in effect for a student who has behavior characteristics that impedes learning

- If there are specific language needs due to the student's limited English proficiency

- For students who are blind or who have low vision, if braille instruction is needed

- If there is a need for assistive technology devices or services[8]

The IEP team must address each and respond to the questions by providing needed services in each circumstance above or by assuring in writing that there is no need based on appropriate evaluation. So if Sam has an ongoing problem that manifests itself by hitting classmates, the team must ensure that a behavior plan is in effect to address this. Similarly if behaviors related to his disability are determined through his evaluation process to contribute to problems that he has on the bus on the way to school, a behavior plan must be incorporated into the IEP to address this. As a result, it may provide additional considerations for transportation (also a related service). If Pedro, who has mental retardation, is a native Spanish speaker, the school must take into consideration his language proficiency and provide instruction so that he can learn. If Jasmine has blindness and reads braille at home, instructional materials may need to be provided in braille for her, and if Roy cannot speak due to a motor problem, the team must consider and evaluate his need for assistive technology, such as an augmentative communication device, that would allow him to express himself.

Behavior and Discipline: Special IEP Factors

Concerns about discipline and behavior have become a major issue for parents of children with and without disabilities, students, and teachers. Schools have begun to implement policies for conduct violations that include suspension and expulsion. The policy intentions have been focused on security and safety for students, but in some cases, the results have had negative effects. Students with behavior issues that are related to their disabilities have sometimes been penalized for their disability more than the infraction. Before such consequences are enforced, there is a need to examine whether a disability characterized by behavior problems may require adapted discipline procedures or behavior modification measures.

In order to address this issue, IDEA implemented regulations mandating that within ten school days of any change of placement for a child with a disability due to a conduct violation (a student may be suspended for under ten days or the school may remove a child to an interim placement for forty-five days if he or she has inflicted serious bodily injury), the IEP team should convene to review the IEP and gather the observations of teachers and parents to determine if the conduct was caused by the disability or if it was the result of the school's failure to implement the IEP. This process is called the *manifestation determination*. If the team decides that the behavior was a manifestation of the child's disability, the team will conduct *a functional behavior assessment* and implement a *behavior intervention plan* or review a current one that exists to modify it. (Again, the immediate exception is when a child inflicts serious bodily damage to another person on the school premises or at a school function.) This process is designed to describe the behavior and the extent to which it interferes with learning, identify possible causes, make recommendations about addressing the behavior and replace it with positive behaviors, and ensure that a child is not further penalized for his disability.

Functional Behavior Assessment

The functional behavior assessment is an organized process designed to collect information on a student's challenging behaviors, causes of those behaviors, and predictors of occurrence or nonoccurrence. The results of the assessment are then used to develop positive behavior interventions. The process has the following steps:

1. Identify the behavior that is problematic.

2. Determine the conditions or circumstances under which the behaviors occur.

3. Collect data from numerous sources about the child's disability and behaviors related to the disability.

4. Develop a hypothesis about the function of the behaviors.

5. Identify positive behaviors that can be taught to replace negative behaviors while still meeting the functional needs of the student.

6. Write a plan for implementation as part of the IEP.

7. Evaluate the change.

The IEP goals and objectives for behavior should focus on positive supports and proactive behavior change, not punishment, which may be counterproductive if there is no plan to assist the child in developing more appropriate behaviors. Behaviors do not occur in isolation and usually have a reason, so any evaluation must take the context into consideration.

Behavior Intervention Plan

This plan, developed by the team and incorporated into the IEP process, is designed to teach positive behaviors and usually includes these components:

- Specific skills training to increase prosocial behavior
- Changes to the child's environment to reduce problem behaviors
- Strategies to replace problem behaviors with appropriate behaviors
- Supplementary aids, supports, or curricular modifications
- A plan to determine progress

In addition, IDEA specifies that states must provide in-service education to school personnel on positive behaviors because implementation of any of these plans requires a team effort. Some sample behavior goals might include being on time for class, working quietly without distracting others, or raising a hand before speaking. Some examples of behavior intervention strategies might include preventive cueing or using cues to alert the student that he or she is doing something unacceptable, proximity control or moving closer to a student, and behavior shaping or rewarding small gains that approximate the desired behaviors.[9]

The Transition Plan

By the age of sixteen at the latest, students with disabilities who have an IEP also must have a statement of transition services in place that identifies supports and interagency connections to assist the student in the movement from school to postschool outcomes. This statement includes the development of "appropriate measurable postsecondary goals based on age appropriate transition assessments related to training, employment, education and, where appropriate, independent skills" and identifies "transition services including courses of study needed to assist in reaching those goals."[10] In addition, not later than one year before the student reaches the age of majority, he or she must be informed of adult rights.

Assessments used to develop the transition plan look at strengths, needs, interests for postschool employment, education, training, and independent living. These assessments can include a variety of measures: interviews, situational assessments, vocational evaluations, assessment of self-advocacy skills, and analysis of natural supports in a student's life situation, among others. The results of the assessments lead to the development of postsecondary goals in areas listed above (training, employment, education, independent living, and sometimes daily living skills) and a plan to match the student with educational, vocational, or independent living options through recommended preparation and training. Postsecondary goals could include plans to investigate college options, pursue vocational training based on the identified strengths and interests of the student, obtain a job, live in the community or other setting, and to prepare for these changes. In order to accomplish the postsecondary goals, the team must identify needed transition services and courses of study that are required.

For example, if Theresa wants to get a job in a department store after graduation, her transition services might include vocational evaluation and specific skill training, job training with a job coach, mock interviews with the school counselor, and instruction in using public transportation. If Hector wants to go to college, transition activities may include investigating college options, setting up visits to colleges, working with the school counselor to arrange for testing accommodations if necessary, and scheduling the SAT or other qualifying tests. Courses of study identified in his plan may include taking algebra or needed science prerequisites.

By the time a student is sixteen years old, he or she should be participating in his or her own transition plan meeting (when appropriate, the school may discuss transition plans with the student before the age of sixteen) because this is a process that should be focused on the student's needs but also his or her strengths, desires, and interests. Not only should a student have an active role in transition planning, but some advocates support transition meetings that are student driven since findings reveal that sometimes the student is the team member who has the least understanding of this meeting. School counselors can help students to prepare for this transition process by discussing student interests and needs with the student and help to investigate future options. Weidenthal and Kochhar-Bryant found that preparing students for their participation in the meeting, talking about their future plans, and facilitating self-determination skills were effective strategies to elicit their involvement in the planning process.[11] This aspect of transition planning may dovetail well with individual planning integral to the ASCA model, as well as career standards and competencies. Representatives of adult service agencies must be invited to attend transition meetings. If the student might use adult public services after school completion, the involvement of these groups facilitates this move.

At the transition meeting, the student, along with other family members, school staff and other specialists, explores options for the future in terms of continuing education or vocational preparation, job placement or exploration, discussions about where the student will live, how he will get around, and whether he is prepared to assume activities of daily living such as cooking, cleaning, shopping, and paying bills. The details of the transition plan are customized to the needs, interests, potential, and goals of the student.

Translating It All into Action

All students are entitled to an appropriate education in an environment most like (or the same as) the learning situation of their typical peers and one in which they can make reasonable progress—for example:

- This means that because Susie has spina bifida and is a wheelchair user, there should not be an automatic assumption that she needs to be in a segregated special class.

- This means that Eddie, a high school student with average intellectual potential and with dyslexia, who wants to go to college, should be able to pursue avenues that his peers pursue in terms of investigating options, taking the SAT (possibly with modifications), visiting colleges, and expecting the assistance and facilitation from school counselors who help other students with this aspect of transitioning beyond high school.

- This means that Frieda, whose IEP stipulates that she can receive double time on tests as a necessary accommodation because of her labored movement, should not fail if the teacher calls time and collects all the exams yet she has not finished.

The school counselor, as a member of the team, can have an instrumental role in connecting people and information in order to ensure continuity and consistency in implementation of the IEP. School counselors attend to the personal, social, academic, career, and resiliency needs of students. Special attention is given throughout this book to recognize the amplified developmental needs of students with disabilities. In the example of Claudia at the end of the chapter, it is evident that there are many amplified developmental concerns and issues. Read her case and try to identify her amplified personal, social, academic, career, and resiliency needs.

Section 504 and 504 Plans

Some students with disabilities have a 504 plan but not an IEP. These are different from each other. Section 504 is not about special education; it is about providing access to programs and is most relevant to students who have a disability that may affect them in school but does not require special education. IDEA and Section 504 are derived from very different regulations. Section 504 is based on civil rights statutes, while IDEA is based on education regulations. A student who requires an IEP qualifies for a 504 plan, but not all students who qualify for a 504 plan require an IEP. Table 4.2 highlights the differences. Section 504 is part of the Rehabilitation Act of 1973 (P.L. 93–112), the first civil rights legislation in the United States designed to safeguard the rights of those with disabilities. It is more closely related to the ADA and states: "No qualified handicapped person shall on the basis of handicap, be excluded from participation in, be denied benefits of, or otherwise be subjected to discrimination under any program or activity which receives or benefits from Federal financial assistance."

Section 504 basically ensures equal access to programs and services that receive any federal monies, which includes public schools and universities, as well as federally funded organizations and programs. Section 504 defines disability in terms of "physical or mental impairment" that "substantially limits a major life activity" like walking, dressing, feeding oneself, working, or seeing and supports the provision of needed accommodations. Section 504 protects individuals who have disabilities (that affect daily activities), have a history of disabilities, or are regarded as someone with a disability. Unlike IDEA, Section 504 has no funding attached to it, so costs must be incurred by the district, and it is legislation with which districts must comply.

Table 4.2 An IEP and 504 Plan Comparison

504 Plan	IEP
Ensures equal access to services and programs that receive federal money	Meets the requirement to provide free, appropriate public education to all
Based on civil rights; falls under Section 504 of the Rehabilitation Act	Based on education regulations; falls under the Individuals with Disabilities Education Act.
Most applicable to students who, because they have a disability, require accommodations to access educational tools or facilities	Most applicable to students who have been assessed and qualify for special education

Sometimes a child has a disability that may not neatly fit into one of the IDEA categories or does not have an impact on learning as long as certain services, treatments, or program modifications are provided during the school day. As an example, Margie has a severe food allergy to milk, wheat, and peanuts. She has no learning problems, but if she ingests one of the substances she is allergic to, she could have a fatal reaction. This is a pretty clear case of the need for a 504 plan. The plan must describe her disability, situations that would be contraindicated, and precautions that need to be taken, and outline emergency procedures in the event of a problem—for example:

- Margie's lunch will be prepared in separate dishes in the cafeteria, served with separate utensils, and use no allergic substances.

- The parents of all other children in the class should be asked not to send peanuts to school because of Margie's reaction.

- The school will maintain an autoinjecter of epinephrine that can be used in an emergency situation.

- Teachers and other staff will be trained to recognize the critical nature of time (even seconds) that can make a difference and the need to act quickly if necessary.

Margie and other children in similar situations do not necessarily need special education. However, there are protections under the law to ensure that they can attend school with the needed accommodations and supports and benefit from an education. Although any child who ends up with an IEP would qualify for 504 by virtue of his or her disability, not every child with a 504 plan needs special education.

While 504 plans explain the disability and need for accommodations and list them, it is a much simpler document than an IEP with few regulations about procedures, team members, or required educational services. So Tony, who has ADHD and has developed excellent self-monitoring skills provided he takes his medication each morning, may need a 504 plan to ensure that he can miss the first five minutes of class each morning in order to get his medication from the school nurse. Some children with ADHD who do not have learning problems can also fall under Section 504; their plans could include items like ensuring that directions are broken down and provided visually and auditorally, or that their seat in class needs to be in the front to minimize distractions for them. Although it appears that there is less prescription in terms of regulations guiding procedures, evaluations, required staff, and therapies, schools nevertheless are legally obligated to comply with 504 requirements. Violations could potentially result in legal action against schools.

NCLB and IDEA

The No Child Left Behind Act (NCLB), enacted in 2001 by President George W. Bush, was designed to increase accountability in schools and improve academic outcomes for all students, assessing progress mainly through increased state testing.

Prior to NCLB, students with disabilities were often excluded from state assessments. Students with disabilities are now required to be included in state assessments, with test scores supplied as part of each school's adequate yearly progress evaluation. Although many advocates for children with disabilities saw NCLB as a positive change—a way to ensure that schools would focus more attention on academic expectations and success for students with disabilities—some have felt that the expectations for some students with disabilities may be unrealistic. The expectation of NCLB is that by 2014, all students will be proficient in reading and math. The stress on the curriculum has had mixed results and in some cases has meant that teachers and students have had to forgo opportunities to engage in innovative learning in order to spend time on state test preparation.

Under NCLB, students with disabilities are required to participate in annual assessments, with needed accommodations, in the grade in which they are enrolled. IEP teams determine how these students will participate in testing. They may take grade-level assessments as other students do, take the same assessments with needed accommodations, or take alternate assessments based on grade level or alternate standards. Each state determines allowable accommodations such as changing the test setting to reduce noise or distractions; changing the schedule of the test; altering the test presentation with larger print, sign interpretation, or other such modifications; or providing a different mode of response, such as a scribe or adapted answer sheet.

Some states also allow adaptive equipment or format. If the student cannot take a grade-level assessment even with accommodations, the IEP team must explain why not and describe alternate ways of assessment, which can include observation checklists, parent interviews, assessments of specific tasks, or portfolio evaluations.[12] Only the most severely involved students with the most significant cognitive disabilities are permitted to take alternate assessments that are based on alternate criteria (these are typically students in a life skills program).

Claudia's Story

This chapter has provided basic information with which school counselors should be familiar in order to best serve students with disabilities. Sample scenarios and case information demonstrate how student needs can be articulated into goals, enacted through the creation of a plan, and tied to real outcomes for students.

Having the actual regulations is important for comprehension and clarification, and these are available online. With the wealth of legal material covered in this chapter, I close with a real example to tie everything together. Claudia's story gives context to this material and highlights the school counselor's role.

Claudia was diagnosed with a seizure disorder at the age of two, a few weeks after receiving a scheduled DPT vaccination. In 1985, she entered first grade, and she was then diagnosed with language-related processing issues and attentional problems. This translated into her need to have information repeated, difficulty in following complex or abstract verbal directions, difficulty processing what she heard when there was background noise, and some difficulty staying on task without additional supports. This was despite the fact that her intellectual capacity fell within the average range. Anticonvulsant medications controlled her seizures but caused fatigue and affected her fine motor coordination. The teacher reprimanded her (reflected in grades) for not paying attention, not following directions, and taking too long to complete tasks.

She was a happy child, loved animals and music, and had an excellent memory for events and excellent decoding skills. After a family relocation to another state, an IEP was developed that identified her as a student with a learning disability and other health impairments. She began to receive help in mathematical reasoning from the resource teacher as well as language therapy from the speech-language pathologist. The teacher and family worked closely together in trying to keep her progress on track. Academic stress that usually does not arise until middle or high school for most students was amplified for Claudia, because she needed to muster increased focus time and cognitive energy in order to keep up with grade-level materials. This needed to be done in the face of the rigors of additional therapies, slowed processing time, medication effects, and the social ramifications of being a nontraditional learner in a class of more typical peers.

In junior high, the family, school counselor, and school nurse worked to ensure that staff had information about seizure disorders and what to do. It was also important for Claudia and others to know that excessive fatigue, too much stress, or extreme physical activity might put her at higher risk for a seizure. The physical education teacher was informed of this so he would be aware of changes during physical activities. The school also provided in-service information to teachers so they would understand what a seizure disorder was and that it did not mean cognitive delays. In addition, the school counselor, as a member of the multidisciplinary team, worked to see that Claudia received additional time for test taking and was scheduled to meet regularly with the resource teacher to work on math and writing assignments and that teachers provided instructional information in multiple formats and included visual information.

Through communicating with the parents, the counselor learned that Claudia's mother spent at least three hours a day with her after school working on school assignments and studying. Demands on Claudia's time were again amplified as school work demands increased despite the fact that her processing time did not and that medication effects continued to cause fatigue. Most of her time after school was spent keeping up, reading, and doing homework rather than socializing, and she missed social opportunities and other opportunities for typical adolescent peer interactions.

In high school, the attitudes, teaching styles, and preparation of her individual teachers were a critical factor in her success and varied from teacher to teacher. Once when she received a poor grade on her geometry test, her parents requested the test so that they could see how to better help her. The teacher refused, saying he would not give back tests because then students would have the answers. The school counselor intervened to point out that although this allowed the teacher to continually administer the same test each year, it discriminated against this student.

On another occasion, the teacher gave an assignment that required completing a math activity about how to hit a hole in one and gave students the task of designing an actual golf hole, building it, trying it, and drawing the angles someone would have to hit to complete the task. He also required that the student physically hit the ball to get a hole in one in order to get a passing grade. The school counselor again intervened when the parents pointed out that this was not reasonable if someone had a physical issue or a perception problem and that the task actually tested a disability rather than math knowledge. The school counselor worked with the resource room special educator and class teachers to arrange for extra time on tests. However, Claudia protested being called out of the class to take the test because she did not want to be identified by her peers as being different. So arrangements were made for her stay and begin the test in the class and then go to the resource room afterward to finish if she needed more time.

Social isolation was an additional issue, amplified by some school policies such as seating children with disabilities at the same lunch table, further segregating them from more typical peers. The school counselor, through discussions with Claudia, found that she was being targeted and bullied in part due to school practices in the cafeteria, and she helped the school to rethink seating arrangements that facilitated more normalized interaction. In addition, the school counselor made sure that teaching and support staff were more alert to identifying bullying and instituting measures that countered such behaviors rather than ignoring them by attributing them to typical (and acceptable) adolescent behavior.

In tenth grade, transition planning included a discussion of Claudia's skills, interests, and future plans. The team decided that a series of mock interviews with the school counselor would help her to practice needed skills and that a part-time job or volunteer opportunity would provide Claudia with job-related experiences and needed skill development. She began to volunteer in a nursing home and took a part-time job in an early childhood center.

The team helped her find out about postschool options, information on college programs, and extended-time accommodations for SATs and ACTs. Her parents and school counselor worked together to complete the paperwork required to demonstrate and document the need, receive advanced approval from the national testing agencies, and make arrangements for a time accommodation on the college exams. The school counselor also worked with Claudia to help her analyze her own strengths and interests in the context of exploring additional career options that might suit her well.

When the ACT was administered, the proctor forgot to provide extra time, and Claudia got to complete only a small portion of the mathematics section. When her parents called the school to complain, the school counselor arranged for a different administration with the time accommodations that had been listed in her IEP/transition plan. The difference between the final scores on the two administrations (one with time accommodations and one without) was five grade levels in mathematics. Claudia completed high school at the same time as her peers and entered a state college.

Chapter 5

Partnering with Parents

The American School Counselor Association's Ethical Standards for School Counselors highlight fundamental principles intended to guide school counselors in their work with parents of students with disabilities (ASCA, 2004):

- Parents need to be the guiding voice in the school's work with children with disabilities. They have hopes and dreams for their child, and they are often the best authority on their child. The school needs to honor their parental rights and responsibilities.[1]

- A collaborative partnership with parents is essential in helping students with disabilities meet their amplified academic, social/personal, and career development needs as they progress through their school experience. This partnership can maximize their success in achieving competency in these critical developmental areas.[2]

Parents of children with disabilities often know their children better than anyone else, and they naturally are the ones who will remain involved year after year. In many cases, parents are experts because of their wealth of information about their child's disability, and they also tend to be well informed about the possibilities that exist for their children. School counselors are wise to value their expertise. Unfortunately, school counselors sometimes overlook the depth of parents' knowledge or are put off by their persistence, communication style, or different opinions. Our focus in this chapter is on how to better understand their perspectives and realize the potential of strong partnerships with them.

A Glimpse of Common Parental Experiences

School counselors must understand some of the salient experiences of parents that often bear on their interactions with them. Some of them are emotional experiences related to having a child with a disability, some have to do with previous experiences with educators and health care providers, and some have to do with ongoing worries, frustrations, and stressors. It is easier to empathize with parental concerns, no matter how they are presented, when we understand more about what they often have gone through by the time we meet them. Here is what one mother had to say:

> I remember really flaring up quickly at one meeting. I am sure they thought I was just one more difficult mother. And I was. What they didn't see was my frustration from the last four years of asking different educators for someone to give my child class notes because he couldn't write. They didn't see how much stress I have on a daily basis, how much I love my child and how worried I have been about him. So when I overreacted to the first sign of stalling at this meeting, I was reacting to all that as well as the fact that I had spent four hours the night before doing homework with my child.

Many parents of children born with disabilities initially experience heart-wrenching feelings of loss. It is as if they had lost the child they imagined they were going to have. Grief may be overwhelming, but it generally subsides, and most parents are able to get beyond it and celebrate the child they have. School counselors need to appreciate what parents have been through in terms of coping with loss. Parents of children with some disorders (such as autism) may find their once-communicative children have lost language and social connection and seem to prefer objects to them.

School counselors will appreciate that some parents experience similar stages of mourning as those described by Elisabeth Kübler-Ross in her seminal work on death and dying.[3] Duncan conceptualized parental reactions to childhood disability as similar in terms of progressing through the stages of initial shock, denial, bargaining, anger, depression, and acceptance.[4] The process of acceptance of a child's disability is not linear; no one moves through these stages once and for all. Some parents easily leave grief behind. But for many, these feelings of loss resurface because they are triggered by certain events, often developmental milestones. For example, the successful attainment of milestones by other people's children can underscore just how far off the mark their own child is according to typical standards. The realization could then usher in a "new" mourning phase:

> You spend years teaching your child how to throw and catch a ball. She finally gets it right and you are ecstatic. It is one of those moments of joy and satisfaction and confirmation that your child can learn and progress with attention and practice. Suddenly your joy is tempered by the realization that while you have spent years mastering the simple task of throwing and catching, your child's peers have worked on batting, basketball, soccer and are now playing football. That very accomplishment that was for an instant a supreme high is now yet another cause to grieve. I realize that this will recur throughout my child's life and makes me realize how emotionally strong parents of children with disabilities need to be.[5]

Stage theories, such as Kübler-Ross's or Duncan's, are sometimes useful as a means to understand that the route to coming to grips with a child's disability often includes phases in which depression or anger is prominent. But frameworks can be used inappropriately when parents' emotional reactions are too quickly attributed to their internal struggles when the problems are actually external. Here is an example of an inappropriate application of the parental grief stages. During an individualized educational program (IEP) meeting, a parent is angry and agitated because of a lack of attention to the child's specific learning needs. The school counselor recognizes the emotional reaction and attributes it to the grieving stage of anger and then responds to the emotions present: "I can understand that accepting your child's disability is producing all this anger. That's a normal grief reaction." In fact, the school counselor dismissed the real cause of the anger: the parent's frustration that the child's needs are not being met.

The route to acceptance of a child's disability varies greatly from parent to parent. Some do not go through a mourning period at all, and sometimes what appears to school counselors as denial is actually recognition of their child's true potential and an understanding of realities that their child faces. For example, a parent who tells the school counselor that her son with Asperger's syndrome wants to go to college may be regarded as "in denial"; in this instance, the counselor lacks information that the parent has about the growing numbers of individuals with Asperger's syndrome who are attending and succeeding in higher education.

Taub cautions that school counselors should not assume generalities about all parents of children with disabilities, although she does mention a few common issues and concerns that more often visit families who have children with disabilities. In addition to grief and loss, she lists feelings of overprotectiveness, concerns about the attitudes of other children and parents, underestimation of the child's potential by teachers, and life transitions as major issues. With respect to feelings of protectiveness, parents are often anxious because they are aware of all the obstacles their child faces.[6] An additional ongoing and deep concern noted by parents was their child's lack of friendships, a concern well illustrated by the following parental anecdote:

> There is a helpless feeling that you get when you pick up your child at 3:00 PM in the school parking lot and watch her going from child to child inviting each one over only to be refused. If you only had the power to create a friend you would do it. How many times can you tell her that they must have other things to do today and maybe they'll be free another day before she catches on they just don't want to play with her? And then what do you do?[7]

Yet not all parents wrestle with negative feelings about a child's disability. Many embrace the child and experiences that have come their way:

> I thought I would change him and make him the boy I wanted him to be. But he has changed me, and helped me become the man I needed to be. He taught me the meaning of unconditional love—to honor his sacred right to be loved for who he is, not what he has achieved lately, how he looks, or how much money he will earn. What a priceless lesson he has taught me in his silence, without words—like a Buddha.[8]

Parents sometimes struggle more mightily with their feelings about professionals than with their feelings about their children. Many others have spent months or even years fearing there is something wrong with their child's learning abilities or health and frustrated or discouraged by being unable to get a clear diagnosis. "When James turned six months old, my husband and I decided to change pediatricians. The second doctor was an angel in disguise. She spotted the problem immediately . . . the reason I call her an angel is that she finally put an end to the unknown. The not knowing exactly what was wrong was driving me crazy."[9]

Many parents have had uphill battles with health care providers, and the stress and frustration have a way of accumulating and affecting other professional relationships as well. This is especially true when they also experience parallel battles with school professionals. Consider the parent who reported to one of us that she was told by a school professional that "if her daughter could go to the store and buy a loaf of bread in ten years, she should be happy." Or the parent who heard a school counselor say, "I don't waste my time with high school students with learning disabilities who want to go to college because they don't belong there." Sometimes parents believe there is a reason that their child is having difficulty meeting the learning and social demands of school, only to be told by school counselors and teachers that the child has been improperly parented and simply is too undisciplined to do well in school.

Although we would like to assert that these negative statements are rare or that these negative beliefs do not exist within the health or education fields, we would be misleading readers if we did. We encourage school counselors to realistically assess their school environments and challenge these beliefs and attitudes. More important, a school counselor who understands and acknowledges how these negative parental attitudes have developed can go a long way to diffusing them. Strained parent–professional relationships may be grounded in the stereotypical beliefs that some professionals hold about parents of children with disabilities.

Stereotypes About Parents

In Chapter Two, we wrote about stereotypes and the lenses that distort how professionals often see students with disabilities. Parents of children with disabilities are often also vulnerable to stereotyped ways of viewing them that are counterproductive and often obscure valid concerns.

Parents of children with disabilities have sometimes been labeled by counselors and teachers as being too aggressive, troublemakers, or unrealistic about their child's abilities and expectations for the future. In fact, the literature cites that parents are more often labeled negatively than the reverse.[10] These stereotypes are sometimes further exacerbated and "confirmed" when parents call the school, ask for meetings, ask for extra accommodations, cite the law at IEP meetings, or complain about unfair treatment, testing, or grading practices that appear to discriminate.

Two of the authors of this book are parents of children with disabilities and are also professionals in the field. Having worn both hats for years, they wish to underscore that many parents have had to become assertive, sometimes even unpleasant, to get their children's needs met from a host of professionals over the years. It is quite likely that school counselors work in a school district where parents are treated fairly. But the reality is that parents of children with disabilities are well aware of many instances in which parental and child rights have been summarily dismissed or disregarded. One parent known to these authors was told by the school district they could not afford speech therapy even though the child needed it. Similarly, another was told her daughter could not attend the appropriate programs because the school was not going to pay for the transportation bill (until she found out through her own efforts that that transportation is a related service under the law and that the school was required to provide it). The reality is that either the schools were knowingly violating the student's rights in order to save money or did not understand the law themselves. Neither scenario is comforting, and these instances are much too common.

Empowered parents of children with disabilities:

- Learn to be assertive to ensure that their child's needs are met

- Are knowledgeable about their child's disability

- Tend to be protective of their children

- Research their child's disabilities to understand the social, academic, and career effects so they can be more effective advocates for the needs of their child

- Put in long hours preparing for IEP meetings finding ways to ask for, and if necessary demand, what they believe their child needs

It is helpful for school counselors to reframe some parental behaviors that strike them as too assertive, too demanding, or too pushy. For example, they could reframe these behaviors as wise parents who are asserting their parental rights and responsibilities and are strongly looking out for their children.[11]

Other stereotypical assumptions may be directed toward families of children with emotional or behavioral problems. These disorders are among the most misunderstood disorders in the sense that their neurobiological base is often disregarded. Many neurobehavioral disorders such as autism, obsessive compulsive disorder, bipolar illness, and others are attributed to the lack of good parenting. It is not unusual for professionals to say, "I can see where the child gets it," after interacting with a particularly harried parent. What they do not see is that the parent's behavior is often reflective of the aftermath of difficult and intense child rearing rather than the cause.

Parental Stress

Parents of children with disabilities often face overwhelming everyday issues and stressors. It should be apparent to professionals who understand these issues that parents can become overwhelmed in trying to maneuver through not only their own reactions and adjustment to the disability, but to the ever-changing landscape of educational and medical testing and evaluations, IEPs and other team meetings, other family issues, and a host of social issues. Studies have shown that the quality of parent-child interactions decreases as the level of parent stress increases and that there is also a correlation between parent stress level and the psychological health of the children.[12] If counselors can successfully engage parents and provide appropriate support services, they will more likely and productively tap into the critical role that family can play in the child's progress.

Parents of children with disabilities may have issues with acceptance or knowing what to expect about their child's prognosis or course of treatment; may have ambitious expectations that may be realistic or not; or may still be searching for a label for their child's atypical learning or behavior. In addition to all of this, they may also be (to name only a few):

- Trying to juggle medical appointments or find specialists for rare disorders
- Keeping their child from falling behind by spending extra time on homework or finding tutors
- Trying to optimize social opportunities for their child
- Helping to investigate options for their child after high school
- Figuring out how to navigate a new service system they will confront after entitlements end at age twenty-one or at high school graduation

These tasks are certainly difficult when considered individually. When viewed collectively, they may be sources of tremendous stress for parents. School counselors who understand the level of stress that parents of children with disabilities face are better equipped to encourage and support them and ultimately help them meet the needs of their children.

Parents do note when counselors make concerted efforts to understand their stressors and respond to them. School counselors who reach out to parents can make a tremendous positive difference, as the following two comments from parents illustrate:

> "The school counselor got heavily involved, was very helpful in crisis situations and proactive advice. She never blamed my son, was very respectful of him, and very supportive of me. She continues to be supportive."

> "The junior high counselor gave encouragement to our child who is now thirteen and is the first professional who made me feel my child is a normal adolescent."

Neglectful and Abusive Parents

Up to now, we have focused on well-intentioned parents who have their children's best interest at heart and are interested in being invested partners in their development. However, a seminal report on the maltreatment of children with disabilities provided evidence that this assumption is unfortunately not always correct.[13]

The incidence of abuse for children with disabilities was reported as nearly two times the rate as those without disabilities. The maltreatment that was identified included both physical and sexual abuse and various forms of neglect (physical, educational, and emotional). Further specific findings of that report illustrate that for specific types of neglect or abuse, the incidence for children with disabilities is higher than that of their typical peers:

- Emotional neglect is 2.8 times more prevalent.

- Physical neglect is 1.6 times more prevalent.

- Physical abuse is 2.1 times more prevalent.

- Sexual abuse is 1.8 times more prevalent.

A more recent study concluded that maltreatment was 3.4 times more prevalent for students with disabilities.[14]

Clearly, the evidence of the association between abuse and neglect and children with disabilities is irrefutable. We present this evidence because school counselors are often on the front line for the identification of neglect and abuse. Our hope is that an awareness of this connection will prompt them to be ever vigilant for signs of abuse or neglect in their work with students with disabilities.

Partnering with Parents and Caregivers

The importance of parent involvement as equal partners in the educational process was underscored in the Individuals with Disabilities Education Act (IDEA). This legislation ensures that parents have the rights of involvement, to ask questions, to agree with or disagree with evaluation results, to give consent for testing, to provide information about the student, and to collaborate to determine appropriate goals. Relationships between parents and school personnel run the gamut, from effective collaborations to contentious to disengaged. Not only is effective collaboration with parents of students with disabilities invaluable in itself, but it is also an important deterrent to mediation and other disputes.[15]

Parents and school counselors who work collaboratively can make a substantial impact on a child's educational and developmental processes. Both have the capability to contribute different yet potentially synergistic components. Parents often know their child better than anyone else and are generally the ones most committed to that child's future. They are the ones who are there year after year as even the most dedicated educators and others come and go through the child's life. Many parents have amassed a great deal of knowledge about their child's disability, have been immersed in it for years, and are better informed about their child than school personnel can ever be.

The role of the school counselor in this partnership is to listen and understand parental concerns and issues, help them problem-solve or offer suggestions, and be a reliable conduit to other important players in the school milieu. Quigley and Studer view school counselors as an important connector among the school, the family, and the community.[16] The goal of successful inclusion is affected by the quality of school counselors' interface with parents and their ability to facilitate cooperative relationships between parents and school staff.[17] Carpenter et al. note that school counselors are essential in establishing partnerships with parents who may have withdrawn from active participation due to previous negative experiences.[18] When a good collaborative relationship is forged, school counselors can be a tremendous resource for the parents. School counselors are developmental specialists who understand the needs of the student and the family, and they are often in a position to be an excellent advocate for their child.

As part of this partnership, school counselors help parents respond to myriad amplified concerns about their child's school experience. These concerns run the gamut from how the child, the child's peers, and the peers' parents react to their child to how the child's friendships will be affected by the disability. Both Taub and Marshak, Prezant, and Hulings-Shirley address parental concerns regarding how peers and other parents will react to their child.[19] One would think that it is safe to assume that other parents, of relatively more typical children, will have good-will toward all children, especially those who have extra challenges. But sometimes other parents see the interventions to assist the child with a disability as a threat to the quality of their own child's school experiences. For example, the mother of a child with severe life-threatening food allergies spoke of the "war" that ensued when other parents were informed that they could not bring home-baked foods to class for treats because of her child's medical needs. This mother was astonished when she started receiving furious phone calls at home asking, "Just who do you think you are, trying to control what other children eat?!" To say the least, this parent was surprised to find herself pitted against the other parents when she was simply acting, like any other parent would, to protect her kindergarten-aged daughter from life-threatening situations. She was even more astounded by the other parents' reactions because she knew that this was her legal right, as was stipulated in her daughter's 504 plan. This is only one example of a negative reaction to a child with a disability; we could list countless others. Parents count on school counselors to take on an advocacy role to address these issues.

What Parents Value in Helping Relationships

School counselors are trained helpers and have developed a repertoire of helping skills that serve them well as they develop helping relationships with parents of children with disabilities. There are key facets to these specific types of helping relationships. For instance, interviews with adults with disabilities and parents of children with disabilities have revealed that at times there is a mismatch between what the provider and receiver of help perceive to be helpful. The classic example is that of the wheelchair user on the corner at a light and the helpful pedestrian passerby who grabs the wheelchair and "helps" the person "cross" the street without ever asking to find out that he did not want to cross and was waiting to meet a colleague there. Similarly, actions that professionals may decide are helpful may not be viewed that way by the recipient of the "help." And at the same time, actions that parents feel would be helpful may not occur at all. In surveying over a hundred families about actions they would like to see occur, Prezant and Marshak concluded that over half of the responses could be listed in three categories:

- Wanting professionals to listen to and respect what parents have to say

- Wanting professionals to be knowledgeable and provide information to parents

- Wanting professionals to collaborate and communicate with them[20]

It was clear that parents value the response of school personnel who seem to listen and respect them and their contributions regardless of whether there was agreement on all issues and that the mutual relationship should foster open communication and joint effort. They also expected school professionals to have information that they did not and could therefore count on the school to be an expert resource.

Parents also identified actions that they found to be unhelpful:

- Ignoring parental input

- Demonstrating demeaning behavior toward student or parent

- Discouragement of inclusion

- Abuse of power

- Having low expectations[21]

When parents experienced these unhelpful actions, they appeared to lose faith in the relationship with the school. The relationships often became counterproductive and at times contentious.

Responding to Parents' Needs for Support and Empowerment

The two most salient ways that school counselors can respond to parents' need for empowerment and support are working to empower parents by helping them navigate the various decision-making meetings and designing and offering support groups for parents.

Decision-Making Meetings: Empowering Parents

Once their child has been diagnosed with a disability, parents quickly learn that they must become knowledgeable about the educational laws, rules, and regulations that guide the schools as they seek to meet the needs of their child with disabilities. IDEA dictates the process for decision making for students with disabilities. Individualized educational programs (IEPs), 504 plans, and transition planning are the vehicles for this decision making. It is therefore essential for school counselors to realize the importance of these meeting for parents and that the process is complex and often confusing for them. Although school counselors are not IDEA experts, they need to be conversant enough to direct parents to the appropriate disabilities expert in the school district and be an advocate for the child in meetings.

School counselors and school professionals need to do all that they can to facilitate a process that is collaborative and to ensure that meetings are inclusive of parents as well as productive with respect to the needs of the child. This process begins with scheduling of a meeting. Legislation stipulates that IEP and 504 meetings need to be scheduled at a mutually convenient time; however, many parents do not know this, and many schools do not necessarily abide by this. Rather, the letter that is typically sent to parents in many districts about the scheduled IEP meeting may seem more like a demand for attendance than a collaborative meeting to discuss the needs of their child. This is a place where a small effort on the school counselor's part can make a big difference. Simply reviewing the communication that is being sent to parents and ensuring that its tone is collaborative and respectful of their schedules communicates appreciation and understanding. This attention to tone can go a long way to lessening the power differential that is easily inferred and parents often feel. Also, school counselors can help make sure that the location of the meeting is in a private and quiet setting, with no interruptions, and in which confidentiality can be maintained.

School counselors who understand group dynamics know that the physical seating at the meeting is also critical. Parents should not be on one side of the table facing the school professionals, and parents should not be seated in a child's chair. Nonverbal behaviors can send unintended messages. We have been at many IEP meetings in which a parent enters a room of professionals, and no one bothers to make introductions. A school counselor can make sure that parents are warmly welcomed to the meeting with handshakes, perhaps even engaging them in some small talk and presenting an invitation for them to join the group. Introductions around the table, as well as an explanation of stakeholder roles, go a long way toward building effective parent-professional partnerships. Whenever possible, a school counselor should prepare parents as to what to expect at the meeting. We recommend that school counselors draw on their group counseling training to help set up positive norms for the meetings that work to empower parents and foster communication and collaboration.

Even under the best of circumstances, there may be times when the child's needs diverge from that of the school. For example, the child may need a specialized residential treatment program, but given the realities of the school's budget, the cost of the program for the school is prohibitive. In these instances, school counselors are presented with a conflict of interest: Do they advocate for the child or the school? We believe they can do both if they simply tell the parents that it is well within their rights to assert their child's needs and insist that the school meet those needs in accordance with the laws. Or they could refer them to other parents (or parent advocates) who have successfully navigated similar challenges (got the school to respond to their child's needs) by being assertive and successfully advocating for their child. These parent-to-parent connections can be valuable and should be encouraged whenever possible.

As much as we have emphasized the importance of parents' guiding voices, there are times when it is in the best interests of the counselor to disagree. The following comment by a school counselor is indicative of a fairly common occurrence:

> I get very frustrated when the family hires a professional advocate to come to the IEP meeting and requests things that are not necessary. Counselors must decide what role they will play in an IEP meeting, and we need to remember we are advocating for the benefit of the child, no one else, including the parent. I once had a parent who was furious with me because I would not agree with what she was asking the school to do. She told me that I was not a proper advocate because I was not backing her request. My reply was that I was advocating for the child and in the child's best interest as I saw the situation. What she was requesting was not in my opinion the best situation for the child.

Expressing disagreement with a parent is certainly sometimes in the best interests of a child. We are not suggesting that parents always know what is in the best interests of a child. Sharing an alternate viewpoint is often essential.

Parent Support Groups

The journey that parents with children of disabilities experience is often challenging. School counselors need to recognize that parents respond to this challenge in a variety of ways and that they should respond to them according to their needs. Some parents are informed and readily prepared to advocate for their child. They are self-reliant and empowered and need little to no support from school personnel. They have developed sufficient personal resources outside the school. Their main request is that the school does its job and follows through with its agreements with them.

There are also parents who are disenfranchised and in need of support from the school. They may:

- Experience shame for their child's disability and seek to minimize or hide it

- Have a child with a low-incidence disability for which outside resources are minimal

- Reside in a rural area in which access to resources is more limited

- Have cultural barriers that prevent them from seeking help

- Believe that they have no time for connecting with others considering everything they have to do

- Withdraw and become an isolated unit (the principle here is, "We can solve this together. We don't need any outside help")

- Be socially isolated

- Lack the capacity to understand the resources available and need more assistance

As we noted earlier in this chapter, parents of children with disabilities have a wide range of feelings and stressors. All too often the only time they are asked to come to school is for required, and sometimes mechanistic, meetings or when their child is in trouble. Limited interactions of this nature do not contribute to a parent's sense of caring or empathy on the part of the school and can add to feelings of disenfranchisement.

To respond to parents, many schools have started support groups that are designed for and by parents of students with disabilities. Such a setting provides invaluable support, camaraderie, information sharing, and a forum for discussion of concerns and brainstorming solutions with other parents. If your school does not have a relevant group, do not overlook the possibility of helping to develop one. The fact that such a group could be facilitated by a school counselor is helpful in several ways. In addition to providing the benefits noted, the counselor is paving the way for constructive parent-professional partnerships.

These local school support groups can be supplemented by national organization support groups. Melissa Thompson, a family support specialist at the Texas School for the Blind and Visually Impaired, has noted an excellent resource for these national support groups: "Each year in the January edition of *Exceptional Parent Magazine* an extensive listing of these organizations, as well as parent-to-parent support organizations is published."[22] This magazine is an excellent resource for both empowered and disenfranchised parents.

Common Barriers to Developing Collaborative Relationships with Parents

Some experiences and behaviors are counterproductive to the development of positive relationships with parents and instead produce difficulty between the parent and the school counselor. Well-intended school counselors and parents may inadvertently engage in these unproductive behaviors. We highlight them here as a caution:

- *School counselors acting as if they are endowed with more power than the parents.* In this case, the parents see the relationship with the counselor as administratively driven, structured, and highly controlled by the school professionals. The parents are seen as "less than" and not on equal footing with the school counselor. This behavior creates a skewed power dynamic and a two-tiered system, with the school counseling professional at the top and parents below.
- *Parents who have had prior negative experiences with other professionals may be cautious and distrustful of the school counselor's efforts to build a positive and collaborative relationship.* In essence, the parents project all their old baggage onto the school counselor. When this happens, counselors should not take the parents' reaction personally and instead make a more concerted and intentional effort to establish trust with them.
- *The school counselor enters into the relationship with a negative attitude.* This attitude could be due to personality clashes with the parents, a professional bias about the student, or information the counselor has heard about the parents. This negativity can have a severe negative impact the relationship. It is critical for school counselors to remain as unbiased as possible and maintain a positive attitude with a primary focus on acting in the best interest of the child.
- *The school counselor works to maintain a professional distance.* School counselors see this as a as a way to remain objective; they are concerned that becoming too emotionally involved with the child could cloud their judgment. Some parents perceive professional distance as being disinterested or detached. School counselors who have this concern can use supervision and consultation to address the issue before it interferes with the parent-professional relationship.

Critical School Transitions and Developmental Stages

As children progress through school and the subsequent developmental stages, many common parental concerns or issues arise. Here we highlight these school transition periods and the corresponding developmental issues that are experienced for identified time periods: elementary school, middle school, high school, and transition. For each of these periods, we provide a table that identifies the transitional issue or developmental concern, the corresponding common parental concern related to the issue, suggestions for the school counselor to use to help parents address their concerns, and reference to other chapters that provide additional helpful information for the school counselor.

Elementary School

The move from the safety of the home into the school environment is filled with many challenges and risks for children with disabilities. This may be the first time that the child and the parents are confronted with realities of the impact of the disability. There are issues of safety, competency, judgmental reactions from others, school demands at home, and social isolation (Table 5.1).

Middle School or Junior High School

Perhaps the best way to describe this transition phase is that it is filled with complexities. It is as if the challenges of elementary school are exponentially increased. There are more teachers, more academic subjects, complex logistics to navigate such as bigger buildings, more classrooms, and more transitions in the day, lockers, and homeroom periods. There are more students, and with more peers come more complicated social issues (Table 5.2).

High School

This transition period corresponds with adolescence and puberty, and it is when students may begin to disengage in school and even consider dropping out. This is also a time when earlier childhood friendships can be lost and peer relationships intensify. There is the possibility of corresponding high-risk behaviors that result from this added peer pressure. Also, some students begin forming dating and romantic relationships that are fraught with social intricacies and present a demand for social skills. Some parents are faced with what sometimes feels like an inner conflict. On one hand, they desire safety for their children (and they are aware that greater socialization entails more risks); on the other hand, they are aware that too much protection may harm their children (Table 5.3).

Preparing for Transition

This refers to the transition that corresponds to leaving the K–12 environment. For school counselors and their work with students with disabilities and their parents, this is really a subphase that occurs later in high school (Table 5.4). We realize that by law, transition planning begins in middle school or junior high (see Chapter Four for more details about transition planning details). We decided to make it a separate section because we believe that many issues surface for parents with respect to this time period. This transition to adulthood is often referred to as "on your own without a net."[23] When students with disabilities leave the safety of the school setting and the supports and entitlements that exist there, they can become overwhelmed and thus begin to rely heavily on their parents and some parents become overly protective.

In closing, one parent of a child with an emotional disorder wrote of the impact of her son's school counselor:

> When my son graduated from high school, my husband and I felt real gratitude to his school counselor. Now and then we still talk about him. Over the years between IEP meetings, calls to the office for disciplinary issues, and a host of problems, we got to know him very well. Although we didn't always agree, my husband and I could count on him to listen to our concerns and express his honest opinion. It was a nice relationship. When he thought my child was taking advantage of a situation, he didn't hesitate telling us. We did not need to feel defensive of our parenting or our son because we knew the counselor respected us and believed our son would eventually get his act together. (He did!) He showed that he liked our son despite his exasperating behavior.

> He saw our child through high school and served as the consistent person we could rely on. These were very hard years for us as a family, but we felt like we had an ally and we felt far less alone in the uphill battle of launching our child. It has been many years since our son has graduated, but we still sometimes talk about his kindness and concern during a time when we were mostly used to being told by other people at school the latest thing our son had done wrong.

Table 5.1 Elementary School Transitions or Developmental Concerns

Important Transitions or Developmental Concerns	Common Parental Concerns or Issues	Helpful Suggestions for School Counselors	Other Helpful Chapters
Being away from home and exposed to more risks if medical needs are involved (for example, life-threatening food allergies, diabetes, asthma, seizure disorders)	Fear of medical emergencies; relinquishing responsibility and control; needing to fully trust that school staff will respond and implement the 504 plan and respond without error to all medical emergencies. Common parental sentiments: "They don't realize how serious this is and that my child might die on their watch!"	Set up a three-way consultation for school nurse, parents, and counselor to review procedures and elicit their concerns and feedback. Be sure that parents understand their 504 rights.	Chapter Four
Dealing with failure, peer and teacher judgments, and negative comparison to classmates	Wanting to protect their child's self-esteem and sense of self-worth. Common parental sentiments: "It breaks my heart to see my child feel so badly about himself, and I feel helpless."	Use classroom guidance lessons to help promote resilience, and if needed spend some one-on-one time with the child to teach resiliency skills. Collaborate with parents to prioritize and protect the child's self-esteem while encouraging the development of resiliency skills. Ask parent to reinforce resiliency at home. Have ongoing communication with the parents, and listen to and address their concerns.	Chapter Seven

(Continued)

Table 5.1 Elementary School Transitions or Developmental Concerns *(Continued)*

Important Transitions or Developmental Concerns	Common Parental Concerns or Issues	Helpful Suggestions for School Counselors	Other Helpful Chapters
Homework creates high home demands and stresses, especially when the disorder interferes with the homework process	Unrealistic workload when considered with other related disability demands such as learning difficulties, medical regimes, and limited attention spans. Common parental sentiments: "This homework task has nothing to do with independent learning. Why don't they understand that it means we'll have three hours (if not more) of coaxing, tears, and tantrums, and realistic frustrations?"	Check in with parents to assess the home-school interface. Work with teachers to provide parents some helpful homework strategies. IEP needs: If homework demands are unrealistic determine what accommodations can to be made.	Chapter Six
First contact with disabilities labels and diagnoses. Also the possibility of their child being diagnosed with a disability.	Fear and sadness; catastrophic thinking about what this means for the child's future; they do not understand the nature of the disability and its implications. Common parental sentiments: "This is a relief; finally we'll be able to get the help we need." Or "I can't believe there is something wrong with my child, and I am worried about what this means for our future."	Provide disability information and resources for the parents. Heighten the need for support and encouragement and possible referral to support groups and counseling. Help them anticipate potential transitions or changes in what the child will need in moving through grade levels.	Chapters Three, Four, Seven, and Eight

| Child feels left out and experiences social rejection or exclusion versus genuine social integration | Worry about their child having friends to play with and being to get along with others.

Common parental sentiments: "You know how cruel kids can be." | Consult with teachers to ensure that they use purposeful strategies to promote social integration and provide strategies to parents so they can work to complement the school strategies at home.

Observe typical social interactions with the child and his or her peers, and develop appropriate responsive interventions if necessary (for example, social skills training, group interventions).

Involve the PTA in developing school-wide strategies to foster genuine inclusion: "I belong, you belong, and we all belong." | Chapters Seven and Eight |

Table 5.2 Middle School Transitions or Developmental Concerns

Important Transitions or Developmental Concerns	Common Parental Concerns or Issues	Helpful Suggestions for School Counselors	Helpful Chapters
Multiple teachers with more academic pressure	Given that their child now has many different teachers, with different expectations, different teaching styles, and different personalities, the potential for problems is exponential. Common parental sentiments: "This is so overwhelming, and I thought that negotiating with one teacher was tough!"	Assist parents by helping teachers understand empathically the need for accommodations. If necessary, help teachers connect with resources needed to implement the IEP.	Chapters Four and Six
New physical environment	Increased environmental complexity leads to logistical concerns (for example, mobility and fatigue for children with physical disabilities); or increased anxiety for children with disabilities such as autism spectrum disorders, obsessive compulsive disorder, and attention deficit hyperactivity disorder. Common parental sentiments: "How is my child going to handle changing classes, remember locker combinations, and not get sidetracked?"	Provide opportunities for orientation and walkthroughs. It may be helpful to use a peer "buddy" for this (this may be also benefit social integration). IEP needs: Accommodations may be necessary, such as leaving class early if extra time is needed or because hallways are less crowded.	Chapters Four and Seven

Increased possibility of bullying	The frequency of bullying increases in middle school. Common parental sentiments: "This is the last thing I want for my child."	Implement classroom as well as small and large group interventions as part of a schoolwide program, with zero tolerance for bullying.	Chapter Seven
After-school activities	Attitudinal and physical barriers threaten to keep their children from having access to the same activities and opportunities as their typical peers. This could snowball and result in diminished opportunities to develop interests and abilities that lead to meaningful avocational and career involvement. Common parental sentiments: "I'm upset that my child is left out of these fun and important activities."	Provide a brief in-service for advisors to promote the attitude that where there is a will(ingness), there is a way (to accommodate).	Chapters Seven and Nine

Table 5.3 High School Transitions or Developmental Concerns

Important Transitions or Developmental Concerns	Common Parental Concerns or Issues	Helpful Suggestions for School Counselors	Helpful Chapters
Possible school disengagement and dropping out	Negative attitudes toward school can be pervasive. Many students have attendance and other issues that are often signs of school disengagement and may foreshadow dropping out.	Create a guidance curriculum unit that addresses the development of proactive self-determination and decision-making skills.	Chapters Six and Eight
	Common parental sentiments: "I can't make my son go to school. If he drops out, I don't know what he'll do or what kind of life he'll have. My hands are tied, and I am ready to give up."	Respond to early signs of disengagement by increasing efforts to keep the student connected. Identify someone in the school environment who is willing to take on an informal mentoring role.	
		Pretransition planning sometimes needs to begin two to three years before graduation to ensure the student has the life skills as well as academic skills to function independently in the community.	
Peer intensity	Increased feelings of social isolation for some and gravitation toward negative peer influences for many others. Potential engagement in high-risk behaviors.	If necessary, address social skills and enhance the school's climate of social acceptance. Also, help parents seek possible social opportunities outside of school.	Chapter Eight
	Common parental sentiments: Social isolation: "I feel like I have to be both a parent and a friend because she has no friends her age and I hate to see her sit home alone."	Understand that many disabled students are more likely to engage in high-risk behavior than their typical peers. Get them involved in responsive	

	Negative peer influence: "After all those years of helping with tutors, homework, and working with the schools, he now chooses to hang with the kids who are smoking pot and going nowhere!"	services as soon as possible. As necessary, make referrals to community counseling.	
Balancing autonomy and safety	Recognition that adolescent children need to experience life and make independent choices, which can conflict with the parental desire to keep them safe. Independence creates higher levels of risks and increased level of parental anxiety. Common parental sentiments: "I know I need to let her grow up, but she doesn't understand the risks that she is taking. With her learning problems, she is often a bad judge of character and doesn't see trouble coming. I couldn't live with myself if something bad happens."	Consult with parents to help them cope with decreasing levels of protection in order to permit more adolescent autonomy for their child. In addition, help them sort out realistic concerns about their child's readiness. Address the young person's deficient skills through individual or group psychoeducational training.	Chapter Eight
Dating and romantic relationships	Intensified parental adolescent conflict can occur during this time, especially with nonvisible disabilities. Students with physical disabilities tend to be left out of romantic partnerships even if they have had success with friendships. They lag behind their peers in this area, and many doubt their future prospects. Those with nonphysical disabilities face diverse and different challenges such as impulsive sexual choices and emotional volatility. Common parental sentiments: "It is sad to see her left out of the prom and other things kids do." "She doesn't listen to anything I say; she listens only to her boyfriend."	Both individual and group counseling interventions could be helpful. Collaborate with the school nurse and local professionals to offer a workshop for parents on dating and sexuality issues of adolescents with disabilities.	Chapter Eight

Table 5.4 Preparing for Transition

Important Transitions or Developmental Concerns	Common Parental Concerns or Issues	Helpful Suggestions for School Counselors	Helpful Chapters
Loss of the K–12 entitlement system based on their disability label	Their child needs to navigate the adult system to obtain educational or vocational services. Parents and their child are facing the prospect of the loss of the team support (IEP and transition). Common parental sentiments: "I am aware that we face the loss of the support from the school; we will be going it alone. It is like being on our own without a net."	As appropriate, connect students and parents with state and federal vocational rehabilitation agencies so that they can begin to navigate the maze. Advise students and parents about the disability support services available at the postsecondary level.	Chapters Four and Nine
Succeeding in work or postsecondary education is the hallmark of adult life.	Apprehension due to recognition that success or failure will soon be in the hands of their son or daughter. Parents can no longer run interference once their child is in the job, vocational training, or college setting. Heightened awareness of the need for planning as graduation approaches. Common parental sentiments: "I hope that my child is mature enough to follow through on the plan."	Self-determination and self-advocacy skill development are critical. Provide additional specialized guidance curriculum units.	Chapters Eight and Nine

Part Two

Meeting the Needs of Students with Disabilities

Addressing the Amplified ASCA Domains

Chapter 6

Meeting Students' Academic Needs

If children don't learn the way we teach,
we must learn to teach the way they learn.

CONSTANCE MCGRATH (2007)

While the concept of a free and appropriate public education has been widely accepted as a right of all children, the application of this concept to children with disabilities has been highly variable through the history of public education. Ranging from exclusion to segregation to mainstreaming, current practices are focused on inclusion of children with disabilities in the least restrictive environment. This chapter focuses on creating inclusive school environments that promote academic, personal/social, and career success.

The Purpose of Education and Academic Success

Considerable time, money, and resources are dedicated to educating the nation's children. Library shelves are filled with volumes of research and information purporting best practices in educating children. Legislation abounds regarding the rights of families in accessing education, as well as the expectations of government, school districts, and school administrations in implementing the current trends in education. Clearly educational systems are pivotal in society, and expectations are high that the products of educational systems are able to make positive contributions in society. The underlying premise is that good academic competence allows one to be a contributing citizen. What has remained unclear is what constitutes an appropriate education for children with disabilities. Consequently, children with disabilities are at higher risk for dropping out of school, of not being as easily able to obtain sustainable employment, and of having unfulfilling lives lived often in isolation, either with families or on the margins of society.

In recent years, many families have drawn attention to the insufficient or inadequate education for their children with disabilities by contesting the value of the education that their children have received. For example, Hechinger and Golden describe a young man who graduated from high school in 2006, only to have his parents mail his diploma back two days later. Their son, who has learning disabilities, according to his parents was able to graduate because teachers inflated his grades, accepted poor work, and awarded him a meaningless diploma to avoid paying for ongoing instruction in the name of "accommodation" for his disabilities. His parents deemed the diploma meaningless because their son lacked the requisite skills to be able to hold sustainable employment or to perform at an acceptable level in a postsecondary program. Without the ability to maintain employment or complete advanced education, he would be unable to support himself in life.[1]

Hechinger and Golden describe in another instance parents of a young woman with cerebral palsy who speaks only with the help of a computer. This student, who graduated with honors in 2002, had language and math skills at only an elementary school level. In this case, her parents were successful in challenging the school to pay $400,000 for a special education program for her after she graduated. Instead of providing such a program for her while she was in school, a judge ruled that the school lowered the curriculum's level of difficulty and removed large and meaningful aspects of the curriculum in an effort to accommodate her special needs.[2]

Both examples highlight that the importance of education is not of having students graduate with a diploma. The issue is whether students are graduating with the requisite skills to be able to obtain sustainable employment or to be academically prepared for postsecondary education.

The Role of High-Stakes Testing

Most conversations today about education tend to have high-stakes testing as a focal point. Parents consult the testing results of school districts when considering where to buy a home. Teachers report feeling restricted by a curriculum that is focused on improving test scores. School administrators and school boards are concerned by performance indicators that have direct implications for school funding opportunities, as well as governance concerns for schools that consistently "underperform." Students feel stressed and overwhelmed by the pressures placed on them to perform well on these high-stakes tests. In essence, high-stakes testing puts more pressure on schools to demonstrate a high level of performance in order to receive funding. Educators are increasingly accountable in high-stakes testing with implications that have included teaching to the test and reports of excluded participation by students with disabilities in some districts—both of which lead to perceptions that students with special needs are a potential liability rather than children who have a right to and an expectation of education in the least restrictive environment.

The implications of high-stakes testing for students with disabilities are profound, and an overarching question for schools is how to account for the performance of students with disabilities in the reporting of test scores. In addition, performance on some tests may determine whether a student receives a diploma or the type of diploma that a student might receive. Hechinger and Golden reported on some complaints received from parents whose students received accommodations on high-stakes tests that led to meaningless diplomas. Among complaints, for example, whereas a reasonable accommodation for students might include extra time on exams, some districts were reported allowing students several attempts to take or pass a test or to be given the answers on multiple-choice tests. Some parents reported that their children received passing grades if they did not make an effort or even skipped school. In some instances, the teachers may have wanted to fail a student receiving special education services only to be overturned by an administration that favors a no-fail approach for students with individualized educational programs (IEPs).[3]

In part, due to controversy that may have been penalizing rather than assisting students with disabilities, NCLB added provisions that require inclusion of students with disabilities, looks at progress of children with the most significant cognitive disabilities who can participate using alternate achievement standards, and provides credit to schools for progress by all children. Readers should refer to www.ed.gov for the most current updates on this issue.

The Purpose of Inclusion

Often the approach to making accommodations for individuals with disabilities involves viewing the disability as a problem that resides within the individual; consequently, the individual must adapt or change to fit with the demands of the learning environment in order to be considered successful. According to Stensrud, the World Health Organization and the U.S. National Institute on Disability Research and Rehabilitation Research are advocating for the concept of disability to be considered in systemic terms that reflect the interaction of the person, environment, and individual factors that are disabling. Viewing disability from a systemic perspective offers more opportunities for leading to a change; as in systems theory, change that occurs in one area automatically leads to some type of change overall.[4] The change does not have to occur within the individual; it could occur in the environment.

In order to be successful in inclusion efforts, schools need to make curriculum relevant. Instruction that takes place in an inclusion classroom makes not just the curriculum but also the learning process relevant to all children. Making the learning process relevant sets the stage for students with special needs to be able to become lifelong learners.

Amplified Academic Needs

Adults with disabilities in the United States face significant barriers to community participation and self-sufficiency. They experience high levels of unemployment and underemployment. For example, in 1997, individuals with disabilities were reported to have employment rates of 31 percent compared to 78 percent of all working-age people between ages twenty-one and sixty-four years and a median earning of thirteen thousand dollars compared to twenty-three thousand dollars of all working people. In addition, compared with the general population, people with disabilities have less formal education than people without disabilities. For example, 38.7 percent of all adults had no more than a high school diploma, but 49.4 percent of adults with disabilities had only this much education. Among all adults, 25.5 percent had college degrees or higher, but this was the case for only 12.5 percent of adults with disabilities.[5]

Less education results in limited job opportunities. This puts many people with disabilities in jobs that pay poorly, offer few benefits such as health insurance, and provide work that is likely to lead to injury and further disability. People with disabilities also face discrimination in the workplace that often results in their quitting or being terminated, further contributing to limited employment prospects and success.[6] McGrady, Lerner, and Boscardi, in their autobiographies of individuals who were diagnosed with learning disabilities as students, found a consistent theme related to the psychological and emotional impacts of their learning disabilities, including behavior problems, low self-esteem, poor interpersonal relationships, drug and alcohol abuse, anger, depression, and job failure.[7]

Hampton and Hess-Rice found that 54 percent of students with diagnosed emotional and behavioral disorders (EBD) dropped out of school, according to the U.S. Department of Education in 2000, and 58 percent of students with EBD are arrested within five years of leaving school, but among dropouts, the arrest rate is 73 percent.[8] Kemp cited general reasons for the increased dropout rate for students with EBD as including academic failure and disengagement from the educational environment. Student disengagement from the educational environment includes multiple unexcused absences from school, minimal involvement in extracurricular activities, and involvement in negative social interactions with both peers and school personnel.[9]

These reasons are themes in research conducted by Stensrud, who compared interview data obtained from young adults with disabilities who had dropped out of the public school system with children who had just completed grade 6 in the public school system. Of the children who had just completed grade 6, one group was composed of those who were considered to have successfully transitioned to middle school, while another group was composed of students who were considered not to have successfully transitioned. The latter group included students who had disabilities. Of the adults who had dropped out of school, participants reported hating school and viewed dropping out as a release from an unpleasant situation. Their experience with school consisted of academic problems, peer-related problems, and problematic relationships with adults in the system. Not only did they not get good grades, they also believed that no one was going to help them. They described themselves as not fitting in, having negative experiences both in and outside the classroom, and believing that teachers blamed them for their negative experiences by siding with other students without hearing their side. By middle school, they had the perception that they were different from other children and felt increasingly isolated from relationships and supports. These characteristics were also reported among students in the unsuccessful transitioner group, who were also less likely than the successful transitioner group to report being involved in extracurricular activities, had more time alone at home after school, and had fewer social relationships to draw on during the school day. Unsuccessful transitioners also described conflicting adult relationships at home and within the school.[10]

Wenz-Gross and Siperstein suggested that middle school students, especially students who experience learning problems, are at particular risk for stress and adjustment problems. They attribute this to changes to more complex learning environments with increased demands: grading practices, amount of material to be organized and mastered, as well as socially having to negotiate larger and more fluctuating groups. And while students with learning problems experience more stress, this is a time in which they may also experience less social support.[11]

Clearly one ultimate goal of inclusion needs to be avoiding the domino effect of early failure that results in compounding failure. Children who become at risk academically then become at risk for failure in life.

Negative Academic Self-Concepts of Students with Disabilities

Students with disabilities experience the challenges related to their disability in addition to the challenges encountered by typical children in the school environment. Consequently, they have more difficulty in achieving school success (as typically defined) and a positive academic self-concept. Self-concept pertains to the thoughts, feelings, and perceptions that one has about oneself. An academic self-concept focuses those thoughts, feelings, and perceptions about oneself in terms of the ability to compete and achieve in typical academic arenas. For example, one student might come to think of himself as being able to learn anything he sets his mind to, and another might conclude that she is good at reading but not able to do math well. This self-concept sets the tone for these students' motivation to engage in the learning process and for the results that they expect.

Children's academic self-concepts are heavily influenced by the feedback that they receive from adults in their environment. Early on, if a child receives a low score on a test, he does not necessarily see that as a reflection of his abilities; rather, it is the messages that his teachers and parents give him about that score that results in his evaluation of himself. Because children lack life experience to draw on, they are not in a position to refute the labels and beliefs that others put on them, and they may conclude that the adult must be right: "I am stupid, lazy, difficult, not able, not worthy." Elbaum and Vaughn conducted a meta-analysis of school-based interventions to enhance the self-concept of students with learning disabilities and found that those who experience severe academic difficulties are considered to be particularly at risk for poor self-concept and its adverse consequences.[12]

Clearly a critical factor contributing to the negative academic self-concept for students with disabilities is the perception of school personnel of these students' abilities to be successful. Other critical factors include overt and covert messages that are sent to the school community in terms of the services a student receives, where those services are located, and how those services are promoted. For example, students may experience academic embarrassment. Students who are diagnosed with learning disabilities and sent to resource rooms or receive learning support automatically have their confidentiality breached: they cannot consistently leave class to receive services without other children knowing. Many are embarrassed to ask for help in the classroom for fear of being accused of being lazy or not paying attention or of being singled out.

Students with disabilities are likely to have more difficulty keeping up with the compounding development of skills for improving learning, including skills for lifelong self-learning. For example, students with reading-related learning disabilities may still have equivalent vocabularies in first grade as their peers without disabilities, but those peers will begin to rapidly outpace vocabulary development beginning in second grade because of what they are introduced to with the greater volume of their reading.

Another mitigating factor for a student's negative perception of school, or of herself in school, pertains to the relevance of school and school activities to life. If school is structured to relate to real life (now and in the future), students will be more committed to being successful in school versus not committing to school success when it feels like a meaningless routine. This is particularly true for routine school activities such as homework. Students with disabilities are likely to require increased effort and time in completing homework compared with their more typical peers. In addition, while homework is designed to give students extra practice with newly learned concepts, it also serves as a stressor and contributes to parent-child conflict. After having spent a day at school, students who struggle academically do not want to do more school work. Many times they have lost recess or other free time at school because of not having completed seat work, so to come home and have to sit more doing work that is unsavory is a difficult emotional challenge for these children. This is particularly true of homework, which they perceive as busywork rather than something with a meaningful and clear purpose.[13]

Social problems also do harm to a child's self-concept in the classroom, particularly when negative behavior interrupts academic learning for the child with a disability and for others. Negative behaviors can result from a child's feeling inadequate in the classroom, confused about what is expected or unable to complete work, feeling singled out, feeling isolated or as an outsider in the classroom, as well as embarrassed or frustrated with frequent unwanted negative attention. Hampton and Hess-Rice suggest that although an objective of inclusion is to help students with disabilities increase social competence and foster positive peer relationships, these are often areas that are most difficult for students with disabilities to develop.[14] The social isolation that pervades many of their experiences compounds. Adding to this difficulty for students with EBD is that adult relationship conflicts also compound. Furthermore, as schools have developed policies such as zero tolerance concerning difficult behaviors, suspension and isolation are typical approaches schools use for dealing with students with these behaviors, which serves to exacerbate the strain between these students and adults.

Unique issues abound for students with hidden disabilities such as learning disabilities, anxiety, obsessive compulsive disorder, and psychiatric difficulties. For instance, obstacles to learning are sometimes less defined or perceived and therefore more complex or involved to resolve. Included in this conundrum are difficulties with clearly explaining the disability and needs to teachers, peers, and others. Because a disability may not be obvious, there may be less understanding, empathy, or acceptance from teachers or peers. Students themselves may have issues related to identifying with the disability and the need for accommodations and special services. Particularly with disabilities diagnosed later in a child's academic career, these students may be faced with questions such as, "Do I consider myself a student with a disability?" "Do I make full use of accommodations and services?" Depending on the severity of the disability and how it interferes with a child's ability to learn, teachers' attitudes toward the student with the hidden disability may have an impact on their inclination to provide accommodations or assistance to promote learning.

Twice-Exceptional Student Issues

In addition to hidden disabilities, twice-exceptional student issues also present with implications for the development of a student's academic self-concept. Nitkin described a "twice-exceptional" student as a bright child who has a learning disability. These are children who could qualify for gifted and talented classes but who could also have an IEP for help with learning disabilities.[15] According to Nitkin, many schools do not yet recognize that children can be both and instead focus on only one aspect of a child. The consequence for this approach is that a child who is gifted but not working to potential because of the learning disability could be written off as lazy or unmotivated. Hertog considered this to be a challenging advocacy situation in terms of trying to get schools to even recognize that gifted children can also have a disability, let alone accommodate them.[16]

In terms of academic approaches, Assouine, Nicpon, and Huber asserted that educational recommendations need to be designed to guide interventions that promote access to challenging curricula matched to a child's academic strengths, while also providing supportive environments where their vulnerabilities are also addressed.[17] One hurdle that school counselors may encounter is the assumption that gifted children do not require special intervention or they buy into the notion of global giftedness, in which is it is assumed that a child is gifted in all areas of the curriculum. Educators look for exceptional strengths or deficits among children but rarely screen for both within children. Failure to recognize that giftedness can coexist with learning disabilities leads to the risk that twice-exceptional children are more likely to be misunderstood, underserved, or invisible.[18] A positive example of a school that effectively met the needs of one student was reported in the *Pittsburgh Post Gazette*. In this example, Gabe Torres was identified in kindergarten as having deficits in speech and language, as well as attention deficit disorder/pervasive developmental disorder (ADD/PDD). By the end of first grade, he was identified as a gifted and talented student. His parents credit their school district with meeting his unique needs, capitalizing on his strengths to form relationships with peers and identify career goals in line with his interests and abilities. In 2008, Gabe became a National Merit Scholarship semifinalist, received the Navy Junior ROTC Academic Excellence Medal for achieving the highest score in the nation on its academic exam, and qualified to attend Ivy League–level schools.[19]

Another group of students who may not be recognized as twice exceptional are students who are both gifted and diagnosed with Asperger's syndrome. According to Neihart, gifted children with Asperger's syndrome may not be identified because their unusual behaviors may be wrongly attributed to either their giftedness or to a learning disability. A complete developmental history in addition to psychological and cognitive testing is necessary to help make this determination. Otherwise a child who is both gifted and has Asperger's may be left to manage alone because teachers will not know how to make the accommodations that are necessary to help the child access the curriculum. Neihart also emphasized that relationships with teachers and peers can be difficult for a child with Asperger's syndrome, and as a result these children may become isolated, depressed, or highly anxious. Behavior problems that might exist include compulsive or hyperactive problems. These are children who may be prone to tantrums or aggressive outbursts, hitting children without provocation, or touching people in inappropriate ways. Some engage adults in endless arguments.[20]

Promoting Positive Academic Self-Concepts with Students with Disabilities

According to Gradel, Jabot, Magiera and Maheady, successful interventions prevent, eliminate, or overcome the obstacles that keep individuals with disabilities from learning and participating actively and fully in school and society.[21] School counselors, who are often the professional liaison among school psychologists, school administrators, teachers, parents, and students, are uniquely positioned to advocate for the educational needs of students with disabilities. They can also serve as supportive adults who understand the unique social and emotional needs of students who are twice exceptional.[22] Given the training of school counselors to work with academic as well as personal/social issues, interventions are recommended in each area. Elbaum and Vaughn suggested that self-concept interventions were more effective for young adolescents than for elementary-aged children or older adolescents, whereas academic interventions were more reliably effective for elementary students, and counseling interventions were most consistently effective for middle and high school students.[23]

Academic Interventions

One area where school counselors can be beneficial to a child's school experiences is to offer suggestions or resources for interventions that are targeted to academic performance. This may include suggestions for accommodations at IEP planning meetings or throughout the academic year as challenges arise. Nitkin suggests that the accommodations do not have to be onerous or complicated.[24] Even students without a recognized exceptional need occasionally may need more time to complete assigned tasks or may need to hear an assignment instead of having it presented in only a visual manner. Or a child diagnosed with obsessive compulsive disorder may take longer to complete work when he is feeling exhausted due to the impact of the disability on school performance. A child with a learning disability may feel increasingly anxious or depressed for not measuring up to the performance of other students or for not being able to overcome the disability in order to focus on school work. Children with dyspraxia, neurological disorders, orthopedic problems, or attention deficit hyperactivity disorder might benefit from using a peer note taker or a computer to take notes in class or complete homework assignments rather than have compounded academic difficulties related to note taking or handwriting.

Neihart advised that children with Asperger's syndrome are strong visual learners and think best with concrete, literal pictures—a disadvantage in most classrooms where the expectation is that students think verbally. These children need instruction that includes the use of diagrams, visualization, visual cues, and pictograms for learning and behavioral management. They also benefit from instruction done without affect, as they react to what they might sense as anger, frustration, or negativism and respond better when the teacher is perceived to be calm and in control.[25] Children with autism or sensory integration difficulties have particular challenges when ordinary stimuli are perceived as more intense or even unbearable than for the typical child, who may be better able to filter out annoying sounds of shrill noises of bells or loud noises in the lunchroom. This may coexist with low tolerance for stress and change. Occupational therapists may need to be accessed for sensory integration therapy, and accommodations in classrooms and school settings may be needed to lessen the impact of such stimuli for these children.

The relevance of academic work, including homework, may be an area for intervention for some children. If schoolwork is increasingly linked to future career or training and education goals, children may be more likely to persevere or commit to completing work. This also makes the case for effective K–12 career planning in all schools in order to link academic work to career and training goals and accentuates the importance of attending to the career development for children with disabilities (see Chapter Nine).

Promoting academic interventions is directly linked to advancing the personal and social skills that children need to be successful in the classroom in terms of how to survive in the academic environment. Baum, Olenchak, and Owen suggested that sometimes difficulties with hyperactivity, attention, and impulsivity increase when the curriculum is perceived as routine and dull—some students are not being taught at their instructional level or do not require as much repetition to master material and skills. Consequently they may be tempted to act out in an effort to direct their boredom with schoolwork to something more engaging or interesting. These authors also indicate that some students have high energy and ability and are more likely to take risks. They may be more motivated to accomplish their own goals and be unwilling to put their own agendas on hold to accommodate the demands of the typical classroom, especially if the environment is too restrictive or inhibits these students' natural energy. They recommend that it is as important to consider the effects of the environment on the student's behavior as it is to consider the student's behavior on the environment.[26]

As an example, Ben, a six-year-old child diagnosed with Asperger's syndrome and identified as gifted and talented, quickly grasps material beyond the abilities of most of his peer group. According to his parents, he is easily frustrated by repetition of material that he already understands. In these instances, his parents report, he is more likely to engage in self-stimulation activities or to become resistant to what the teacher has assigned because he sees the material as annoying. If he is engrossed in a project that interests him, he is unlikely to want to put the project on hold to make a transition to a different subject or activity, preferring instead to finish his project. If he is forced to make an unwanted transition, he is more likely to have a tantrum or resist the request.

Counseling Interventions

School counselors can perform counseling interventions designed to fit a variety of personal and social needs that a student may have that impede his or her academic performance, including individual and group counseling and classroom guidance interventions. McEachern and Bornot suggested that school counselors can do individual and group counseling to help improve classroom behavior, increase self-esteem, develop positive interpersonal relationships, and foster social acceptance and self-confidence, while Neihart advised that social skills training may be necessary.[27] Some students may benefit from concrete visual cues to convey expectations, such as social stories or comic strip conversations, mirror and imitative exercises, and videotaping to teach new behaviors in addition to teaching about affective experiences—particularly of others. For students with Asperger's syndrome or others on the autism spectrum, brief, concrete directives are most effective, as are pictograms or other visual cues regarding expected behaviors.

Wenz-Gross and Siperstein emphasized the need for skills and interventions that address peer stress, which includes difficulty making friends, handling peer pressures, and being victimized.[28] Students with disabilities may encounter more challenges in getting along with their teachers and in controlling their behavior, managing multiple teacher relationships, negotiating issues of increased autonomy, and demonstrating self-regulation. These students also benefit from help with time management, organizational skills, prioritizing multiple tasks into more manageable units, assertiveness training, conflict resolution, and refusal skills to help with peer pressures and victimization. Furthermore, school counselors can assist students by helping them to recognize their own personal stress triggers, identify physical and emotional responses to those triggers, and practice stress-reduction techniques to manage their stress. This includes assisting them with identifying their own circle of support and increasing a sense of belonging and connectedness to their learning communities.

In addition, school counselors can work with students and parents to ensure that school life reflects the balance of real life (that is, not simply academics but also extracurricular, social, leisure, and part-time work) and that school-related opportunities are being capitalized on in order to broaden a student's experiences. The school needs to cultivate within students the sense of being an active member of a larger community rather than simply being part of a segregated group.

Modeling Self-Advocacy

Stephen Covey, in his best-selling book, *The Seven Habits of Highly Effective People*, includes the habit of "beginning with the end in mind" as a critical trait to cultivate.[29] If the ultimate goal of education is to graduate productive, independently functioning citizens, it stands to reason that the interventions implemented in school settings are designed with that end in mind. Children are expected to become increasingly independent as they mature. However, students with disabilities are often sheltered from asserting themselves, and adults in their lives advocate on their behalf. In the short run, this may be easier, but the consequence in the long run is that these students may not know how to advocate for themselves effectively in adulthood.

One student who requires the use of a wheelchair for her disabilities reflected on her school experiences. She reported that her parents did not just tell her what she should do; they taught her the skills that she would need to advocate for herself one day. When they made phone calls or had conversations surrounding ways to meet her needs, they would explain why the conversation was necessary, how to work within the framework of the system, and why it was important. When she went to a college far from home, she found that she was able to use those skills to effectively advocate for herself. Whether it was in terms of getting a schedule changed so that she could attend class in a more accessible building or taking on a safety issue on campus, she felt competent and capable to effect change for herself. The risk of not modeling effective self-advocacy is the development of a learned helplessness mind-set in which individuals do not see themselves as being able to have their needs met and are dependent on others or systems to meet their needs for them.

Promoting Inclusion

Perhaps the most effective activity that a school counselor can be involved in is the promotion of inclusive classrooms. A truly inclusive classroom promotes not only independence in academic functioning but also social success and physical independence, which contribute to increased self-worth.[30] When students believe that they make a difference in a learning community, they feel valued and then also want to do well in the community. As a result, there are fewer behavioral issues and increased academic success.

McGrady, Lerner, and Boscardin identified a common approach to inclusion as placing students with disabilities in the general education classroom along with recommendations that accommodations be made by the general education teacher or the special educator based on the child's ability to participate in general curriculum. In this model, the accommodations are made on a case-by-case basis; however, the accommodations themselves do not necessarily make the curriculum accessible to the child. For example, if a child has an accommodation that reduces the workload, it does not necessarily mean that the child comprehends or understands the work itself if the material has not been presented in a way that is consistent with his or her learning style.[31] McGrath defines an inclusive classroom as structuring the room to accommodate all children in it versus trying to make the child change to fit into the classroom. She advocates permanent accommodations that make the curriculum accessible to all children using curricular, physical, and social supports so that no child can be identified as having a special need. The advantage to making permanent accommodations is that all children benefit, even children who are not identified as having a special need but for whom the curriculum is not necessarily accessible.[32]

Efforts should not be made to lower the bar. Rather, the bar should be kept realistically high while the environment is reasonably altered to allow a student to learn and achieve success. These inclusion practices promote a positive classroom learning environment:

- Working with teachers to foster inclusive attitudes and teaching practices by helping them develop permanent accommodations rather than respond to case-by-case situations[33]

- Explaining the need for and legitimacy of accommodations (developing teachers' willingness and attitudes in complying with accommodations)

- Encouraging differentiated practices that make the curriculum accessible to all students, such as visual prompts, auditory directions, and reminder steps that students can refer to in the classroom

- Assisting teachers with positive behavioral supports and discipline issues

- Assisting in determining the proper use of paraprofessionals in the classroom so as not to isolate children with disabilities

- Fostering supportive, friendly, interdependent classrooms in which children can form relationships with peers that then allow them to work collaboratively with, sit with, and help each other—for instance, helping teachers to find tasks that students with disabilities can do to enable them to make meaningful contributions to the learning community versus having children feel like outsiders in their environment[34]

An example of a reasonable accommodation that can be easily implemented at little to no cost came from one student with a disability that restricts her ability to write well. She suggested pairing children who are unable to write or to write well with a child who can, so that the child's aide does not always have to be present—something that can further isolate a child from peers. Alternative means to accomplish the same goal exist, such as using a rubber stamp for putting names on papers or signing yearbooks. Another individual with a disability cautioned that teachers need to use care that children do not over assist or become "mothering," which can draw an unwanted amount of focus or attention on the child and can be overwhelming or stressful. Other inclusive practices are useful as well:

- Maintaining connections between the class and the student with a disability during periods of prolonged absences from school. One student who had frequent, protracted absences from school due to her disability found that her relationships with peers were severed during times of home-bound instruction or hospitalizations and then needed to be reestablished with each reentry back into the school. This can be overwhelming for children who are also struggling to keep up with academic work. Feeling awkward can affect a child's motivation to be engaged at school.

- Promoting the inclusion in music, art, gym, library, computer class, and extracurricular activities. A woman reported, in reflecting on her school experiences when she was young, that after-school activities were not accessible to her because of where students had to enter the school to go to the activity, which meant entering by a side door and negotiating a stairwell that she could not do in her wheelchair. That automatically meant that these activities were not available for her and served to further limit her connectedness with school and peers.

- Making the class a psychologically safe place as well as a physically safe place for children. One student recalled that many children with disabilities have no social connection at all and were isolated in school. "We think about inclusion as being a way to eliminate isolation but sometimes the inclusion is so overwhelming for some kids that it actually creates more isolation. They don't have a safe place." Hehir reported that friendships for many students with disabilities do not develop as naturally as they do for other children.[35] Educators can provide approaches for the development of social relationships between children who have disabilities and those who do not. This includes assisting with fostering supports in the community that will last beyond one's school experience. Care must be taken not to sabotage naturally occurring friendships by making a friend a caregiver and thereby upsetting the balance in peer relationships inadvertently by creating a power imbalance.

Developing inclusive environments is not without challenges, primarily in terms of changing paradigms about service delivery of special services and educational practices for students with disabilities. Currently practicing educators may be more familiar with a segregation model of special education, and thus may be reluctant to see the value of a fully inclusive school environment. Schwarz identifies salient differences between these two approaches to meeting the needs of students with disabilities (Table 6.1).[36] A side effect of the different approaches to fully including students with special needs in all aspects of the school environment is that the school counselor will encounter resistance in many forms while trying to advance inclusion.

Mind-Sets that Resist Inclusion and Responses to Challenge Them

An important role for school counselors is to consult with teachers as needed to implement a student's IEP in a manner that meets both the spirit and the letter of the law. Realistically, many teachers see IEPs as a burden, although it is a tool to maximize a student's success. Many also form impressions of students based simply on the IEP. School counselors may find it beneficial to develop a set of talking points to use when encountering teachers who resist making inclusion a priority for their students who have disabilities. Sample talking points are included here to facilitate productive discussions surrounding inclusion.

Lack of Awareness

While the purpose of IEPs is to make specific to all parties involved with a child's education what accommodations are needed in light of a student's disability, there exists a misperception in some school districts that IEPs are confidential and off-limits to the teachers who need to use the information in order to assist the student. One teacher stated, "Sometimes a teacher never sees an IEP. There

Table 6.1 Inclusion Versus Segregation Approaches to Accommodating Children with Disabilities

Inclusion	Segregation
Requires collaboration, openness to new ideas	Leads to isolation
Knowledge of curriculum, differential instruction, ongoing planning	General education separate from special education
Equitable coteaching	Double standard: not giving consequences because of disability
Zero-rejection policy	Labels, focus on differences, failures
Focus: the factors or criteria that determine when a child returns to general education classroom	Focus: the factors or criteria that determine if a child returns to general education classroom
Special education as a service	Special education as a place.
Curricular adaptations and differential instruction strategies, innovative approaches to learning Universal design: invites, includes, fosters belongingness and success For every student in the classroom; includes the entire spectrum of learners	Risk of static IEPs: no changes in goals, objectives, and benchmarks
Benefits all students with everyone else in the school community—including specials, recess, lunchroom	Benefits few
Fosters an us mentality All children included in the same opportunities School and parents on same team General education teachers and special education teachers as a team Families valued for expertise	Fosters a we-them mentality Children with disabilities separate from typical children School versus parents General education teachers versus special education teachers Families viewed as the "enemy," thwarting what the school wants to do
Promotes independence and encourages "Dignity of risk"	Promotes learned helplessness; provides constant care and supervision and stifles risk taking that would naturally occur with peers.

Source: Schwarz (2006).

was one year when I asked for the IEPs and was told, 'I'm sorry, you can't have them because of the right of privacy!'"

Another misperception occurs when teachers are given a copy of the IEP or a summary of one, with the assumption being that the teacher knows about the nature of the disability and therefore will know exactly what types of accommodations are going to be beneficial to the student. School counselors can be invaluable in providing information and support to teachers in these instances. For example, one teacher spoke of her trepidation when initially reading the IEP for a child with obsessive compulsive disorder: "I was given a handout as were all of his teachers on what we should expect in the classroom and the different accommodations that we were required by law to make. When I saw this piece of paper, I almost fell over . . . and I was nervous and I thought about it all night long, actually all weekend long." As it turned out, the school counselor was instrumental in helping this teacher become comfortable with her knowledge base related to OCD and the nature of the accommodations needed. Eventually this teacher was not only able to implement the student's accommodations effectively but she developed a uniquely positive relationship with him. She explained:

> One thing I've learned about obsessive compulsive disorder is that these children tend to seek out safe places or safe people that they can go to when they are really in need. I had always thought that at the beginning of the year if Sam [a pseudonym] needed to go to a safe pace, I should send him to his counselor. But it turns out that my classroom has kind of been a safe place for Sam. If he's having trouble in another class, he tends to come here not really to talk about it but just to be somewhere where he feels comfortable. . . . He doesn't take advantage of it but he knows that if something's going wrong, "I can go there."

In these types of situations, school counselors can remind teachers and administrators of the legal requirements to implement a student's IEP and provide support as well as information about particular disabilities to the team involved with implementing accommodations.

Accommodations Are Too Difficult or Time-Consuming

One of the valuable roles a school counselor can play is to help teachers be more willing to make the accommodations that students with disabilities need. Certainly refusal to make necessary accommodations can be addressed at an administrative level (if all else fails). However, it is better for all involved to help reluctant teachers resolve the obstacles they experience with regard to making accommodations. Sometimes the reluctance comes from a belief that they are too difficult or time-consuming. Certainly there are some permanent accommodations that may initially be time-consuming to put into place but in the long run serve to save time.[37] Some teachers may not know how to go about making an accommodation or do not see how an accommodation can be implemented without expending tremendous amounts of energy, initiative, or money. In these instances, the school counselor can be a useful resource in brainstorming options, providing support, looking for ways to simplify the process, or identifying alternative resources.

Many teachers and counselors feel they need to reinvent the wheel rather than turn to other sources that have more experience solving logistical problems. For instance, the parents of young students or older students themselves often are the best source of ideas and can suggest useful accommodations. Sometimes special education resources or ideas can be easily located or adapted from resources on the Internet. It is useful to model the aphorism, "Where there's a will, there's a way," and work collaboratively with others to find one.

Many educators make required accommodations with enthusiasm. The teacher of one student, Linda, who was a wheelchair user due to having quadriplegia approached accommodations as if it was simply natural to include her. When we interviewed her for this book, she fondly described her teacher's efforts:

> I was in choir for years. In middle school we had concerts three times a year. But in middle school we did a lot of traveling. The choir director wanted me to go so she made the arrangements to get the extra van to take me because she felt it was important." Linda's mother added, "That was only because this teacher chose to be my daughter's advocate and to have her involved in all the concerts. If they were traveling, she chose that my daughter was going to go. So she took it upon herself to insist the school pay for the transportation."

This teacher serves as an exemplar. Linda's mother noted that this educator approached accommodations without any hint of patting herself on the back for doing so, adding that this was in contrast to some teachers whose manner sent the message: *Hey, look at me. I have a disabled kid in my class, and look at what I am doing for her.* Moving from a "we have to do this" to a "we can do this" mind-set instills in the school community an expectation that it is natural to include children with disabilities in all aspects of school life and that it is undesirable or unnatural not to do so.

Accommodations Discriminate Against Other Students

A mother who is an educational advocate as well as the parent of a child with a disability shared this story with us about an incident at her school that epitomizes this common obstacle:

> We had a student in our school that lost his left arm above the elbow, in fact, almost up to his shoulder. He did not have any prosthesis. He was taking one of the required courses in our school (keyboarding), and the teacher of it was a very thorough, rigid person. At the end of the first semester, the guidance counselor saw that he had failed, and she called the teacher down to find out what the problem was. His explanation was that the student didn't meet the time requirements for the speed he needed to pass the course. The counselor said,

"But he only has one hand, so how can you actually time him?" The teacher's explanation was, "Well, I can't discriminate because that is the rule for every other student in the classroom." The counselor was so angry that she ended up saying, "What would you be able to do if I just cut your arm off? Would you be able to pass your own class?"

As effective as this might have been (or not), there is a more direct way to talk about why accommodations are fair and emphasize that sameness is not fairness. The reality is that students who have disabilities are not the same as their typical peers and often have to overcome significant physical, social, or emotional challenges that their more typical peers do not, and they are expected to meet the same learning goals that their typical peers do. Accommodations acknowledge these challenges and provide a context in which to take these differences into account. While some teachers are willing to make accommodations for students with visible disabilities, advocating for accommodations for those with less apparent disabilities can be daunting. For example, the mother of a student with dysgraphia, a learning disability that affects writing abilities such as spelling, poor handwriting, and difficulties putting thoughts on paper, shared her struggle with getting teachers to follow through on providing notes to her daughter: "It was an uphill battle. Most teachers initially had a reason why this couldn't be done. One said she couldn't figure out the best way to do it. Then there was the one that said 'okay' but didn't follow through. Another said it depended on if she could find a student who would volunteer for this task. One even told me his notes were protected by copyright! Truly!"

Unfortunately, the person who stands to lose the most in this type of situation is the student, who needs the assistance the most. School counselors can help by facilitating the discussion and process by which accommodations are made.

Accommodations Get Students off the Hook with Easier or Lighter Workloads and Increase Opportunities for Cheating

Sometimes resistance to implementing accommodations for students comes from the perception that the student with a disability is getting a free ride, while more typical students have to work harder. Students with a disability, however, spend time and energy in dealing with the effects of a disability above and beyond the requirements for school work. A child with a learning disability requires more time to understand and demonstrate learning. A child with physical and mental health concerns may be challenged by the side effects of medications or treatment regimes that interfere with the ability to concentrate, focus, or learn. In this respect, this mind-set is akin to the *sameness is fairness* doctrine. A student who demonstrates mastery of a new skill or knowledge while receiving accommodations is not getting a free ride; rather, she is getting consideration for the obstacles she must overcome in order to demonstrate mastery.

Accommodations do not mean simply lowering expectations or watering down the curriculum. In fact, to do so removes the meaningful aspects of the curriculum and does not lead to learning. Rather, accommodations require discerning between essential and nonessential tasks and requiring the tasks that are essential for accessing the curriculum. For example, does requiring a student to have excellent penmanship matter to a child's future? If not, should a child with writing problems lose points for penmanship as part of showing proficiency on a writing assignment? Similarly, being overly accommodating is not beneficial to students, as to do so sends the message that the student is not capable of anything and that nothing should be expected from them.

Rigidity: "This Is How I do Things"

Some teachers feel so uncomfortable deviating from their rigid ways of managing classes that they see requests as unreasonable. Linda (introduced above) provided an example of this obstacle when she related how a teacher responded to her request for a seat that would enable her to exit a class quickly and unobtrusively for a variety of reasons:

> On the first day of classes at the beginning of our senior year, like I usually do, I went into my classes and I picked where I wanted to sit. It is usually by the door because we have fire drills. So my aide sat down and I sat next to her. And the teacher was new to the district and she was like, "You can't sit there. You'll mess up my seating chart." I said, "Okay, but I still need to sit there so I can get out of the door." So I had to call and talk to her about that because she wouldn't leave it alone.

In this instance, persistence was the key. The teacher found that changes in her rigid structure did not cause the upheaval she anticipated. Attitude change followed quickly, and as Linda added, "And then after that . . . she loved me. But I had to put myself first." Table 6.2 summarizes the mind-sets that suppress or promote inclusion.

Identifying Useful Accommodations and Technology

One way to make the curriculum accessible to students is by ensuring useful accommodations through appropriate and adequate accessibility to assistive technology. An assistive technology device is "any item, piece of equipment or product system, whether acquired commercially off the shelf, modified or customized, that is used to increase, maintain or improve functional capabilities of individuals with disabilities."[38] The intent and benefit of assistive technology is to improve access to educational content and increase independence in functional activities.

Table 6.2 Inclusion Mind-Set Comparison

Mind-Sets That Suppress Inclusion	Mind-Sets That Promote Inclusion
Accommodations are too difficult or time-consuming.	Permanent adaptations save time in the long run.
Accommodations discriminate against other students.	Differentiated instruction, curricular adaptations, universal design, and cooperative learning benefit all students and make differences ordinary.[a] Inclusion and possibility thinking expose children to forms of diversity they will encounter in society. Differences are seen as attributes.
Accommodations get children off the hook with easier or lighter workloads and increase opportunities for cheating.	Fairness is defined as each student getting what he or she needs to be successful and includes removing barriers in the environment that might prevent a student from fully accessing the curricular and social experiences in the classroom.
Rigidity	Flexibility.
Assumptions of how students will be based on their IEP.	Getting to know the individual student, listening and asking questions, and then making decisions based on knowledge of the individual.
The IEP is a burden.	IEP is a plan to maximize a student's success.

[a]Schwarz (2006).

Assistive technology is different from educational technology, which is used to deliver academic content to both students with and without disabilities. Examples of educational technology include computer programs to teach a specific topic or subject as well as devices such as electronic whiteboards. Assistive technology is also different from medical technology, including that which supports physiological functioning, such as a ventilator. Rather, assistive technology includes any items, not just electronic items, that improve access or increase independence. Such items range widely:

- Low tech (a plastic cuff to hold a pencil for a student who cannot grip it)
- High tech (robotics)
- Free tech (computer software adaptations)
- Mainstream tech intended for the general public (a trackball is easier to use than a computer mouse for some people with physical disabilities)

- Specialized tech designed for disability (a wheelchair)
- Adapted or customized tech (a trackball attached to a desk with custom-designed mounting hardware)

The Individuals with Disabilities Act first named technology as a separate service that must be addressed in IEPs.

Assistive technology is nearly always combined with other accommodations that are designed to allow students with disabilities to participate more fully in the school setting by allowing them to accomplish a similar task in a different way (for example, being given extra time on assignments due to slow writing), independently or with the minimal amount of human assistance needed to be as independent as possible (for example, setting up and maintaining a laptop computer to complete seatwork or homework), or to modify the environment to minimize the impact of a disability (for example, moving a desk so a student in wheelchair can sit among other students and use his wheelchair lap tray as a desk).

Individual assistive technology is less necessary when classrooms and curricula are well designed. *Universal design* allows use by people with a variety of abilities, sizes, or needs. For example, if coat racks are hung low, students in wheelchairs as well as students without disabilities can reach them to use them independently. If chairs of different sizes are available, a student with mobility limitations can find one she can get into and out of independently. *Universal design for learning* applies the same idea to curriculum: if all worksheets are printed in a large font, students with visual impairment will not need a magnifier or an enlarged version. Unnecessary attention is not drawn to the child's disability, and the concept of preparing for all types of needs becomes commonplace for all students. Some examples of accommodations based on universal design include these:

- Adjusting instruction, testing accommodations, homework and assignment accommodations
- Accessing common and current forms of assistive technology
- Creating a stable, organized backdrop that benefits all children, including physically organizing the room according to types of information (math corner, writing center) where prompts and reminders are kept to facilitate independence
- Creating areas conducive to maintaining focus through engaging or interactive activities

- Arranging desks and tables for independent work, places for the whole class to gather that include supports for children to lean against or get up and down from the floor as well as in private places for individual and group meetings and resource areas

- Having adequate and pleasant lighting available in the environment, not just overhead fluorescent lighting, which can cause glares or buzzing that interferes with some students' learning

- Establishing seat change routines to prepare those who are unsettled by unpredictable change

- Presenting lessons that appeal to more than one of the senses to accommodate the learning styles of those who are not primarily auditory learners[39]

In addition to knowing the purpose of assistive technology and being able to identify appropriate types to promote inclusion in the classroom, school counselors need to maintain sensitivity to some of the human issues that affect assistive technology selection and implementation. For example, there is a tendency for people to think that high-tech solutions are superior to simpler ones when in fact this may not be the case. In addition, school counselors may encounter some resistance to assistive technology by students based on their reluctance to appear different from peers, by teachers based on technophobia, by administrators based on expense, and by everyone based on resistance to change. There may also be some unrealistic expectations for technology, including the notions that assistive technology is automatically the best solution, can solve everything, can stand alone, or is a quick fix.

School personnel are crucial in assisting with the selection and procurement of assistive technology, the first step of the process. Once the devices are obtained, the student and team members need to be trained in how to use them. Only then are deliberate efforts needed to implement the technology in the classroom and at home, including working out logistics such as where devices are to be used and who will be responsible for tech support, training, or troubleshooting. Appropriate and adequate funding sources need to be identified as well. For example, schools are required to fund assistive technology for students with disabilities up to age twenty-one, who are eligible for special education or who are considered to be "handicapped" under Section 504.

The technology must be education related, including needs for using it at home to do homework. Vocational rehabilitation may, depending on individual state regulations, become involved with students in making a transition from K–12 to postsecondary training and education or to work. Such transitions may include the last one, two, or three years of high school depending on the nature of the student's disabilities.

Including Families and Other Natural Supports

Another way for school counselors to promote inclusion and create opportunities for students with disabilities to have positive school experiences is to make use of natural supports in the child's life. Examples of these activities include fostering collaborative parental involvement, helping teachers work with parents, facilitating the parent's home-based role in the student's academic achievement, serving as a liaison between school and home, encouraging natural supports, and planning for effective transition after night school.

Fostering Collaborative Parental Involvement

Often parents report that "collaborative" in the school means doing things the school's way rather than working with parents as members of the team. The temptation may be to tell parents what they need to do rather than solicit their ideas, concerns, or localized knowledge about their child to promote the child's success. Consequently, parents may be viewed as "resistant," and an adversarial relationship results. Palmer, Fuller, Arora, and Nelson emphasized that is important to hear and respect parent concerns related to inclusion for their child with disabilities.[40] While some parents may be "told" what the accommodations will be for their child, they may not necessarily believe those accommodations are best for their child. They may have concerns that their child's education will be sacrificed for the sake of inclusion when he or she might be better placed in a classroom with a smaller student-teacher ratio or fewer children for their child to have to interact with if peer or other social relationships create stressors that could impede their child's ability to learn. Some might believe that their child will be better off learning life skills that have practical applicability to life outside school even after graduation. Frederickson, Dunsmuir, Lang, and Monsen found that school staff, rather than parents or students, tended to emphasize the social benefits of inclusion, whereas students, and to some extent parents, brought issues to the table related to bullying. When the bullying concerns were mentioned, they tended not to be taken as seriously by school staff.[41]

Helping Teachers Work with Parents

While teachers may have ideas about the curriculum, families also have ideas about their child. Hehir advocated for working with families in the process of developing IEPs as students and families can give educators important insights about the impact of their disability and the most effective ways that they learn.[42]

It is important that as children get older and become more independent, they begin to take appropriate responsibility for their education by understanding and expressing the nature and impact of their disability as well as by participating in their transition and career planning.

Facilitating Parents' Home-Based Role in the Student's Academic Achievement

Parents may be receptive to knowing how they can advance their child's academic achievement at home. Some helpful suggestions are training them on the curriculum or expected outcomes so that they know what is expected; notifying them in advance of deadlines and due dates to allow for extra time needed to complete larger assignments; ensuring that they can troubleshoot assistive technology problems; and provide them with supplemental resources.

Serving as a Liaison Between School and Home

Some parents are strong advocates for their child, highly involved, and possess a heightened responsibility in an area (education, pedagogy). Some might become so overwhelmed or not understand the system that they give up and are not very involved. School counselors can be a link between the family and the system to promote the needs and interests of the child or could serve as a referral source to advocates who can guide parents in the process of advocating for their child.

Encouraging Natural Supports

Peers can be a natural support as well. While peer support and acceptance can be invaluable, being sensitive to how the child interprets assistance is critical. For instance, L'Amoreaux found that children may be resistant to having a peer tutor as they may come to view themselves as "less than or stupid" compared to peers.[43] In addition, the peer may serve as a distraction, trying to get child off task. Sometimes students find that having an older child help may be less stigmatizing. Communities may also contain some natural supports by providing mentoring opportunities with others with disabilities, like older students or adults in the community.

Planning for Effective Transition After High School

Often the focus on accommodations or inclusion is limited to the immediate school experience, but academic transition planning for after high school warrants consideration as well. One college counselor who works with assisting students with disabilities in their transition to college life explained, "I work with students who have had IEPs all through their school experiences, and when they get to college they are blown away because they don't have an IEP that reduces expectations or workloads. There is no link between the accommodations made in school and the accommodations available in college. Some students are also certain to fail in college because of this disconnect." It is critical to include students as well as parents in planning the transition by encouraging them to take increasing responsibility and empowering students and parents to be able to ask for what they need—essentially, to self-advocate.

Promoting Academic Resilience

Although all students at one time or another face challenges that exceed their ability to cope, some use those challenges to adapt and grow, while others succumb to the challenges. This difference between thriving and succumbing often boils down to resilience.

Medina and Luna concluded that children who feel marginalized in society and then again in school come to see themselves as ineffective in meeting the demands or rigors of school, and they disengage from the learning process.[44] Wenz-Gross and Siperstein also highlighted the notion that students with learning problems are a group at risk in middle school and experience higher stress, lower peer social support, and poorer adjustment than other students.[45] In terms of academic stress, they had more difficulty keeping up with new learning and following directions. As they experienced increasing failure in school, their problems with academics became internalized into their conception of self and may have contributed to problems that these students have in terms of self-concept and depression. The types of interventions needed include not only academic interventions but also interventions to increase self-concept and lessen depression.

Not all students who encounter challenges due to disabilities end up disengaging from the learning process. Some remain hopeful and tenacious, expansively realistic, goal driven yet flexible, possessing a clear understanding of competencies and goals aligned with competencies, or empowered.[46] Brooks and Goldstein defined resilience as the focus on strengths in helping overcome adversity and the capacity to deal successfully with obstacles to maintain a path toward one's goals. Children face different challenges in life, and those who are resilient will handle these challenges with greater effectiveness and success. School counselors can promote resilience in children with disabilities by fostering within them the ability to:

- Feel optimistic
- Feel appreciated in the eyes of significant others

- Set realistic goals and expectations for themselves

- Believe they have the ability to solve problems and make decisions

- View mistakes, hardships, and obstacles as challenges to confront rather than as stressors to avoid

- Rely on coping strategies that are growth fostering rather than self-defeating

- Be aware of weaknesses and vulnerabilities

- Recognize strengths and talents

- Be empathetic and possess the skills to develop satisfying interpersonal skills[47]

Fostering resilience in students also means that students need to know that there will be adults who will advocate for them.[48] An example is Linda's music teacher who, when arranging concert trips for the school choir, consistently advocated to the school on her behalf to pay for the transportation costs associated with having her attend and be included too. Another student described how her school counselors advocated for her: "I think they really just looked ahead at problems in my life with teachers or whatever and tried to prevent them from happening all together . . . I look at many other people's stories and because they didn't have a good advocate in the system, they didn't get what they needed." Sam's director of special education and general education teachers also served this role for him. Their approach of "meet him where he is today" gave him acceptance and safe places to be who he was. Fostering resilience means combating mind-sets that say "we can't do this for her, because what will we do if other students come along who also need this level of accommodation and the precedent has been set" and replacing it with the expectation that "this is our student, and whatever it takes, we will do it."

Ultimately the school counselor is uniquely positioned to emphasize the need to consider approaching instruction from a multiplicity of perspectives, bearing in mind not just meeting the requirement of an IEP but also its spirit by recognizing that the impact of the diagnosis can have a damaging impact on the child's self-perception, and of others' expectations of the child's abilities, for peer relationships, or being able to fully participate in all aspects of school life.[49] Effective interventions can reduce the impact of disability and enhance access to quality education. However, interventions can also exacerbate the impact of disability—for example, inappropriately segregating students, pulling them out of opportunities to interact with their peers, or focusing on their disability when doing so would not be beneficial or necessary.[50]

House and Martin, in their work on social advocacy and social justice, suggest that counselors must work as change agents for the elimination of systemic barriers that impede academic success for all students and work to remove institutional barriers that continue to result in an achievement gap. This means working to help all students gain access to rigorous academic preparation and support for success, which helps them become prepared to work and move toward becoming active, involved citizens.[51] While House and Martin's work is focused on working with minority youth, we believe this applies to working with all students who encounter disadvantages in educational settings.

Because issues related to failure, problems, and challenges are brought to their attention more readily and frequently than perhaps any other educator or administrator, school counselors are uniquely positioned to challenge issues related to equity, access, and lack of supports for academic success concerning students with disabilities. As Stensrud wrote, "A disability matters only when it matters. The goal is to create environments in which they do not matter."[52] Or as McGrath stated, "When you believe you will always have children with different learning styles . . . you know that the effort you put into designing curricular supports is an investment, not a stopgap for a unique situation . . . you are ready for any student."[53]

Chapter 7

Meeting Elementary Students' Personal and Social Needs

We all need competence and confidence.

PATRICK SCHWARZ, 2006

Developmental tasks for children with disabilities include additional challenges that they often initially face in childhood and whose mastery continues on throughout adolescence and young adulthood. Studies of self-concept and social adjustment in adults with a wide range of disabilities indicate that their adjustment is not predetermined by the type of disability and does not correlate with the severity of disability.

Developing a healthy self-concept is one example of how personal and social development becomes more complicated for children growing up with a disability. Young children with disabilities initially are not concerned with their differences, but often learn to feel badly about them because they live in a social environment that eventually gives them the message that to be different is to be less than or bad. Children with physical disabilities are used to seeing other people stare or hearing children ask their parents, "What's wrong with her?" Many students with disabilities are aware that some skills come easily to their peers but not to them.

Some children with disabilities have the perception that they are repeatedly being fixed by parents, cadres of therapists, and medical professionals. These sociocultural factors make it harder to view themselves as worthy as well as to identify personal strengths and assets.

Frye provided a cogent overview of studies that document the unique personal and social needs of students with a range of physical, emotional, and learning disabilities in the context of her discussion of the role of elementary school counselors with students with disabilities.[1] This body of research notes increased levels of stress and anxiety, learned helplessness and self-esteem, external locus of control, more negative school experiences, and deficits in anger management skills.[2]

The needs of children with disabilities naturally vary greatly from child to child and are not determined solely by the disability. For example, the specific personal and social needs of one child with spina bifida are likely quite different from those of another. The same holds true for children with specific learning disabilities. With this in mind, it is important to recognize that there are commonly experienced personal and social needs that often arise due to commonalities in experiences. Considerations in addition to the American School Counselor Association (ASCA) National Standards for personal/social development must be taken into account with the following amplified needs:

- To incorporate a child's disability as one facet of his or her identity but not the single or most important one.

- To not overgeneralize the child's limitations. Beatrice Wright described this as *containing* disability effects.[3]

- To build up a sense of self that resists stereotypes and devaluement.

- To appreciate all children's abilities and differences.

- To teach children to accept help but not fall into learned helplessness.

At this point, we have only touched on self-concept. The developmental process of acquiring interpersonal skills also becomes more complicated. This occurs even if the disability does not directly interfere with social skills. Due to social stigma, many children with disabilities have few friends in school, and fewer chances to socialize outside school, and they are often rejected or victimized. In addition, they are more likely to be involved in friendships that lack healthy reciprocity.[4] For such reasons, these children often require stronger or additional social skills. The interpersonal skills of children with some disorders are significantly affected by the direct effects of the disability itself. This includes students with autism spectrum disorders, specific learning disabilities, as well as conditions that cause difficulties with mood or self-control.

Because self-concept and socialization are interwoven, difficulties are often compounded. In addition to making self-worth more difficult to obtain, students who struggle socially generally dislike school; this is most pronounced in students who feel they are social misfits, are teased, and are often rejected.[5] This chapter focuses on the many ways that school counselors can facilitate the personal and social developmental needs of students with disabilities. One of the meaningful roles that school counselors can play is to help classroom teachers find ways to facilitate this much-needed social integration. Some of these methods include those that create a favorable climate for social integration to occur: promoting regular contact between typical and atypical children by removing barriers, using proximity to encourage interaction and possible friendships, and strategies that enhance the likelihood of greater acceptance. This chapter also focuses on developing inclusive social atmospheres throughout the school environment, social skill development, protecting emergent friendships, and fostering resiliency.

Fostering Social Integration in the Classroom

Social integration is really a cycle, when children don't have social encounters, they don't learn how to interact with others, and then, ultimately, others don't want to interact with those children"

KRISTA HOPSON, 2003

From a young age, children spot differences. This is natural; in fact, identifying which one is different is often a learning game because it is a precursor for reading and other skills (Figure 7.1). Children as early as kindergarten are aware of physical and behavioral differences and are often initially reluctant to engage with those children they perceive to be different from themselves.[6] Young children recognize differences in behavior even in the absence of information

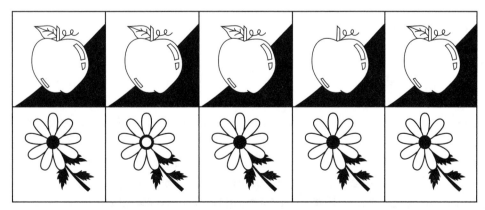

Figure 7.1 Which of These Is Not Like the Other?

identifying a child as having a disability.[7] They begin to choose playmates without disabilities over those with disabilities. Nowicki found that young children were often particularly negative about classmates with intellectual disabilities and wrote, "Peers who do not learn new things easily may be viewed as globally bad by younger children."[8]

Kindergarten is an important time to facilitate more positive attitudes because attitudes generally have been found to become more progressively negative with age. For this reason, children with disabilities are more likely to establish new friendships during elementary school than in middle school.

Social integration in the classroom is fundamental to the principles espoused in the Individuals with Disabilities Act (IDEA) and the requirement to place a child in the least restrictive environment possible. As we discussed in Chapter Four, this is derived from an understanding of the harmful effects of segregating people with disabilities and excluding them from the mainstream of society.

Terpstra and Temura clearly articulate the potential of an inclusive classroom:

Young children learn many skills through play and social interactions with their peers. Skills such as understanding social roles, sharing, communicating and appropriate responding to situations are learned in this manner. In an inclusive educational program, children with disabilities are placed in a setting with typically developing peers who serve as same-aged models with whom they can interact and learn through natural behavior modeling format.[9]

Opportunities for meaningful interaction and social development do not occur simply because a child has the opportunity to be with typical peers in a regular classroom setting.[10] Kemple is one of many researchers who found that placement in a general education setting does not necessarily increase the frequency of interactions because typical children prefer to play with similar children.[11]

Creating a Classroom Climate Conducive to Social Integration

First and foremost, the manner in which educators regard a child's differences sets the stage for young students who are in the process of developing their ideas about who belongs in their social circle. Diamond points out that the manner in which a classroom is organized communicates powerful messages to students.[12] School counselors can encourage teachers to think about ways in which their interactions with a student with disabilities set that student apart or communicates that it is natural for everyone to be included. The idea is to establish a learning community in which all students are valued and to avoid the "us" and "them" division that may occur. This practice in turn assists all students with becoming comfortable with and accepting of the various types of diversity they will encounter not just in school but in society in general.

Bringing Students Together

In *The Tipping Point*, Gladwell refers to research by Milgram and others to underscore the importance of proximity and shared activities in friendship formation in general.

> In one well-known study, a group of psychologists asked people living in the Dyckman public housing project in northern Manhattan to name their closest friend in the project; 88 percent of the friends lived in the same building, and half lived on the same floor. In general, people chose friends of a similar age and race. But if the friend lived down the hall, age and race become a lot less important. Proximity, in other words, overpowered similarity. Another study, done with students at the University of Utah, found that if you asked someone why he is friendly with someone else, he'll say it is because he and his friend share similar attitudes. But if you actually quiz the two of them on their attitudes, you'll find that what they actually share is similar activities. We are friends with the people we do things with as much as we are with the people we resemble. We do not seek out friends, in other words. We associate with the people who occupy the same small physical spaces that we do.[13]

Resources on encouraging friendships between typical and atypical children emphasize the same two points: proximity and shared interests are vital to the development of social relationships. There are many ways to capitalize on this in the classroom. For example, peer interaction is facilitated when teachers form small groups that include students with and without disabilities. Bringing students together in unobtrusive ways is helpful and increases proximity and the likelihood of interaction. However, this needs to be subtle. Trying too hard to have children interact with students with disabilities can backfire. Baker and Donelly describe the process as one of informal facilitation that capitalizes on many casual opportunities to bring typical and atypical students together.[14]

School counselors can work with teachers to develop creative ways and activities to bring typical and atypical students together. One recommendation is for the school counselor to develop a mini in-service/workshop on how to bring students together. The school counselor starts with a brief overview on the importance of social integration and the heightened need for it for students with disabilities, especially at the elementary level. Then he or she could introduce the key factors to consider in bringing students together and have participants discuss them. Possible discussion items include:

- Given the specific learning objectives on my lesson plan, can I foster social integration in my classroom by having students work in pairs, small groups, or teams and still not sacrifice my educational goals?

- How do I create classroom norms (expected behaviors) that welcome and accept diverse social interactions?

After the discussion, the school counselor can give the teachers a few examples of creative ways or activities to increase social integration in the classrooms. Teachers can then brainstorm to develop more ways to engage students in diverse social interactions. They could do this in groups that the school counselor forms by using an activity that illustrates how to increase social integration within the workshop group. At the end of the workshop, teachers could share the activities developed, which could then be put into a booklet for all teachers to use.

One of the best ways is to create an environment with many opportunities to play and learn together and to foster the sharing of interests. This includes removing barriers to interaction. Sometimes, in the interest of providing help, programs pull students out of the classroom at times during which they can best socialize. For example, one student mentioned that she cannot interact with her classmates at lunch because she is taken out for a lunchtime group (that focuses on socialization) with other students with disabilities. Physical barriers can also exist in the learning environment that serve to isolate children with disabilities. Consideration should be given to factors that promote the independence of children to move about as freely as possible.

Studies of friendships between students with and without disabilities reveal the key role of shared interests.[15] Thinking about this finding can lead to useful strategies that can foster friendship formation. It is helpful to make sure that students are aware of common interests they share with a particular student with a disability. (This is not to say that friendships between students with disabilities are not as valuable; it is just that they do not face the same barriers.) The benefits of classroom guidance lessons that focus on shared interests and friendships can greatly facilitate the development of these relationships. Simple adaptations may need to be added to lesson plans so that they are inclusive of a variety of interests and span the scope of the interests to increase the matches and commonalities across typical and atypical students. Small, heterogeneous groups designed to promote friendship-making skills can accomplish similar goals on a smaller scale, and they may be particularly beneficial for children whose disability may make it difficult to connect easily with others.

Although most often a low-key approach is helpful, sometimes a child's differences are so apparent that more explanation is useful, such as when a new child is entering a class. It is not unusual for a parent to initiate a discussion of how best to introduce a child with a disability into a classroom. There is a fine line to walk between demystifying a child's disability while not setting him or her even further apart from the other students. The focus needs to be on obvious differences that children will easily notice. Therefore, this pertains to students with physical differences such as orthopedic disorders as well as disorders that result in conspicuous behavioral differences. The Muscular Dystrophy Association raises an important point about which students may need to have some help in educating peers about their differences: "Ironically children who are less disabled by neuromuscular disease can have a tougher time with peers. Children who seem 'OK' and don't use wheelchairs, but whose conditions cause them to be clumsy and weak, often suffer taunts, jibes and accusations of being lazy or not trying hard enough."[16] It is important that any conversation about a child's disability with classmates be discussed collaboratively and reflect the opinions of the parents, the teacher, and the student. A good example of this collaboration initiated by the educators follows:

> "In preliminary meetings about his Duchenne Muscular Dystrophy, the school staff expressed concern about his social inclusion. Nicholas is ambulatory but moves slowly and has trouble climbing stairs. They wanted to know if it was OK if they told the other children that Nicholas had a problem with his muscles and that that is why he couldn't keep up," Larkin [Nicholas's mother] said. "They felt it might help if the kids knew there was a reason. By not knowing they might think he was lazy or just didn't want to keep up with them." Larkin asked Nicholas, age five, if it was all right to tell the other children his muscles were different, and he said that was OK."[17]

Sometimes parents take the lead and the student welcomes this. Other times, students prefer their parents not to be present. We emphasize six guidelines for this process:

- Ensure that the student with the disability is present for the discussion. This is to be an empowering experience, not perceived as if the class is being talked to behind the child's back.

- Emphasize the process of doing the same things differently rather than how they cannot be done. For example, say, "She uses a wheelchair to get around," rather than, "She can't walk."

- Help the class see the whole child and not just the disability: "Billy loves to watch baseball, and his favorite TV show is *Jimmy Neutron*."

- Encourage empathy, seeing the world through the eyes of their classmate as opposed to sympathy.[18] Empathy begins with understanding one's own feelings and reactions and then beginning to generalize feeling awareness to the experiences of others.

- Always share information in an age-appropriate manner.

- Bear in mind that information alone about a disability does not always promote more positive attitudes.

This last point, that information may fail to effect a change in attitude or willingness to interact with atypical peers, may be surprising to readers. In fact, it can sometimes have a negative impact by underscoring differences. Swaim notes, "With certain conditions, such as epilepsy, obesity and blindness, presentation of such information has even had a negative effect on attitudes or behavioral intentions."[19] The impact of information about disability on attitude change is somewhat complex. For example, Siperstin and Bak used video and information in order to have a positive impact on attitudes of sighted children toward those with blindness. They found that the information resulted in more positive attitudes but more negative behavioral intentions.[20] These studies should not be considered definitive; however, they underscore the importance of thinking about the quality of information used. Certainly, information is helpful, and we do not want to unintentionally dissuade readers from using it. It is likely that children do better with descriptive information that points out similarities (despite differences) than information that is considered to be explanatory in terms of the cause of these differences.[21]

The question of whether it is helpful to encourage the disclosure of hidden disabilities is often debated. Although disclosure opens the door for stigma, it may also open the door for increased support and understanding.[22] Ochs, Kremer-Sadlik, Solomon, and Sirota found that full disclosure regarding autism to peers and educators resulted in better support in the classroom and the playground. Children who are older at the time of diagnosis with a less conspicuous or obvious disability may wish to have more control over disclosures to peers.[23] For example, a student who is known to one of the authors was a preadolescent when initially diagnosed with Asperger's syndrome. He had endured years of bullying and social isolation in elementary school, but in middle school, the teasing and bullying had finally decreased and he felt socially safer. His fear of having his peers become aware of his diagnosis was that he might once again become the target of bullying. At the same time, he wanted a select few of his peers to know about his disability so that he could know who his reliable and safe friends were.

An important aspect of sharing information pertains to helping peers learn how to interact with a classmate. For example, school counselors and other individuals often learn to communicate well with a child who has a communication disorder but forget the importance of teaching the child's classmates the same skills. It is important to teach students how to communicate and play with any particular student. This can include teaching peers to understand nonverbal cues and other ways a child may be communicating with sounds, gestures, signs, and facial expressions. For example, if a peer does not get a verbal response from the student with a disability, the educator can model trying again and explain the child's nonverbal response such as that he talks with his eyes or smiles rather than using words.[24]

The School Counselor's Guide to Helping Students with Disabilities

The Antithesis of Social Integration:
Bullying and Social Rejection

The hope is that the efforts made to enhance social integration create a safe and supportive learning environment for students with disabilities. Unfortunately, data suggest that this not always the case. The reality is quite different for students with disabilities. The hard truth is that these children are targets of bullying and social rejection more often than their typical peers are. This is defined as bias-based bullying—bullying that occurs simply because of one's disability status.

It is important that school counselors and school administrators understand how this bullying plays out in classrooms and other school environments because the harmful effects of bullying and social rejection can be long lasting. School counselors need to make every effort to address the issue and deal with this behavior. Although a full appreciation of the magnitude of the correlation between disability status and bullying is not known, the U.S. Department of Health and Human Services, Health Resource and Service Administration, through its Stop Bullying Now Web site, provides an overview (Table 7.1) of the evidence found (http://stopbullyingnow.hrsa.gov/HHS_PSA/pdfs/SBN_Tip_24.pdf).

The impact of this bullying can be serious. The U.S. Department of Health and Human Services reports that students who are bullied report troubling emotional responses from depression to abandonment; they can become suicidal. They begin to dislike school and disengage or even withdraw from it, as is evidenced by their high rates of absenteeism and decreasing academic functioning; they can experience a multitude of physical symptoms: headaches, stomachaches, fatigue, or poor appetites, for example.

As school counselors face the reality of bullying in their schools, it is helpful to have a framework on which to build interventions. The New Jersey Cares About Bullying program, part of the state of New Jersey's Office of Bias Crime and Community Relations, has created a chart (Table 7.2) that defines three levels of bullying, from least to most severe, across three types of bullying: physical, emotional, and social. The chart denotes verbal and nonverbal components of bullying and gives specific examples too. This framework gives school counselors an excellent tool to assess both the nature and severity of the bullying that is occurring and to construct interventions.

The best intervention for bullying is preventing its occurrence, as much as possible, in the first place. Many school counselors have led efforts to develop schoolwide bullying intervention programs, and there are well-developed curriculums and programs available, such as the highly recognized Olweus Bullying Prevention Program OBPP (http://www.olweus.org/public/index.page). Although this program is not exclusively targeted to students with disabilities, it is inclusive, supplying community, school, classroom, and individual components. The PACER Center, a parent training and information center for

Table 7.1 The Reality of Bullying and Disability

The Disability	The Bullying Reality	The Supporting Research[a]
Learning disabilities	There is an increased risk for being the victim of teasing and being physically bullied.	Martlew (1991); Mishna (2003); Nabuzoka (1993); Thompson (1994)
Attention deficit hyperactivity disorder (ADHD)	There are two bullying realities: being bullied, which is "more likely," and being the bully, which is "somewhat more likely"	Unnever (2003)
Appearance-affecting medical conditions (for example, cerebral palsy, muscular dystrophy, and spina bifida)	When the disability affects their physical appearance, "they are more likely to be victimized by peers." Also, they often report experiencing name-calling because of their disability.	Dawkins (1996)
Hemiplegia (paralysis of one side of the body)	The impact is on their peer relationships. They are more likely to be bullied by peers, are seen as less popular than their peers, and have fewer friends.	Yude (1998)
Diabetes and dependence on insulin	These children are "especially vulnerable to peer bullying."	Storch (2004)
Stuttering	They are "more likely" to be bullied.	Hugh-Jones (1999)

[a]The sources cited here are noted on the Web site.

families of children and youth with all disabilities, supports the National Center for Bullying Prevention, which provides resources. It developed an age-appropriate Web site for elementary students entitled Kids Against Bullying (www.pacerkidsagainstbullying.org), which offers a lesson plan designed to interface with the many Web-based activities supplied. Children are encouraged to take the oath to "be a kid against bullying" and can even print an "official" certificate to highlight their commitment (Figure 7.2). In addition to schoolwide strategies, school counselors can work individually with students who are the targets of bullies or with those who do the bullying. School counselors can be an incredible asset in working with all school constituents to ensure that the school is a welcoming place that fosters positive social interactions.

Table 7.2 Levels, Types, and Examples of Bullying

Level 1 bullying

Physical verbal	Expressing physical superiority, blaming the victim for starting the conflict
Physical nonverbal	Making threatening gestures, defacing property, pushing or shoving, taking small items from others
Emotional verbal	Insulting remarks; calling names; teasing about possessions, clothes, or physical appearance
Emotional nonverbal	Giving dirty looks, holding nose or other insulting gesture
Social verbal	Starting or spreading rumors; teasing publicly about clothes, looks, relationships with boys or girls
Social nonverbal	Ignoring someone and excluding that person from a group

Level 2 bullying

Physical verbal	Threatening physical harm
Physical nonverbal	Damaging property, stealing, starting fights, scratching or biting, pushing, tripping or causing a fall, assaulting
Emotional verbal	Insulting family; harassing with phone calls; insulting size, intelligence, athletic ability, race, color, religion, ethnicity, gender, disability, or sexual orientation
Emotional nonverbal	Defacing schoolwork or other personal property such as clothing, locker, or books
Social bullying verbal	Ostracizing using notes, instant messaging, or e-mail; posting slander in public places
Social nonverbal:	Playing mean tricks to embarrass someone

Level 3 bullying

Physical verbal:	Making repeated or graphic threats; practicing extortion such as taking lunch money; threatening to keep someone silent: "If you tell, it will be a lot worse!"
Physical nonverbal	Destroying property, setting fires, exhibiting physical cruelty, repeatedly acting in a violent or threatening manner, assaulting with a weapon
Emotional verbal	Harassing based on bias against race, color, religion, ethnicity, gender, disability, or sexual orientation
Emotional nonverbal	Destroying personal property such as clothing, books, jewelry; writing graffiti with bias against race, color, religion, ethnicity, gender, disability, or sexual orientation
Social verbal	Enforcing total group exclusion against someone by threatening others if he or she does not comply
Social nonverbal	Arranging public humiliation

Source: Reprinted in full with permission from New Jersey Cares as adapted from Atlantic Prevention Resources.

Some bullying prevention programs focus the intervention on the bystanders —those who are aware that bullying is occurring but may feel powerless to become involved for fear of becoming a bully's target themselves. In these programs, the bystanders are given options for taking action to reduce bullying in their learning environments. Another area where school counselors can effectively address the issue of bullying is by working with adults in the school to recognize and accept that bullying exists. Sometimes actions that are passed off as "kids being kids" or victims "asking for it" are really tacit acceptance of peer aggression. Small group interventions designed to promote treating others with respect, increase conflict resolution, and increase assertive communication can assist all students with the skills needed to have more prosocial relationships in the learning community.

Paraprofessionals and Social Integration

The use of paraprofessionals in the classroom can be beneficial in some regards and detrimental in others. Students with disabilities are the school's responsibility and should not be delegated to the care of a paraprofessional alone. This is not to say these professionals cannot be a key component in a child's success. Snow's description of this common problem illustrates some of the issues in terms of social integration and the lack of opportunity for personal and social development:

> The child and the para may sit together in the back of the class (so they don't "disrupt" the rest of the class). The regular ed teacher may take little or no responsibility for the child—the para is the "expert." When the para and child always work together, the child may be excluded from group activities, free choice time, and other opportunities to work and learn with other students. The student may be physically integrated in the classroom, but he or she is not *part* of the classroom, and the other students may see him or her as an outsider. The aide may be more like a "guard" than a helper, working diligently to prevent the child from "doing anything wrong." This is a terrible situation for the child, and he is not given the opportunity to learn self-discipline or self direction. He learns helplessness.[25]

If a child has a paraprofessional in the classroom, it heightens the need for enhanced social integration activities. One parent advocate said, "Often what happens when a child uses a wheelchair is that they are like an island; they are taught around rather than interacted with directly." Every effort needs to be made to genuinely and consciously include the student and encourage direct interaction with peers. This situation presents an excellent consulting opportunity

Figure 7.2 Antibullying Oath

for the school counselor to intervene in a proactive way. The focus of the consultations could be to:

- Increase awareness of the child's social interactions and social skills

- Identify how the teacher and the paraprofessional could work in concert to increase and enhance social opportunities

Meeting Elementary Students' Personal and Social Needs

- Develop strategies to increase direct peer interactions and to teach social skills
- Collaborate with parents to reinforce the development of social skills outside the school environment

In group counseling activities, efforts need to be taken to ensure that the child can participate without the presence of the paraprofessional. This assists the child in functioning independently in the group and also ensures the confidentiality of the child as well as the other group members.

Common Integration Missteps

The value of being part of the social fabric of the classroom cannot be overemphasized. Angela Wrigglesworth, an elementary school teacher with a neuromuscular disease (she was also Ms. Wheelchair Texas in 2004), wrote about one way her third-grade teacher fostered a genuine sense of inclusion through a simple action: "I recently came across a pile of letters that my third-grade teacher had my classmates write me during one of the many hospital stays of my youth. They are a priceless compilation of overused crayons, misspelled words, and sincere get-well wishes. They remind me that I was once part of a little community that missed my presence, my positive influence and my example that we should always search for the abilities within our disabilities."[26] This is true also for children who have chronic illnesses that lead to extended absences from school. Children diagnosed with cancer, for example, may be out of school for months at a time with treatment or illness issues. Returning to school after extended absences may be especially difficult without a connection to the class or their peers. Although getting back to school can be important to help children feel less isolated, they can have difficulties with fatigue, ongoing treatment, or the impact of their illness that create disruptions in their social relationships with peers.[27]

According to the Muscular Dystrophy Association, research has found that children with serious chronic illnesses struggle with feelings of isolation, inadequacy, and lack of self-worth. Nevertheless, "Children's natural resiliency allows them to bounce back from these negative emotions, especially if they feel accepted, supported and secure. Helping children verbalize their feelings, focus on their strengths and make friends with peers can enable them to incorporate a realistic awareness of their disabilities into their self-concepts."[28]

Being part of the social fabric of a classroom includes not having undue attention directed to you. Being the center of attention is often uncomfortable for children with disabilities. Thinking they are making sure a child feels welcomed, the educator may be overdoing it so that the child feels awkward and even more different from his or her classmates. In Chapter Two, we noted the phenomenon of children being typecast as mascots. Undue attention contributes to typecasting, as illustrated in the following example provided by a woman who used a wheelchair due to a progressive degenerative disorder that affected her muscles: "I had a wonderful teacher who was very embracing. The only problem was she didn't quite understand the importance of not making a child so 'pointed out.' Every time I would come or leave, she would have the whole class say 'hi' or 'bye.' She was an older teacher, and she felt like doing this would include me better."

A parent provided a clear example of how undue attention became problematic for her child. She spoke of how the school principal routinely made a beeline when he spied her child in the hall. The principal was overly friendly and inadvertently kept the child from proceeding with the other students down the hall. In this case, the mother and child came up with the idea to add the phrase, "I have to go now," on the child's adaptive technology device used for synthesized speech. Gleeson's study, based on interviews of mainstreamed children with illnesses and physical disabilities, led her to the conclusion that "essentially, pupils wanted teachers to understand enough about the condition so that appropriate arrangements could be made, *without making a fuss* [italics added]."[29]

Handling the curiosity of other students is also an aspect of fitting in. Even when careful efforts are made to provide a class with information about a student and his or her disability, questions often keep coming. For example, one mother spoke of paving the way carefully for her child who has multiple severe food allergies. Nevertheless, he spends many lunch periods with children gathered around him holding up food and asking, "Can you eat this? Can you eat this? What about this?" An adult with a disability reflected back on her elementary school years: "At that age, kids are a little more accepting, but you also get the curiosity that it brings. I was being continually analyzed, and I think that went on through the second grade where they were open about asking questions, which in a sense is good, but it gets a little overwhelming. Like they were obsessed with my three-wheeler, they were obsessed with my trachea, or my nurses or whatever. They even asked if I was going to die."

It is important for educators to prevent children from being bombarded with questions. The Circle of Inclusion Project, funded by the U.S. Department of Education's Office of Special Education, provides excellent guidance on handling questions from peers. These recommendations include conveying information in a manner that contributes to an understanding and acceptance of the child. "For example, a child may ask, 'Will Jacob ever learn to walk?' A reply might be, 'I don't know for sure. He may not learn to walk in the same way we do, but he is learning to use his wheel chair so he can move around by himself. He really wants to learn how, so let's help him practice every day!'"[30]

Helping and Its Side Effects

Having students help the student with a disability needs to be done judiciously. Remember to emphasize the caveat of *doing the same things differently*. The essential messages about helping should be, "We all need help," and, "We all can be helpers." Many educators suggest a buddy system to help students with disabilities in the classroom. These systems are helpful but only if all students, not just the student with a disability, are matched with buddies. One college student with a physical disability offered these personal reflections about some of the unintended effects of having typical students help those with disabilities. They were based on her experiences being a wheelchair user:

> There is a point where you want the other children to help assist the kids but you don't want them to become their mothers in the classroom. I've actually heard my professors teach people to create buddy systems where there would be another kid helping a kid with a disability. If the world was perfect that would be great. But there starts to be a pitying aspect, a mothering aspect. Honestly it is hard to develop friendships then because you are always "the child with the disability." So I kind of discourage that buddy system approach. Teachers and parents didn't recognize it as a problem because they don't foresee such young kids becoming mothering.

Nevertheless, having all class members form buddy pairs is a natural, unobtrusive way for help to be given and received. Peer helpers and peer helping programs are very common among many school counseling programs. These programs can be used to normalize the concept of helping and caring for each other. When designing these intervention programs, school counselors can easily integrate typical and atypical students' needs. Goodwin described experiences with peer assistance for children who required the use of wheelchairs as beneficial if the peer interactions were instrumental, caring and consensual. Instrumental support included assistance with mobility, equipment, and the increased ability of the child to participate with peers in a shared activity (such as running bases for a child in a game). Assistance perceived as caring occurred through acts of patience, sharing time and interests, and social support within the group such as staying with the child, not leaving him unattended, alone, or unsupported. Consensual assistance included classmates asking the child if assistance was needed before providing it. Assistance that was perceived as threatening included interfering with a child's ability to complete a task independently, offering assistance in a reckless or unsafe manner that could lead to injury or embarrassment for the child, and disregarding the child's request to cease helping.[31]

Children with disabilities also need to get a chance to help. Certainly the opportunity to help others themselves—rather than be the perpetual recipient of help—plays a role in the development of a positive self-identity. This is also instrumental in terms of learning friendship skills. Middleton emphasizes having opportunities to help others because it enables children to understand about reciprocity within friendships: "Children need to learn the skills involved in making and keeping friends. In this respect there are traps into which a disabled child is more likely to fall than a non-disabled child. Their chances of lasting friendship, in childhood or later in life, are based on understanding reciprocity. It is important that disabled children are not conditioned into dependent roles, and learn to give as well as receive."[32]

One woman identified a simple yet effective accommodation for her to be able to sign class books with her peers even though she had difficulties with handwriting. With the use of a rubber stamp, she was able to contribute at the same level as her peers without difficulty.

Protecting Friendships

Friendships that occur between children with and without disabilities need to be protected. All too often, budding friendships are turned into ones in which the child without the disability is encouraged to eventually become the helper of the student with a disability. Van der Klift and Kunc wrote:

> Over-emphasizing the "helper-helpee" relationship between children with and without disabilities can easily skew the delicate balance of giving and receiving that is a critically important parameter for friendship. They don't deny that help-giving contact may reduce an initial sense of strangeness or fear that some typically developing children may feel towards their peers with disabilities and that it may lay the groundwork for future friendships between children. However, they adamantly argue that it is essential to acknowledge that help is not and can never be the basis of a friendship. The reciprocity between friends is what makes friendship authentic.[33]

Staub spoke of educators who make the mistake of interfering with the natural development of friendships by paying too much attention to the child's disability. She notes that if a typical child is commended for such a relationship, "we inadvertently make friendship a big deal and imply that all children are not created equal." Staub also wrote of the frequency with which educators often ask the typical friend to help their friend with the disability. In this manner, a reciprocal friendship can change into one that is more helper-helpee.[34]

One mother we interviewed for this book shared with us a wonderful strategy she used in order to protect the friendships her child established with other children in his class. At the IEP meeting for her child, who was moving to middle school, she asked that he be placed with his friends in classes. (Her child needed assistive technology to communicate.) She understood that protecting friendships was of great importance and that proximity was one important aspect of this. This is one idea that school counselors can add to their repertoire of creative ideas that help students with disabilities.

Resiliency and Self-Concept

Being accepted as part of the social fabric of the classroom fosters resiliency, but there are several additional strategies that foster resilience in young children with disabilities. The importance of this is better understood in the context of the amplified needs students with disabilities often have regarding the development of a positive self-concept. These include not seeing their disability as all encompassing or the major aspect of their identity. In addition, they often need to appreciate their abilities and talents in the context of societal attitudes that often see them as "less than" others. Some key aspects of fostering resilience that are easily incorporated in elementary school settings follow. Of course, these concepts are good for all children to develop, but they represent critical issues for students with disabilities. Having resiliency skills can greatly contribute to their eventual success in social integration and social interactions.

Developing Islands of Competence

Brooks described many children with disabilities as finding themselves "drowning in an ocean of inadequacy." He adds that adults can help identify and reinforce the islands of competence that every child has. In this way, they can be sources of pride and accomplishment. He continues, "Doing so may create a ripple effect, motivating the child to venture forth and confront tasks that have been difficult."[35] School counselors can assist students in developing islands of competence by encouraging them to view hardships and obstacles as challenges that they can surmount. Small group experiences in which students give and receive feedback about their unique contributions to the group process, their strengths and talents, and their successes in interpersonal encounters also serve to promote their sense of competence.

Encouraging Contributions

Being able to use one's abilities to make a positive difference does a great deal for self-respect and school motivation. Brooks states this is particularly true for students with ADHD or learning disabilities, but it is helpful for all. He provided a clear illustration of this process:

> An elementary school child, who has no use for school and whose self-perceived island of competence was taking care of his pet dog, was enlisted as the "pet monitor"

of the school. The position involved taking care of various pets in the school, writing a brief manual about pet care that was eventually bound and placed in the school library, and speaking to all classes about the care of pets. Until the manual was proposed, this boy disliked writing, but with the encouragement and assistance of his teacher he wrote the manual because he believed he had a message of value to offer.[36]

Model a Resilient Approach to Mistakes and Struggles

The fear of making mistakes can limit a student's growth by leading him or her to avoid challenging situations. Some students struggle with tasks that would lead most students to feel self-defeated at times. Mistakes and failures need to be seen as a natural and expected part of the learning process.[37] Educators need to communicate their belief in the child's ability to succeed while being empathic to the struggle. The focus needs to be on the value of persistence rather than trying harder because students are often trying their best. It is more helpful to say something like, "I really admire how you are hanging in there. I am sure it is frustrating. Let's keep working together to find some new ways to make learning this a little easier." This approach also models the importance of using a creative problem-solving approach to struggles.

Encourage Interests and Hobbies

Helping a child with a disability develop interests and hobbies builds resilience in several ways. It provides opportunities for enjoyment, recognition, and self-esteem. In addition, this can result in attributes that others can recognize and, most important, share. A large proportion of friendships formed by typical and atypical children are based on shared interests. Because children with disabilities often have less leisure time than others due to multiple appointments and services, they may have less opportunity to be exposed to a range of activities. An added benefit of this encouragement of interests and hobbies to increase social interactions at an early age can be reflected in the child's career development. Areas of interests that are fostered early on may well blossom into occupation or work interests. In addition, all of these key aspects of resiliency can be expanded into classroom guidance activities or focused on in group or individual counseling sessions.

Social Integration Beyond the Classroom

Our emphasis to this point has been on the personal and social needs of students with disabilities as they relate to the classroom. Assuredly, the classroom is the primary environment for personal and social interventions in the elementary school. But the elementary school social environment extends to more than individual classrooms. Seen through the eyes of a child, the school is quite an expansive social setting. For them, this social environment includes the playground, the school bus, the cafeteria, the gym, the music and art rooms, the hallway, the restroom, and after-school activities, both school sponsored and nonschool sponsored, such as sports and birthday parties.

These areas provide both personal and social opportunities and challenges for children with disabilities. It is essential that school counselors understand these opportunities and challenges. The following sections highlight the important issues for school counselors to take into consideration when helping to integrate children with disabilities into the school environment.

Critical Social School Environments Outside Class

The three most important social environments outside the classroom for young children are the playground, the school bus, and the cafeteria. In these environments, peer interactions are less structured and more child-to-child focused than other environments in the school. Ask any young child what their favorite part of school day is, and you will often resoundingly hear, "Recess!" or "Lunch!"

The Playground

The playground is a wonderful, playful, and carefree place of activity, but it can often be experienced very differently by students with disabilities. In many cases, especially for students with physical disabilities, the very structure of the playground prevents them from joining others in play. These missed play opportunities are also missed social and personal opportunities because the interactions on the playground often facilitate communication skills and the development of friendships.

When school counselors view the playground as an essential place for learning social skills, they take an active role in ensuring that students with physical disabilities can fully participate in the playground and in playground activities. In 2004, the U.S. Access Board (http://www.access-board.gov/news/ada-aba.htm) issued new accessibility guidelines for the Americans with Disabilities Act and the Architectural Barriers Act of 1968 that include a section for play areas. The main purpose of the guidelines is to provide access for all children to the play area and to play components located on the ground or on the play structure. These guidelines provide an excellent resource for school counselors to help their school evaluate playgrounds accessibility. The U.S. Access Board also produced *Accessible Play Areas: A Summary of Accessibility Guidelines for Play Areas* (http://www.access-board.gov/play/guide/intro.htm), a handbook that delineates these guidelines. Should there be accessibility issues for the child, it is important that the school counselor advocate for their removal.

Removing the physical barriers on the playground for children with disabilities increases their opportunities to experience social connections with their peers, which in turn can increase corresponding advances in their social skill development. When the playground becomes a place where children with disabilities experience a sense of independence, when they have an "I can do this" attitude, they are free to experience and interact with their peers in new ways. It is these free interactions that provide the social learning environment. Independent interactions with peers in unstructured environments such as the playgrounds provide opportunities for children to resolve differences and practice social skills and friendship-making skills without direct adult mediation and to evaluate the success of these interactions based on their own efforts. For these reasons, while it may be more convenient in many respects for school counselors to schedule groups during nonacademic or unstructured time, it is critical that children be able to use these times to develop and maintain peer relationships.

Because playgrounds also serve as opportunities for bullying to occur, teachers and school counselors need to be on the alert for possible peer aggression and recognize that a student's reluctance to engage in play during recess or playground opportunities may be a sign of problems that need adult intervention.

The easiest way for a school counselor to understand how an individual student with a disability will interface with the playground is to consult with the child and his or her parents (Figure 7.3). Create a dialogue, and elicit their help.

The social barriers on the playground are not only physical; cognitive and social stigma barriers also play out in this environment and can prevent students with disabilities from being fully engaged in the playground's social environment. For example, students with cognitive disabilities may be at a loss because they

Figure 7.3 Consulting with Parents and Children About the Playground

simply do not understand the rules of the games that are being played, or they may not have the social skills to read the nonverbal communications of their peers and react inappropriately. Social stigma can be heard in the very language that children use on the playground: "We don't want to play with Billy because he's weird" or, in a whining tone, "Do we have to play with Billy?" Both types of barriers can distance a child with disabilities from the social interactions on the playground.

One school that addressed some of these issues in an inclusive manner developed a process to discuss the playground and the games played there. From these discussions emerged a list of appropriate playground games that would be acceptable and make the school playground an inclusive place. These games were then taught to all students by the physical education teacher. The special education teacher supplemented the instruction for children with special needs. With this extra instruction, the special education teacher basically ensured that students with disabilities understood the rules of the games and could easily join in the play. This exemplar school also understood that there is an additional element of the playground experience: the selection of sides for games or choosing who will be "it" for a game. These essential playground skills might be challenging for children with cognitive disabilities. They could struggle to understand the rules and also might not understand the cognitive concept of one-to-one correspondence that they require. So a simple children's counting rhyme like *eeny, meeny, miny, moe* may be a play barrier for them. Again, the students with disabilities were taught these choosing activities by the special education teacher. As all children developed these playground skills and a full understanding of the games, the playground became a truly accepting place where the children with disabilities had the freedom to join in and be part of the social environment.

This is an excellent example of how the school counselor's collaborative efforts worked to enhance the overall school experience for the students with disabilities. In addition, this collaboration resulted in addressing the amplified social needs of the students with disabilities. In doing so, it is more likely that they will gain the social competencies.

The School Bus

The school bus can be seen as simply a means to transport students to school or as an additional opportunity for learning, practicing, and gaining competency with social skills. Most children begin and end the school day on the school bus. In addition, some spend a substantial amount of time traveling to and from school on the bus, sometimes up to an hour or two every day. To them, the bus is clearly more than a transportation device. It can be a hub of social interactions and can set the tone for the beginning and ending of the school day.

In determining appropriate school counselor roles, many, including ASCA, advocate that bus duty is a noncounseling activity and therefore not a high-priority role. We suggest that school counselors need to see the school bus as a critical social environment and that they can intervene to help improve all children's bus experiences, including attending to the specialized needs of children with disabilities. Here are some simple suggestions:

- Help the school administration focus on the school bus as an extension of the school environment where positive social interactions are valued.

- Train bus drivers how to establish and reinforce good social norms on the bus. These norms should support and enhance the social integration being fostered in the classroom.

- If paraprofessionals accompany students with disabilities on the bus, help them see the importance of using this environment to increase the child's social autonomy and to increase opportunities for direct peer interactions.

- Immediately confront all derogatory references to school buses.

- Create an antibullying program that recognizes that the school bus can be a place where inappropriate and aggressive behavior occurs with higher frequency. This is verified by the informal poll on the Kids Against Bullying Web site (http://www.pacerkidsagainstbullying.org/). Forty-two of the children identified the school bus as the place where bullying occurs most often.

The Lunchroom

Similar to bus duty, lunchroom duty is often viewed as a noncounseling activity. But like the playground and the school bus, the school cafeteria is a social environment for children with many opportunities for relaxed, stress-free peer-to-peer interaction. This environment presents personal and social challenges for some students with disabilities, especially those with food allergies or with diabetes. Imagine the social isolation felt by an elementary student who must sit at the peanut-free table every day for lunch and with its limited opportunities for easy, friendly lunchtime interactions. Again, the atypical child's difference becomes pronounced. The very intervention designed to assist the children calls attention to them and puts them in the spotlight. In effect, the children stand out because of their disability. Unfortunately, some other children use such differences to taunt their atypical peers. Sometimes children even use food to threaten or bully the allergic child. For a student with diabetes, the lunchroom experience can highlight their difference by bringing attention to their food choices. For these students, the cafeteria can create stressful social interactions because they may be teased or taunted for their need to make food choices.

In both, school counselors need to be cognizant of not only social issues that are present for the children but the medical issues as well. It is imperative that a working and consultative relationship be developed with the school nurse and the student's parents. Most important, the school counselor must understand, and in many cases help others understand, that for these children, their interaction with food can have serious consequences and could even result in life-threatening situations. There are several ways that a school counselor can assist:

- Working in collaboration with the school nurse and parents, create educational outreach programs that help the school community understand food allergies and diabetes.

- Encourage the awareness of health differences by recognizing National Diabetes Month (November) or Food Allergy Awareness Week.

- Use the resources of the American Diabetes Association (ADA) or the Food Allergy and Anaphylaxis Network (FAAN) to add a unit on food issues to the school's classroom guidance curriculum. (See the FAAN's Be a Pal program, http://www.foodallergy.org/pal.html, or the ADA's Planet D Web site, http://tracker.diabetes.org/index.php, for suggestions.)

- Solicit teachers and staff in the school who have food allergies or diabetes to serve as role models or mentors.

- Offer support groups specifically designed for children with food allergies and diabetes with special attention on how their disability affects their sense of self and interactions and friendships with peers.

Students with sensory integration disabilities such as autism may find the lunchroom an experience in sensory overload and may have an adverse reaction to the smells and sounds routinely found in a school cafeteria—stimuli that typical children are easily able to ignore or filter out. In these instances, the child with autism may draw attention to himself by acting out his reaction to sensory overload, which often results in humiliation and despair. This child may appreciate the option of a calm, quiet environment with fewer peers.

Schools are hubs of social interaction. School counselors are urged to assess their school's total social interaction climate with respect to the needs of students with disabilities. In addition to the classroom, the playground, the bus, and the cafeteria, the school's social environment includes the gym, the music room, the art room, the hallway, restrooms, and after-school sponsored activities.

Facilitating Social Integration: Fostering Social Skill Development

Social skills are infrequently addressed in standard educational curriculums because of the assumption that these skills, which in many ways are part of an unwritten curriculum, develop naturally through play and social interaction with peers. For students with disabilities, however, the various school environments are challenging, and as a result these students sometimes do not gain the skills in this unwritten curriculum. Nevertheless, these skills can be taught, and as students with disabilities gain skills for interacting in the school's environment, they can achieve many benefits:

- They are more likely to develop healthy peer relationships and friendships and feel more connected to the classroom and school community.

- They are less likely to feel lonely and socially isolated.

- They are able to respond to teachers in a more positive manner and are less likely to experience teacher rejection.

- They are able to be assertive and communicate their needs and wants. This skill could greatly enhance their ability to resolve conflicts and help them become better self-advocates.

- They are better able to respond to various social cues.

Of course, not all students with disabilities have social skill deficits, and conversely, not all students without disabilities are able to gain social skills through the unwritten curriculum. School counselors can advocate that the unwritten curriculum be replaced by intentional efforts to assist students in achieving social skill competencies. They can lead this effort by working with the school administration to develop a schoolwide social skills curriculum emphasis or by increasing the focus on social skills in the school's guidance curriculum.

Students with appropriate social skills have a greater chance of succeeding both personally and academically. However, good social skills are not a panacea. They are necessary for students with disabilities to have to increase interpersonal success, but they are not a cure-all. Social skills acquisition needs to be combined with other accommodations and interventions.

Some of the key amplified social skill needs of young children with disabilities are listed in Table 7.3, and there are many ways that school counselors can help to address the social skill needs of students with disabilities. We recommend that these skills be emphasized as part of the overall school's guidance curriculum and that students with disabilities are included in those educational experiences.

Table 7.3 Amplified Social Skill Needs

Joining, introducing yourself	Listening and empathy
Making conversation	Making friends
Giving compliments	Self-advocacy
Responding and dealing with being bullied or teased	Self-acceptance
Developing problem-solving skills	Playing skills
Understanding how to arrive at conflict resolution	Resiliency skills

Source: Cook (2003).

However, as we saw in the exemplar playground example, there will certainly be a need to augment their learning with more targeted interventions. A school counselor could develop specialized small groups that facilitate social skills development. For example, a school counselor could create a friendship group designed to develop students' ability to use social skills to create positive peer relationships. This type of group could be an ideal way to help a student with a disability gain increased competency in social skills without being singled out as different. A more intensive intervention could involve the school counselor working individually with the student to facilitate the learning of social skills. Many commercial programs exist, although they are not usually written solely for students with disabilities. It is possible that the school counselor could modify or adapt the programs to include students with disabilities.

For many students with disabilities, the development of social skills can be quite a challenge, and therefore we advocate that the school counselor couple these skills with the development of resiliency skills. The Oregon Resiliency Project identified programs that have been effective in promoting social and emotional resiliency. Two are readily available as resources for school counselors:

- *Dare to Be You*, by Jan Miller-Heyl, Davis MacPhee, and Janet J. Fritz, Colorado State University, Fort Collins, Colorado. (See http://www .coopext.colostate.edu/DTBY/ for additional information.)

- *Strong Kids*, by K. Merrell, and others, University of Oregon, Eugene, Oregon. (See http://strongkids.uoregon.edu/ for additional information.)

Social Integration, Resiliency, Social Skills, and the IEP

The IEP rightly has its focus on the academic and educational issues that students with disabilities face. Frequently the social and personal needs of the student are an afterthought. Nevertheless, a direct connection to how the services provided by the school counseling program can help address these needs must be more salient. It is here that school counselors' involvement in IEP meetings puts them in an ideal position to advocate for the personal and social needs and emphasize the importance of fostering resiliency, which will have a positive impact on the student's academic success. In this role, school counselors can help identify these needs and ensure that the plan adequately addresses them. In preparation for the IEP, we suggest that the school counselor:

- Focus on the student's competence. Gather information on the student's personal and social strengths from a variety of school constituents: the student, teachers, the paraprofessional, cafeteria staff, and, if applicable, the bus driver or other activity leaders.

- Gather the same type of information from the student's parents. It is critical to ascertain if the personal and social issues observed in school are pervasive across environments. Also, help the parents identify possible interests and hobbies that could be supported in the IEP.

- Meet with the student to brainstorm ways that he or she contributes to the school community and suggest that these activities be included in or supported by the IEP. Understanding the student's goals and interests that can be incorporated into the plan in ways that can benefit the student will help him or her to feel more connected to the planning process as well.

- Create a list of the identified personal and social needs of the student.

- Develop three suggestions for how the school counseling program can be used to help address the personal and social needs of the student.

Children with disabilities have amplified social integration and social skill needs. This is illustrated by the story of Teddy Willis, a fifth-grade boy diagnosed with autism who requested sharing his experience with autism during the school's autism awareness month. After initially being denied and then after a community swell of support, he eventually got to share his experience with having a disability with his classroom, the rest of the school, and the school board. Given the opportunity, he made a powerful statement about the social experience of students with disabilities. He said, "I would like more people to understand my disability about having trouble with social skills," he said into the microphone. "If they did that, then I wouldn't be the least popular kid at Goodnoe [his elementary school] and I would just be like everybody else."[38]

School counselors can use formal activities such as classroom guidance and group interventions to address the special personal and social needs of students with disabilities, and they are especially positioned to observe and facilitate personal and social growth in informal settings such as playgrounds and lunchrooms.

Chapter 8

Meeting Adolescent Students' Personal and Social Needs

To be different when every adolescent instinct begs for sameness is to be denied the protective coloration that helps other kids endure the teen years, the mean years.

LESLIE MILK KRIEGSMAN (1992)

Personal and social competencies are especially critical for secondary students with disabilities. Blum called such competencies *protective factors* and added, "The difference between youth who successfully adapt and those who do not is believed to be related to their ability to develop coping behaviors and to acquire and maintain needed resources for managing the added demands of a chronic illness or disability."[1] Secondary students with disabilities often experience more complex and intensified developmental demands than more typical students and perhaps more than at any other time of their lives. During this time, these youth are often even more socially isolated in school than they had been previously. Friendships established earlier in school are more vulnerable. Some weather this period of time but many do not, and new friendships are hard to form. "With a few exceptions, my closest able-bodied friends are people I first met when I was very young. For a child with a disability, it becomes harder to make new friends in late grade school and high school. . . . Why is it so hard for teenagers to form same-sex friendships crossing ability boundaries?"[2]

Adolescents are notorious for banding together and excluding those who are different. Sometimes their rejection is overt, but sometimes it is more subtle though every bit as real. For example, it may take the form of social distance. It is not unusual for adolescents with disabilities to find themselves sitting alone at school gatherings. Having a disability often relegates students to a lower social caste. As one student recently remarked to one of the authors, "Don't you know? Having ADD in high school puts you just one level above being retarded?"

Self-acceptance also often changes dramatically during adolescence. This is reflected in the words of one teenager with spina bifida: "I don't know what happened to me. I used to be fine with myself. Now, all of a sudden, I hate my body. I hate who I am. I never used to think of myself as disabled. I don't know why." This girl retained close friends from a church group, but as they began to date and she did not, she not only derided her very being but also lost her belief that she could get what she wanted in life. As an adult, she is well on her way to attaining her dreams and views herself much more positively. Adolescents with invisible disabilities also experience a sharp increase in personal and social problems. Students with learning disabilities face increasingly complex social and academic demands and have problems responding to this increased stress. This is also true for students with other disorders as well. Those with Asperger's syndrome are at much greater risk of being bullied and excluded as their social deficits become more striking.

This chapter focuses on understanding and addressing the personal and social adjustment needs of secondary students with disabilities. Many of the recommendations made earlier in this book also function to lay the groundwork to benefit students later in adolescence, so in some ways, this discussion began in earlier chapters. It is critical that schools are seen as inclusive and welcoming environments and that negative attitudes and beliefs about students with disabilities are challenged and not tolerated. This is especially true for high schools because adolescents' ability to interact with peers and form positive peer relationships is highly influenced by these prejudicial beliefs and attitudes. They often prevent the typical student from reaching out in social ways to the student with the disability. Students with disabilities may become self-isolating to protect themselves from hurt or because they internalize these negative beliefs and attitudes. We have also stressed the importance of fostering resilience. We believe that students with disabilities who develop resilience in their early years will be better suited to face the challenges that adolescence brings. We do acknowledge that many students with disabilities, even those forearmed with enhanced resiliency skills, will more than likely struggle with the heightened personal and social demands of adolescence.

Identity and Self-Esteem

Like their typical peers, one of the most salient tasks of adolescence for students with disabilities is developing a sense of self and establishing one's own identity. A school counselor who has a disability himself pointed out, "If you don't develop a sense of self—if you don't define who you are . . . the world becomes your definer. You will become a second class citizen at best. Once you have a sense of self, you can handle the world . . . you can handle the looks and laughter (behind your back) and the obstacles." This counselor is emphasizing the need for what has been described as a *durable self*: a self that enables one to resist internalizing devaluing comments and actions.[3]

School counselors can contribute to a more positive sense of self for students with disabilities in several ways. The most fundamental way is to be conscientious about how they regard each student and advocate for them to have access to the same quality of life as other young adults. Chapter Two detailed some common stereotypes that are projected on students with disabilities, like regarding them as heroes, tragic figures, mascots, and eternal children. Being careful to avoid these projected identities is essential to helping students with disabilities establish healthy self-images.

Self-Esteem Development

Although many counselors assume that greater degrees of disability correlate with lower levels of self-esteem (or psychological adjustment), this assumption contradicts research findings.[4] In fact, many researchers have found that students with relatively milder disabilities may experience more difficulties. Beatrice Wright postulated that this occurs because "persons with a mild disability may, because they are *almost* normal, have a greater need to hide and deny their disability, thereby thwarting adjustment, whereas those whose disability is so severe as to be undeniable have little recourse but to grapple with the problem of accepting themselves as a person with a disability."[5]

There are three important points to emphasize about self-esteem and disability: self-esteem levels are individual despite disability, disabilities can amplify self-esteem struggles, and environmental factors can influence self-esteem. Although they may appear contradictory at first, they really are not.

Self-Esteem Levels are Individual Despite Disability

In aggregate data, students with physical disabilities generally do not report lowered self-esteem despite their social isolation.[6] There are several reasons that self-esteem can remain positive despite social stigma and other social barriers. These include the fact that many youth who have grown up with physical disabilities have developed ways of maintaining self-worth in the face of societal devaluement. This often involves placing relatively less value on physical than internal attributes. Wright has identified this process as conducive to adjustment and requiring a deviation from society's emphasis on appearance.[7] Furthermore, parents often work intentionally with their children to develop resiliency, knowing they will need this increasingly as they become older and social judgments become harsher. One man who knew this from his own experiences with childhood polio provides an illustration of how he taught this aspect of resiliency: "I've tried to teach my children that handicap is a relative thing. There is no such thing as perfectness; we are all handicapped. Some is visible and some is not"[8]

Disabilities Can Amplify Self-Esteem Struggles

We should not underestimate the magnitude of self-esteem struggles for some students with disabilities. Feelings of shame and inferiority can pervade their sense of self no matter how solid their sense of self was in younger years. Emily Rapp's memoir about life with an amputation and a prosthetic leg describes this well as she recalled an event that occurred while playing tetherball:

> It was on the school playground that the pride I felt in my body began to dissipate, when I realized how it was viewed by some in the able-bodied world. . . . I saw a girl in my class, Rita, limping along nearby in an exaggerated way. She was bent over and trailing her hands along the ground like a monkey. She hobbled and then looked over her shoulder at me. I slapped the ball back to my partner. After taking a few more labored, limping steps, Rita stopped and looked at me again. I realized it was me she meant to imitate. The ball returned and I held it in my hand. I clutched the ball to my chest and felt my heart pound against the smooth leather. *Do I look like that? Like an animal?* . . . The strength of my shame confused me then, because it felt like a physical force—it was overwhelming. I didn't know exactly how to name it or know it. But I felt the same hot, stirring motion in my chest that I felt in my stomach before vomiting. I thought *I'm ugly; I'm a bad person,* even though I knew I was wrong to think such things.[9]

Environmental Factors Influence Self-Esteem

We want readers to bear in mind that many of the problems experienced in adolescence are due to external factors that need to be addressed. In other words, if a young adult is excluded from after-school activities and social opportunities, it is misguided to primarily focus on feelings of lowered self-worth. The issue, of course, is not intrapsychic. It is external and pertains to the need for advocacy for genuine inclusion. True self-acceptance is very hard for students with disabilities, and school counselors need to pave the way by making sure the school environment does not send the devaluing message that students with disabilities "are less than" other students. Although up to this point we have emphasized the identity struggles of youth with physical disabilities, adolescents with invisible disorders have been found to have relatively more emotional problems than those with more visible disabilities or deformities.[10] Blum explains this phenomenon: "Think, for example, of an elevator where someone enters at the third floor and presses the second-floor button. You think to yourself, 'Why doesn't he walk?' If someone looks healthy we assume they are healthy; and if they can't meet our expectations the psychological price they pay is failure."[11]

Forming Identity

Adolescent students who feel ashamed because of their disabilities may see them as the single most defining aspect of themselves. The developmental challenge is to integrate a disability as one part of the self and without seeing it as devaluing despite the fact that disability is stigmatized in society. Some people speak of the process of "overcoming" a disability. We prefer the concept of *overcoming barriers* related to having a disability. The difference is not just semantics. Sometimes adolescents (but more often adults) reach a point in adjustment in which their disabilities are incorporated as a valued aspect of their identity.

Josie Badger, an accomplished adult with a severe disability, often reflects on her own life when speaking to youth with disabilities. She asserts that maturity and a healthy personal identity are contingent on the acceptance of one's disability rather than denial. She states that the turning point in her life was attending a large meeting of the National Youth Leadership Network: "For the first time in my life, I met people who accepted their disability. They embraced it and were strong because of it. It made me realize that everything I had done up to that point in my life was to mask my disability." Referring to her own development, she stated she had reconstructed her view of herself, including the view of her disability as "not just as a limitation, but as a part of who I am."[12] This is key to positive identity and is echoed by many others, including Luke Jackson, an adolescent with Asperger's syndrome and the author of *Freaks, Geeks and Asperger Syndrome*. Jackson shared his view in response to a question about whether there is a cure for autism. He wrote, "Well, sorry if you don't like that answer, but 'no' there most definitely is not. For those of us who have learned to accept our differences this is a very good thing. To cure someone of AS [Asperger's syndrome] would be to take away their personality and some real cool abilities too."[13]

Finding value in one's disability is also clearly expressed by a nineteen-year-old graduate of a program focused on building resiliency in adolescent girls with disabilities. She wrote, "I am not so different. I actually see my disability as a gift now, a different way of seeing things. I no longer limit myself to one way of doing things and therefore have created some good problem-solving skills. I am luckier than others because I can see many ways of doing things."[14]

Rodis, Garrod, and Boscardin's discussion of identity formation for persons with learning disabilities provides a valuable way to understand the pathways many students travel in attempts to come to terms with a disorder that is stigmatizing:[15]

Stage 1: The problem-without-a-name

Stage 2: The diagnosis stage

Stage 3: The alienation stage

Stage 4: Passing

Stage 5: Crisis and reconfrontation

Stage 6: Owning and outing

Stage 7: Transcendence

This model serves as both a way to understand where a particular student may be at in this journey as well as how students can eventually integrate their disabilities as valuable parts of themselves.

People's reactions differ when moving from stage 1 to the diagnosis stage. Some experience a relief: "When I was first diagnosed with the disability, I felt that a weight had been lifted from my back . . . learning that many of the problems that I encountered were actually not caused by lack of intelligence or lack of effort, but by a learning problem that I could not control." Others struggle with despair: "After being diagnosed at around eight with dyslexia, I thought that was it that was as far as my learning was going to go. I was never going to learn anything again. I felt that I was stupid, dumb, and incompetent."[16]

According to Rodis, Garrod and Boscardin, the alienation stage (stage 3) often occurs during early to midadolescence. Even if the disability had been accepted earlier, it is often recast during this stage as alienating the young person from others. It is seen as a barrier that determines a negative fate in the world: "Like invisible glass walls . . . learning disabilities seem to demarcate the inner world from the outer world, the individual from the group, the actual from the desired, yet always in ways that leave one feeling shut out and undervalued." Students who are alienated may disengage from educational supports. The alienation stage also provides the substrate for turning toward students others designate as not fitting in, and it can open them up to more involvement in substance use as well.[17]

Stage 4, passing, involves concealing one's learning disability in order to avoid stigma. Rodis, Garrod, and Boscardin illustrate this stage with the comments of one adolescent: "The whole angry world I created around me was to protect me.

The clothes and makeup were a disguise: I hoped that people would see me as a freak, instead of stupid. I would have everyone think I had done too many drugs, and that was why I was slow, instead of them knowing the truth."[18]

Crisis and reconfrontation (stage 5), which often occurs in late adolescence, centers on coming face-to-face with the negative consequences of denial and evasions regarding one's learning disabilities. The disadvantages of concealing a condition become untenable, and this may lead to stage 6, of *owning and outing*, which involves integrating disability into one's self-identity. As one student wrote: "LD [learning disability] is a label, and as a label, stereotypes will always surface. But the label is also part of me. It's as much part of me as my middle name, as my smile, as my love of lilacs."[19] The final stage is *transcendence*. This is when disability is seen as a valuable intrinsic part of self. This process describes common stages. Variations hold true for some students, and some, naturally, have very different ways of dealing with who they are.

Although these developmental stages were meant to describe the paths of students with learning disabilities, many of the stages fit equally for students with physical disabilities. Many students with physical disabilities also go through the stages of trying to pass, alienation, reconfrontation, and owning and outing. For example, an adolescent with juvenile-onset diabetes may attempt to pass by not being forthright about her dietary restrictions and diabetes management when around peers. They may show alienation in terms of their future and opportunities due to their feelings about the serious medical complications they may eventually face, as well as how they feel about being different from others. Dangerous metabolic crises and other aversive consequences often call an end to this risky passing behavior. The student faces the impossibility of passing while staying healthy and often progresses to owning and outing. None of this is meant to imply that it is a smooth progression through the stages. Rather, this sketches out a direction of movement that many take in individual courses of identity formation and adjustment. Although we speak of direction, this is fluid and changes with life events. Others have conceptualized models of adjustment to disability that are similar.[20]

School counselors who are cognizant of this adjustment process are in a better position to help facilitate students' movement move through the stages. In addition, school counselors can help normalize the developmental process by providing students with mentors who have navigated these stages. One resource is the National Youth Leadership Network, which is devoted to developing the leadership skills of youth with disabilities and is an excellent affirming resource for professionals who work with students with disabilities. (For information on this network, see http://nyln.org/.)

These stages are important to consider as school counselors work with students in other American School Counselor Association (ASCA) standards such as academic and career development. This developmental information can also help individualized educational program (IEP) team members understand and appreciate the world of the student and help them factor in the impact of these stages as they consider possible interventions. An understanding of these stages can also be useful in interactions with parents who are experiencing the ramifications of their children's reaction to the various stages or a somewhat parallel journey to acceptance.

One final consideration regarding identity formation of which school counselors should be aware is the pressure some students with disabilities feel to be "inspirational" or extraordinary. We often project this image onto people with disabilities. In addition, some strive to be inspirational to compensate for their feelings regarding having a disability. Either way, it is a pressure that is not necessarily healthy. As Rapp wrote, "I did not want to be abnormal *or less than* because of my grievous, irrevocable physical flaws, so I had to be absolutely fantastic in order to compensate. The paradox: Being extraordinary was the only way to be ordinary."[21] It is easy to imagine the intensity that this adds for adolescent students with a disability, and school counselors need to be careful not to add to it inadvertently.

Sexuality Issues

Sexuality is a critical part of the identity and adjustment of all adolescents. "The success or failure encountered by children in their sexual development significantly contributes to the potential success or failure of their adaptation to adulthood."[22] We sometimes stereotype students with disabilities as eternal children and regard them as childlike in their interests and desires. But no student is asexual, no matter how severe his or her disability, including cognitive disabilities. Although we often speak of students classified as having mental retardation as having mental ages that are far below their chronological age, this masks the fact that they are indeed adolescents or adults. They may act out their desires differently or suppress them, but they do exist. Sexuality is central to one's sense of self and cannot be ignored in any student.

Many researchers have found that students with disabilities are as likely as typical peers to engage in sexual activity. This body of research included Mantsun Cheng and Udry's study of adolescents with physical disabilities as well as their study of males with IQs that fell in the range of mental retardation. It is important to note that the parents of these males overall were largely unaware of their rates of sexual activity. Furthermore, these parental data indicated their sons received less sex education at home than did typical peers.[23] Greydanus, Rimsza, and Newhouse also report rates of sexual activity being as high as peers (or higher) for youth with chronic or life-threatening illnesses. So even if parents and professionals do not acknowledge the sexuality of youth with disabilities, these young people certainly are sexual.[24]

Students with physical or medical conditions often think about the impact on their sexuality, including having children someday. Greydanus, Rimsza, and Newhouse point out: "Even mildly disabled adolescents may have significant problems with identity consolidation, particularly if periodic or prolonged hospitalization and medical care are necessary. The same chronically ill adolescent who openly expresses the desire not to become a parent may privately mourn a perceived (though often not real) loss of reproductive potential."[25]

Adolescent girls with physical disabilities often struggle with society's emphasis on their appearance, and this can manifest itself in compensatory behaviors.[26] "For adolescent girls," write Greydanus, Rimsza, and Newhouse, "sexual adequacy is often measured in terms of physical attractiveness. Unattractive physical features caused by a disease process or necessary medical treatment often pose a severe threat to self-esteem, sometimes resulting in promiscuous attempts to prove femininity."[27] Grealy's autobiography provides a clear example of how her physical disfigurement affected her sexual choices: "Not surprisingly, I saw sex as a salvation. If only I could get someone to have sex with me, it would mean that I was attractive, that someone could love me. I never doubted my ability to love, only that love would never be returned. The longing for someone and the fear that there would never be anyone intermingled to the point where I couldn't tell the difference."[28]

It is also useful for school counselors to be aware that students with some disorders are more likely than typical peers to experience precocious puberty (that is, early puberty). This often occurs due to central nervous system injury or dysfunction and may affect students with cerebral palsy and females with spina bifida and other neurodevelopmental disorders.[29] Levey wrote that youth with neurodevelopmental disorders are fully twenty times more likely to develop very early puberty. He added that almost 20 percent of girls with spina bifida enter puberty before they are age eight. Female students who enter puberty far before their peers often experience teasing, so this adds one more layer of concern for some children and adolescents. Conversely, males often have more adjustment difficulties when they appear less physically developed than their age-mates. Males with some chronic medical conditions, such as cystic fibrosis or chronic renal illnesses, often look younger than their age.[30] Elaborating on this point, Blum writes, "As a consequence, young adults with these conditions may be treated as much younger children—a response less socially tolerable for males than females."[31]

We are not advocating that school counselors provide sex education. That is not part of their role. Rather, it is within their role to be aware that issues related to sexuality are likely to have an impact on these students relatively more often than on typical students and to consult with health educators and health professionals to help ensure that the sexual education needs of adolescents with disabilities are addressed. Also, as these sexual issues surface, it is important that school counselors use brief counseling and make referrals to appropriate community professionals. In addition, it is important that the school counselor heighten the IEP team's awareness of these issues.

Personal Self-Determination and Self-Advocacy

In addition to the heightened struggles with identity issues, students with disabilities need to acquire a sense of self-determination and to be able to advocate for themselves. More specifically, they need to learn to make decisions based on a desired future vision that they have for themselves. They also need to have an underlying belief that they can have control over their fate. This is the essence of self-determination. They need to learn to be aware of their needs and assertively seek ways to get these needs met (self-advocacy). All adolescents and young adults face these aspects of development, but students with disabilities often feel relatively less empowered in this regard. This lessened sense of personal control over their lives is sometimes a by-product of having parents, school administrators, and other professionals "telling them" what to do and also from generally having less peer support.[32]

The concept of self-determination as defined by Field, Martin, Miller, Ward, and Wehmeyer underscores its importance to personal and social development.[33] "Self-determination is a combination of skills, knowledge and beliefs that enable a person to engage in goal-directed, self-regulated, autonomous behavior. An understanding of one's strengths and limitations together with a belief in oneself as capable and effective are essential to self-determination. When acting on the basis of these skills and attitudes, individuals have greater ability to take control of their lives and assume the role of successful adults in our society."[34]

A survey of the literature with respect to self-determination shows a strong correlation between adult success and self-determination.[35] This evidence suggests that with increased self-determination come greater financial independence, employment, and an enhanced quality of life. The concept of self-determination has historically been used primarily in the area of career development and refers to the student's ability to make decisions related to his or her future in the world of work. (Vocational self-determination and vocational self-advocacy are detailed in Chapter Nine.) Self-determination, however, extends beyond the career domain. For example, it may extend to the choice to pursue healthy friendships or to work toward more intimate or romantic dating relationships. This would include exercising independent decision making so that they are neither taken advantage of nor unduly influenced by others.

Luke Jackson, an adolescent with Asperger's syndrome, epitomizes self-determination and self-advocacy while he exhorts others to follow suit in actively handling bullying, a common problem of adolescents with Asperger's: "Remember, the most important thing is to tell someone. It may not be that easy. I know, I've been there! But from my experience I have learned that you can't just sit around and wait for it to stop. You have to do something. If teachers won't listen, then make them. Keep on and on. Go to the head of the school. Get your parents to come in and talk to the teachers. Remember, now is the time for it to stop. From now on, take no more crap!"[36]

Moloney, Whitney-Thomas, and Dreilinger explored aspects of self-determination in the lives of adolescents with and without disabilities. They interviewed adolescents about their "difficulties in their lives—with family, friends, drugs, and health." The researchers were examining students' "sense of purpose, knowledge of one's own strengths and weaknesses, and the ability to communicate this information to others." They found that students fell into four self-determination categories related to these variables: peer dominated, parent dominated, replacements, and full array. *Peer-dominated* youth "had independence but insufficient support, struggled with their families, had difficulty reaching out or using support, and consistently relied on their peers for most of their needs. These factors often led to emotional distress and poor decision-making." *Parent-dominated* youth "had insufficient independence. They tended not to be well connected with their peers, and their parents often made decisions for them and dominated their relationships with school personnel. While these students face fewer overt struggles, they may have difficulty building self-directed adult lives." *Replacements* "lacked strong parental or family support. They 'replaced' these missing support figures with friends, teachers, or other school personnel. In that sense, these students seemed fairly self-sufficient in attracting and building their own resources for support." *Full-array youth* "had multiple sources of support they felt comfortable using. They consistently made daily and long-term decisions that were well thought-out and had positive consequences." Students with disabilities fell primarily into the peer-dominated and parent-dominated categories.[37] In essence they were overly influenced by either their peers or their parents.

School counselors are in a good position to foster self-determination. They can:

- Always make sure to elicit a student's opinions on the choices he or she is facing.

- Follow the essence of the principle embraced by the disability rights movement: "Nothing about us without us." This offsets the tendency of professionals to decide what is in the best interests of someone with a disability.

- Teach and encourage assertiveness (self-advocacy skills).

Many students with physical disabilities lack assertiveness skills because in a society that values self-sufficiency, they have been socialized to not want to be "a burden" to others. Often their parents have advocated almost too well for them, and they have not developed this skill themselves. Nonetheless, they need well-developed assertiveness skills because they are often in situations in which they need to speak up in order to get some needs met, refuse unwanted assistance, or protect their rights when faced with inadvertent or conscious acts of discrimination. The time spent helping students learn to be assertive will enable them to self-advocate, a skill they will need throughout their lives. This includes students who need to self-advocate for educational accommodations (Chapter Six) and to protect their career dreams (Chapter Nine).

Kriegsman, Zaslow, and D'Zmura-Rechsteiner address the rationale and skills of assertiveness in a guide for teenagers with physical disabilities. Among their seven reasons that assertiveness is needed, they include the importance of asserting independence with parents: "Parents and teenagers are going to have differences of opinions. This is part of growing into adulthood. If you have to physically rely on your parents for help, it's a difficult struggle. It's tough to say 'No!' to a parent who had just lugged your wheelchair out of the car trunk. But you do not have to go along with everything they say just because they sometimes help you." They also suggest that adolescents ask themselves the following questions:

- Do you assert yourself?
- How do you assert yourself?
- Do you assert yourself in certain situations?
- Can you assert yourself with certain people and not with others?
- Can you assert yourself at home and not in public?
- Or out in public but not with your parents?
- Does it feel okay to speak for yourself when it comes to disability issues but not while on a date?[38]

Assertiveness is one of a wider array of social skills that are important for personal and social development, and all are necessary for self-determination.

Social Skills: Basic and Specialized

Whereas many students with disabilities have strong social skills, some have more persistent skill deficits that need attention. Some disabilities, like learning disabilities, attention deficit disorder or attention deficit hyperactivity disorder, and autism spectrum disorders, directly affect the development of social skills and, in turn, peer relationships. Like their typical peers, most adolescent students with disabilities seek out ways to fit in with their peer group and gain acceptance. The following anecdote, based on a boy known to one of the authors, illustrates some of the many ramifications of social skill deficits.

Billie was fourteen years old. He had been diagnosed with attention deficit hyperactivity disorder at an early age and had been taking medication for several years. He struggled with peer relationships. Most of his peers found him intolerable and quite juvenile, and all of his social efforts to fit in were thwarted. As a last resort, he started to cheek (*cheeking* is a slang term for hiding one's pills in a cheek while pretending to actually swallow) and hoard his medicine. He then started to share his medication with his "friends" and accumulated more and more so-called friends. This pleased him; he felt part of the peer group.

It is easy to see that Billie used his prescription medicine to literally buy friendship. The peers who had ignored him for years now found that he had something to offer them. These new-found friends were all into drugs, and Billie found himself immersed in the drug culture. In order to maintain his acceptance with this peer group, Billie joined them in their drug use. Stronger social skills might have increased his chances to enter a healthier peer group.

Individuals with disorders such as Asperger's syndrome are also at risk of significant problem with peers due to social skills deficits. One of the problems is that they have more difficulty accessing the hidden curriculum, that is, the social skills that many people seem to learn without being directly taught—for example:

- "People do not always want to know the honest truth when they ask your opinion. Your best friend does not want to hear that she looks fat in the dress she just bought for the high school dance.
- When the teacher is scolding another student, it is not the best time to ask the teacher a question.
- What may be acceptable at your house may not be acceptable at a friend's house. For example, although it is acceptable to put your feet up on the table at home, your friend's mom may be upset if you do that in her home.[39]"

It is important that educators understand that youth with Asperger's often require direct instruction on the hidden curriculum. Otherwise they break these unspoken rules and are ostracized by peers or run into trouble with adults.[40] Morrissey's discussion of this included the example of how some adolescents with Asperger's thought they were simply flirting when their behavior was actually perceived as perilously close to stalking by the objects of their romantic interest. She also spoke of problems such as expressing common phrases at inappropriate times, for example, greeting someone with, "Hi, how are you doing?" when standing beside that person at a urinal. Morrissey said that young adults with Asperger's are 25 to 50 percent more likely to have run-ins with the legal system if they are not taught critical aspects of the hidden curriculum.[41] Myles and Southwick recommend the use of carefully selected peer models who can discuss the hidden curriculum (as they see it) with teachers and perhaps the student's parents as well.[42]

Research evidence attests to the long-term impact of social skill deficiencies. Goldberg, Higgins, Raskind, and Herman conducted a twenty-year longitudinal, qualitative study of individuals with learning disabilities and found that these individuals "reported a general shyness or difficulty trusting others in various contexts, such as work, recreation, or family settings." They added, "Many told us they did not know where and how to meet new people, or make or sustain friendships. Most reported late development of romantic relationships compared with their non-disabled peers. Finally, participants mentioned difficulties in personal or marital relationships as a result of dependence and/or lack of reciprocity."[43] These findings emphasize how important it is for school counselors to help students acquire the skills they need for positive peer relationships and for functioning more effectively within the complex social layers in the middle and high school environments.

There are formal assessments of social skills and self-determination. (For an overview of these formal assessments, see the Self-Determination Technical Assistance Centers developed by University of North Carolina at Charlotte [http://www.sdtac.uncc.edu/].) Often a more informal social skills assessment is sufficient by observation and discussion with the student about the kinds of situations that may be problematic with peers and teachers.

ASCA's 1999 position statement described "providing social skills training in a classroom setting, in small groups or individually teaching social skills" to the student with special needs as an explicit and inherent responsibility of the school counselor. However, in 2004, ASCA revised its position statement and offered a more inclusive statement that services, including individual and group counseling, are a part of the overall program activities.[44] Although the more recent inclusive language is positive, we are concerned that this new language lessens the emphasis for teaching these essentials skills specifically to adolescents with disabilities.

In addition to basic social skills, students often need what can be thought of as specialized social skills for handling some unique situations that other students generally do not face: for example, having others stare at you, losing your balance in public, feeling an aura that indicates a seizure is about to occur, or being at a school dance in a wheelchair. Helping students develop personal strategies for handling these specific kinds of situations is what we are calling *specialized social skills training*, and such techniques can be learned through role playing. Both individual and group settings are useful for this; however, groups have the advantage of providing camaraderie and a pooling of ideas on how to handle tough social situations that students may have in common.

Students with physical disabilities may benefit from the art of normalizing the manner in which others perceive them and putting others at ease, a skill set described as *stigma management* or *deviance disavowal*.[45] These skills include initiating conversation on topics that could help others realize their commonalities and offset the stereotype that people with disabilities are so different. These skills also include learning to make casual reference (sometimes through the use of humor) to their disability so others do not feel uncertain about whether they are supposed to entirely ignore a disability as if it were taboo to acknowledge it in any way. In this manner, interactional strain is eased and barriers to interaction diminished.[46] The better equipped students are to handle socially demanding situations, the more likely they are to feel confident and to face, rather than avoid, them.

The impact of adolescent students' disabilities on their peer relationships is somewhat disability specific. For an example, some disabilities interfere with verbal communication abilities and require that students use assistive technology for communicating. McCarthy, Light, and McNaughton found that as a result of using this technology, students with disabilities feel isolated and experience "barriers in getting to know peers, barriers to meeting and making friends, frustrations with respect to initiating and maintaining relationships with peers, and extreme frustration with negative experiences related to attempts at peer acceptance and socialization."[47] With this specific type of disability, it may be important for school counselors to work with the student and the classmates to teach them how to communicate with each other. The solution may be as simple as creating a peer training program to help them understand the technology and making sure that the student with the disability is adept enough with the technology to engage in peer interactions. Peer training has been shown to increase the frequency and extent of the communication.[48]

Kriegsman, Zaslow, and D'Zmura-Rechsteiner provided suggestions for adolescents with disorders that impact their speaking abilities:

> Speak clearly and distinctly in whatever way you can. If you have a speech disability, calm your anxiety by trying to relax the muscles of the body, taking in deep breaths of air and exhaling slowly. Speak slowly and as distinctly as you can. Sometimes it helps to calm yourself by visualizing a soothing image, such as a mountain stream or a quiet meadow in springtime. You will find that your whole body will relax and that you will be able to focus on your thoughts and your message. If you are calm, the other person will relax and be able to concentrate on what you are saying. If you use a speech synthesizer to speak, you may want to give the person a little note explaining this device. You will think of other ways to communicate . . . . Do not be overly polite (obsequious).[49]

Even if they have very strong social skills, students with disabilities are often rejected by their peers. The stigma associated with a disability is not always surmounted. Some secondary students with disabilities will be able to find friends more readily outside the school environment through social groups connected to religious organization or volunteer groups. It is also helpful to know what local disability organizations have activities specifically for adolescents with disabilities. Rebecca Klaw spoke of the value of social groups composed of youth with autism spectrum disorders and developmental disabilities who were faced with the demands of coping with inclusive environments at school: "[Inclusion] is not a halfway road. We're expecting them to go all the way. It's exhausting to always be adapting to other people's standards. They need opportunities to be themselves, to talk about what's going well or not so well."[50] Some disability organizations also have camps and weekend retreats that are important resources for some students with disabilities.

High-Risk Activities

Like their typical peers, adolescents with disabilities face the same societal issues as drug and other substance abuse, sexual behavior resulting in unwanted pregnancy and sexual abuse, delinquent behavior, and dropping out of school. These issues are exacerbated by their disability or their response to their disability.

Most school counselors maintain a community resource directory that they use to facilitate making referrals of students to outside school programs, agencies, and professional services. We suggest that school counselors in a district work together to create a central resources directory that highlights agencies and professionals particularly well suited to providing services to students with disabilities and their families. This would include professionals who understand the needs of these students and demonstrate the ability to help them achieve their potentials (rather than succumb to stereotypical thinking about them). This type of directory would be an excellent resource when consulting with parents and for the IEP team to reference for identifying potential additional services.

In addition to the responsive services of the school counseling program and referrals to outside agencies, school counselors often help address these high-risk behaviors through prevention programs and educational programming. Let's revisit the exemplar practice for addressing playground issues and managing the games on the playground that was presented in Chapter Seven. In that case, a multilayer approach addressed the collective playground needs of all the children. Their assumption was that the students with disabilities would have additional learning needs when it came to understanding the rules for the games, how to play the games, and also other play-related issues like dividing into teams. They planned a multilayer response that helped students with disabilities gain the competencies necessary to succeed in the high social environment of the school playground.

Many of the intervention and prevention programs for adolescent high-risk behaviors are one-dimensional. Basically they are designed for typical students and do not have any modifications or adaptations to help students with disabilities gain the necessary competencies to deal with the complex social pressures and issues they face during adolescence. We recommend that each prevention or educational program that is implemented in the school be assessed for its appropriateness for students with disabilities. School counselors, in collaboration with other school professionals, are urged to create multilayered prevention and intervention programs that respond to the specialized learning needs of students with disabilities.

Substance Abuse

Students with disabilities are at risk for alcohol, tobacco, and other drug use. The U.S. Department of Health and Human Services, Office of Disability, reports that "the prevalence rates for substance abuse among persons with disabilities are very alarming" and that "a conservative estimate of the number of adult individuals with a substance abuse problem and a co-existing disability is approximated at 4.7 million Americans."[51] Similarly, Hollar and Hollar and Moore report a growing body of evidence that students with disabilities have a comparable or higher level of substance abuse risk than their typical peers.[52]

Although these statistics are widely known, very few prevention programs have been developed specifically for this population.[53] School counselors who recognize the disability and substance abuse connection can work to help address the problem.

Unwanted Pregnancy and Sexual Abuse

Adolescents with disabilities are often sexually active, and this sexual activity, combined with their disability, puts them at high risk for unwanted pregnancies. Although there are no specific data related to the prevalence of pregnancies and parenting for this special population, it is speculated that it may be as high as, if not higher than, their typical peers.[54] Moreover, prevention programs and strategies to help adolescents students with disabilities deal with this issue are virtually nonexistent.[55]

School counselors also need to be aware of heightened risk of sexual abuse for students with disabilities. Gordon, Tschopp, and Feldman found that students with physical disabilities often lack essential information about their sexuality: "The limited information provided to adolescents with disabilities puts them at risk of receiving biased messages with little knowledge to refute these ideas."[56] This is particularly important in light of evidence that people with disabilities are at far greater risk of sexual abuse and partner abuse.[57] Sullivan and Knutson found that children with disabilities were more than three times as likely to be sexually abused as children without disabilities.[58]

Juvenile Delinquency

The connection between juvenile delinquent behavior and disability is widely accepted.[59] Mears and Aron found that "youth with disabilities are overrepresented in correctional settings." More specifically, they report the following estimates for the juvenile corrections environment population:

- Specific learning disabilities: 10 to 36 percent

- Emotional disturbance: 50 percent

- Serious emotional disturbance: 20 percent

- Mental retardation: 12 percent

- Attention deficit hyperactivity disorder: 20 to 50 percent

They caution that these data are not precise because the diagnosis of disabilities is not always clear-cut, there were some methodological flaws, and state laws differ in how they define juveniles in terms of their ages. Even with these caveats take into consideration, the correlation between juvenile delinquency and disabilities is clear. Mears and Aron suggest three theories to explain this connection:

- Susceptibility theory: "Youth with disabilities are more likely to engage in delinquency because of particular characteristics putatively associated with disability (e.g., impulsivity, suggestibility)."

- School failure theory: "A youth's disability may contribute to difficulties, frustration, and failure in school, which in turn leads to criminal behavior."

- Differential processing theory: "Youth with learning disabilities are no more likely than youth without disabilities to engage in delinquency, but . . . they are more likely to be arrested/referred, convicted, and formally processed."[60]

School Dropout

The prevalence of dropping out of school for students with disabilities is high and quite comparable to rates for juvenile delinquency. Lehr, Johnson, Bremer, Cosio, Thompson, and the National Center on Secondary Education and Transition reported: "On average, students with disabilities are at greatest risk of dropping out of school. According to the 23rd Report to Congress, only 57% of youth with disabilities graduated with regular diplomas during the 1999–2000 school year. The dropout rate for students with emotional or behavioral disabilities is approximately twice that of general education students.[61] Of youth with disabilities who drop out of school, the highest proportions are students with learning disabilities (32%) and students with emotional/behavioral disabilities (50%)."[62]

One explanation for this high dropout rate is school disengagement. The choice to drop out of school is often seen as a hasty one, but in reality, it is often preceded by a gradual school disengagement that is evidenced in school withdrawal and school difficulties.[63]

Dignity of Risk and Resiliency

We conclude this chapter by discussing two key concepts that school professionals can use to help students with disabilities navigate the challenging personal and social issues that arise in adolescence: the dignity of risk and resiliency.

Dignity of Risk

Risk is inherent in growth and development and necessary to achieve goals, desires, and some dreams. Adolescents with disabilities have the same aspirations as other students, but their experiences have lowered their levels of success due to a range of barriers.[64] Blatt has long argued for the rights of people with disabilities to include choice and risk, even if those choices result in harm, and notes that the freedom to make such choices has been a cherished value and ideal in our society.[65] "Why then, asked Blatt, should we hold a different set of ideals and values for people with disabilities?"[66]

School counselors can help students with disabilities develop a healthy risk-taking attitude in two ways. First, we can stop overprotecting them. As an advocate and adult who grew up with a severe disability, Josie Badger put it very well: "The adults must step aside and let them take risks and make mistakes."[67] Second, we need to help students learn to take reasonable risks and teach them to handle unfavorable outcomes. We can do this by helping them learn to reframe what they perceive as failures. We agree with the often reported quote: "The truth is that if you can't make a mistake, you can't make anything." Here are ways to help students with disabilities in this regard:

- Encourage students to redefine failure. School counselors can work to emphasize that the act of going after one's desires is a success in its own right.

- Have students think of the worst possible outcome that could occur and how they would cope with it.

- Explain that succeeding in life is a numbers game in which some thwarted outcomes are expected on the road to positive outcomes. An example is exemplified in a quote often attributed to Thomas Edison: "I have not failed. I've just found 10,000 ways that won't work." For the sports-minded, we add that Michael Jordon espoused a similar viewpoint: "I've missed more than 9000 shots in my career. I've lost almost 300 games. 26 times, I've been trusted to take the game winning shot and missed. I've failed over and over and over again in my life. And that is why I succeed."

The perspective that some negative outcomes are predictable rather than catastrophic is part of the process of encouraging healthy risk taking and one important aspect of resiliency. One adolescent with a neuromuscular disease illustrated the value of this well: "As a male, my disability most strongly affected my self-image when I hit puberty and got really interested in girls. I thought, 'Who's going to like me in a wheelchair?' So I asked some girls out and got some rejections. But then some girls said, 'yeah.' If I'd stopped at the rejection stage, I wouldn't have gotten very far."[68]

Resiliency

We have emphasized that building resiliency skills and resiliency competencies is good for all students, and we advocate that they be added to the ASCA standards. We believe that these are essential needs for students with disabilities because resiliency is the capacity of an individual to bounce back from adversity. By its very definition, a disability is a hardship and an obstacle. Henderson stresses that resiliency is the antithesis of "at risk." She reports that "longitudinal research has corrected an inaccurate impression left by earlier risk research: Many children identified as 'high risk' do not develop the litany of problems educators have come to expect. Although exposed to high-risk environments, they have proven resilient. In addition, a significant number of those who do experience problems in childhood demonstrate resiliency in adulthood."[69]

As students with disabilities cope with adolescence, school counselors who invest in fostering resiliency in these students will see a substantial increase in their ability to adapt and navigate challenges. The following resiliency characteristics were identified by Morin and Linares: "Persistence, motivation, goal-oriented qualities, adaptability, optimism, self-esteem, and appropriate social skills."[70] We recommend that school counselors build classroom guidance lessons around these key characteristics.[71]

More specifically, secondary school students with disabilities need resilience to do the following:

- Maintain their self-esteem when faced with social exclusion or the projection of stereotyped images onto them.

- Persist toward valued goals despite encountering social or physical barriers.

- Engage in problem solving when logistics appear to prevent valued opportunities.

- Retain hope for the future even when adolescence is quite tough.

- Appreciate what they have gained in terms of personal strength or life perspective while coping with some of the most difficult aspects of living with a disability.

Integrating Personal and Social Competencies

In our work with adolescents with disabilities, we often take a multifaceted approach that integrates many of the concepts discussed in this chapter: strengthening self-esteem, expanding adolescents' repertoires of social skills, and helping them hold onto their dreams for the future despite the difficulties of having a disability in a secondary school setting. Sometimes we also talk with discouraged adolescents about the fact that the high school years are simply harder than others for making friends. We add that whereas it is important to keep trying, they can realistically expect more social acceptance when their peers mature. This is actually an imparting of (realistic) hope, a key element of resiliency.

While the personal and social challenges associated with adolescence are many, the rewards for developing personal and social competencies are invaluable for adolescents with disabilities.

The following quote from a woman with a neuromuscular disease illustrates many components of resiliency:

> As an actress, many times my self-image has been put to the test. The first time I was only 5 years old. I was asked by the director of a children's theatre group to introduce the show rather than play a role. I didn't understand then that this would be just the first curb I'd encounter due to expectations others have in theater. High school brought other hurdles, like automatic exclusion from lead parts and show choir, all of which were reported to me matter-of-factly . . . . I've learned that it's my job to sustain my self-image. Acting is a thick-skinned profession; as a wheel chair user, I have to be a rhinoceros.[72]

Her comments show resiliency in action and how it is interwoven with self-determination. When she refers to having the need to develop the thick skin of a rhinoceros, she is echoing the advice of the school counselor who grew up with a disability and urged young people with disabilities to define themselves so that they can resist internalizing the second-class citizenship often conferred on them. In other words, she created a durable self. Her belief that she could maintain her self-esteem in the face of rejection and discrimination enabled her to take the healthy risks that are an inherent part of pursing challenging and meaningful goals. And her overarching resilience enabled her to hold onto her dream of being an actress long enough for this possibility to become a reality.

Chapter 9

Meeting Students' Career-Planning Needs

"I want to be a pilot. I dream about it at night!" This comment was made by a student who uses a wheelchair due to a rare illness that resulted in an amputation. In fact, his fondness for flying developed as a by-product of his frequent need to visit distant medical facilities able to perform the surgeries required for him to live as well as possible with the condition. It was clear that he had begun some preliminary work to shape this dream into a realistic goal. He said, "One of the obstacles to what I want is, What if I might still be a wheelchair user? Will I be able to walk to the cockpit? When I have episodes of phantom pain, it will distract me. This could happen while flying a plane. People tell me I'm funny. Perhaps I will be a comedian and a pilot. Or I might be an elevator operator in a fancy hotel."

This student's stage of career development well illustrates some of the amplified needs of students with disabilities. He has meaningful dreams and some awareness of the potential obstacles. Without assistance in career development, it is likely that he will have trouble in this aspect of transition to life beyond secondary school because the complexities he faces are much greater than those of more typical peers.

The topics of career development and the transition beyond secondary school are intertwined. All too often students with disabilities lose their way in the difficult transition from secondary school to becoming a productive member of society. This is generally not due to a lack of effort; rather, it is due to the fact that there are so many complexities and barriers.

Amplified Career Development Needs

Career development for students with disabilities typically takes additional and concerted efforts that include a realistic understanding of predictable obstacles in the world of work. Students with disabilities share the same basic set of career developmental needs as students who do not have disabilities. They need to develop career awareness and employment readiness, acquire career information, identify career goals, and obtain the knowledge and skills needed to achieve those goals. However, their unique experiences with having a disability can cause them to have amplified—even additional or unique—career development issues. Some result from predictable complexities in the developmental process, while others exist due to the fact that they are often entering a tougher world of work: they do not face a level playing field when it comes to competition for jobs.

Individuals with disabilities have these work realities:

- They are only about half as likely to be employed.[1]

- Up to two-thirds of those who are currently unemployed report that they would rather be working.[2]

- Employers fear that accommodating them is prohibitively expensive and thus refrain from hiring them. The reality is that the costs of accommodations are zero or minimal.[3]

Students with disabilities often have other complications and obstacles in terms of career development. These children may have a more difficult time imagining themselves being involved in a wide variety of work, and so they may prematurely foreclose various career dreams. Because there are few visible role models of adults with disabilities thriving in careers, these youngsters' misinformed, lowered expectations often go unchallenged. Furthermore, students with disabilities may experience fewer opportunities for social and extracurricular activities that increase their interests, and thereby miss the indirect benefits to career development provided through such activities.

Students with disabilities also have transition hurdles to get through as they plan for and attempt to move beyond high school into careers. For instance, attempting to pursue accommodations (if needed) for college entrance exams can sometimes be confusing and frustrating to obtain. There are numerous legal matters to be knowledgeable about, such as the Americans with Disabilities Act and Section 504 of the Rehabilitation Act, as well as the potential impact of workplace accommodations or technology on vocational options. Complicated questions and issues exist, such as whether to disclose a hidden disability to a college or an employer, how to request and negotiate accommodations, and how to locate and make use of supportive resources as needed. These are just some of the factors that complicate the career development process for children and young adults with disabilities that merit consideration when assisting such students and designing school counseling programs.

Before we move on to these and other related matters, it is important to consider what the overriding mind-set of a school counselor should be when addressing the career development needs of students with disabilities. School counselors can influence how students and their parents look at the suitability of future career options. The goal is to empower them with the support and tools needed to make increasingly independent and potentially satisfying career decisions. The career development process needs to be based on a rational self-understanding of abilities, functional limitations, values, interests, and aspirations. We call this *expansive realism*. It is akin to teaching and inspiring students with disabilities to explore the world of work without fear yet instill a sense of good judgment and decision making.

In attempting to help students with disabilities in their career development, school counselors can sometimes take one of two unhelpful and extreme mind-sets. The first and more common extreme can be described as an *antiexpansive* approach. This mind-set has low expectations of people who have disabilities and views individuals with disabilities who are gainfully employed as exceptions rather than the norm. The employed individual is seen as a hero who is doing something exceptional. Statements that you might hear from people who hold an antiexpansive mind-set include, "Yes, we can grant them [students with disabilities] special services or accommodations while in school, but seriously, what are they actually going to be able to do when they get out into the real world? Aren't we just delaying the inevitable?" or, "That student is not college material because of his learning disability. He needs to consider finding a job immediately after high school." School counselors with antiexpansive mind-sets do not encourage students with disabilities to move fully through the developmental stages of dreaming about and exploring what they want to be when they grow up. The disempowering effects of this are apparent in this comment from a state vocational rehabilitation counselor who works with adolescents in transition to the world of work: "They have continually been given the message over and over that they do not have the ability to do much of anything. So when I finally get them I hear them say things like, 'I was told I can't do that. My learning disability won't allow me to do that kind of job.' It bothers me because when I ask them, 'Have you ever tried?' I always get 'no' for an answer."

The end result of this mind-set is the premature foreclosure of possibilities and options. This is the phenomenon in which the child closes off a full consideration or imagination of his or her options in life. "This is a particular risk for adolescents with disabilities if they have internalized societal injunctions about their place in society. They lose the freedom to explore personal desires. They may fail to dream about their future or may be too quick to compromise their dreams away rather than works towards them."[4]

Working with elementary school children with disabilities, school counselors can facilitate an expansion of possibilities. Inclusive classroom guidance activities can create awareness of the world of work that shows how individuals with disabilities function within the various job clusters. These types of activities can go a long way in helping to prevent a premature foreclosure of options in adolescence. Adolescents with disabilities may foreclose their vocational options because they have incidentally acquired from society and others the assumption that their career possibilities and expectations are limited. *Ableism* is a term used to describe the belief that it is better not to have a disability and that it is better to do things according to how people without disabilities do things. This naturally leads to the belief that certain careers or activities are impossible for people with disabilities if they cannot engage in them "normally."[5]

Then there is the *unrealistic* mind-set. This mind-set maintains that the sky is the limit and does not truly account for a realistic assessment of a student's abilities and limitations. People holding this mind-set often say to students, "You can do anything you want as long as you try hard enough." While foreclosing on students' dreams is undesirable, it is equally important to guide students in the ongoing development and maturation of their dreams so that their eventual career goals and actions line up in a direction and plan that will offer them a reasonable chance of attainment and success. The unrealistic mind-set ignores the real-life limitations associated with a person's disability as well as the societal and environmental challenges that such a person might face in the world of work. The unrealistic helper does not prepare a student to deal with predictable obstacles. School counselors and others with a sky-is-the-limit stance do not actively seek out or make use of the practical information, strategies, or services such as vocational rehabilitation services, advocacy skills training, or assistive technology that students with disabilities will need in order to succeed in the world of work. Like the antiexpansive mind-set, the unrealistic mind-set is also disempowering for students with disabilities. As one college student with a physical disability put it, "I think that people need to strive for who they want to be regardless of a disability, but there is one group of people who are saying, 'Oh, just go for whatever you want,' and then there is the other group that says, 'You can't do anything.' There is a real fine line there."

Both the antiexpansive and the unrealistic mind-sets suffer limitations that ideally school counselors should always avoid. Acknowledging, however, that all err from time to time, the better side on which to err is that of possibility. It will always be easier for students to recover from a mind-set that is perhaps overly ambitious than one that is constrictive and leads them to foreclose on career possibilities prematurely. One counselor who works in transition illustrates his approach that is consistent with this philosophy: "I'm not saying I always agree with some students' unrealistic work goals, but I never straight out tell them they can't do it. I believe in at least letting them have a shot at it before concluding with them that they can't do something. Sometimes though, I am surprised at what they can do once they start seeing themselves as adults."

What Is Realistic?

The question of what is realistic for a student with a disability comes up routinely when addressing career development needs. Without appearing to sidestep this issue, one of the best answers for school counselors is, "I'm not sure." This lack of certainty is often wise because careers that often appear unrealistic may indeed be realistic, but we are not in the position to see this for several reasons:

- Assistive technology and accommodations can resolve many obstacles.

- It is hard to accurately predict the future performance of some students with disabilities who may have a longer learning curve than others.

- Most standardized tests do not fare well in terms of predicting future career outcomes.

The comments of a college student with a disability reinforce this philosophy:

I don't think it is the place of a guidance counselor to say directly, "You cannot do that." Because unfortunately a lot of times guidance counselors are misinformed or underestimate someone's potential. I feel that there are too many chances for them to be wrong. For example, I am involved with a national disability organization and our executive director was an amazing person who had a traumatic brain injury in high school, and it drastically affected her learning, writing and verbal skills. And she was talked down to and told that she needed to get involved with her toys and dolls because that was all she would ever do. But now she's the executive director of our national organization. She has even worked for the United Nations!

Some of the best resources about possibilities are those written by insiders: people with disabilities who found ways to work in their professions or organizations devoted to accessibilities in professions. For example, several organizations have been devoted to recruiting more people with disabilities into the sciences. The American Association for the Advancement of Science has publications that provide information on career paths and on role models.[6] Also, DO-IT, Disabilities, Opportunities, Internetworking, and Technology (www.washington.edu/doit/), is an organization based at the University of Washington that provides a wealth of career/vocational and disability information in various formats (electronic/online resources, free publications, videos, training materials, workshops, presentations, events, and others). DO-IT's mission is to assist persons with disabilities to face the challenges of pursuing academic and career goals.

Two other key Web sites provide useful information for school counselors:

- Job Accommodation Network (JAN), a service of the Office of Disability Employment Policy of the U.S. Department of Labor. JAN provides free consultation to persons with disabilities, employers, and other interested parties (www.jan.wvu.edu/).

- ABLEDATA is a project funded by the National Institute on Disability and Rehabilitation Research of the U.S. Office of Special Education and Rehabilitative Services. It provides information about assistive technology products and rehabilitation. ABLEDATA may be useful in providing a tutorial of the types of assistive, adaptive, and rehabilitative devices that could be available for students with disabilities if such equipment would enable them to perform work tasks (www.abledata.com).

Many resources can provide useful information for the IEP and transition teams to facilitate the student's career planning. These Web sites represent a small fraction of the organizations and resources that exist. In preparation for team meetings, it would be helpful for the school counselor to do a little homework. Here are some helpful tips to prepare for the individualized educational program (IEP) and career and transition planning meetings:

- Have a conversation with the student about his or her career interests.

- Do a preliminary search comparing characteristics of the student's specific disability and of the identified career cluster. Print general information found. We recommend that the counselor do this with the student when feasible.

- Do a preliminary search of JAN to see what accommodations could be made to help this student work in his or her area of interest. We recommend that the counselor do this with the student when feasible.

- Take time to develop three steps that the student could take to enhance his or her career planning.

Expansive Realism in Action

Expansive realism allows the inclusion of all occupations as part of the career development process and then uses a series of decision-making steps to filter this expanded reality into realistic career goals. Expansive realism needs to be the primary guiding tenet of career development for all school counselors who work with students with disabilities. In practice, school counselors should follow these key ideas:

- Listen to all ideas, and refrain from foreclosure of the student's options, and encourage students not to foreclose too many options.

- Provide information about all the careers of interest.

- Research whether there are rules or regulations that restrict access to a specific occupation. For example, there may be requirements for a job that are unable to be addressed with accommodations. However, for many occupations, accommodations can be made to make that job available to an individual with a disability. For assistance with identifying possible job accommodations, the Job Accommodation Network's SOAR (Searchable On-line Accommodation Resource) Web site is an excellent resource that matches specific disabilities with possible accommodations (http://www.jan.wvu.edu/soar/index.htm).

- Given the possible occupations of interest, help the student find examples of a person with the same disability working in the profession. Search a wide variety of resources. The purpose of finding real-life examples is to help both the student and the counselor challenge their assumptions about whether a person with a specific disability can do a specific type of work. This provides an assessment of the realities and a role model for the student. Just because an example cannot be found does not mean that the job option should be discarded.

- If possible, find a local mentor in the occupation or profession.

- Use career clusters to explore a variety of possibilities within the profession.

- Work with the student to assess his or her capacity to do the job in question.

- In conjunction with career assessment, facilitate the development of an individualized career plan.
- Mesh this career plan with the mandated transition plan.

What about students whose career dreams cannot work by any stretch of imagination? For example, the first sentences of this chapter told of a student whose physical condition absolutely precludes his dream career. He was part of a small focus group composed of students whose physical disabilities were so severe that their needs could not be met in a public school setting. When we asked these students for their advice to school counselors when working with students whose career goals might not be realistic, the response was excellent: "First we need to dream; *then* we need to see if it's realistic." Another student added that this would include considering physical limitations. The aspiring pilot agreed and added that reality enters the picture when they meet with school counselors. The combined wisdom of this group was congruent with our own professional beliefs:

- Respect career dreams.

- Think creatively, and do not assume something is impossible without clear evidence.

- Do not take away someone's dreams without helping shape alternative valued goals that are both realistic and relatively attractive.

The last point is one that school counselors and all helpers should emphatically follow. Pulling away someone's dreams without helping to shape a new one can cause great harm. The youth may lose hope for a better future, and it is often that hope that makes the present bearable. There are ways to agree to disagree about whether something is possible in the future.

Other Career Development Issues

A *vocational self-concept* is the ability to envision oneself in the world of work. This becomes the personal context from which to consider future possibilities in this part of life. It becomes refined over time and ideally incorporates a positive sense of self, an awareness of interests and values, and an appreciation of aptitudes, skills, and limitations. This process of vocational imagining begins in childhood and can be fostered by a child's educational experiences. Elementary school counselors often develop classroom guidance lesson plans designed to facilitate this vocational development. However, children with disabilities may experience more difficulty than typical children in developing a positive vocational self-concept. Part of the reason is that they grow up amid a culture that by and large underestimates the vocational possibilities for them. Children with disabilities sometimes incorporate into their own self-concepts the lowered expectations that society holds for them and consequently have a low or nonexistent vocational self-concept. Conscious thought and deliberate action are essential to help young children with disabilities develop a positive vocational self-concept. The adults in their lives must seek out ways to help them attend to their vocational selves. The simple act of asking a young student with a disability, "What do you want to be when you grow up?" communicates the affirming message that the world of work has a place for them.

Role Models and Mentoring

One of the amplified needs of children with disabilities is that they often lack role models of employed adults with disabilities with whom they can identify. The absence of such role models is even apparent in young children's books. Two of the authors of this book, Marshak, Prezant, and Hulings-Shirley (2006), analyzed the thematic content related to the topic of disability of 173 children's books published between 1995 and 2006. They found that only 3 percent of the books included an employed character with a disability.[7] One noteworthy recently published exception is *One of the Gang*. This book for elementary-aged children helps those with food allergies explore what they want to be someday and presents pictures of seven people with food allergies who pursued their dreams. In this manner it provides vocational role models of people in fields such as sports, medicine, music and broadcasting.[8]

School counselors might also find it helpful to subscribe to *Ability Magazine* (http://www.abilitymagazine.com/), a bimonthly publication that is an excellent resource and provides many examples of role models. A student with a disability who notices this on a table in the counseling office will see it as affirming. Being proactive in this area is important and easy. School counselors can encourage teachers to seek out images of successfully employed adults with disabilities and infuse these into the classroom. Some simple examples include the use of specific children's books, placing images and stories of employed adults with disabilities on bulletin boards, and finding appropriate guest speakers from the community. School-based career development activities for all students should regularly include references to people with disabilities.

Unlike many other minority groups, children with disabilities often do not have the benefit of growing up with parents, older siblings, or relatives who share their particular minority group's characteristics or status and therefore have not coped with the stigma or logistical problems they deal with in having a disability. If a student identifies as having a disability, encourage mentoring. A student who has multiple sclerosis remarked on the benefits: "I'm very fortunate because I play wheelchair basketball and all the guys on my wheelchair basketball team have jobs and work . . . and they're all successful and they're all doing the kind of thing that I want to do." Mentors can serve as the gateway into social and professional networks where opportunities often arise based on those relationships. One school counselor has instituted the practice of having graduates with disabilities come back and speak to students. This is an example of how a simple idea, put into practice, can provide important help to students in their career development. One school counselor said, "To see our students with disabilities get into colleges brings great joy to me. So we invite our special education graduates to come back and talk to our current students about their experiences in college. It is so great to hear about how successful they are!"

School counselors can take advantage of Disability Employment Mentoring Day (DMD) in October, a result of a partnership between the U.S. Department of Labor's Office of Disability Employment Policy and the American Association of People with Disabilities. This is a perfect opportunity to focus annually on mentoring initiatives for students with disabilities. DMD is a national program that provides free and detailed resources online for developing mentoring programs, matchmaking, and implementing recruitment tools. A list of state and local DMD coordinators and contacts can be accessed at http://www.dmd-aapd.org/. School counselors who work in a rural school district or some other locality where recruiting mentors or particular types of mentors might be difficult can consider using Connecting-to-Success. Since 1999, this electronic mentoring program has coordinated e-mentoring opportunities for youth with disabilities and adult volunteer mentors (http://ici.umn.edu/ementoring/).

Standardized Career Assessment Instruments

School counselors are trained to administer and interpret standardized assessment instruments to assist students in understanding their abilities, interests, and values related to career development. However, these instruments often result in inaccurate portrayals of students with disabilities, yet another complexity in the career development process.

Clarifying a student's career interests is fairly central to career planning. Many career assessment batteries are based on the practice of finding areas of correlation between interests, abilities, values, and world-of-work practicalities. Interest inventories are a fairly standard way to explore interests of students in general. They are not necessarily as useful with students who have disabilities. Often the profiles of students with disabilities reveal very few interests. A profile may be flat, designating few and low interests, for two reasons that often confound the results: it may reflect a lack of exposure to a full range of activities, and students sometimes do not endorse items that reflect specific career interests because they assume they will not be able to enter those professions.

The main problem with standardized testing is that many instruments are not normed for groups of individuals with certain types of disabilities. These problems become pronounced when assessing aptitudes and measures of general intelligence. For example, many aptitude tests are timed, and a student's score is based on how many items can be completed in a limited period of time. If a student's disability interferes with motor functioning, such as cerebral palsy, the relative slowness at documenting answers may obscure the student's strong aptitude. This is also seen on the performance sections of IQ tests. By the time test pieces are manipulated, allotted time runs out, and it appears the student's performance IQ is lower than it may actually be. For this reason, untimed versus timed tests are sometimes more appropriate. For students with emotional disabilities, the lack of a relationship with the test administrator may be problematic in that a student might react in an inappropriate interpersonal manner, thus making the test results inaccurate. However, a test administrator who has a strong interpersonal connection to the student might be able to use the established rapport to put the student at ease, which could have a dramatic affect on the outcome of the assessment. Many assessments rely heavily on reading skills and comprehension, the ability to understand detailed instructions and abstract language, timing, and similar skills. If a student's disability interferes with any of these basic test-taking requirements, then what the test is actually attempting to measure would be indirectly hampered, and any result would not be accurate for the student.

This does not mean standardized assessments should be avoided altogether. Rather, as with any other diverse groups, use the results from standardized measures as but one source of career guidance information for students with disabilities, not a primary or sole source. Consider a wide range of features to achieve equity in the assessment of students with disabilities, including the aspirations they themselves voice and their expressed interest and values, aptitudes, and talents as reported by their teachers and parents. Less reliance on standardized batteries is often more helpful to students. As one school counselor said, "When in doubt, take your time helping students with disabilities to make career decisions, and ask a lot of questions. Also, take time simply to get to know your students with disabilities."

Self-Determination and Self-Advocacy: Critical Assets in Career Planning

Self-determination and self-advocacy are integral to the process of career success for students with disabilities. *Self-determination* is defined as "the attitudes and abilities required to act as the primary causal agent in one's life and to make choices regarding one's actions free from undue external influence or interference."[9] *Vocational self-determination* (VSD) is the attitudes and abilities required to be the primary decision maker with regard to one's vocation. *Vocational self-advocacy* is the ability to promote one's own career needs and interests and to use assertive skills to ensure that necessary accommodations or modifications are made to access the job, educational institution, or activities. This is a highly important skill that students with disabilities will need in order to be empowered participants in the workforce. Like all other workers, they will eventually need to take responsibility for making independent career-related decisions and actions. In addition to these typical career decisions, people with disabilities need to be able to assertively explain their disability-related needs to employers (which may include explaining the nature of their impairment, depending on whether they choose to disclose it), negotiate with employers for various accommodations, and assertively but diplomatically explain their legal rights under the ADA, for example.

Many students with disabilities often are not fully aware of what their disability entails or are unable to clearly define for other people their strengths and weaknesses. This seems to be more common for students with learning disabilities. School counselors may find that no one has ever actually sat down with them to fully explain their diagnosis in lay terms or practiced with them how to explain their disability to others. School counselors can help students acquire this ability. They can also help students identify strengths as well as relatively weaker abilities. One college student with a disability reflected on his high school experiences: "I don't think it's common to find a guidance counselor who will really sit down with a student who has a disability and help them with their self-exploration by helping them understand things like, "Okay, these are the things you are good at, these are the things that you are not, and these are the types of accommodations you are probably going to need when you work."

School counselors should work with students with disabilities to develop these skills. There are many programs designed to teach them. An excellent example of a self-determination and self-advocacy skill development program at the K–12 level is one developed by the state of Alaska, "Teaching Self-Determination in Alaskan Schools: A Toolkit for Teachers" (http://www.alaskachd.org/toolkit/index.html). Also, Postsecondary Innovative Transition Technology (Post-ITT) has a section for teachers and parents to help them foster and develop the self-advocacy skills students with disabilities need to make a successful transition to the postsecondary environment (http://www.postitt.org/).

Transitional Planning

Transition planning became a federal mandate as a result of the widespread, unacceptable postsecondary outcomes for students with disabilities. Many students with disabilities fall through the cracks in an attempt to navigate from an educational system in which accommodations and services were mandated to the wider world in which that is not the case. Good transition planning can point a student in the right direction without pigeonholing them into a specific career and close the gap for them between the highly structured environment of secondary schooling and the independence they will need to assume as an adult.

Transition planning should be designed as a general springboard, supplying the tools students will need to venture into life after high school, whether that takes them directly into the world of work or into postsecondary training. It also includes linking students with agencies and programs that can provide critical and needed assistance. Vocational Rehabilitation Services (VRS) are key to the transition process. In addition, local centers for independent living are valuable for students with relatively severe disabilities.

State and Federal Vocational Rehabilitation Services

Perhaps the most important agency with which to form a strong partnership is the state VRS. Each state has a VRS program that is partially funded by and adheres to regulations and oversight by the federal government. The purpose of these state agencies is to provide vocational-related assistance to state citizens whose disabilities substantially limit their employability and could reasonably be expected to benefit in this regard from VRS assistance. Those who qualify for VRS services may be able to access various forms of rehabilitative assistance—for example: career counseling, medical or psychological evaluations, restorative services, vocational training or retraining (including funds or grants to help pay for postsecondary schooling), assistive technology, interpretive services (for individuals who are deaf), mobility services (for individuals who are blind), transportation services, and job placement.

In order to access these services, students with disabilities need to apply for them. After being deemed eligible for services, the student with disabilities is assigned a VRS counselor, who should play an increasingly involved and important role as the student moves closer to graduation. VRS can be particularly useful for help with transition planning activities, and this counselor should attend IEP meetings once transition planning begins. After graduation from high school, the school counselor and the school cease any formal involvement with the individual, but the VRS counselor has the potential to remain in the student's life as an advocate and will see him or her into the next stage of employment or further education or training.

It is particularly important that school counselors stress the need for students with disabilities to explore eligibility with VRS. If a student's IEP team and parents are not making active use of VRS services, the school counselor should

One CIL Perspective

Centers for Independent Living (CIL) across the country hold this as one of their highest standards: "Nothing about me without me." CILs are not institutional settings; they are support networks made up of 51 percent or more of the staff themselves having a disability. Although each CIL has different programs and services, all offer these core services: peer support, advocacy, information and referral, independent living skills training, and nursing home transition services.

A CIL (its staff and volunteers) works with and on behalf of an individual or group to take **ACT**ion by **A**mplifying the voices of those who have disabilities; **C**onnecting people to opportunities and resources; and **T**ransforming lives. When a CIL and people with disabilities **ACT**, they are dedicated to working on the success of children, youth, and adults with disabilities at home, at school, at work, and in the community.

There are several important considerations for students with disabilities:

- CILs can offer role models through peer mentor programs and through the CIL dynamics that 51 percent or more of its staff are people who have disabilities.
- It is important that students find opportunities to apply their skills (math, problem solving, reading, and social) in volunteer or employment settings.
- Counselors can assist through school programs to provide employment readiness experiences. This includes practicing interview skills role plays, practicing completing a job application, developing a set of basic information that students can use as a guide to complete application, and development of a résumé that profiles the student's skills and interests.
- Older students may want to consider working in AmeriCorps VISTA (Volunteers in Service to America). These positions offer a stipend and do not have an impact on Supplementary Security Income or Social Security Disability Insurance earnings, but they

> do allow for work experiences to be generated and for possible scholarship for further learning opportunities.
>
> - Advocacy skills need to be reinforced at IEP meetings. All students should be asked to share what they want for themselves and what they think about the plan that the team is developing. These skills can be reinforced by requesting students to go out into the community and practice making requests for necessary services. Every time we advocate, we will not be successful in getting what we want, but we need to work at being successful in how we share our concerns and ask for change.
>
> By Carolyn Grawi.

suggest that they do so, especially in the last couple of years before a student's graduation. (A listing of state vocational rehabilitation programs is available at http://ovr.ky.gov/StateVRPrograms.htm.)

Centers for Independent Living

Centers for Independent Living (CILs) emerged in the 1970s in response to the independent living movement, asserting that people with disabilities, not professionals, are the best experts on their needs. Carolyn Grawi provided "One CIL Perspective," her thoughts and recommendations based on her valuable vantage point as the director of advocacy and education at the Ann Arbor Center for Independent Living. Her view is also informed by having grown up with juvenile-onset diabetes, which eventually resulted in blindness.

On Your Own Without a Net

This phrase aptly describes what every student with a disability experiences in leaving the safety of the K–12 environment.[10] It also speaks to the high level of risk and, subsequently, fears that students with disabilities may experience as they leave the comfort of school behind. It is not surprising that this time of transition is very difficult for the parents of students with disabilities. In many ways, they become a pseudo-net for their children. It is critical that school counselors recognize that this transition period will be challenging for parents and reach out to assist them as they assist their children. The following sections contain important information for school counselors to consider when helping students make the transition from high school to work or postsecondary education.

Transition to Work After High School Ends

Students with disabilities transition to the world of work in one of two ways: they complete school and receive their diploma or drop out of school. The dropout rate for students in special education is nearly 29 percent, and for students with emotional disturbances, the dropout rate is even higher, at 51 percent.[11] For these students, the transition to work often happens without any assistance and is not very successful. They find themselves in low-paying, temporary jobs earning less than their peers, and frequently without benefits.[12] School counselors can be mindful of these statistics and bring them to the attention of IEP teams with the hopeful goal that the IEP and transition teams, armed with this information, can work to facilitate students' completion of school.

For the dropouts and the graduates, the most important and critical information that they need to understand as they make the transition to the world of work is their legally protected rights. In short, they need to understand the Americans with Disabilities Act (ADA) and its importance for them.

Students with Disabilities and the ADA

The ADA defines an individual with a disability as someone who has a physical or mental impairment that substantially limits one or more major life activities, has a record of such impairment, or is regarded as having such impairment. Major life activities are those actions or pursuits that an average person can perform with little or no difficulty, such as walking, breathing, seeing, hearing, speaking, learning, or working.

The ADA directly addresses discrimination, and students with disabilities need to understand that Title I of the ADA makes it illegal for private sector employers, employment agencies, and labor unions with fifteen or more employees to discriminate against qualified individuals with disabilities in all facets of employment: hiring and firing; compensation, assignment, or classification of employees; transfer, promotion, layoff, or recall; job advertisements; recruitment; testing; use of company facilities; training and apprenticeship programs; fringe benefits; pay, retirement plans, and disability leave; or other terms and conditions of employment. Discrimination under the ADA can also include harassment on the basis of disability; retaliation against an individual for filing a charge of discrimination, participating in an investigation, or opposing discriminatory practices;

employment decisions based on stereotypes or assumptions about the abilities, traits, or performance of individuals with disabilities; and denying employment opportunities to a person because of marriage to or association with an individual with a disability.

The ADA provides some key protections. Students need to know that an employer may not directly ask a job applicant about the existence, nature, or severity of a disability. Applicants may be asked about their ability to perform specific job functions. Job offers may even be offered conditionally, pending the results of a medical examination, but only if such an examination is required of all prospective employees in similar positions. Also, required medical examinations must be strictly related to and consistent with the position in question and the employer's business requirements.

The ADA also defines the term *qualified*. The ADA considers an individual with a disability (an employee or job applicant) to be qualified if he or she meets the skill, experience, education, and other job-related requirements of the position in question and can execute the essential functions of the job with or without the use of reasonable accommodations. An accommodation is generally not considered reasonable if it would constitute an undue hardship to the employer.

Supported Employment for Students with Significant Disabilities

This chapter has mostly considered the needs of students with disabilities who are most likely capable of living and working independently, albeit with some transitioning assistance. For the most part, these form the majority of students with disabilities with whom school counselor work. But what about students with more significant disabilities who may require some form of lifelong support, such as students with significant cognitive disabilities or some forms of autism? Can these students eventually work too? Although obtaining and maintaining employment can be especially difficult for these students, many with significant disabilities can experience career success and be highly appreciated by their employers if they are given appropriate vocational supports.[13]

One effective approach that has been used for workers with significant disabilities is *supported employment*. It assesses both the worker with the disability and the job environment during competitive work in integrated, typical settings. It also provides varying levels or types of ongoing vocational support for the worker with a disability and his or her work environment, such as behavioral specialists and job coaches. A *job coach* is a specialist who works at an integrated work setting assisting the person who has a disability to learn the job. Depending on the needs of the worker with the disability, the services of the job coach may slowly diminish, or they may change to a more intermittent or as-needed-only basis, or the coach may assist the worker regularly on a long-term basis at the work site. Numerous studies have found favorable outcomes for the supported employment approach in terms of vocational development and quality of life for workers with significant disabilities and also in terms of employer satisfaction.[14] Supported employment services are usually acquired through involvement with a state vocational rehabilitation agency that may assist in contracting behavioral specialists and job coaches.

A good illustration can be found in Henn and Henn's discussion of their thirty-one-year-old daughter with severe autism. She is nonverbal and considered to be functioning in the lower 10 percent of adults with autism. She relies on sign language, gestures, and only a few words to communicate. She can exhibit severe behavioral issues at times, including kicking, screaming, biting, throwing tantrums, and other dangerous behaviors. In spite of being considered to be on the lower functioning end of the ASD spectrum, she works forty hours each week for her local county's department of human services, at union-scale pay, and receives full benefits. Her duties include microfilming, catching metered mail, delivering inter- and intradepartmental mail, and making notepads. She has maintained this job for over nine years (as of the writing of Henn's and Henn's 2005 article) and is considered to be the most productive microfilmer in her department since she executes this duty roughly two-and-one-half times faster than the next best-producing, nondisabled coworker. She use a full-time behavior support specialist–job coach to assist her in achieving her sustained employment success.[15]

Transition to Postsecondary Education

Since school counselors are very familiar with helping students make the transition to postsecondary education, it makes sense to build on this foundational expertise while addressing areas that are exceptionally different for students with disabilities.

Entrance Exams

The College Board, the organization that administers the SAT, PSAT/NMSQT (National Merit Scholarship Qualifying Test), and Advance Placement exams, has specific services for students with disabilities. Students with disabilities must apply for and be deemed eligible to receive accommodations. This process takes approximately eight weeks to complete, so school counselors should urge the IEP and transition teams to recommend that the student start this process well in advance of the posted test date, because the student must adhere to submission deadlines for the accommodation application and its supporting documents. Four general types of accommodations can be made, based on the student's disability: presentation accommodations such as large print, a reader, and braille; responding accommodations such as verbal dictation to a scribe or a large-block answer sheet; timing or scheduling accommodations such as frequent breaks or extended time; and setting accommodations, such as a private room or adaptive furniture. The College Board Web site is essential reading for complete details (http://www.collegeboard.com/ssd/student/accom.html).

Disclosing Disability Status

Students who need accommodations must disclose their disability status during the application process. And after they are admitted to a postsecondary institute, they will need to disclose again in order to request accommodations. Perhaps the most common misperception among students with disabilities and their families (and even some teachers, special educators, and school counselors) is that a student's high school IEP or 504 plan simply transfers to their postsecondary school setting, where their rights, responsibilities, and services will essentially be the same as they were in the K–12 setting. This is incorrect and accounts for a general lack of planning and preparation by many students bound for postsecondary education.

The federal Individuals with Disabilities Education Act (IDEA) does not follow students beyond high school, which explains part of the reason for the differences in disability rights and responsibilities. In postsecondary educational settings, the federal laws that primarily affect students with disabilities are Title II of the ADA and Section 504 of the Rehabilitation Act of 1973. Although the ADA and the Rehabilitation Act are the same laws that protect elementary and secondary students from discrimination, they do so a bit differently for postsecondary students. Postsecondary schools are not required to provide free and appropriate public education (FAPE) or to ensure the educational success of their students with disabilities. Postsecondary schools are required only to provide equal access to the institution and its programs through "appropriate academic adjustments" or reasonable accommodations in order to ensure that students with disabilities are not discriminated against. This is a major difference. The focus in elementary and secondary schools is one of programming for students with disabilities, and places more responsibility on the school for determining needs and providing specialized services in order to ensure FAPE. The postsecondary school focus is primarily one of ensuring equal access for students with disabilities (that is, avoiding discrimination) and places more responsibility on the student to identify and substantiate his or her accommodation needs to the postsecondary institution, make use of accommodations that may be available, and meet the same essential requirements of the school or program as any other student (with or without disabilities).

Most postsecondary institutions require students who are registering for disability services or accommodations to submit recent documentation of the disability (for learning disabilities, *recent* is usually considered three years old or less). An IEP or 504 plan usually does not suffice as documentation for most institutions. Postsecondary schools usually ask for a letter or report prepared by an appropriate professional qualified to make the diagnosis of the particular disability, and it is the student's responsibility to do so. Postsecondary schools are not required to pay for or conduct evaluations. In order to aid in the transition process to postsecondary training, some high schools are willing to conduct updated evaluations as the student nears graduation. The student's regional VRS office might also be willing to pay for or provide such. If not, parents may need to pay for this evaluation and documentation. In light of this information, school counselors can act as an advocate for students with disabilities who wish to attend postsecondary school by having the high school conduct a timely, professionally documented evaluation appropriate for postsecondary use.

Choosing a College or University

It is important that students research the types of accommodations and services available for people with disabilities at the school they wish to attend. Depending on the student, this could be one of the most important factors to consider in picking a postsecondary institution that will be a good fit. Some institutions may provide services above and beyond the minimum requirement of ensuring equal access. There is a lot of inconsistency between one postsecondary institution and the next with regard to disability services offered. Although appropriate academic adjustments (accommodations) are the financial responsibility of the postsecondary institution, any services offered above and beyond these minimal requirements may or may not impose additional costs or fees on the student. Therefore, students with disabilities who are bound for postsecondary schooling (and their parents) should be made aware of this issue.

Postsecondary schools are generally not required to lower or waive the essential requirements of programs or curriculums or even to make substantial modifications. They are also not required to provide such services or items such as personal attendants, assistive devices for use outside the institution (for at-home or personal use or for performing homework), readers for personal use or homework, tutoring, or typing. The focus is on providing equal access to the institution itself and its programs. In that vein, some common accommodations provided by postsecondary institutions (depending on the nature of a student's disability and their particular details) might include priority registration; reduced course loads; in-class note takers, recording devices, sign language interpreters, or testing accommodations such as extended time, an isolated/quiet environment, reading or transcribing; and screen-reading, voice recognition, or other assistive technology for school computers.

Planning

For many students with disabilities, postsecondary schooling can be a logical next step in their career development after high school. Such training is becoming increasingly more important in the world of work, especially for individuals with disabilities. However, students, parents, and their IEP and transition teams need to be aware of and plan ahead for the differences that exist in disability-related rights and responsibilities between K–12 school and postsecondary settings. Three excellent resources to consult are:

- *The Counselors' Toolkit: Advising High School Students with Disabilities on Postsecondary Options*, produced by the Heath Resource Center: Post-ITT (Postsecondary Innovative Transition Technology), a Web-based resource for high school students with disabilities considering college. The site includes forty-five guidance activities designed to facilitate the transition planning process. There is also companion information for parents and teachers to use to support this planning process.

- *Opening Doors to Postsecondary Education and Training: Planning for Life After High School* (http://dpi.state.wi.us/sped/pdf/tranopndrs.pdf) is a handbook published by the George Washington Heath Resource Center to "assist students, parents, school counselors, and others on the IEP team in planning for postsecondary experience" (http://www.heath.gwu.edu/). It has easy-to-read charts showing many of the differences between high school and postsecondary life.

The Intangible Benefits of Work for Students with Disabilities

The importance of effectively helping students with their amplified career development needs cannot be overestimated. It requires creativity and an ability to see the potential in students, when sometimes they have trouble seeing it themselves. However, the benefits are far reaching. It is largely through work that they become a more recognized part of society, with a means of support, a social identity, and, ideally, a broader social network.

Part Three

Disability-Specific Information

Implications and Practical Applications

Attention Deficit Hyperactivity Disorder

Todd A. Van Wieren

Indiana University of Pennsylvania

General Background Information About Attention Deficit Hyperactivity Disorder

Attention deficit hyperactivity disorder (ADHD) is a condition affecting between 3 and 5 percent of children. It is usually first noticed during the preschool or early school years, and the primary characteristics are inattention, hyperactivity, and impulsivity. Students with ADHD are usually able to focus on things they really enjoy but may struggle with staying deliberately focused on less interesting topics or details or on one thing, and thus they may find it difficult to complete tasks or stay organized. They may appear fidgety and always on the go. They may seem to act before they think, often blurting out inappropriate comments, not waiting their turn, acting without regard to later consequences, or displaying unrestrained emotions. Because the symptoms associated with ADHD are often present to a lesser degree in many children without the disorder and because these symptoms can sometimes be caused by other medical problems or stressors in a student's life, children should undergo thorough medical and psychosocial examinations as part of the diagnostic process.

There are three types of ADHD: predominantly hyperactive-impulsive type (displays hyperactivity and impulsivity, but nonsignificant inattention), predominantly inattentive type (displays inattention, but nonsignificant hyperactivity and impulsivity), and combined type (displays all three: inattention, hyperactivity, and impulsivity). Treatment often involves a combination of medication, behavioral modification, lifestyle change, and counseling. In an elementary or secondary school setting, a student with ADHD will typically not qualify for an individualized educational program (IEP), but may qualify for some services with a 504 plan.

In preparing for postsecondary education, it might be helpful to know that students with ADHD may qualify for limited accommodations (such as extended time and isolation for exams and note-taking services for class lectures).

What Students and Parents Wish Their Teachers and Counselors Knew About ADHD

- "I really do try to focus on what the teacher is saying. But sometimes all it takes is a bird chirping outside the window, other students clicking their pencils on their desks, and before you know it, my attention turns to that, or I start daydreaming, and then I haven't listened to the last few minutes of what the teacher was saying."

- "I'm hoping that I'll outgrow my ADHD."

    - While it is true that improvements are often seen in the area of hyperactivity, issues such as attention and focus, organizational skills, and impulsivity may be lifelong symptoms that the student will need to continue dealing with and learning how to compensate for.

- "I think that the special services I get at school, and the medication I'm supposed to take, are a sign of weakness and dependence. It's embarrassing, and I don't want to be singled out any longer as being different."

    - In part because ADHD could be considered an invisible disability of sorts, many students with ADHD may not be forced to come to terms with their disability (at least, not to the same degree as students with more obvious and pervasive disabilities) and thus may not truly self-identify with the concept of having a disability. They may thus feel embarrassment and frustration in having to be formally associated with disability-related services at school or with medical or therapeutic treatment. They may wish to deny the extent that ADHD is an issue for them. However, particularly as such a student is moving closer to graduating from high school and facing greater independence, it is important for them to move toward a healthy acknowledgment of their strengths and weaknesses and to take responsibility for managing their disability.

- "I feel like I can't do anything right. When I think about school, I get anxious and worried."

- "My friends sometimes get annoyed with me because they don't feel like I'm paying attention when they talk to me, or I cut them off in conversation."

- "My child is able to pay attention to things they're involved in at home that interest them, but they can't seem to do it at school or when they're working on homework."

- "My son is a really great kid. I think he's so talented and creative in certain areas. But it breaks my heart to see him struggle in school like he does. I really worry about his self-esteem. And I worry that he's not going to be successful in college or later in a job."

- "I feel guilty for how I treated my daughter before she was diagnosed with ADHD. Looking back, I thought she was just lazy and unmotivated, and I regret that. I didn't realize she was actually struggling with a disability."

- "I realize that my child's ADHD behavior can be annoying to his teachers, and I worry that they're just going to write him off, and that they won't take the time to really see his potential and cultivate his abilities."

- "I wish my child would learn to organize herself better and become more independent with keeping track of things."

Practical Applications

Personal Applications

- *Emotional issues:* When interacting in a one-on-one counseling fashion with students with ADHD, a school counselor should be sensitive to and deal with emotional issues that may include the hidden nature of the disability and the student's self-identity associated with it; potential embarrassment with having special services at school or a disability diagnosis; feeling academically inadequate; or feeling typecast by others as lazy or unmotivated.

- *Organizational strategies:* Students with ADHD should be taught compensatory strategies for organizing and managing their time and responsibilities, with progressing levels of responsibility the older they get and the further they progress in school. The goal is to enable them to be as independent as possible in using their organizational strategies before they graduate from high school.

Social Applications

- *Problematic social-behavioral issues:* Acknowledge for the student and parents that some of the student's problematic social-behavioral issues (not waiting for his or her turn, cutting other people off when talking, inattention to what others are saying, fidgety and impulsive behavior) are directly related to the disability and difficult to control. This doesn't mean the or she is a "bad" kid. However, the student also needs to understand that to have a successful and satisfying academic, vocational, and social future means taking progressive responsibility for these behaviors and learning to modify them. The school counselor can work directly with the student and in consultation with teachers to develop strategies for encouraging positive social behavior inside and outside the classroom.

Academic Applications

- *Seating in class:* When possible, students with ADHD should generally be seated near the teacher and away from distractions: other disruptive or talkative students, items in the classroom that could be played with or could divert the student's attention, and so forth.

- *Interactive teaching methods:* Particularly when a student with ADHD is present in the class, teachers should be encouraged to make use of interactive teaching methods that involve the students as much as possible throughout the lesson (as opposed to passively listening and absorbing a traditional lecture).

- *Note-taking assistance:* During the secondary school years when students begin to take notes in class, students with ADHD should be encouraged to take their own notes, but it may be beneficial to supplement their notes with photocopies from other students in the class who are academically strong.

- *Test taking:* Extended time and a quiet or isolated room away from the other students in the class are often useful for students with ADHD in order to perform to the best of their ability on exams and quizzes.

- *Stability and routine in environment and schedule:* When possible, the overall physical layout of the classroom should remain unchanged and constant. A predictable routine for the school day and class periods should be established and kept to as much as possible. The routine should be reinforced for students with ADHD so they know what to expect and can better manage themselves and their schedule.

- *Directions and homework assignments:* The manner in which teachers give directions in class should be consistent from assignment to assignment. They should be presented in the form of a list (step by step, when possible), and expectations should be stated as clearly and unambiguously as possible, including stages of the assignments and due dates. Teachers who have a student with ADHD in the classroom should probably restate the directions and expectations to the class more than once, checking to make sure everyone understands. An open atmosphere for asking questions to clarify directions should be cultivated. It might be beneficial for a written version of the directions to be given separately to students with ADHD.

- *Homework completion:* If the student with ADHD is consistently having trouble with completing homework on time and in a satisfactory manner, it may be beneficial to modify the amount of homework given and then slowly increase the level as the student is able to handle it. The school counselor or teacher should check in regularly with the student to monitor progress and performance and thus help the student increasingly acquire this organizational skill. It might also be beneficial to help the student conceptually break large homework assignments down into smaller, more easily manageable chunks and perhaps develop due dates for each of these progressive chunks.

Career Applications

- *Proper environmental and work demand fit:* In guiding students with ADHD through career counseling and development, it is particularly important to help them consider the types of environments and tasks in which they function best and to gain self-awareness for those in which their ADHD symptoms interfere. Career environments and work demands that tend to be better fits for many individuals with ADHD are those that do not require prolonged periods of quiet focus on single items; allow a level of predictability in schedule and work demands yet a healthy level of regular activity; and capitalize on the person's interests, which tends to enable the individual with ADHD to focus on to a greater degree.

Resources with More Detailed Information About ADHD

- CHADD (Children and Adults with Attention Deficit/Hyperactivity Disorder): A national nonprofit clearinghouse of evidence-based ADHD information (online resource center, online store for educational books and videos, conferences, online support communities, and more), geared toward individuals with ADHD, their families, and professionals working with them. www.chadd.org

- ADDA (Attention Deficit Disorder Association): A national nonprofit organization, geared primarily toward providing information for adults with ADHD and professionals working with them. Of use to the counselor working with school-aged children, ADDA's Web site also provides access to important articles about school, family, career, and legal issues related to ADHD. www.add.org

Anxiety Disorders

Nadene A. L'Amoreaux and Nicole Reed
Indiana University of Pennsylvania

General Background Information About Anxiety

Anxiety disorders affect approximately 13 percent of children and teens and are therefore one of the more common psychological or emotional disorders children experience. The primary characteristic of anxiety disorders is a mismatch between an actual threat of a situation and a child's emotional or physiological response to a perceived threat that interferes with academic, family, social, or emotional functioning.

Symptoms of anxiety can include increased frustration; irritability; increased heart rate; clamminess or sweating; shaking; shortness of breath; a chocking sensation; nausea or vomiting; faintness; chest pain; overall bodily discomfort; or fears related to losing control of self, "going crazy," or dying. Anxiety disorders in children may also be marked by somatic symptoms and complaints (headaches or stomachaches), poor sleeping, extreme shyness, refusal or reluctance to participate in otherwise enjoyable activities, and continuous worrying about concerns over which the child has no control. Symptoms related to anxiety disorders can sometimes coincide with various medical conditions, drug and alcohol problems, or increased stress or dysfunction in a home environment or other area of a child's life (in such a case, this would not necessarily qualify the child for an actual diagnosis of an anxiety disorder).

Although many family medical practitioners are becoming increasingly aware of anxiety disorders, a child who is suspected as having one should be thoroughly evaluated by a qualified mental health provider to determine if the child's anxiety has been long term (six or more months), if it has interfered with the child's day-to-day functioning, and the impact the anxiety appears to have on the child.

Some of the more common types of anxiety affecting children are:

- *Separation anxiety* usually affects younger elementary-aged students and involves an intense fear of being separated from a primary caregiver or home environment. Stressors that contribute to separation anxiety may include a recent divorce or separation, an unexpected death of a loved one (including pets), a catastrophic event (house fire or tornado), or the military deployment of a loved one.

- *Specific phobia* is a consistent and intense fear of a particular object or situation, such as a fear of dirt or being unclean or fear of heights, and could include intense fears of testing situations.

- *Generalized anxiety disorder* involves excessive and uncontrollable worries about situations beyond their control or that do not pose a specific threat, such as worries that there will be inclement weather, that friends will not play with them on the playground, or that they will not get into college despite good academic performance.

- *Social anxiety disorder* is a fear or worry about social situations, often accompanied by a fear that the child will embarrass himself or herself or will be judged and rejected by others. Students may avoid playgrounds, lunchrooms, locker rooms, public speaking, or situations involving larger groups of peers.

- *Posttraumatic stress disorder* is an extreme experience of anxiety and panic that may be experienced by children who have been exposed to traumatic events such as abuse, a catastrophic event, or witnessing a traumatic or catastrophic event (witnessing a crime, being in a hurricane, feeling in danger by a large dog) and usually include symptoms of nightmares, hypervigilance, or a persistent worry that the concern will reoccur.

- *Obsessive compulsive disorder* is characterized by persistent and recurring thoughts that are also paired with a repeated behavior that temporarily relieves the obsessive thoughts. In addition to ritualized behaviors or reoccurring thoughts, other manifestations might include preoccupation with organization, structure or Tourette's symptoms.

Treatment for anxiety disorders can include medications; individual counseling such as behavioral, cognitive, or play therapy interventions; group counseling; family counseling; or a combination of all or some of these. School counselors may need to work with a highly anxious child to use self-calming strategies or increase positive self-talk in anxiety-provoking situations. They may also need to assist school personnel in understanding the effects anxiety can have on a child and his or her school performance. For example, a child with obsessive compulsive disorder may spend hours writing or rewriting a sentence in an effort to get it "perfect" before moving on to another sentence. Homework can conceivably take hours, with the child returning to school exhausted and frustrated. Adults may be tempted to tell the child to move on, without understanding the intense emotional response to the anxiety that the child may be experiencing. In the school setting, a child may qualify for an individualized educational program under emotional disturbances once he or she has been fully evaluated. If not, some services might be implemented through a 504 plan.

What Students and Parents Wish Their Teachers and Counselors Knew About Anxiety Disorders

- "I get really nervous when I have to do presentations in class. Teachers will take points off of my grade because my voice shakes or I shake, and I can't help it. I really can't control it; it's like they don't understand."

- "I get angry when people tell me to just calm down. I really want to. I don't like feeling this nervous, and I can't control it. They don't know what it feels like, so how can they tell me to calm down?"

- "I hate that I have to be so reliant on taking a pill every day. I just want to be normal. I wish my teachers understood that just because I take my medication doesn't mean it completely cures my anxiety. It's not a magic pill that makes all my anxieties go away."

- "I really do just want to make friends, and I try, but then I get so nervous and embarrassed, and I feel lonely a lot of the time."

- "My daughter is very intelligent, caring, and friendly, but this sometimes can be hidden by her anxiety. I just wish teachers would take the time to try and understand what she is feeling and going through, to ask her questions. So many of the teachers don't acknowledge anxiety as a true disorder and make her believe she is just doing it to herself and should control it, which isn't true."

- "My son misses school sometimes because of his panic attacks. They scare him, and me too, but that doesn't mean he is defiant or just likes to skip school. I know he doesn't want to feel that way."

- "My daughter doesn't like to admit that she has an anxiety disorder. She just wants to feel independent, but her anxiety can keep her from doing that, and it is hard for her to accept help. That doesn't mean she doesn't need assistance, though, or someone to talk to. She just needs to feel like she is still an independent person. You don't need to coddle her, or do things for her; that would only embarrass or anger her. Just point her in the right direction or give assistance without being authoritarian."

Practical Applications

Personal Applications

- Students who struggle with anxiety may also experience social isolation and depression. Individual and group counseling may assist them in identifying the myriad feelings and reactions they are having to their school experiences and the impact that anxiety has on them personally.

- Students with anxiety disorders may experience fatigue and malaise in response to coping with the impact of anxiety. They may need accommodations such as a flexible school day, modified assignments, or places within the school to go that are "safe" to allow them the opportunity to manage their symptoms.

- Students with anxiety disorders may seek constant approval, validation, or support from adults who understand the nature of their disability and its impact on them, and can benefit from conversations that enhance their self-concept and provide opportunities to learn as well as practice self-calming skills.

- Cognitive-behavioral interventions are often recommended for anxiety disorders. Since anxiety involves fearful thoughts and behavioral responses that are incongruent with their actual context, both areas need to be addressed.

Social Applications

- Students with anxiety disorders may show poor attendance or continued tardiness. They may tend to visit the nurse's office frequently for physical complaints. Behaviors such as these can be misinterpreted by others as intentional avoidance, and the student could be labeled as noncooperative or defiant. Understanding that these symptoms are very real and intense to the child can assist school personnel in helping the child to manage the symptoms. Students with anxiety disorders tend to avoid peer interactions or in-class group activities, which leads to social isolation and misinterpretation as defiance or noncompliance with assignments. Loneliness can increase a child's problems and may develop into additional psychological and emotional diagnoses such as depression.

Academic Applications

- Establishing a point person who might be willing to allow the student to check in with him or her at the beginning of each day when the child arrives at school (sometimes a very anxiety-provoking activity) may help prevent frequent absences and tardiness. This individual might also serve as a safe person for the child to return to throughout any given day when the anxiety feels out of control, which may serve to decrease some anxious episodes.

- If possible, assist the student with developing and maintaining a consistent daily schedule and routine (unsuspected changes may increase anxiety and throw the student off for the remainder of the day). However, as unexpected changes in routine are a part of life, students with anxiety disorders can benefit from preparation in anticipation of upcoming changes. For example, inclement weather often leads to modified schedules or disruptions in expected school routines.

- Tests and oral presentations may evoke particularly strong anxiety and may require possible accommodations, such as testing privately without being timed or being allowed to remain in one's seat when delivering a presentation to class (instead of standing in the front, facing everyone). Assigning a peer note taker or providing notes to a student with concerns related to obsessive compulsive disorder may help the child accomplish the task in a less threatening way and still meet the spirit of the assignment. The student may have some suggestions in identifying possible useful accommodations and interventions.

- Students with anxiety disorders may benefit from a modified school day to help deal with exhaustion or emotional reactions at the start of the school day.

Career Applications

- When discussing career options with a student who has an anxiety disorder, remember that such disorders may be lifelong, requiring ongoing treatment or medication. And yet a student with an anxiety disorder can become fully functional in the work world. Therefore, it is important in career counseling to make sure a student is not unnecessarily limiting or foreclosing career options due to anxiety or fear.

Resources with More Detailed Information About Anxiety Disorders

- ADAA (Anxiety Disorder Association of America): The only national nonprofit organization dedicated to promoting awareness and education about anxiety disorders. Attempts to decrease negative public perceptions of the disorders, offers resources to seek help, and encourages scientific research to advance treatments for anxiety disorders. For individuals with an anxiety disorder, their family and friends, and professionals in the field. www.adaa.org

- Taylor, J. *Recognizing anxiety disorders in school-aged youth*. http://www.guidancechannel.com/default.aspx?index=2016&cat=13.

- Watkins, C. E., & Brynes, G. Anxiety disorders in children and adults. http://www.ncpamd.com/anxiety.htm

Asthma and Allergies

Kristen M. Bernot

Indiana University of Pennsylvania

General Background Information About Asthma and Allergies

Asthma

Asthma is the number one cause of missed school days for children, accounting for approximately eight days missed for every child.[1] It affects almost 5 million children under the age of eighteen. Asthma attacks can be lethal.

Asthma varies in form: allergic asthma or nonallergic asthma. Although many of the symptoms are the same, the differences lie in the triggers of an attack. Both forms of asthma are the result of the bronchi becoming inflamed and swollen, mucus shutting off air passages, or the muscles tightening around the airways, cutting off air.[2] Allergic or extrinsic asthma is usually caused by inhaling dust mites, pollens, molds, pet dander, and cockroach droppings. Nonallergic or intrinsic asthma is caused by airborne aggravates (smoke, perfumes, paint), respiratory infections (colds, pneumonia, and flu), exercise, cold air, experiencing strong emotions (anger, fear, excitement), and some medications (aspirin).[3]

Asthma-related events can range from having symptoms twice a week to several times a day. Symptoms can be managed through inhalers or long-term daily medications, or both.[4] Hospitalization may be needed to treat severe attacks.

Over time asthma may also cause permanent narrowing of the bronchial tubes (airway remodeling), and medications used to help treat it that are taken for long periods of time may cause problems.[5] Most asthma attacks give the sufferer warning signs before the actual attack. The child may cough, feel his or her chest tighten, or feel tired. At the first sign of an attack, the student should be excused to the school nurse's office to take medication rather than wait for a full-blown attack to occur.[6]

Allergies

Allergies can be fatal. They can present specific and major difficulties in school settings. Food-related allergies are a major problem for allergic students who want to eat in the school cafeteria, participate in classroom celebrations, or attend social events with peers. Some common food allergies that students may have are egg, shellfish, milk, wheat, and nuts. Given the prevalence of food allergies, school personnel are likely interacting with many children who have food allergies.

Food allergy symptoms can range from eczema, hives, asthma, allergic rhinitis, and digestive symptoms to life-threatening anaphylactic shock. Prevention of allergic reactions can occur through avoiding the allergen as well as products that contain it; however, some children are so highly allergic that a reaction can occur through accidental cross-contamination, such as by coming into contact with a utensil that had previously been in contact with the allergen. Even cross-contamination has been sufficient to cause a severe health crisis or death for highly allergic children.[7]

Latex allergies can also be problematic for children in schools. They can cause dermatitis and hypersensitivity immune system response, including itching, redness, swelling, sneezing, wheezing, and anaphylactic shock.[8] Latex exposure can occur through direct contact or inhaling latex particles, which can occur when a pair of latex gloves is removed and the powder lining the gloves is released into the air.[9]

Latex products include products made into hardened rubber (such as athletic shoes, tires, and rubber balls) or dipped latex (including rubber gloves, balloons, and rubber bands). Children with latex allergies are more likely to have reactions to dipped latex products. Other common products that contain latex are dishwashing gloves, carpeting, waistbands on clothes, rubber toys, hot water bottles, sanitary pads, erasers, swim goggles, racket handles, and bicycle handgrips.[10] Items commonly found in school settings include balls, workout mats, weights, gym uniforms, and protective masks, plus items commonly found in the school nurse's office, such as blood pressure cuffs, stethoscopes, syringes, bandages, gloves, and surgical masks.[11] Students with spina bifida may be more prone to latex allergies.[12] Although there is no cure for these allergies, avoidance can be effective in preventing latex allergic reaction.[13]

With any allergies, school personnel need to work with parents and children to determine appropriate responses to potential allergic reactions, including having medicine on hand in the case of an asthma attack or a reaction to food. Educators may underestimate the severity and urgent nature of an allergic reaction. Mere seconds can mean the difference between life and death. If state law permits, students can carry epinephrine (such as an Epipen) for immediate use. Otherwise, Epipens must be readily available and educators must be trained in proper use.

What Students and Parents Wish Their Teachers and Counselors Knew About Asthma and Allergies

- "When I start to wheeze and can't breathe, I know everyone is watching me, and that makes the asthma attack worse."

- "I had a classmate accuse me of faking my allergy to peanuts because she thought I just wanted attention and special treatment."

- "It breaks my heart to see her turn down a piece of birthday cake because there might be nuts in it. She has to eat something she brought from home, while the rest of her friends can eat the cake."

- "What teachers and school personnel may not realize is that foods that are commonly enjoyed by most children could be deadly to mine. Chicken nuggets fried in peanut oil, hot dogs with fillers, jelly beans processed in plants that also process nut products . . . . It's not convenient to check all packages, but it is necessary, and in some cases a matter between life and death."

- "One of the scariest moments in my life was when I got a call from the school nurse saying my daughter had an attack from a cookie a friend gave her and was being taken to the hospital."

Practical Applications

Personal Applications

- Some children with food allergies have a realistic fear that they could have a fatal reaction at school. This can result in tremendous anxiety, which can cause them to linger at the nurse's office.

- It may be helpful to discuss with the child the implications the asthma or allergy has on day-to-day life and how it affects self-esteem, relationships with siblings and peers, and parents. Children with allergies and asthma need to be vigilant of the products around them. They may need to talk about what it is like to be different from other children.

Social Applications

- Children with allergies to certain foods may feel exceptionally out of place when the rest of their friends are able to eat snacks or birthday cake at school or at a private party, and they must refrain. It can also be quite embarrassing for the child to explain to those providing the food why he or she cannot eat it. If the child and parents consent, it may be helpful to send a letter to other parents in the child's class describing the allergy. It may be necessary to ask parents to refrain from sending snacks or treats for class functions that contain the food allergens. If the allergy to a certain type of food is severe enough, it may warrant requiring the child to eat in a place separate from others because the allergen is present, which may cause the child to feel isolated or unable to participate in more social aspects of the school day.

- Asthma can be quite embarrassing to a child. If the child must use an inhaler during class, other students may be curious as to why and what it feels like to have asthma. In this situation, it may be helpful to educate other students about asthma and why it is necessary for the child to stop what he or she is doing to use the medications. Peers can alert adults to the onset of asthma symptoms if the child is unable to do.

Academic Applications

- Although food and latex allergies and asthma may not be directly related to a child's success in the classroom, they are not completely separate from it either. It may be helpful to require all students to wash their hands after lunch before they return to the classroom to prevent the child with the allergy to be indirectly or accidentally exposed to the allergen. After a child has had an asthma- or allergy-related incident, he or she may feel fatigued and may struggle with concentrating on class work or completing assignments. Because asthma is the primary cause of missed school days, children may get behind in their work if they miss several days because of an attack.[14]

Career Applications

- It may be helpful to make students aware of professions in which exposure to allergens or asthma triggers may be more prevalent. For example, a student with egg allergies may have problems being a baker, and a child with allergies to dust may have problems working at a construction site. Students may benefit from considering what it would be like to inform an employer about his or her asthma or allergy and how it could potentially affect his or her daily work day.

Resources with More Detailed Information About Asthma and Allergies

- Allergy and Asthma Network Mothers of Asthmatics. http://www.aanma.org

- Association of Allergists and Immunologists of Quebec. http://www.allerg.qc.ca

- Asthma and Allergy Foundation of America. http://www.aafa.org

- Canadian Society of Allergy and Clinical Immunology. http://www.csaci.ca

Autism

Scott Shaw

Indiana University of Pennsylvania

General Background Information About Autism

Autism is one of a group of developmental disorders that make up autism spectrum disorders (ASDs), also commonly referred to as pervasive developmental disorders.[1] ASDs commonly include autistic disorder, Asperger's syndrome, and pervasive developmental disorder, not otherwise specified (PDD-NOS). Rett syndrome and child disintegrative disorder are two additional but very rare pervasive developmental disorders.[2] ASDs are characterized by impairment in the areas of social interaction, communication, and behavior.[3] They are frequently associated with unusual, repetitive behaviors such as tics and self-stimulatory behaviors like hand flapping and unusual interests, as well as sensory problems.[4] Asperger's syndrome is typically characterized by relatively high cognitive function, adequate language development, and impaired social interaction and behavior.[5] Autistic disorder is typically characterized by impaired social interaction and behavior, profound communication impairment that may or may not include a lack of verbal speech, and delays in reaching developmental milestones.[6] PDD-NOS is diagnosed when symptoms are severe and persistent, but do not meet the diagnostic criteria for a specific pervasive developmental disorder.[7] Seizures are the most common comorbid symptom, typically developing in early childhood or adolescence, and affect 25 percent of people with ASDs.[8]

The symptoms associated with ASDs may also be seen as a spectrum, or continuum, of behavior. Impairment in social interaction, for example, may be as mild as poor eye contact and lack of social initiation, or as severe as a profound inability to interpret social cues or even meaningfully interact with others. Communication difficulties can range from a child with a large vocabulary but difficulty using it conversationally, to a child who never develops oral language and uses a picture board or sign language alternative. Most children with an ASD have difficulty using and interpreting facial expressions, gestures, tonal inflection, sarcasm, and humor. They tend to be very literal and will attribute the same meaning to a given set of words without contextual or situational consideration. For example, the phrase, "That's just great," may mean something is great, or it may be used sarcastically to imply the opposite. A child with an ASD will not likely be able to interpret the meaning of this phrase when used sarcastically. Behavioral issues are perhaps the most complex, as children with ASDs have difficulty tailoring their behavior to the demands of the social setting. While some children with ASDs are very quiet and compliant with prompts, others exhibit self-stimulatory behaviors, extreme reactions to a change in routine or sensory input (for example, the sound of a siren, or the texture of a food), or physically aggressive behaviors. Children with ASDs commonly inhibit emotional regulation, resulting in exaggerated displays of emotion, including crying in class and verbal outbursts.[9]

ASDs affect children across racial and socioeconomic groups but are four times more common in boys than girls. They begin before the age of three and occur in approximately 1 of every 150 children. While most children with an ASD will require some type of educational services to accommodate differences in learning, their academic abilities vary greatly, from gifted to severely challenged.[10]

What Students and Parents Wish Their Teachers and Counselors Knew About Autism

- "I am interested. I cannot always let you know in conventional ways that I am understanding and comprehending what's happening around me."

- "I can get frustrated if you make things too easy as well as too hard. I don't know how to show my frustration, and that may scare or confuse people."

- "I want to belong. I need to be understood. It takes time, education, and compassion, but I am worth it."

- "My son is bright. He can learn and understand if you take the time to see how he learns. The work you put into helping him understand will pay off greatly."

- "Behaviors disappear when he is engaged appropriately. He CAN contribute to your class."

- "I worry about how my son will do in school. Things that are part of a normal school experience are painful for him: the sound of the school bell, fire alarms, noises in cafeterias and playgrounds can set off a tantrum. I'm worried the other kids won't understand."

Practical Applications

Personal Applications

- Children with an ASD face many challenges in an academic setting. In addition to the difficulty they face in forming relationships, many have other health or medication issues that complicate their adjustment. For example, children with an ASD are frequently on medications that have an impact on their energy level, their appetite (and weight), and their ability to attend to tasks.[11] Balancing these medications to maximize benefits and minimize negative side effects is a difficult task that may require frequent adjustment or changes in medications.

- Changes in routine can be a source of frustration for children with an ASD. School settings typically have a regular schedule, but there are frequent deviations in that schedule for school assemblies, special classes, fire drills, inclement weather, and others. While it is important for children with an ASD to learn strategies to cope with changes in routine, many will need significant one-on-one support for unexpected changes. Anticipated changes in routine can be addressed by giving advanced warning of the change and using social stories and picture schedules to prepare the child.[12]

- Another significant issue is behavior modification. While many unique behaviors may not be significant enough to warrant intervention, others, such as self-harm or physical aggression, have to be addressed. Behavioral analysis is commonly used to determine the antecedent and consequence of a given behavior. A behavioral intervention plan can then be implemented to increase desired behaviors and decrease or extinguish problematic behaviors.[13] In addition, applied behavior analysis special education programs can address behaviors and learning skills both reactively and proactively.[14]

Social Applications

- The very nature of ASDs makes it difficult for children with autism to have normal interactions with their peers. While there is some debate among professionals and people with ASDs about the impact this has on children with an ASD, most believe it is beneficial for children with an ASD to have as many opportunities as possible to interact with their nonautistic (or neurotypical) peers.[15] In addition to promoting the development of social relationships, these interactions provide valuable opportunities to teach social pragmatics and address inappropriate behaviors.

- Children on the autism spectrum are at risk for social isolation, bullying, and rejection by peers. They are also at risk for being exploited or taken advantage of by peers because they tend to be very literal in their communication and may not know to question motives or intentions of peers.

Academic Applications

- Children with ASDs generally benefit from an environment that accommodates their sensory needs. Classrooms with few distractions (windows, posters, loud noises, frequent interruptions) allow children with ASDs to invest more of their energy on required tasks. The specific sensory and learning needs of a child with an ASD should be considered when assigning seats in a classroom, choosing teaching methods (auditory, visual, tactile/kinesthetic), creating homework assignments and directions, designing testing methods, and developing a classroom schedule.[16]

- Academic accommodations for children with ASDs commonly include extended testing time, alternative testing formats, modifications to the environment, schedule modifications, specific methods of instructional delivery, break periods, and sensory rooms.[17] In addition, consideration must be given to the impact that medications have on the child's ability to attend in class and complete homework assignments within a given time period. Children with ASDs tend to respond better to situations that offer predictable structure, so consistency in routine, personnel, and the type and quality of interaction is critical. When a child with an ASD is involved in the individualized educational program process, the same considerations for structure and sensory input should guide the location and format of the meeting.

Career Applications

- Because there is such a tremendous array of abilities among children with ASDs, one child may go on to become a successful scientist, while another may thrive with job coaching or government- or community-supported employment. Careful consideration needs to be made for transition planning and the promotion of independence to the greatest extent possible.

Career exploration should accommodate the child's unique abilities and challenges in order to offer the widest possible selection of vocational opportunities.

Resources with More Detailed Information About Autism

- Autism Speaks: A national nonprofit organization geared toward providing information, education, resources, and national advocacy. http://www.autismspeaks.org/

- Autism Society of America: A nonprofit member-based organization with state and local chapters creating connections between people on the spectrum, families, and professionals. http://www.autism-society.org/

- National Institute of Mental Health: Its Web site provides information on symptoms, treatment, current research, and links to other resources. http://www.nimh.nih.gov/health/topics/autism-spectrum-disorders-pervasive-developmental-disorders/index.shtml

- National Dissemination Center for Children with Disabilities (NICHCY): NICHCY is a project of the Academy for Educational Development and is funded by the U.S. Department of Education. It provides a wealth of information on specific disabilities and disability issues, including the Individuals with Disabilities Act and No Child Left Behind. Disability fact sheets may be printed from the Web site. http://www.nichcy.org/index.html

Bipolar Disorder and Depression

Rebecca A. Seybold
Indiana University of Pennsylvania

General Background Information About Bipolar Disorder and Depression

Depression is a mood disorder affecting between 2 and 4 percent of children and adolescents in the United States.[1] The disorder is characterized by considerable feelings of sadness, lethargy, guilt, low self-worth, and a slowing of thought processes. The symptoms vary in intensity for many children and can include changes in appetite and sleep patterns, difficulties in concentration and decision making, as well as frustration, withdrawal, anger, and anhedonia. Often depression causes significant disruptions in one's life physically, emotionally, motivationally, and cognitively.[2] Depressive symptoms can occur at any time. Due to the impairments that can result from depression, children suspected of having depression should undergo physical and mental evaluations as part of the diagnosis screening to ensure an accurate diagnosis. Treatment options include medication, as well as individual and group interventions.

Major risk factors associated with depression in children and adolescents include suicidal ideation and self-destructive behaviors. For individuals at risk for harming self or others, inpatient hospitalization is recommended to achieve symptom stabilization and reduce risks. If left untreated, depression is considered the number one cause of suicide among young people.[3]

Bipolar disorder, also a mood disorder, affects approximately 7 percent of children and adolescents.[4] An increasing challenge for accurate diagnosis of this disorder lies within many of the characteristics that are prominent features in other childhood disorders. This disorder is characterized by shifts in mood ranging from depression (see symptoms above) to mania (a significant increase in thought processes and activities, more talkative or pressured speech). The intensity and frequency of mood changes can differ in individuals.[5] Typical symptoms of a manic episode in children or adolescents include irritability, hyperactivity, distractibility, elated mood, grandiose behaviors, flight of ideas, decreased need for sleep, impulsivity, risk-taking behaviors, and hypersexuality.[6] Treatment options include medication, as well as individual and group interventions. For individuals at risk for harming self or others, inpatient hospitalization is recommended to achieve symptom stabilization and reduce risks.

With regard to impact that symptoms of depression and bipolar disorder have on academic performance, students with either diagnosis are likely to qualify for school accommodations under a 504 plan or in an individualized educational program.[7]

What Students and Parents Wish Their Teachers and Counselors Knew About Bipolar Disorder and Depression

- "I don't try to be a bad kid. There are times when I feel like I just want to talk to everyone because I have so many things that run through my head."

- "It's so hard for me to get out of bed in the morning. People think that it's just me, but I don't feel like me. I'm always so tired."

- "I can usually make a lot of friends, but I can never keep them."

- "I'm not a bad parent or person. I set boundaries for my child. I can't control whether they work."

- "Just because counselors and teachers have more education than I do does not make them the experts on my child."

- "I don't feel that my child is getting the best education available considering that she has been moved to a special school program due to her behaviors. She is incredibly talented, and I'm afraid she will not reach her full potential."

Practical Applications

Personal Applications

- *Emotional issues:* Children with depression and bipolar disorder experience many emotional struggles given the nature of the mood disorder. School counselors can provide invaluable assistance by conveying empathy. Multiple factors can have an impact on emotions within the school setting and at home. Having a diagnosis alone creates many difficulties for a student, such as receiving special services, feeling different from their peers, and dealing with the stigma of having a mental illness. Effective interventions include medication and individual and group counseling experiences.

- *Organizational strategies:* A symptom of depression and mania is difficulty concentrating and possible forgetfulness. With this in mind, it is likely that a student will struggle with organization. For this reason, students with mood disorders benefit from strategies that address organization. Some strategies include creating task lists, keeping a date book for assignments and obligations, and breaking large tasks into smaller ones. Initially counselors may find success in providing some form of reinforcement for a student's initial efforts since many students experiencing a depressive episode also have low motivation.

- *Medication side effects:* Students who are prescribed medication for treatment of a mood disorder may experience side effects that impair concentration, increase fatigue, create dry mouth, or impair sleep quality, which can have a negative impact on their ability to learn or complete school work.

Social Applications

- *Problematic social-behavioral issues:* Some typical problematic social behaviors that may emerge in a manic episode are difficulty concentrating, rapid thoughts, irritability, and a lack of reserve. These symptoms can all have negative impacts on peer interactions. A child who is having difficulty concentrating likely may be perceived as not listening or not caring. Rapid thoughts may lead to difficulty with turn taking, monopolization of discussions, and not being able to stay on topic. These characteristics may lead to social isolation or peer rejection. Having a mood disorder makes controlling behavior more difficult; however, behavior can still be managed if students are able to identify triggers and engage in self-reflective behaviors. Collaborative efforts on behalf of the student, counselor, and teacher can foster successful strategies to promote healthy peer interactions.

Academic Applications

- *Seating in class:* Students with bipolar disorder or depression will likely benefit from preferential seating in close proximity to the teacher. This will decrease possible distractions and limit negative interactions with peers.

- *Interactive teaching methods:* Interactive teaching methods will enable students in a depressive episode to stay more focused than if a teacher employed only lecture strategies. Forcing peer interaction is likely to increase anxiety and negative emotions in students with a mood disorder. This can greatly be reduced by allowing students to pick their own role within the group. Tasks geared to the student's ability level increase their experience of success when working with other students, which can also serve to increase motivation.

- *Note-taking assistance:* Note-taking assistance for students with a mood disorder may be necessary to promote the student's concentration and free his or limited reserves of energy to focus on instructional activities.

- *Test taking:* Students experiencing a depressive episode may need to have extended time on tests due to difficulties with concentration. Other strategies to increase success in school performance include having assessment materials read by staff or conducting assessments in a quiet room.

- *Stability and routine in environment and schedule:* Abrupt changes in routine are likely to produce feelings of anxiety in students diagnosed with a mood disorder. Changes to the schedule or classroom environment should be subtle or announced in advance so the student can anticipate changes.

- *Directions and homework assignments:* Directions for assignments should be clearly communicated to students in order to eliminate confusion and stress. Teachers should be encouraged to observe the students for signs of difficulty and provide assistance if needed. Students with mood disorders may need to have adjustments in homework, especially if they are experiencing low energy or fatigue as a result of the disorder or from side effects of medications.

Career Applications

- *Proper environmental and work demand fit:* Modifications are provided in many working environments. In career counseling, counselors and students should work together to identify potential struggles that may emerge as a result of a mood disorder and collaborate on strategies to use in order to accommodate special considerations that result from having a mood disorder.

Resources with More Detailed Information About Bipolar Disorder and Depression

- NAMI (National Alliance on Mental Illness): This nonprofit organization provides support services for people living with mental illness, as well as services for their families. It also provides comprehensive resources about diagnoses, medications, and other services. www.nami.org

- CABF (Child and Adolescent Bipolar Foundation): This nonprofit organization is established to provide resources and support to families with a child who is diagnosed with bipolar disorder. www.bpkids.org

- HealthyPlace: This is a comprehensive Web site that provides information regarding mood disorders and other types of mental illnesses found among children, adolescents, and adults. This site provides a plethora of resources ranging from recovery to support groups, as well as symptom information and treatment modalities. www.healthyplace.com

- NASP (National Association of School Psychologists): This site provides free handouts and publications regarding children's mental health issues in the school setting. It also outlines important aspects of children in the school setting that educators and health care professionals should be mindful of. http://www.nasponline.org/resources/freepubs.aspx

Cancer

Katherine A. Piscopo
Indiana University of Pennsylvania

General Background Information About Cancer

Approximately 240,000 children are diagnosed with cancer each year. Cancer occurs when abnormal cells grow rapidly. Examples of common types of childhood cancer are leukemia, brain tumors, lymphomas, Wilms' tumor, neuroblastoma, bone tumors, and retinoblastoma.

Cancer treatment affects children physiologically and psychologically. Common types of treatment are chemotherapy, radiation therapy, and surgery. These treatments can have a negative and sometimes painful effect on the child's body, including difficulties with the cardiac system, liver damage, and loss of a limb. They can also have potential side effects, including severe fatigue, swelling, increased risks for fractures, paralysis, cardiac arrhythmias, pain, lesions, or amputations. While going through treatments, a child diagnosed with cancer may have a significantly impaired immune system, making him or her especially susceptible to and vulnerable to infection and illnesses that may be prevalent in the school environment. Chemotherapy has many detrimental immediate and long-term side effects. Short-term side effects can include hair loss, low energy, nausea, and higher rates of infection. Long-term effects, such as infertility and growth problems, may also affect children who receive treatment for cancer. Children with cancer may experience prolonged absences from school during treatment and may find returning to school difficult due to interrupted relationships with teachers and peers.

What Students and Parents Wish Their Teachers and Counselors Knew About Cancer

- "One time some kids at school said I was chubby. I cried a lot, and the teacher told my mom. So Mommy and I put together a presentation for the class about how some of the medicines I take make me gain weight and appear different. After that the kids never made fun of me again."

- "I just hated being treated differently! If I were in charge of the school, I would make sure everyone was treated equally." http://www.lehman.cuny.edu/faculty/jfleitas/bandaides/libby.html.

- "In one of my classes, the teacher yelled at me when I interrupted him to tell him I was having heart problems. He yelled at me so hard and told me in front of the class I wasn't really sick. I ran down to the office crying and told the nurse, who told the principal, who called my mom. She came right away and talked to the principal and the teacher. He apologized to me, but the damage was already done, and I really didn't want to go to school too much after that." http://www.lehman.cuny.edu/faculty/jfleitas/bandaides/libby.html

- "It was hard to catch up with school work. My teachers were very understanding and willing to work with me, so that was good and a big help." http://www.teenslivingwithcancer.org/dealing/stand/deal/school.asp

- "You have to think that your child is going to get better." http://news.bbc.co.uk/1/hi/health/3244991.stm

Practical Applications

Personal Applications

- *Emotional issues:* Because treatment can leave the child with a changed or damaged physical appearance, body image issues are common. Poor body image has been known to lead to depression and a decline in school performance. Treatment also causes students undergoing cancer treatment to miss school, which can affect social relationships.

Social Applications

- *Return to school:* The child's classmates may have questions about cancer or about the changed appearance of the child since treatment. The diagnosed child may also have concerns and anxiety regarding acceptance by classmates. To make the child's return to school easier, the teacher and class can stay in contact with the child through treatment. The classmates can draw pictures or cards and send them to the home or hospital. In addition, the diagnosed child can send pictures of himself or herself and updates to the classroom. Also, the teacher or school nurse can make a presentation on cancer for the classmates to answer any questions before the child returns. Attending school helps the child to feel he or she is working toward something—most important, a future.

- *Social life:* Children with cancer are more susceptible to infections and have a harder time fighting them off. Because of this, many times they are kept from large crowds. This affects their social life because large crowds include school, malls, and theaters. Time that could be spent with peers in school or in a social setting is usually taken by doctor visits and treatment. This makes the diagnosed child feel left out, and often they have feelings of depression and isolation.

Academic Applications

- *Absenteeism:* A child diagnosed with cancer will most likely miss more days of school than the average child. Because of this, some children with cancer are eligible for special education services: counselors, speech pathologists, physical therapists, and special attention from the school nurse, as well as home-based instruction, tutoring, or a reduced school day.

- *Learning:* Cancer treatment can result in learning disabilities in children. When tested, the child may have a lower IQ score than the score before treatment. They may also have memory and attention deficits. Because of this, the child may have trouble in math, reading, writing, and organization.

- *In class:* The teacher needs to be sensitive to the child's physical needs and allow multiple breaks throughout the school day. The teacher should be sensitive to the child's learning needs, such as allowing extra time for take-home assignments. If the child has difficulty concentrating or is fatigued, the teacher can allow the child to complete an exam in a quiet environment.

- *Homework:* The school can send homework and class activities to the child's home so the child can complete assignments at his or her own pace. Also, a teacher or tutor might be used after school or on weekends to help the student stay on course.

Career Applications

- Career implications with this disease are unique to the specific needs of the individual. School counselors are encouraged to consult Chapter Nine for career and work place considerations.

Resources with More Detailed Information About Cancer

- Association of Cancer Online Resources: Provides current information and community support for those affected by cancer. www.acor.org/

- American Cancer Society: Provides information, resources, and physician and community support referrals. www.cancer.org

- The Oncology Nurse's Patient Guide:. Provides patient information for a variety cancers, including pediatric cancers. www.onconurse.com

- Outlook: Life Beyond Childhood Cancer: Addresses ongoing issues and concerns related to survivors and families. www.outlook-life.org

Cerebral Palsy

Kristen M. Bernot

Indiana University of Pennsylvania

General Background Information About Cerebral Palsy

Cerebral palsy can be defined as movement and posture disorders that restrict activity; it is attributed to damage to the fetal or infant brain, particularly areas of the brain that control motor functioning. Cerebral palsy (CP) can be experienced with seizures or problems with sensation, cognition, communication, or behavior.[1] Because the brain damage occurs only once, the problems that are experienced do not get progressively worse. Symptoms can change, however, with therapy; a child may be able to gain some use of limbs he or should could not use before. Symptoms can also change for the worse. As children age into adulthood, their muscles may tighten and they may lose some dexterity they once had.[2] Often there are other problems that occur with cerebral palsy, such as pain, musculoskeletal problems, fatigue, bladder and bowel problems, reduced bone mass, seizures, spasticity and contractures, impaired oral-motor functions, and hearing and vision problems.[3] Controlling spasms can be fatiguing for students with CP. Because of problems with their oral motor functioning, those with cerebral palsy may have dysarthria. Dysarthria is the result of weak muscles of the face or a weak mouth, so a child with CP may have problems moving his or her mouth to create words, chew, or swallow. Drooling or problems producing speech can result, as can difficulties with projecting speech, slurring speech, mumbling, or having problems controlling tone or inflection.[4] School personnel and classmates may need assistance or instruction in what to do if they are unable to understand what a child with CP is saying (such as asking the student to repeat what he or she said, not interrupting or finishing the child's thought).

Movement impairment can be manifest as spastic-type movements such as tight muscles that are unable to move properly, which can cause awkward, hindered movements. Often surgery, physical therapy, medications, or other mobility aids are used to help children with this type of cerebral palsy. Athetoid cerebral palsy, a rarer form, can result in constant, uncontrollable movements or problems directing movement. Ataxic cerebral palsy (the rarest form of cerebral palsy) results in problems with balance and depth perception. Affected children often have problems walking and may have poor muscle tone and shaking or trembling hands. Movement and speech impairments have led to teens with CP being mistaken for being under the influence of drugs or alcohol.

Treatment is determined on a case-by-case basis. The following therapies are available to treat the symptoms of cerebral palsy: physical therapy, orthotic equipment, occupational therapy, speech therapy, hearing supports, eyeglasses or eye surgery, Botulinum toxin injections, baclofen, surgery (some children have multiple surgeries resulting in frequent or extended absences from school), electrical stimulation, and bodysuits to stabilize muscles.[5] Baclofen has side effects, which include extreme drowsiness, muscle weakness, headache, nausea, vomiting, infections, cerebrospinal fluid leaks, and seizures.[6]

The school must be sure its faculty and staff are well informed about the student's manifestations of cerebral palsy. Other accommodations such as braces, wheelchairs, or scooters must be considered when maneuvering around the school environment. Because of the child's possible problems with mobility, it may be helpful to allow the student to leave class a few minutes early in order to travel in an empty hallway to ensure his or her safety. These children also need accessibility to their classrooms; ramps and elevators must be accessible to get to their classes.

What Students and Parents Wish Their Teachers and Counselors Knew About Cerebral Palsy

- "It is hard for me to make friends because I have trouble swallowing, and I sometimes drool. People who don't know me laugh at me or they stare."

- "Because I am different, I am afraid other kids will make fun of me, so I try to act like I'm not different from the other kids."

- "Because I can't speak clearly, people treat me like I'm dumb."

- "It is difficult for me to deal with people who treat her like she is incapable, or mentally handicapped, and I cannot imagine what it is like for her."

Practical Applications

Personal Applications

- *Improved self-efficacy and independence:* The counseling relationship with a child with cerebral palsy can be used to discuss self-efficacy and developing independence and autonomy. Overall, students with cerebral palsy have low self-efficacy compared to traditionally developing children. Also, these students have been found to have very close and overprotected relationships with their parents. It may be difficult for the students to become close to their peers when they are so accustomed to their parents' protection.[7]

- It may be helpful to discuss with parents how their child is changing and how their relationship may need to be adapted as they age. It may also be helpful to help students exert their independence. This could mean having a student be responsible for getting to classes unassisted. Improving the student's self-esteem is also important.

Social Applications

- *Friendship:* It is important to promote interaction of students with cerebral palsy and other students. Students with cerebral palsy are less socially active, tend to have fewer friends, and spend less time with their friends.[8] In addition, the friends they do have may be less caring and less validating than those of traditionally developing children.[9] Other students may think that children with cerebral palsy are "weird" or "different" because of their speech and language problems. They may also treat the student with cerebral palsy differently if the child has motor function problems and cannot chew or swallow properly, causing drooling.[10] It may be helpful to educate other students about cerebral palsy and explain to them that inhibited motor function does not make their peer unintelligent or stop him or her from wanting to have friends and be part of social groups.

- *Hiding behaviors:* Students with CP may use hiding behaviors or nonparticipation as ways to protect themselves from teasing, bullying, or peer rejection, or they may try to project a more typical self-image in an effort to fit in with peers. Some may struggle with issues related to body image, self-perception, and limited autonomy.[11]

- *Sexual identity and education:* Adolescents with cerebral palsy have less knowledge of sexuality and fewer life experiences. Experiences with sexuality are especially hindered when the students have problems with mobility and speaking.[12] Counseling issues could include sexual identity, sex education, and sexual development.

Academic Applications

- *Classroom integration:* Students with cerebral palsy need to be integrated in the classroom with their more typical peers. Being only with other students with disabilities may create difficulties with coping and independence when they are the only person with disabilities in other life situations.[13] Being separated may also promote feelings from other students that these children are different. Being integrated into the classroom includes identifying contributions that these students can make independently.

- *Completion of work and other tasks:* Children with cerebral palsy may encounter challenges with task completion in school. Although school personnel may think assigning an assistant may be best, a personal assistant may actually decrease the child's independence and interaction in the classroom with others. Rather, making environmental changes may help the child remain engaged with others and focused on his or her work.[14] Children with cerebral palsy may also have adaptive devices to help them in the classroom to complete their assignments, as well as to communicate with others. These interventions may be as simple as hearing aids or eyeglasses or as complex as computer equipment used for communication.[15] Desks that are designed for the student's height and prosthetic devices are also helpful, as are instruments to help the student hold and use pens or pencils.[16] Teachers should work with students to see if they need extra time to take tests or complete assignments. Working with the student to make specific accommodations is the most important piece to the student's success.

Career Implications

- Career implications with this disorder are unique to the specific needs of the individual. School counselors are encouraged to consult Chapter Nine for career and workplace considerations.

Resources with More Detailed Information About Cerebral Palsy

- United Cerebral Palsy: Provides information on resources for patients and families, has an online newsletter, and provides referral information for local community supports. http://www.ucp.org

- Pathways Awareness Foundation: For children with movement difficulties. Provides information for parents and physicians related to early detection and early intervention for children with motor delays. http://www.pathwaysawareness.org

- March of Dimes Foundation: A nonprofit site dedicated to the prevention of birth defects, premature births, and infant mortality. www.marchofdimes.com

Cystic Fibrosis

Danielle Wolfe

Indiana University of Pennsylvania

General Background Information About Cystic Fibrosis

Cystic fibrosis (CF) is a genetic, chronic, noncontagious disease that causes the body to persistently produce thick mucus and creates respiratory and gastrointestinal problems. It affects approximately thirty thousand people in the United States. People who have CF often do not appear to be ill, and the type and severity of its effects is unique to each person. Common characteristics are a chronic cough, shortness of breath, poor digestion often requiring enzyme supplements, increased appetite, susceptibility to dehydration, fatigue, excess gas, increased urination or bowel movements due to malabsorption, vulnerability to infections, slow growth rates, or the appearance of a barrel-shaped chest. With a median life span of almost forty years, CF requires that diet be carefully monitored, that precautions be taken against overexertion, and that daily medical treatments are provided, which often include using antibiotic inhalers or breathing equipment, sometimes during the school day.

What Students and Parents Wish Their Teachers and Counselors Knew About Cystic Fibrosis

- "Sometimes I feel that I have to go over and above what other people do just to prove that my CF is not going to hinder what I can do or how far I can go in life."[1]

- "I have a unique need to care for my disease yet live an active life alongside typical peers."

- "Multiple hospitalizations, daily medical treatments, and doctors' visits characterized our childhood. But so did chores, swim teams, girl scouts, sibling rivalry, camping trips, and homework."[2]

- "My child may cough frequently and at times violently. The cough is related to the Cystic Fibrosis and is not infectious."[3]
- "I did have the 504 plan meeting with the school. I highly recommend it. They made sure my son has his own everything so he doesn't have to share germ filled crayons, instruments, etc. It also allows for a private tutor to be sent to me either at home or in the hospital any time he misses more than three consecutive days of school."[4]

Practical Applications

Personal Applications

- Counselors can help school members respect the individuality of a student who has CF and its effects, especially when a family chooses not to make the condition known. This degree of confidentiality nevertheless requires that teachers know the student's needs and guard privacy requests.

- The malabsorption caused by CF requires enzyme supplements. Counselors can acknowledge that parents may prefer that the student self-monitor this. In such cases, counselors can advise teachers to discretely supervise intake or send the child to the school nurse in case the child forgets or refuses to take them in order to try to be like friends or being tired of always taking supplements.

- Slow growth rate, pale complexion, barreled chest, distended belly, and latent puberty are possible symptoms of CF that are physically obvious and can invite taunts from peers, increase susceptibility to depression or low self-worth, and may require exclusion or adaptations to participation. School counselors can schedule consultations to evaluate what social, emotional, or environmental help is needed.

Social Applications

- Some characteristics of CF may require accommodations that other students see as favoritism, such as the need for high-fat, high-calorie foods; unlimited lavatory privileges; rest during gym class; or even school absences. Educating peers about CF can ease tension and help the student with CF to be understood.

- The chronic coughing typical of CF can be an annoyance. Therefore, educating teachers, staff, and other students about the purpose of the coughing; the discomfort it can cause for the child; and the need for the child with CF to have his or her own school supplies can increase tolerance and ease embarrassment for the child, as can allowing the student to leave class during severe coughing episodes.

Academic Applications

- Some symptoms affect the academic progress of the student with CF, and others require adaptations for classroom participation. Although CF does not affect cognitive functions, unavoidable symptoms like fatigue may require accommodations such as testing during the student's most alert hours or extra time for assignments. A second set of textbooks can ease physical exertion.

- Frequent medically required absences can cause a child to lag academically and socially. The school may need to provide a tutor or alternate instruction. A school counselor might encourage using videotapes of missed activities to help students keep up with class in a way that feels more inclusive. People with CF do not have an increased risk of contracting a virus, but they are more likely to suffer more severe reactions when they have one. Washing hands frequently is the most important prevention, and promoting schoolwide awareness, including strategically placed signs, is one way a counselor can help the student with CF feel less singled out.

- Symptoms that can cause academic confusion or disruption include airway clearance treatments. Some can be scheduled around the school day (for example, using equipment before school, after school, and before bed), but some cannot. Scheduling should be done with the child's class routines in mind.

- Frequent urination and bowel movements or excess gas can require class absences and cause embarrassment for the student with CF. Allowing the student unlimited lavatory access and encouraging teachers to place the student's seat near the door will help the student exit quietly. Excess mucus production may require the student to keep tissues and a disposal container nearby to help discretely eliminate mucus and discard it to encourage germ containment.

- Shortness of breath may require reduced participation in some activities; physical activity nevertheless keeps lungs clear and strengthens breathing muscles. Students with CF often participate in physical activities with their peers, even outperforming them.

Career Applications

- Adults living with CF work in a wide variety of careers and occupations. Career exploration and planning need to take into consideration the nature and progression of the individual's disease, as well as accommodations needed for medical treatment and independence.

Resources with More Detailed Information About Cystic Fibrosis

- "Cystic Fibrosis in the Classroom": This twenty-page guide concisely details the most important, school-specific issues regarding students with CF.[5] A free copy can be requested from CFRI at 650–404–9975 or Digestive Care at http://www.digestivecare.com.

- Cystic Fibrosis Information: A Web site that provides information including hundreds of links like "school," which lists numerous sources regarding elementary, secondary, and postsecondary issues surrounding students with cystic fibrosis. http://www3.nbnet.nb.ca/normap/CF.htm

- Digestive Care and Cystic Fibrosis Research. (2007). *Cystic fibrosis in the classroom*. Mountain View, CA: Cystic Fibrosis Research, Inc. Retrieved Dec. 10, 2008, at http://www.cfri.org/PDF%20files/2008CFintheClassroomEnglish.pdf. This site provides resources for parents, teachers, school nurses, and school administrators.

Deafness and Hearing Disorders

Angela Orbin

Indiana University of Pennsylvania

General Background About Deafness and Hearing Disorders

Deafness refers to the complete loss of ability to hear in one or both ears. This impairment can be permanent or fluctuating, and it adversely affects a child's performance in school and education. *Hearing impairment* is the term that refers to reduced ability to hear, which can range from mild to severe and affect one or both ears. *Conductive hearing loss* affects the outer or middle ear, and it is experienced by a reduction in ability to hear speech and other sound, though faint sounds are audible. Ear infections are among the most common causes, along with allergies, fluid, impacted earwax, and foreign bodies. Medication or surgery may be used to correct the problem, which may be temporary. Even temporary hearing loss, though, can have negative effects on language learning, socialization, and academic learning during critical developmental periods.

Sensorineural hearing loss is caused by damage to delicate cells of the inner ear or supporting nerves. Loss of hearing ranges from mild to profound. Sensorineural hearing loss affects the ability to hear frequency and may occur with age and exposure to loud sounds. This type of hearing loss is permanent and affects the understanding of speech. *Mixed hearing loss* is a combination of conductive hearing loss and sensorineural hearing loss. The problem is located in both the middle and outer ear. *Central hearing loss* refers to hearing impairment related to the nerves of the central nervous system.[1] *Auditory processing disorder* (APD) occurs when a person is unable to recognize subtle differences between words and sounds and is sometimes known as *word deafness*. It is especially difficult to understand language when the environment is loud or the information being presented is complex. Students with APD have a normal intelligence level, but following directions and listening to oral information is difficult for them. Poor listening skills, lower grades, behavior problems, and language difficulties are often present in school. Because APD is also associated with childhood dyslexia, attention deficit disorder, autism, autism spectrum disorder, and specific language and development disorders, it is possible that some students without hearing problems are inaccurately categorized as having APD.[2]

In the year 2000, 28.6 million Americans had some type of deafness or hearing impairment. During the 2000–2001 school year, 70,767 students ages six to twenty-one received disability services primarily for hearing loss.[3] Ninety percent of children with hearing impairments are born to hearing parents.[4] Hearing loss has three general causes:

- *Ear infections*, or a buildup of fluid in the middle ear. Ear infections can cause fluctuating hearing loss and are the most common cause of hearing loss in children. Sounds are received as muffled or inaudible. Hearing loss due to ear infection becomes permanent when the damage is done to the eardrum, bones of the ear, or the hearing nerve or if the infection occurs several times.

- *Congenital hearing loss* is present at birth and ranges from mild to profound.

- *Acquired hearing loss* occurs after birth, typically at the onset of a disease, condition, or injury.[5]

Early detection and intervention are important for children experiencing hearing loss or deafness, and approximately half of all hearing loss and deafness may be preventable.[6] The first six months of life are crucial to the development of language, and all newborns should be screened for deafness.[7] Children with deafness or hearing impairments typically display delayed communication skills and academic achievement, which often lead to social isolation. Vocabulary develops more slowly than it does with typical children, and the gap continues to widen with age. Intervention and therapy are necessary.[8] Deaf children of hearing parents often have more pronounced delays in language compared to deaf children of deaf parents, who typically follow a normal pattern of development. However, deaf children of hearing parents often have a more active social life, which helps them to acquire and develop language skills.[9] Deaf and hearing-impaired children often use a combination of oral and manual communication skills. Oral skills include speech, lip reading, and use of residual hearing. Manual communication skills include signing and finger spelling.[10]

Although some people are able to use residual and limited hearing abilities, certain sounds are very difficult to detect with significant losses. For example, words ending with *es* or *ed* are difficult to hear, along with words beginning with high-frequency sounds like *s, sh, f, t,* and *k*. Tense, possession, and pluralization are often confused. A deaf or hearing-impaired person does not use what he or she cannot hear and may not hear his or her own voice when speaking.[11]

American Sign Language (ASL) is a complete language that uses hand signing, facial expressions, and use of the body and is the first language for many deaf people in North America. It is separate from the English language with its own syntax and does not translate exactly.

Another option that can be considered for those with profound loss is the cochlear implant, a small electronic device. A portion of the device sits behind the ear and another portion is surgically implanted under the skin. The cochlear implant includes a microphone, speech processor, transmitter, and electrode array. The electrode array collects noise impulses and sends them to different parts of auditory nerve. The implant does not restore hearing but helps the individual to understand speech by directly stimulating the auditory nerve. Therapy is necessary for recipients to learn how to use the hearing sense and interpret sounds. Most children who receive the cochlear implant are between the ages of two and six. Early implantation leads to earlier exposure to speech, language, and social skills.

What Students and Parents Wish Their Teachers and Counselors Knew About Deafness and Hearing Disorders

- "I am able to learn just like everyone else. My level of intelligence is normal."

- "Sometimes I think my child is functioning in two worlds: the hearing world and the deaf world. His education takes place in the hearing world, but he communicates best in the deaf world."

Practical Applications

Personal Applications

- Students with deafness or hearing impairment often have difficulty acquiring skills in vocabulary, grammar, and language.[12]

- Reading and math are typically the most difficult subjects for children with deafness and hearing impairments, and without proper intervention, these students are not likely to get past the third- or fourth-grade academic level.

- Student success depends on parental involvement and quality of services received.

- Students with deafness or hearing impairment may need assistance adjusting to their disability or with issues related to self-concept and seeing themselves as capable as their more typical peers.

Social Applications

- Children with hearing loss or deafness often feel socially isolated and unhappy at school.

- Students with mild to moderate hearing loss tend to have more social problems than students with profound hearing loss.[13] School counselors can provide assistance through individual and group interventions that promote the development of social and friendship skills, particularly in teaching social nuances that are communicated through vocal qualities that are more subtle and difficult to perceive, such as communication of sarcasm, irritation, and annoyance.

Academic Applications

- Helpful classroom accommodations include seat placement, amplification systems, a sign language interpreter, closed captioning for media materials, or a personal note taker.[14]

- Individual counseling is recommended for students, along with training sessions with an audiologist and language skills exercises.

- Auditory trainer devices help students focus on the teacher. The teacher speaks into a microphone that goes directly to a headset worn by the student.[15]

- Speech and language therapy are often indicated to enhance communication skills.

- Teachers should be sure to face the child when speaking so the child can get visual feedback.

Career Applications

- Career implications with this disorder are unique to the specific needs of the individual. School counselors are encouraged to consult Chapter Nine for career and workplace considerations.

Resources with More Detailed Information About Deafness and Hearing Disorders

- NIDCD Directory: This is a directory of organizations that can answer questions and provide information, and is maintained by the National Institute on Deafness and Other Communication Disorders. www.nidcd.nih.gov/directory

- America Society for Deaf Children: Offers support for families and teachers of deaf or hearing impaired children. www.deafchildren.org

- ASHA (American Speech-Language-Hearing Association): A professional organization for speech language pathologists, audiologists, and hearing specialists. Its Web site has informative and scholarly resources helpful for professionals working with individuals who are deaf or hearing impaired. www.asha.org

Degenerative Orthopedic Diseases (Muscular Dystrophy)

Kristen M. Bernot and Erica Zinsser

Indiana University of Pennsylvania

General Background Information About Muscular Dystrophy

Of the different types of degenerative orthopedic diseases affecting school-aged children, muscular dystrophy (MD) is most prevalent, with Duchenne MD the most commonly found. Duchenne's is a fatal genetic disorder affecting approximately one in every thirty-five hundred males.[1] This form of MD results in muscle weakness and a wasting away of muscle fiber. The fiber breakdown usually starts with the child's shoulder, upper arm, and hip and thigh muscles.[2] By age twelve, most children use wheelchairs for mobility due to their muscle weakness. The disorder also greatly affects respiratory and cardiac system functioning. These problems associated with cardiac function are devastating and result in death by late adolescence or early adulthood.[3]

Each kind of muscular dystrophy results in differing symptomology; however, most often children are seen with muscle weakness, lack of coordination, and loss of mobility as a result of contractures.[4] Contractures are fixations at the joints that make moving difficult and painful.[5] Specific to Duchenne MD, those affected may have numerous falls, large calf muscles, problems standing up when lying or sitting, and weakness in leg muscles, which make walking problematic and results in an awkward gait. Some children have mild mental retardation as well.[6]

Because there is no cure for MD, treatment revolves around symptom relief and slowing the progression of the disease. Possible treatments may include physical therapy and occupational therapy to keep the muscles fluid and mobile; corticosteroids may strengthen muscles and delay progression of the disease; surgery may be used to treat spine curvature or contractures; orthotic devices improve mobility; ventilation machines help children in later progression of the illness to breathe.[7] There are side effects to medication used to slow the progression of MD. Steroids, though helpful to increase muscle tone and energy level, have significant side effects: "weight gain, short stature, delay of puberty, facial 'puffi-ness,' osteoporosis, and cataracts." It can also cause children to become irritable, hyperactive, emotionally volatile, and distractible.[8] Because of their physical limi-tations and treatment regimes, these children are at risk for social isolation and rejection as well as frequent and extended absences from school, and they require academic accommodations.

What Students and Parents Wish Their Teachers and Counselors Knew About Degenerative Orthopedic Diseases

- "MD is so frustrating! My friends go camping, play baseball, throw a foot-ball, and I am stuck in this wheelchair. Sometimes I can't even dress myself!"

- "When he was diagnosed with MD, I felt my whole life slipping away. I thought, how can I go on . . . knowing that he will likely die before he reaches adulthood?"

- "It's very hard for me to let go and have someone else care for him. I think that if I take time for myself, I am losing time I could be spending with him."

Practical Applications

Physical Applications

- Because of the physical manifestations of the disease, children with MD have problems with mobility. The school environment should be adequately equipped to handle wheelchairs and scooters. Students with MD need ramps or elevators. Automatic door openers might also be accessed to help improve their sense of independence. Because children with MD are prone to falls, it may be important in the elementary set-ting to keep the floors as uncluttered as possible, with pathways open and clear. It may be helpful to coordinate gym class activities with these students' physical therapy. Child who are mobile without the assistance of wheelchairs or scooters may become easily fatigued walking and climbing stairs. Attention to classroom placement, as well as allowing these students to leave early to navigate hallways while they are clear, are recommended.

- Children affected by MD know they are facing a life-limiting disorder. They may want to talk about what the disease is doing to them and what they can do to manage it. As these children age, they may lose their mobility or their ability to perform daily tasks for themselves. So while other children are gaining independence, these children are regressing in their level of care. They may also be experiencing anxiety, feelings of loneliness, or depression.[9]

Social Applications

- Because these children have certain physical limitations, they will likely experience social isolation. These children lose muscle tone while their classmates are gaining it. It may be very frustrating for them to realize that they cannot do the things they once were able to. They may also experience depression or anxiety because of MD. Students with MD will likely need assistance in being included in class and activities.[10] Peers need to be instructed about how to provide assistance in a supportive and respectful way to their peers with MD so as not to embarrass their peer or cause accidental injury.

Academic Applications

- Because these children lose muscle tone, they may need assistance navigating in hallways or getting books and materials to their classrooms and may need a "buddy" to provide assistance. Students with MD may need special grips for pens or pencils to be able to take notes. It may be helpful to allow recordings to be made of class lectures or to provide the student with a copy of notes from class. Alternate tests may be needed if students are unable to write. These children should also have supportive chairs with armrests to promote upright posture. A desk should be provided to allow the student to feel comfortable taking notes in his or her supportive chair. Also because of the risk of mental retardation, children should be assessed and placed in appropriate learning environments for their ability level.[11] Students with degenerative orthopedic diseases often have interruptions in their education due to the nature of the disease, as well as experience significant side effects from medications used to treat their disease. These medications may interfere with their ability to concentrate, learn new material, or retain previously learned material.

Career Applications

- Career exploration and planning need to take into consideration the nature and progression of the child's disease.

Resources with More Detailed Information About Muscular Dystrophy

- MDA (Muscular Dystrophy Association): Resources include information about clinics, equipment, support groups, summer camps, and chat groups. Other information about advocacy and current research is also available. http://www.mda.org

- Muscular Dystrophy Family Foundation: This site provides families affected by MD with emotional support, social support, and adaptive equipment. It also provides research updates on muscular dystrophy and information about the illness. http://www.mdff.org/

- Parent Project Muscular Dystrophy: Information for parents, teachers, and school administration. This site also provides information about research and ways to donate to or become involved in the support of MD research. http://www.parentprojectmd.org

- "About Duchenne." (2008). Retrieved November 12, 2008, from http://www.parentprojectmd.org/site/PageServer?pagename=under-standing_about.

- "Diseases: Duchenne muscular dystrophy." (2006). Retrieved November 13, 2008, from http://www.mda.org/disease/dmd.html.

- "MDA publications: Facts about Duchenne and Becker muscular dystrophies (DMD and BMD)." (2006). Retrieved November 13, 2008, from http://www.mda.org/publications/fa-dmdbmd-what.html#whathappens.

- "What Is Duchenne/Becker Muscular Dystrophy (DBMD)?" (2006, September 1). Retrieved November 13, 2008, from http://www.cdc.gov/ncbddd/duchenne/what.htm.

- "Muscular dystrophy: Symptoms." (2007, December 8). Retrieved November 13, 2008, from http://www.mayoclinic.com/health/muscular-dystrophy/DS00200/DSECTION=symptoms.

- "Muscular dystrophy: Treatments and drugs." (2007, December 8). Retrieved November 13, 2008, from http://www.mayoclinic.com/health/muscular-dystrophy/DS00200/DSECTION=treatments-and-drugs.

- "Seeking treatment." (2008). Retrieved November 17, 2008, from http://www.parentprojectmd.org/site/PageServer?pagename=caring_care_treatment.

- Parent Project Muscular Dystrophy (2006, Summer/Fall). "Education matters: A teacher's guide to Duchenne muscular dystrophy." http://www.parentprojectmd.org/site/DocServer/EdMatters-TeachersGuide.pdf?docID=2403

- Rohrer Durham, M. (2007, April 19). "Managing cognitive problems." Retrieved November 19, 2008, from http://www.anapsid.org/cnd/coping/managecognitive.html.

Diabetes

Rebecca A. Seybold
Indiana University of Pennsylvania

General Background Information About Diabetes

Diabetes mellitus is a metabolic disturbance that causes an increase in blood sugar levels (hyperglycemia). It affects about one in four hundred to six hundred individuals under the age of twenty. This condition is caused by a lowered supply of insulin within the pancreas or from intolerance to insulin. Although diabetes is a treatable condition, it is incurable. Two types of diabetes (type I and type II) are found among children and adolescents. Both conditions are marked by periods of hyperglycemia or hypoglycemia if blood sugar levels are improperly regulated.

Hyperglycemia occurs if an individual does not get enough insulin, consumes too much food, does not get enough exercise, is under stress, or has an illness. Symptoms include extreme thirst, frequent urination, blurry vision, and heavy breathing and can lead to diabetic ketoacidosis, which causes nausea, vomiting, and a high level of acid in the blood and urine.[1] If left untreated, diabetic ketoacidosis can cause death. Hypoglycemia occurs when an individual gets too much insulin or not enough food, or exercises too much. Symptoms of hypoglycemia include tremors, sweating, light-headedness, irritability, confusion, and drowsiness. If left untreated, hypoglycemia can be life threatening and may lead to unconsciousness and convulsions. School personnel must be mindful that students with diabetes may not always recognize symptoms for hyperglycemia and hypoglycemia and may not be able to alert an adult for assistance. Safety plans need to be developed with student and parental involvement to be followed in the event of a health crisis.

Type I diabetes mellitus is the more common of the two types of diabetes found in children. It is an autoimmune disease in which an individual's body destroys the cells in the pancreas that are responsible for developing the hormone insulin. Children living with type I diabetes must check blood sugar levels at regular intervals and must have insulin injections. Insulin injections are frequently completed with the use of insulin pumps, and school personnel need to be informed of management routines for children who require insulin injections. As children enter adolescence, they may experience increased crises related to their diabetes management as this is a stage at which hormonal changes or fluctuations may affect insulin stability. Another complicating factor includes adolescents' becoming less medication compliant in an effort to be more similar to their nondiabetic peers.

School counselors must be sensitive not only to diabetes management routines at school, but also aware of how home routines affect a child and his or her family. For example, at times diabetes management creates particular stressors for the child and caregivers, such as on initial diagnosis when insulin levels are being established or during periods of stress or illness when insulin levels may become unstable. In addition, diabetes is more difficult to control with some children. In these instances, children may require more testing, even during the night, which may cause them to attend school more fatigued or less rested. School parties or other situations in which children may be exposed to sugary treats may create social as well as physical challenges for children. Teasing or bullying may become problematic for these children, including for male children with diabetes, who may be smaller in build and stature than their more typical peers. Body image issues may require the need for individual or group counseling interventions.

Type II diabetes, which used to be diagnosed most commonly in adulthood, is increasingly diagnosed in children, and this increase is thought to be due to more children being overweight or obese. Whereas type I diabetes is due to a lack of insulin production, type II is due to insulin resistance or reduced sensitivity to insulin. Type II diabetes can be reduced with improved nutrition and exercise programs, although some children need to manage their insulin levels with oral medication or, in more extreme cases, insulin injections. Due to obesity, these are children who may struggle with body image issues and may benefit from individual and group counseling interventions as well. Obese children are also vulnerable to teasing and bullying by peers.

With regard to the impact that symptoms of type I and type II of Diabetes Mellitus have within the school setting, students with diagnosis of either type of diabetes qualify for school accommodations under a 504 plan under the Americans with Disabilities Act of 1990.[2]

What Students and Parents Wish Their Teachers and Counselors Knew About Diabetes

- "I hate getting the teacher's attention when I know my sugar level is not where it should be. I feel like my teacher blames me for not managing my diabetes better."

- "I feel different than the other kids because they don't have to worry about what they eat. I just don't think it's fair."

- "I get so tired of testing my blood sugar; it makes my fingers really sore. Sometimes I just want to give up."

- "I feel like no one really understands how important it is for my son to be monitored for his diabetes. I had to pick him up from school so many times due to a bout of hypoglycemia."

- "My son misses out on a lot of school functions like holiday parties because everyone assumes that because he has diabetes he can't have anything with sugar in it."

- "I feel like a lot of people blame me because my child was diagnosed with diabetes at such a young age."

Practical Applications

Personal Applications

- *Emotional issues:* Children diagnosed with either type of diabetes may experience emotional issues as the result of having a lifelong condition that requires self-management. It is important for counselors and teachers to be receptive to a student's feelings. Having a diagnosis of diabetes creates many difficulties that emerge in the school setting, such as feeling different from peers, receiving special services, being required to check glucose levels, dietary restrictions, and the stigma surrounding diabetes. A student with diabetes is likely to gain strong benefits from involvement with a diabetes support group.

- *Organizational strategies:* A student who is experiencing hypoglycemia or hyperglycemia finds it extremely difficult to concentrate even after treatment. For this reason, instructions for tasks should be written down and broken into smaller parts to aid concentration.

Social Applications

- *Problematic social-behavioral issues:* A key characteristic in hyperglycemia is frequent urination. In the school setting, a student experiencing high blood glucose may need to leave the room numerous times, which is not considered a prosocial behavior. Irritability is a characteristic for individuals experiencing hypoglycemia. For students with diabetes, irritability may have a negative impact within interpersonal relationships, causing peer conflict. Collaboration between the student and teacher is essential for proper diabetes management.

Academic Applications

- *Seating in class:* Students with diabetes should have preferential seating. A student needs to be seated close to the board due to the potential for vision problems associated with diabetes. It is also important for a student to be seated close to the teacher so that he or she is more likely to notice signs of hyperglycemia or hypoglycemia. A student who is seated close to the exit door will be able to go to the bathroom without disrupting the class. A student requiring insulin injections must be permitted to go to the nurse's office for injections or administration assistance.

- *Interactive teaching methods:* Interactive teaching methods are useful in promoting student concentration and focus. Students experiencing blood sugar that is too high or too low have difficulties focusing solely on lecture-based instruction.

- *Note-taking assistance:* Students with diabetes may need note-taking assistance as they attend to self-management routines or experience side effects related to fluctuations in blood sugar levels.

- *Test taking:* Students with diabetes should be given some flexibility in test taking. They should be permitted to have water or snacks if needed. They may also need to have testing adjusted depending on their glucose level.

- *Stability and routine in environment and schedule:* It is very important that a student's schedule for meals remains the same. Changed mealtimes may have implications for a child's blood sugar levels and diabetes management.

- *Directions and homework assignments:* Directions must be brief and clear to promote understanding and concentration. Flexibility must be given on homework assignments because a student may be experiencing fatigue or poor concentration.

Career Applications

- *Proper environment and work demand fit:* Students must be made aware of laws requiring workplaces to make accommodations based on the Americans with Disabilities Act.

Resources with More Detailed Information About Diabetes

- Children with Diabetes: This organization provides information regarding both types of diabetes and more detailed explanations for the causes and implications of the condition. It also provides support links and chatrooms for people with diabetes and parents of children with diabetes. www.childrenwithdiabetes.com

- National Diabetes Education Program: A comprehensive site that provides information related to the detection, treatment, and care of diabetes, including diabetes in the school and workplace. This government organization provides information about helping children and adolescents manage diabetes. This site also includes a plethora of resources for health, business, and education professionals regarding diabetes education. http://ndep.nih.gov

- American Diabetes Association: Provides information and social networking opportunities for those touched by juvenile diabetes. www.diabetes.org

- Juvenile Diabetes Research Foundation: www.jdrf.org

Fetal Alcohol Syndrome

Erica M. Askey

Indiana University of Pennsylvania

General Background Information About Fetal Alcohol Syndrome

Fetal alcohol syndrome (FAS) results from prenatal exposure to alcohol, a known cause of mental retardation and birth defects. FAS can occur when alcohol in the mother's blood crosses the placenta and enters into the umbilical cord, causing brain damage and structural defects. FAS is a preventable lifelong condition that causes physical and mental disabilities.[1] Characteristics of FAS are growth deficiency for height and weight, distinct pattern of facial features and other abnormalities, organ dysfunction, and central nervous system dysfunction. Distinct facial features may include small eyes, an underdeveloped area between the nose and upper lip, thin upper lip, and a flat midface. A short nose, small chin, and other facial anomalies may be present as well. Central nervous system damage may include small head circumference, poor coordination, lower-than-average IQ, hyperactivity, attention problems, learning difficulties, developmental delays, and motor problems.[2] The nature and extent of damage to a baby can depend on when during pregnancy the mother drank, the pattern of alcohol abuse, whether other drugs were involved, and other biological features of the mother and fetus.[3]

Significant school placement issues exist for FAS students. They often are underserved or undetected by school programs, as many state educational systems do not recognize FAS as a handicapping condition or separate funding category. "Students are typically characterized as having mild, moderate, or severe retardation, or as suffering from an emotional or behavioral disability." These generic categories and broad labels do not adequately define the individual needs of students or appropriate interventions for them.[4] Students with FAS can be recognized by looking at both external and internal signals. External signals are daydreaming for over 50 percent of class time, biting fingernails and lips, being silent, exhibiting forgetfulness on an hourly or daily basis, and anger. Internal signals include confusion regarding day, time, or class period; emotional breakdowns including retreating from social situations; and high levels of sexual activity, including impulsive acts or inappropriate touching. Other signals are laziness, falling asleep in class, tardiness, poor eyesight, and a history of other physical problems.[5]

What Students and Parents Wish Their Teachers and Counselors Knew About Fetal Alcohol Syndrome

- "I like people, but I don't have many friends because I don't know how to keep a relationship. People can take advantage of me without me realizing it, and I can be led in the wrong direction by someone promising me affection or friendship."[6]

- "I like to be independent, but I also need to be carefully watched because I can't always control my behavior. I don't have good control of my impulses and I have poor judgment when it comes to making decisions, and making bad decisions gets me into a lot of trouble. I can't plan ahead or solve problems very well, and I have a hard time remembering things like rules and consequences."[7]

- "I become easily frustrated with myself sometimes, and I feel bad when I hurt people or make them angry. I always try to make people happy but my FAS can get in the way."[8]

- "To communicate with an FAS child effectively, you must offer simple directions, break tasks into small steps, and teach each through repetitions and concrete rewards. This strategy can be used at home and in the classroom."[9]

- "Because children with FAS have trouble understanding behavior and consequences, they are usually the child in the group that gets caught. This does not necessarily mean that they are the child that initiated or carried out the action, so avoid automatically blaming that child."[10]

- "Talk to the student himself/herself. Some students with FAS can provide useful insights into their own strengths and their input can assist teachers to determine which strategies have worked in the past."[11]

Practical Applications

Personal/Social Applications

- *Emotional and behavioral issues:* Students with FAS often have poor socialization skills, such as difficulties building and maintaining friendships. Because they tend to have a lack of imagination or curiosity, they consequently have difficulty engaging in play with other children. Problems encountered at school are typically behavioral. FAS students should be taught behavioral coping skills, including how to prevent crises and avoid situations that cause them to lose control.[12] Behavioral problems in the classroom can include hyperactivity, inability to concentrate, social withdrawal, stubbornness, impulsivity, and anxiety.[13]

- *Anxiety and depression:* Students with FAS often deal with anxiety and depression. School counselors may need to refer these students to counseling to help deal with these problems. Counselors and teachers can also encourage students to get involved with sports, clubs, or other structured activities to perhaps lessen depressive symptoms.[14]

- *Lying, stealing, or other antisocial behavior:* Students must be closely monitored to ensure this behavior is not occurring. Simple and consistent rules with immediate consequences help to curb this behavior, and counseling often helps as well.[15]

- *Inappropriate sexual behaviors:* Sexual issues are a source of concern for adolescents with FAS. Inappropriate behaviors that are sexually explicit can result in scapegoating and victimization from other students. These behaviors must be monitored and modified as necessary, preferably by a school-based advocate such as a school counselor.[16] Teens with FAS should be taught about birth control and sex using language and concepts appropriate to their developmental level.[17]

- *High risk for chemical dependency:* Children with FAS are at high risk for this because of their family history of alcohol dependency. Parents, counselors, and teachers should work together to teach these children that there are alternate ways of having fun and dealing with their feelings.[18]

- *Trouble with the law:* As children with FAS reach adolescence, they are at increased risk for involvement with the justice system because they often have poor judgment and the inability to anticipate consequences. People with FAS can also be easily led and manipulated, and they often end up in the wrong place at the wrong time. They must be closely monitored by parents and school personnel to prevent involvement with the justice system.[19]

- *Culturally relevant:* FAS abuse is more widespread in cultures where alcohol abuse is prevalent, such as within Native Americans and Alaska Natives. Children within these cultures need to have access to the wisdom and tenets of their cultures so that they can learn to live within them.[20]

- *Community-based education:* FAS students often lack the skills to make logical decisions. Therefore, they must be taught how to make reasonable choices and be given opportunities to practice. Students with FAS should have the opportunity to practice new skills in situations in which they will use them, for example, using money at a grocery store.[21]

Academic Applications

- *Learning difficulties* for students with FAS can include poor memory, inability to understand concepts such as time and money, poor language comprehension, and poor problem-solving skills.[22] Parents report that their children perform more poorly than expected on IQ and achievement tests, and their academic and vocational outcomes are frequently poor as well. Students with FAS tend to have poor attention, impulsivity, and difficulty making transitions.

- *Classroom environment:* Although this is sometimes difficult, teachers should create a structured classroom environment that allows students with FAS to have clear choices and predictable routines.[23] If possible, tasks in the classroom should be broken down into meaningful steps, with each step taught through repetition and reward. Skills should be taught in the context in which they are to be used, as FAS students have trouble generalizing from one situation to another.[24]

- *Supervision:* In school, FAS children should be vigilantly watched so they do not place themselves in dangerous situations.[25] Teachers should plan ahead for change, and transitions should be closely supervised.[26]

- *Communication:* Directions should be simple, brief, and specific. Conversations should begin using the child's name and making good eye contact. Educators should know that children with FAS can be very literal in their understanding of word meanings and expressions; thus, these different meanings will need to be taught.[27] Teachers must also learn to recognize and honor any communicative attempts made by FAS students, verbal or nonverbal. For example, a student may crumple up a math test because that is his way of telling the teacher it is too difficult. "By recognizing the message behind this behavior, educators can respond more effectively to a student's needs and help them learn appropriate methods of communicating those needs."[28] Communication skills should be developed alongside social skills instruction, as the two are essential to functioning in a community setting.[29]

Career Applications

- People with fetal alcohol spectrum disorders (FASDs) are at high risk for unemployment and dropping out of school. Diagnosing a child early and allowing that child to receive special education services will make that child more likely to achieve their educational potential.[30]

- School counselors can help students in high school find employment opportunities with employers who understand that they have hired an individual with a disability. Early job environments with structure, order, and routine can help set the stage for steady employment for an FAS person after high school.[31]

- Volunteer placement can help teens with FAS enhance their sense of participation within the community.[32]

- Educational programs should target functional skills. To be independent, FAS students must know how to ride buses/other transportation, prepare meals, pay bills and budget money, and hold a job. Educational goals should go beyond classroom limits and extend to communities so that FAS students can become productive citizens.[33]

Resources with More Detailed Information About Fetal Alcohol Syndrome

- FAS Community Resource Center: The Web site provides information on the characteristics of FAS and FASDs, statistics on the incidence and prevalence of FAS and FASDs, links to online support groups, and articles and other resources for both parents and school personnel. http://www.come-over.to/FASCRC/

- Family Resource Institute: A nonprofit educational organization whose goal is to identify, understand, and care for individuals with prenatal alcohol exposure and their families. The Web site provides many publications useful to school counselors. www.fetalalcoholsyndrome.org

- National Organization on Fetal Alcohol Syndrome: Dedicated to working to eliminate birth defects from drinking during pregnancy and give information and support to those affected with FAS and FASDs. The Web site also provides resources useful to parents and school personnel. www.nofas.org

- The Arc: An organization that provides resources for those affected by intellectual and developmental disabilities, and their families. www.thearc.org

Learning Disabilities

Angela Orbin
Indiana University of Pennsylvania

General Background Information About Learning Disabilities

A learning disability is a neurological disorder, meaning the brain is wired differently for an individual with a learning disability.[1] *Learning disability* is a term that is often misunderstood by the general public; it does not indicate low intellectual capacity and generically refers to a range of neurological difficulties.[2] Learning disabilities are not the result of sensory, emotional, or intellectual deficits, although they may co-occur with other disorders. The National Institutes of Health report that one in seven Americans has some form of learning disabilities. Eighty percent of students with learning disabilities have difficulty reading. Early intervention is necessary for students. The majority of students with reading difficulties who receive intervention in early grades will go on to read at or above normal levels.

There are some characteristics that may indicate a child has a learning disability. However, it is important to remember that several of these characteristics must be present over a long period of time, and even that does not guarantee that a child has a learning disability. Early language problems often predict learning disabilities.

Other common characteristics include:

- Begin speaking later than other children
- Difficulty pronouncing words
- Problems with vocabulary
- Slow vocabulary development
- Difficulty rhyming words
- Problems learning the alphabet, numerical order, and the days of the week
- Restlessness

- Easily distracted
- Difficulty interacting with peers
- Difficulty following directions
- Difficulty following routines
- Slow developing motors skills

There are different forms of learning disabilities, and no two students are exactly alike. Some of the types of learning disabilities that may be encountered in school include:

- *Various math learning disabilities.* These range from mild to severe and may overlap with other difficulties. Language difficulties can interfere with a student's ability to understand math instruction word problems. Memorization is often difficult, and therefore so is learning number facts. Some students may be able to understand complex math concepts but be unable to organize the formal instruction received in school to match their abilities. It is also possible for students to understand complex math concepts but have difficulty or inconsistency with calculating (for example, difficulty using the correct operational sign or difficulty memorizing basic number facts). Students with math-specific learning disabilities rarely get the services they need because most school programs are based on reading disabilities, and the math-specific students do not get called in for evaluation.

- *Dyslexia.* This is a language-based learning disability with difficulty reading and pronouncing words and difficulty understanding written words. It is sometimes difficult to remember letter symbols, sounds, and meanings. It is a myth that a person with dyslexia reads backward. The severity of dyslexia varies, but early identification helps with school success. Dyslexia often runs in families. Other signs include difficulty learning to speak, difficulty learning letters and language, difficulty memorizing number facts, and difficulty with reading comprehension. Only a formal test can be used to diagnose dyslexia.[3]

- *Nonverbal learning disabilities.* This originates in the right hemisphere of the brain and leads to difficulty understanding facial expression and body language. It is common to bump into people or things. Because these students possess strong verbal skills, there is often the misperception that they do not have a learning disability.

- *Dyspraxia.* This includes problems with motor coordination such as poor balance, hand-to-eye coordination, and difficulty coloring between lines or putting together a puzzle.[4]

- *Dysgraphia.* This processing disorder specifically affects writing and causes difficulty with spelling, handwriting, containing writing into a defined space, and writing thoughts on paper. Signs include tight pencil grip, illegible handwriting, becoming tired quickly when writing, speaking out loud when writing, omitting words, problems with grammar, and a noticeable gap between spoken understanding of language and writing ideas on paper.

- *Auditory and visual processing disorders.* These are indicated by difficulty understanding or processing language despite normal hearing and vision. Some accommodations to help these students include using visual materials in class, allowing think time before responses, and not asking the student to write and listen and the same time.

- *Central auditory processing disorder.* This learning disability is signaled by a student who is easily distracted by background noises and may appear to ignore people when concentrating.

Attention deficit hyperactivity disorder is not a learning disability; however, the two often occur together.[5] Up to 30 percent of students with ADHD may also have a learning disability.[6]

What Students and Parents Wish Their Teachers and Counselors Knew About Learning Disabilities

- "I know what my teacher wants me to do, but I don't know how to do it."

- "I was easily distracted. It was impossible for me to take in everything the teacher was saying—not because I wasn't trying to pay attention but because other things were going on that took my concentration away from the teachers. I just couldn't process what she talking about and check out what was going on in the back of the classroom at the same time."[7]

- "My child is just as smart as the other students."

Practical Applications

Personal Applications

- Because these students often need emotional support, mental health specialists should be part of the individualized educational program (IEP) team.

Social Applications

- Students with poor social skills have difficulty making friends, which can lead to social isolation. Students with learning disabilities are often unable to accurately perceive what others say and do.

- Students may need extra instruction to learn school manners, classroom behavior, anger management, and conflict resolution.

Academic Applications

- Schools should provide evaluation and assessment (with parental consent) and identify the individual student's strengths and weaknesses.

- Math-specific students are in danger of being held back or put into lower-level math classes in early grades when basic facts and memorizing are heavily stressed. Strengths and weaknesses should be assessed so that the full scope of math is still accessible. Accommodations such as a pocket math fact chart should be used for complex math applications instead of holding a child back.

- Test-taking accommodations include allowing students extra time to take tests, offering tests over an extended time, testing in a different order, providing special test preparation, and taking a test in a setting with minimal distractions.

- Academic supplements include interactive materials such as games, frequent academic practice sessions, reading out loud, taping lessons, and providing a watch with a timer and alarm.

- Dysgraphia-specific students may need special ergonomic pens and pencils, extra time for written assignments, tape recorders, or oral and visual assignments as alternatives to written projects. Teachers may be encouraged to allow students to use a mix of cursive and printing when writing and to not grade based on neatness.

- Students may need tutors or specialized therapists that should be a part of the IEP team.[8]

Career Applications

- Many students with learning disabilities do not consider two- or four-year colleges (but may be able to) because they are not encouraged to or prepared. Learning disabilities are the largest disability category represented in the college population. A successful transition after high school requires focusing on career interests, strengths, college or vocational training options and necessary prerequisite skills, modifications, and test requirements.

- School counselors should be part of the IEP team and begin discussing career plans as early as age fourteen. College transitions are easier for students who have been active participants in career planning and IEP conferences.

- Individual psychoeducational training to prepare for the transition to college after high school should be provided. Examples include time management and how to seek necessary support.[9]

Resources with More Detailed Information About Learning Disabilities

- Learning Disabilities Association of America: Provides support for individuals, families, teachers, and other professionals. www.ldanatl.org

- National Center for Learning Disabilities: Includes a parent center and grade-specific learning information. www.ncld.org

- LD Online: A comprehensive Web site offering in-depth information on learning disabilities, advocacy, and advice. It offers specific information for educators, parents, and students. www.ldonline.org

- Great Schools: Addresses learning disabilities basics, including tips for parents and assistive technology recommendations. http://www.great schools.net/articles/67/LD/Identifying-a-Learning-Difficulty /LD-Basics

Mental Retardation

Nadene A. L'Amoreaux and Kelly E. Webb
Indiana University of Pennsylvania

General Background Information About Mental Retardation

Mental retardation is the term used in the Individuals with Disabilities Act (IDEA). However, many find it to be pejorative and use *developmental disability* instead.

Mental retardation (MR) affects 3 out of every 100 people in the United States. Nearly 613,000 children between the ages of six and twenty-one have some level of mental retardation and require special education services in school.[1] Diagnosis is made based on a child's intellectual functioning (IQ) and adaptive functioning. Children with IQ test scores below 70 are considered to have mental retardation. Scores between 55 and 70 are considered to be in mild range, and students who score in this range may appear typical compared to their nondiagnosed peers. Mild MR affects primarily intellectual functioning and is not associated with substantial behavioral problems.[2] Those who fall into the moderate category are considered to be trainable, learning best through repetition. (See Chapter Two related to the work of Marc Gold.) These individuals are likely to require lifelong assistance, as are individuals who fall into the severely and profoundly retarded categories. Individuals who score in between these levels also require varying degrees of assistance and support throughout life, which may include continued training with life skills, social skills, and job skills. Individuals who test in the severely and profoundly retarded categories also tend to display more significant behavioral problems.[3]

In order to measure adaptive behavior, children are compared to age-related peer groups to determine if, and how much, they differ from expected tasks for a developmental level. For example, children may be compared to their peers in terms of daily living skills (independence in getting dressed, toileting routines, and feeding), communication skills (understanding what is being said and being able to respond), and social skills (initiating interactions with and engaging in appropriate or expected social interactions with same-age peers). Deficits in both intellectual functioning and adaptive behavior are required for an MR diagnosis. A child who has deficits in only one area does not meet the criteria for MR. School counselors should consider other variables that could contribute to deficits in only one area, such as cultural factors or a child's life experiences.

Some common causes of mental retardation are genetic conditions, problems during pregnancy (such as exposure to high levels of mercury) or at birth (such as anoxia), and childhood health problems (such as exposure to lead, infections, or injury). Children with mental retardation may display certain signs: sitting up, crawling, or walking much later than expected for their developmental age; learning to talk later or having problems with speech; finding it hard to remember things; having trouble understanding social rules; not comprehending the consequences of their actions; and having trouble solving problems and thinking logically. Many children with mental retardation are not diagnosed until they are school aged and fail to meet the increasing intellectual requirements of the school environment.

Children diagnosed with mental retardation qualify for special education services under IDEA. Some children can attend a regular school with learning support and life skills training. Others may benefit from education and training in more structured alternative education environments. School personnel need to work closely with parents or other caregivers to determine the most appropriate educational environment for the child. In addition, children with MR will likely require intervention services such as occupational, physical, and speech therapy to achieve maximum functioning.

Special education and learning support classrooms are designed to help students learn both academic and independent living skills. Special education is tied closely to social and vocational training; these classes are designed to encourage self-determination. Teachers and parents can help a child to work on these skills both at school and home. Some of these skills include:

- Communication
- Taking care of personal needs (dressing, bathing, going to the bathroom)
- Health and safety
- Home living (helping to set the table, cleaning the house, or cooking dinner)
- Social skills (manners, knowing the rules of conversation, getting along in a group, playing a game)
- Reading, writing, and basic math[4]

What Students and Parents Wish
Their Teachers and Counselors Knew
About Mental Retardation

- "Please do not hug or show special affection to my child. Not every adult she meets will be safe and friendly, and she needs to learn boundaries and appropriate ways to interact."

- "Don't just assume my child can't do things. Take the time to show him what to do in a way that is meaningful to him."

- "Teaching strategies intended for children with intellectual disabilities will help my child learn better and make her easier for you to deal with."[5]

Practical Applications

Personal Applications

- Students with MR are at risk for social isolation, depression, teasing, and bullying. School counselors can provide effective interventions to promote social interaction, self-esteem development, and schoolwide anti-bullying response services to address these concerns.

- Children with MR are at increased risk of child abuse and sexual abuse. School personnel need to be attentive to signs of abuse and take steps to protect this particularly vulnerable population.

Social Applications

- Students with MR often need ongoing social skill development interventions, including assistance with feeling identification and expression, empathy development, respecting social boundaries, conversation skills, and turn-taking and self-management skills. Effective training strategies include repetition, turn taking, immediate feedback, and modeling of expected skills.

Academic Applications

- Students with impaired intellectual functioning need services and classroom accommodations to make the curriculum accessible to them. This includes teaching methods and adaptations that help the student understand the material. Concrete demonstrations that include visual cues rather than relying on verbal delivery of information are critical to relay new information and give directions. Breaking complicated or more involved processes into smaller tasks or steps is also necessary and may require additional assistance.

- Students with MR benefit most from curricular experiences that have relevance to life experiences, such as reading street signs and menus, managing personal finances, and establishing and keeping a schedule. Educational opportunities should not be limited to these activities; however, these activities should be built into the student's IEP.

- Applied behavioral analysis or concepts derived from behavioral approaches are effective in reinforcing mastery of steps involved in learning new skills.

Career Applications

- Students with impaired intellectual functioning often need assistance in acquiring life skills such as tasks of daily living (dressing or eating independently, grocery shopping, managing personal expenses), which increase and become more complex as the child ages; social skills (interacting appropriately with peers and authority figures), as well as career exploration. Students should be encouraged to participate as appropriate in group activities or experiences to develop these skills.

- Students with MR are likely to need a high level of assistance with completing job applications and interviewing skills. They also benefit from job coaching and on-the-job training in actual work settings. Some communities provide government-funded job opportunities for individuals with intellectual disabilities.

- The diagnosis of MR becomes less relevant once a student leaves school and finds sustainable employment, blending in well within communities and job sites.

Resources with More Detailed Information About Mental Retardation

- Centers for Disease Control and Prevention (n.d.). *Intellectual disability*. Provides information and resources to parents with children diagnosed with intellectual disabilities. http://www.cdc.gov/ncbddd/dd/ddmr.htm

- Special Needs Children: Provides information to caregivers related to parenting children with intellectual disabilities. http://specialchildren .about.com/od/mentalretardation/a/MRschool.htm

Oppositional Defiant Disorder/Conduct Disorder

Shanna Rovida

Indiana University of Pennsylvania

General Background Information About Oppositional Defiant Disorder/Conduct Disorder

Oppositional defiant disorder (ODD) and conduct disorder (CD) fall into the category of behavioral disorders of childhood and adolescence. This disorder is marked by negative behaviors that are harmful or annoying to others, noncompliance, defiance, and hostility toward adults beyond what one would expect to see for the child's developmental level. These children genuinely have problems at school with teachers, other authority figures, and peers. Because of their issues with authority figures, peers may not accept them, leading to lower functioning with peers of their age group. Other disorders may be a result of or contribute to a child's diagnosis of ODD/CD such as depression and attention deficit hyperactivity disorder. As children age, more troubling issues often begin to surface, such as physical aggression, destruction of property, alcohol and drug use, truancy, and running away. This disorder tends to interfere with individualized educational programs set in place because children diagnosed with ODD/CD are often noncompliant with services being offered. A child with ODD/CD may have issues related to self-esteem, emotional regulation, and conflictual relationships in home, school, and community. These children find it very difficult to compromise and resist redirection from adults. They are limit testers and will push boundaries set by adults in most settings. Because of their disruptive classroom behavior, their academic achievements may be low, they may become bullies, and they are less likely to respond to conventional consequences in the school setting. While children with ODD/CD may seem to be willfully engaging in misconduct, other considerations for these behaviors could include side effects of medication (irritability, fatigue, restlessness), stressors in school or other areas of their lives (moving, parental conflict) in which they do not have the emotional regulation skills to handle, or other mental health issues including depression.

There are protective factors, though, that tend to help a child deal better with ODD/CD, some of which are positive self-esteem, learning to be empathic to others, setting goals for the future, participating in recreational hobbies that are supervised, and a strong support system at home and at school. Students of lower socioeconomic status and of disruptive homes are more likely to have this diagnosis. Parental behaviors are often mimicked, and parental mental health issues often contribute to a student's diagnosis of ODD/CD.

There are many treatment options for ODD/CD, such as medication in addition to counseling. There is not medication specifically for ODD/CD, but there are medications that help decrease anxiety, depression, and irritability, which may be underlying contributions to the disorder. Other treatment options include parent management training, smaller class sizes with academic accommodations, and cognitive behavioral skills training. The more treatments used at one time, the more likely they are to be effective.

Some educators or school officials may still believe that ODD/CD is an "excuse" for a "bad kid." This may be because of the rapid increase of the diagnosis or misdiagnosis of this disorder in the past twenty-five years. What makes a child with ODD/CD different from a "bad kid" is that typical consequences do not work on children with ODD/CD, sometimes because the consequences do not make sense to the child. Children who have ODD/CD have difficulty regulating their own emotions, which makes it difficult to see how others feel. This may be seen as having lack of remorse or not caring about what they have done, especially when it involves hurting others' feelings or violating others' rights. A disability is considered "physical or mental impairment which substantially limits one or more major life activities." Although children with ODD/CD do not have a physical impairment, their mental and emotional states are not typical of those of their peers. Children with ODD/CD may require special attention, such as an IEP, therapeutic staff support, or a teacher's aide to better navigate their learning environment in regard to the social and emotional aspects of the school experience.

What Students and Parents Wish Their Teachers and Counselors Knew About Oppositional Defiant Disorder/Conduct Disorder

- "I get angry at myself when I can't do the right thing. I feel like everyone hates me, or they are ganging up on me. Then I feel even more mad."

- "Teachers don't get me. They don't listen to me."

- "I feel really frustrated when I can't tell people what I feel. I get so mad that I want to scream. My teacher will tell me to do something, and

I'm just focused on something else. Then when I actually do something right, I don't even get a smile."

- "My child has a real disorder. I'm not just a bad parent."
- "I do not know how to help my child. He/she will not listen to me either."
- "I feel very inadequate as a mother/father."

Practical Applications

Personal Applications

- *Emotional issues:* Children with ODD/CD have emotional regulation issues, which may make it difficult to calm down when they are angry, sad, or frustrated. Emotional support classrooms, time-out rooms, and quiet corners may be helpful for teachers to direct the child to as needed. These spaces offer privacy and time away from an activity so that the child can process in quiet isolation what is upsetting him or her so as to be able to return to the activity or class.

Social Applications

- *Problematic social-behavioral issues:* Children with ODD/CD have difficulty playing with and socializing with peers. They may be argumentative and need to feel that they are in charge. Many peers do not agree with this type of friend and dislike the company of a child with ODD/CD. Teachers should be as inclusive as possible so that other children can find the positive qualities within a child who has ODD/CD rather than the symptoms of the disorder. School counselors may want to present information about children with difficulties in this area to other students in the ODD/CD child's class. They may do well by asking for the ODD/CD child's input so that there is more inclusion and a form of positive adult attention as well.

Academic Applications

- *Limit setting:* Children with ODD/CD have a tendency to push the limits in any setting. They should always be given a choice between at least two options. Even when two options seem to be unavailable, a small modification to the first option may be the second option. The child may attempt to make up his or her own option, but the child must choose an option given by an adult. If the child refuses to choose, he or she should have time to reflect on the two choices. Until the choice is made, the child should not return to or participate in the activity he or she was drawn away from. This situation may become emotionally draining to adults, who need to remember to stay in control of the situation by using a soft and calming voice so as not to keep the situation from escalating.

- *Reinforcement of positive behaviors:* Children with ODD/CD respond well to positive praise. When a child does something positive, large or small, it should be expressly valued and talked about.

Career Applications

- *Proper environmental and work demand fit:* Because these individuals are at high risk for unemployment, underemployment, or frequently changing jobs, students diagnosed with ODD/CD need guidance in identifying their abilities, developing skills in relating to coworkers, and receiving instruction from supervisors.

Resources with More Detailed Information About Oppositional Defiant Disorder/Conduct Disorder

- AACAP (American Academy of Child and Adolescent Psychiatry): A national organization supporting children with mental illness. This Web site contains articles with information about ODD/CD, as well as linkages to physicians, meeting information, and resources. www.aacap.org

- Behavioral Neurotherapy Clinic: A Web site with information on all types of behavioral disorders, as well as signs, symptoms, treatments, and other information about ODD/CD. www.adhd.com.au

- About.com: Special Education: A Web site explaining ODD/CD with behavior support resources, classroom management techniques, and discipline techniques. www.specialed.about.com/od/specialedacronyms/g/ODD.htm

- Education Articles: This Web site offers many articles on ODD/CD for educators and those working in the academic setting. There are articles on tools for ODD/CD children, safety information, treatments, and threat for violence. www.edarticle.com/special-education/ODD

Other Orthopedic Impairments

Scott Shaw

Indiana University of Pennsylvania

General Background Information About Other Orthopedic Impairments

For the purposes of this section, other orthopedic impairments (OOI) can be defined as weakening, damage, or deterioration, especially as a result of injury, disease, or disorder of the skeletal system and associated muscles, joints, and ligaments, exclusive of cerebral palsy, spina bifida, and degenerative orthopedic disease (muscular dystrophy). OOI may commonly include fractures, amputations, burns that cause contractures, fibrous dysplasia, poliomyelitis (polio), rheumatoid arthritis, metabolic bone disorders (osteogenesis imperfecta), osteomyelitis, bone tuberculosis, arthrogryposis, scoliosis, and spinal cord injuries.[1]

Although orthopedic impairments may occur with other disabilities that affect cognition, they themselves do not have an impact on cognitive abilities. OOI primarily result in physical limitations but may secondarily cause social and emotional problems.[2] Physical manifestations of OOI range widely from limited use of one appendage or joint (fractures, monostotic fibrous dysplasia) to quadriplegia with respiratory involvement (severe spinal cord injury).[3] Common manifestations are loss of range of motion, impaired gait, loss of mobility, balance problems, fine-motor impairment, physical deformities or disfigurement, fractures, hearing loss (in metabolic bone disorders), and acute or chronic pain.

OOI may occur in conjunction with or be the result of trauma (brain injury, vehicle crashes, child abuse) or result from a disease process. Regardless of the cause, the child with an OOI experiences significant adjustment issues and barriers to success. Children who experience an OOI resulting from trauma, which can also be induced by painful medical procedures or treatments, may also experience posttraumatic emotional problems.[4] While students with OOI represent a relatively small percentage of the population, their needs can be significant and must be met in an individualized fashion.

What Students and Parents Wish Their Teachers and Counselors Knew About OOI

- "I can't do what other kids can do, at least not as easily as they can, but that doesn't mean that I don't have the same interests that they do. I may not be able to play football, but love watching it, and I know all the players!"

- "I get tired easily and have a hard time doing school work after going to lunch and recess. It takes more time for me to get there [lunch/recess], and then I'm worn out. I can't do as well on tests or homework in the afternoon."

- "I don't mind when the other kids ask about my hook [prosthesis], but I wish they wanted to know more about me than that and asked about normal things about me."

- "My son has missed a lot of school this year for surgeries and treatment. It helped him to come back each time after getting notes from his classmates. It let him know that he mattered."

- "Every year I have to explain what accommodations my child needs to her teachers. Some understand and really want to do what is best to help her, but others don't want to be bothered. They act like it's too much work for them. They don't realize that they are sending the message to her that she is not worth the extra effort, when she has to put forth extra effort all the time."

Practical Applications

Personal Applications

- Respecting issues related to a student's wheelchair or other mobility aid can be an important first step in forming a collaborative relationship. Using a person's wheelchair as a leaning post or footrest is extremely disrespectful as it violates his or her personal body space.[5] Similarly, crutches, canes, and walkers should not be used for alternative purposes and should be kept as close as possible to the student.

- Students with OOI may benefit from individual or group counseling that addresses adjustment to disability, trauma, and coping strategies. Support groups or counseling groups composed entirely of children with physical disabilities can create a system of social support and help students generate solutions to common problems.[6]

- OOIs frequently create the need for adaptive or assistive technologies. Mobility aids (wheelchairs, walkers, crutches), braces, modified or adaptive art supplies, and custom physical education equipment may be required. In addition, mobility impairments may necessitate that classrooms, buildings, and physical activities be modified to provide the student access to programs.[7] Older students can be involved in this process through the participatory action research model (PAR), which involves participants in defining problems, collecting and analyzing data, and creating solutions. PAR can offer the additional benefit of creating a sense of empowerment and independence.[8]

Social Applications

- In a small percentage of cases, the results of chronic pain, social isolation, frustration, and trauma will manifest in behavioral problems. Students who exhibit behavioral problems may benefit from counseling sessions or a combination of counseling and behavioral interventions.

- Mobility impairments can be an isolating factor for students with OOI. They may not be able to sit in bleachers, ride the school bus, climb stairs, or engage in physical games and other activities with their peers. These barriers create both physical and emotional separation from peers and can be a source of frustration, anxiety, and depression.[9] Peer support groups, adult mentors, and social activities that are designed to be inclusive may help students develop relationships and combat isolation. In addition, some students find social connections and empowerment in student clubs that address disability issues. For example, student organizations could identify modifications to the environment that would lead to more inclusion (for example, using school buses with lifts to transport students to away games) and present those suggestions to school administrators.

Academic Applications

- Students with OOI may require academic accommodations to make education accessible to them. Accommodations should be determined individually, as each student's need is different.

- Special seating in class to accommodate mobility aids or a change in the layout of the classroom to accommodate navigation through the room may be necessary.

- Alternative methods of teaching and communication may be required if the student has auditory or speech impairment. The method of expressing and receiving information that is best for the student should be used to maximize learning opportunities. Homework should also be provided in this format.

- Accommodating communication impairments can be accomplished through the use of sign language interpreters, multiple formats (printed and oral), communication devices, or note takers. Note takers or recording devices may also be necessary for students that have difficulty writing.

- Physical education should be provided in normal settings with adaptations whenever possible.[10]

- Additional time to complete assignments or alternative assignments might be appropriate.

- Testing modifications may be appropriate for students with writing problems or other motor impairments, fatigue, chronic pain, or communication problems. Testing accommodations could include extended or untimed tests, a scribe to record answers given orally, the use of a computer to type instead of writing manually, multiple choice instead of essay (or the opposite), or as an alternative to a test, students could be allowed to develop a portfolio that demonstrates their knowledge.[11]

- Establishing a classroom routine that takes into account the student's physical and health care needs can minimize distractions and maximize learning time. For example, if a student has an impaired gait and tires easily, scheduling a bathroom break when other classes are not in the hall is a better choice than asking the student to expend the extra time and energy required to navigate through crowded hallways. In addition, the time and energy the student saved can be put to good use in the classroom.

Career Applications

- Some of the primary concerns in career counseling for this population are accessibility, transportation, and physical requirements. Accessibility is widely viewed as an issue of physical access, and while this is a significant issue, it is not the sum total of accessibility. Students also need to be able to access the primary method of communication used by an employer. For many companies today, that method is e-mail. For students with fine-motor impairments, access might mean using adaptive software that allows them to use verbal commands to control their computer. Students should be encouraged to visit a potential work site and read an official job description to determine accessibility needs.

- School counselors can assist students with OOIs by connecting them with state vocational rehabilitation agencies. These agencies can provide information on a variety of accessibility issues and conduct assessments related to transportation and cognitive and physical abilities. School counselors should encourage students to investigate workplace culture to determine if a specific company is inclusive and accepting of all people. Finally, students with OOIs may benefit from learning to self-advocate when their accessibility needs are not being met.

Resources with More Detailed Information About Other Orthopedic Impairments

- Osteogenesis Imperfecta Foundation: A nonprofit organization providing disability-specific information and support. http://www.oif.org

- National Institute of Arthritis and Musculoskeletal and Skin Diseases: One of the National Institutes of Health. Provides information on treatment and research related to specific disabilities. http://www.niams.nih.gov/Health_Info/Bone/Osteogenesis_Imperfecta/default.asp

- National Association of Parents with Children in Special Education: A nonprofit organization dedicated to providing the information parents need to become good advocates for their children. http://www.napcse.org/

- NDRN (National Disability Rights Network): A nonprofit organization providing legal advocacy services to people with disabilities as part of the federally mandated Protection and Advocacy and Client Assistance Programs. The NDRN works to create equal opportunity and freedom of choice for people with disabilities by providing legal advocacy, legislative advocacy, technical assistance, and training. Areas of focus include "health care, education, employment, housing, transportation, and within the juvenile and criminal justice systems." http://www.napas.org/

- National Dissemination Center for Children with Disabilities (NICHY): A project of the Academy for Educational Development and funded by the U.S. Department of Education. NICHY provides a wealth of information on specific disabilities and disability issues, including the Individuals with Disabilities Act and No Child Left Behind. Disability fact sheets may be printed from the Web site. http://www.nichcy.org/index.html

Seizures

Scott Shaw

Indiana University of Pennsylvania

General Background Information About Seizures

A seizure is a brief event that can include change in consciousness, awareness, and physical activity. The vast majority of seizures are epileptic seizures, which occur due to an electrical disturbance or abnormal misfiring in the brain. There are also nonepileptic seizures, which are the result of physiological processes originating outside the central nervous system; they include pseudo-seizures, syncopal episodes, and seizures resulting from events that include high fevers or drug withdrawal.[1] Seizures can manifest in different physical, cognitive, and behavioral symptoms and may or may not include a loss of consciousness.[2] The period during which a seizure occurs is referred to as the *ictal state*, while before and after are referred to as *pre-* and *post-ictal*, respectively. Seizures may last for as little as a few seconds, or as long as a few minutes. Seizures lasting longer than five minutes or occurring one after another may be a medical emergency known as *status epilepticus* and require immediate medical attention.

Seizures can take many forms but typically include a loss of consciousness. Other symptoms may include a brief period of rigidity and arching of the back, followed by a lengthier period of contractions of the extremities. Seizures may begin with a loud grunt, gasp, or cry as the thoracic muscles contract and forcefully expel air from the lungs. Interrupted breathing and loss of bowel or bladder control are common. Symptoms may also be characterized by a sudden loss of muscle tone that may involve a localized area, such as the neck or an extremity, or the entire body, as well as sudden contractions of localized muscle groups. There is typically no warning that a generalized seizure will occur. However, some individuals report an aura that may include abdominal discomfort, olfactory hallucinations, a sense of déjà-vu, or any number of other unique experiences. Generalized seizures are usually followed by a state that may include confusion, disorientation, fear, extreme fatigue, and emotional upset.[3]

There may be other symptoms that range from subtle to very dramatic and include changes in cognition, loss of memory, odd behavior, or a change in personality. Attempts to disrupt the behaviors exhibited during partial seizures may result in undirected aggression and agitation.[4] Simple and complex partial seizures are unique in that the child may appear to be conscious and self-directed, but these changes are the result of seizure activity.

Although seizures are discreet, time-limited events, they can have profound long-term consequences for children. There is no correlation between seizure activity and IQ, but seizures may be associated with cognitive dysfunction, behavior problems, attentional difficulties, learning disabilities, social isolation and stigma, anxiety and mood disorders, and a high rate of suicidal ideation.[5] These factors can be affected by age of onset, frequency of seizures, course of treatment, medication compliance, home and school supports, and pre- and comorbid conditions.[6] Proper medical treatment and home and school supports are necessary protective factors to reduce or manage the occurrence of these comorbid conditions.

Controlling seizures with medications frequently involves trading seizures for side effects. In general, physicians attempt to identify one antiepileptic drug (AED) with as few side effects as possible to control seizures. However, children who experience multiple types of seizures or do not respond to a single medication may be required to take multiple medications. These medications have potentially serious side effects, including cognitive dysfunction, behavioral problems, drowsiness, hyperactivity, weight gain or loss, confusion, irritability, loss of balance, bone marrow suppression (a potentially life-threatening condition), and depression.[7] Children on antiseizure medications require constant medical monitoring, which may include blood tests for serum levels, complete blood count, and tests of liver function. Some nonpharmacological interventions have been shown to decrease the frequency of seizures. Progressive muscle relaxation training, improved self-monitoring, family training, and biofeedback may all help to reduce seizures by addressing psychosocial factors that contribute to seizure activity.[8]

School personnel are advised that a seizure action plan be developed for all children who experience seizures and should involve parental input as well as medical recommendations.[9] Seizures can be frightening and disorienting for the child, who may require comfort and reassurance, as well as a period of rest.[10] Education and debriefing with peers who might witness a seizure is also recommended, not only to address concerns of the peers but also to assist in the reentry of the student who experienced the seizure to the classroom.

What Students and Parents Wish Their Teachers and Counselors Knew About Seizures

- "Having seizures doesn't mean I can't think or that I have mental retardation as well. Most young people with seizures do the same things that other kids do most of the time."

The School Counselor's Guide to Helping Students with Disabilities

- "For most people who have seizures, the cause is unknown, and they do not necessarily have abnormal EEGs [electroencephalograms]. In most ways, they may function as anyone else does."

- "Sometimes the medications I take may make me tired, and it may take longer for me to get work done."

Practical Applications

Personal Applications

- In addition to the need for care during and after a seizure, children who experience seizures may need help dealing with feelings of embarrassment, isolation, frustration, anxiety, and depression. Children who experience seizures are more than twice as likely as their peers to have suicidal ideation, though the rate of suicidal acts does not appear to be elevated.[11] Having seizures at school can be a traumatizing and isolating experience for children. Offering support to the child and family can help to mitigate these negative experiences.[12]

- Children may require the services of the school nurse to administer medications and coordinate the seizure action plan.

Social Applications

- Helping the child who has seizures individually and directly is an important first step, but there are indirect actions that can also be beneficial. Because seizures can be frightening to watch and because they sometimes cause unusual behavior, there is a stigma associated with having them. Children who experience seizures at school are more likely to be teased and to be socially isolated.[13] Peer and staff education programs can increase knowledge, decrease fear and encourage acceptance.

Academic Applications

- Normal intellectual functioning is common in children who experience seizures. However, some may require academic accommodations due to the direct effects of the seizures, the underlying cause, the effects of antiepileptic drugs, or comorbid conditions.[14]

  - Because many seizures cause memory loss, directions and homework assignments should always be provided in written form.

- Students may need preferential seating so the teacher can monitor for seizure activity.

- Additional time may be required for homework and testing due to attentional difficulties.[15]

- A regular routine can minimize the impact of memory loss and provide stability for the child.

- A note taker for class time lost to seizures may be required. Modified physical education may be necessary.

- Because no two students who experience seizures will have exactly the same needs, an individualized approach is absolutely necessary.

Career Applications

- It is important that the frequency and type of seizure, as well as the resulting impact, be considered when doing career counseling.

  - Many individuals with good seizure control have few or no limits in terms of career pursuit or participation.

  - Most adults with epilepsy are capable of driving, but those who have seizures not controlled by antiepileptic drugs cannot.[16] If seizure control is an issue, then a job that requires driving would not be a good choice.

  - Comorbid conditions like cognitive dysfunctions, anxiety, and mood disorders should be taken into account. If these conditions are pronounced, one might consider jobs that offer relatively low stress and flexible schedules.

Resources with More Detailed Information About Seizures

- Epilepsy Foundation: A national nonprofit organization geared toward providing information, education, resources, and national advocacy. Useful forms can be downloaded from its Web site. http://www.epilepsyfoundation.org/

- NDRN (National Disability Rights Network): A nonprofit organization providing legal advocacy services to people with disabilities as part of the federally mandated Protection and Advocacy and Client Assistance Programs. The NDRN works to create equal opportunity and freedom of choice for people with disabilities by providing legal advocacy, legislative advocacy, technical assistance, and training. Areas of focus include "health care, education, employment, housing, transportation, and within the juvenile and criminal justice systems." http://www.napas.org/

- National Dissemination Center for Children with Disabilities (NICHCY): A project of the Academy for Educational Development and funded by the U.S. Department of Education. NICHCY provides a wealth of information on specific disabilities and disability issues, including the Individuals with Disabilities Act and No Child Left Behind. Disability fact sheets may be printed from the Web site. http://www.nichcy.org/index.html

Speech and Language Disorders

Angela Orbin
Indiana University of Pennsylvania

General Background Information About Speech and Language Disorders

Speech and language disorders refer to difficulties with receptive and expressive communication. These difficulties range from problems such as sound production errors to more complex problems such as difficulty with oral motor functioning or understanding speech.[1] By first grade, approximately 5 percent of students have evident speech disorders without a known cause. Children with speech and language disorders exhibit normal levels of intelligence and have otherwise normal development or may present with other disorders and disabilities, including autism, cerebral palsy, and Down syndrome.[2] Hearing loss and deafness are commonly associated with speech and language disorders since lack of audition during critical developmental periods can interfere with language development.[3]

Children with speech disorders may have difficulty producing intelligible speech sounds; trouble using appropriate vocal pitch, volume, and quality; or problems with speech fluency. Language disorders are characterized by difficulty understanding or using verbal language skills at an age appropriate level. Students with language disorders may have trouble understanding or following directions, may experience difficulty following verbal classroom content or socializing using language, may be unable to express ideas, or may have trouble communicating with others. Someone with a language disorder may hear or see a word, phrase, or sentence but not understand what it means or the correct way to use it. Students with language problems often have difficulty with idiomatic expressions or jokes. Research has shown that the critical period for children to acquire language is during the first few years of life.[4] Because brain development makes learning language easiest before age five, early intervention is critical for children with speech and language disorders.[5] Normally children have naturally acquired language skills by this age. Early identification of a disorder by age three increases the likelihood of successful improvement.[6]

Speech and language disorders can affect learning in many ways. Students often have difficulty understanding what is being said and are unable to respond and participate in class discussions. Students often miss important information during lessons and can misunderstand assignments. Reading comprehension difficulties affect both reading-related classes and other subjects, such as word problems in math class. Students also have problems communicating with and working with their classmates as it is often difficult for others to understand what they are saying.[7] Some of the speech and language disorders teachers and counselors may encounter are as follows:

- *Developmental apraxia of speech* (also known as *verbal apraxia* or *dyspraxia)* causes a person to have trouble saying what he or she wants to say correctly and consistently. It is not related to speech muscles or delayed speech, and it is present from birth as a motor planning disorder. Apraxia is more common in boys than girls and is characterized by difficulty with volitional sound production to form words and sentences. The child may appear to be searching for the correct sound. The ability to use words and language is markedly inconsistent. What may come easily one day will be difficult the next. Children with apraxia may have normal comprehension skills.

- *Stuttering* refers to disrupted speech flow and repetition of sound. Stuttering may be accompanied by eye blinks, trembling lips, or other visible struggles in the face or upper body that are used in the attempt to speak. Three million people in the United States are affected by stuttering. It is three times more common in boys than girls. It is most common between the ages of two and six, when language is developing. Children often outgrow it.[8]

- *Phonological disorder* is the failure to use speech sounds in a way that is developmentally appropriate. Symptoms include the inability to produce and use sound correctly, substituting one sound for another, and omitting sounds. Phonological disorders are more common in boys than girls, and affect 3 percent of preschool-age children and 2 percent of six and seven year olds. Early intervention through speech therapy is very successful in correcting these disorders. By the age of seventeen, less than 0.5 percent of students have a phonological disorder.

- *Developmental expressive language disorder* occurs when a child has lower-than-normal vocabulary proficiency and an inability to produce complex sentences, use correct tense, or find appropriate words. Approximately 3 to 10 percent of school-age children are affected.

- *Mixed receptive-expressive language disorder* is an impairment of both understanding (receptive) and expression of language. Three to 5 percent of children have one or both disorders. These symptoms include problems with language comprehension and expression, numerous articulation errors, and difficulty recalling early sight or sound memories.[9]

- *Cleft palate* is a birth defect defined by an incomplete closure of the roof of the mouth that can be surgically repaired at a very young age. Cleft palate often leads to speech difficulty, including problems with articulation. Speech development is complicated when adult teeth come in.[10]

- *Orofacial myofunctional disorders* affect children whose tongue moves forward in an exaggerated way during speech, affecting the sound. Normally tongue thrusting is outgrown during infancy. Children with this disorder may become self-conscious about the way they look and sound.

- *Speech sound disorders* are characterized by difficulty with making sounds and forming sound patterns. This may include substituting sounds formed in the back of the mouth for sounds formed in the front (for example, *tup* instead of *cup*) or using only one consonant instead of two (for example, *poon* instead of *spoon*).

- *Selective mutism* (formerly known as *elective mutism*) often occurs in childhood when a child does not speak in at least one social setting. However, this child can and does speak in other situations. This disorder typically occurs when a child is starting school, usually before five years of age. It is not a communication disorder and is not related to lack of knowledge. Children with selective mutism often have anxiety disorders, excessive shyness, fear of social embarrassment, or social isolation and withdrawal.[11] Pediatricians and psychologists should be included in the team when working with a student with selective mutism.

- *Social language use (pragmatics)* refers to lack of knowledge about the appropriate way to use language and facial expressions in social situations. These children may offend others when they mean no harm. They have difficulty knowing how to speak in the classroom versus the playground, difficulty taking turns in a conversation, and struggle to stay on topic. A student with a pragmatic disorder may say inappropriate things, display disorganized storytelling, and use little variety in language. In the classroom, these students often have lower social acceptance from classmates and may avoid talking to their peers.[12]

- *Nonverbal.* Some students are totally nonverbal due to motor involvement that prevents them from using their speech musculature or brain damage to the motor parts of the brain. This may occur in types of cerebral palsy, paralysis, or neurological disorders that have an impact on movement. Being nonverbal does not mean that these students have limited cognitive skills, although uninformed teachers may believe this is the case. Alternative and augmentative communication devices may be appropriate for these students who should be evaluated by specialists who usually have backgrounds in speech language pathology and occupational therapy. Due to advances in technology, nonverbal students who use these devices and computer adaptations may be included in regular programs, attend college, and succeed in many careers and employment settings but may be steered into limited options by counselors who do not understand their potential.

Treatment for speech and language disorders is under the direction of a speech and language pathologist. Parents, teachers, counselors, pediatricians, and school psychologists may work together with the speech and language pathologist. The team approach is recommended because children with speech and language disorders often have social and academic problems due to their inability to communicate basic needs and difficulty being understood by others.[13] Augmentative and alternate communication devices provide ways of communicating for students with severe disabilities who are unable to use speech to interact with their peers, teachers, and families. Using a device minimizes the separation students feel from their classmates and allows them to participate in class and enhance their educational experience.[14]

What Students and Parents Wish Their Teachers and Counselors Knew About Speech and Language Disorders

- "I'm just a normal kid."

- "I'm afraid the other kids will make fun of me if I try to speak in class."[15]

- "I don't know what any of them are talking about."

- "Everyone assumes he has behavior problems, but he's not a bad kid."

- "I want to help my child succeed in life, but she has very low self-confidence."

- "I'm doing everything I can at home to support my child's speech development, but we need support from the teachers too."

Practical Applications

Personal Applications

- Students with speech and language disorders frequently do not perform at grade level. They struggle with reading, understanding, and expressing language. They often misunderstand social cues.[16] Speech-language pathologists can work with students and teachers to develop effective ways of communicating in the classroom.[17]

- Children can learn how to use language better by talking to others and practicing.[18] Teachers can facilitate this by providing opportunities for the children to speak in a relaxed environment, such as a small group, without criticism.

Social Applications

- If difficulties with social interaction are not dealt with, they may lead to problems with social interaction into adulthood.[19] Most speech and language therapists focus on enhancing communication in social settings.

Academic Applications

- Speech-language pathologists can work with teachers to integrate language goals with functional performance and academic goals.

- Teachers may be encouraged to use small groups in order to reduce anxiety in the classroom.[20]

- When it is developmentally appropriate, students should be encouraged to write down words they do not understand or try to use new words in conversation.

- One-on-one work: Teachers or assistants may be encouraged to work individually with students. An example would be to have the students paraphrase oral directions given by the teacher, repeat directions again, and explain the directions in their own words.[21]

Career Applications

- Career implications with this disorder are unique to the specific needs of the individual. School counselors are encouraged to consult Chapter Nine for career and workplace considerations.

Resources with More Detailed Information About Speech and Language Disorders

- ASHA (American Speech-Language-Hearing Association). A professional organization for speech language pathologists, audiologists, and hearing specialists. The ASHA Web site has several informative and scholarly resources that are helpful for professionals working with individuals with speech and language disorders. www.asha.org

- NIDCD (National Institute on Deafness and Other Communication Disorders): A branch of the National Institutes of Health that is focused on research, support, and prevention for communication disorders. It offers an extensive online collection of research and helpful information for those who are interested in learning more about communication disorders. www.nidcd.nih.gov

- DynaVox: An augmentative and alternate communication solutions provider that provides electronic communication devices and support information for families. www.dynavoxtech.com

Spina Bifida

Katherine A. Piscopo
Indiana University of Pennsylvania

General Background Information About Spina Bifida

Spina bifida, a congenital disability that develops in approximately the fourth week of pregnancy, occurs when the embryo's spine does not fuse completely, resulting in an opening. This opening can result in spinal cord or a membrane protrusion. There are two major types of spina bifida: spina bifida occulta and manifesta. Spina bifida occulta often results in minimal symptoms, and some people do not even know they have it until later in life when they experience back pain. Spina bifida manifesta results in functional limitations and there are two subtypes: menigocele and myelomeningocele.

Spina bifida menigocele occurs when the membrane that provides protection for spinal cord (the meninges) protrudes through the vertebrae, resulting in a sac called the *meningocele*. Spina bifida myelomeningocele results when the meninges and some of the spinal cord protrude through the deformed spine. Because the spinal cord is involved in this type of spina bifida, it is probable that the individual will be paralyzed in some capacity. The paralysis is more extreme the higher the opening is on the spine. A common side effect of this type of spina bifida is hydrocephalus, or fluid surrounding the brain. Individuals with hydrocephalus usually have a thin tube that drains the fluid from the brain called a shunt. It is important to be aware if the child has a shunt because the symptoms of shunt malfunction can be confused with other sicknesses. For example, shunt malfunction may result in vomiting and headache. In rare cases, a shunt malfunction might result in seizures and a difference in personality and ability to accomplish schoolwork. Shunt malfunctions can also be fatal.

In some cases of spina bifida, a phenomenon known as Chiari malformation can be present. This malformation occurs when part of the brain stem is combined with the cervical spine. The number of symptoms associated with the Chiari malformation depend on how far down the spine the brain stem descends. In this case, the farther down, the more severe the symptoms. Chiari malformation symptoms differ by the age of the child. School-aged children with the Chiari malformation may experience severe stiffness in the arms and hands that limits control and mobility. Children with spina bifida may also experience full or partial paralysis, difficulties with bowel and bladder control, learning disabilities, latex allergies, and mental health issues including depression. They are at increased risk for social isolation, bullying and rejection by peers as well as lower self-esteem.[1]

What Students and Parents Wish Their Teachers and Counselors Knew About Spina Bifida

- "I had learning problems that went undiagnosed until I was an adult, so at times even I thought I was stupid."[2]

- "Due to my hydrocephalus, I have a non-verbal learning disability, which causes me to have some problems with math, comprehension and other subjects."[3]

- "We don't pity her or treat her any different—she can get into trouble just as our other daughter can and of course does! Treat your child different and they will be different."[4]

- "Seeing my daughter tackle her challenges and take life head-on has been such an inspiration. She has an amazing inner strength and deals with problems and limitations most adults couldn't handle."[5]

Practical Applications

Personal Applications

- Symptoms of depression can be especially concerning in those with spina bifida. This is because depressive symptoms can be related to a malfunction in a shunt or caused by an infection. Symptoms of depression include a difference in amount of sleep and food intake, attentiveness, and lack of interest in leisure activities. Individuals with spina bifida are also more susceptible to attention deficit hyperactivity disorder, especially those with spina bifida and hydrocephalus.[6]

Social Applications

- Making friends in school might be more difficult for a child with spina bifida for many reasons, including limited opportunities to interact socially with peers. School counselors can assist by limiting the number of times these students are pulled out of naturally occurring social opportunities during the school day, capitalizing on common interests shared by students in the classroom, providing group opportunities including friendship or social skills groups, and encouraging teachers to incorporate positive group interactions within the classroom.

Academic Applications

- Individuals with spina bifida and hydrocephalus commonly are of average intelligence, usually possessing strengths in reading rather than in math. They can have difficulty with writing due to motor activity deficits. There are eight general areas related to learning that individuals with spina bifida may have difficulty with: perceptual motor skills, comprehension, attention, hyperactivity, memory, organization, sequencing, and decision making skills. In order for the student with spina bifida to benefit from education, the following accommodations should be considered for the child's individualized educational program: allowing the child extra time to copy notes, assigning a peer mentor and giving the child more time to complete class work, and permitting the use of educational tools such as a calculator or computer to complete assignments and tests.

- Teachers should be aware of their classroom setup. Many students with spina bifida need assistance with movement, such as wheelchairs or leg braces. Because of this, the teacher should be mindful of physical obstacles the child might encounter. Some children with spina bifida have a catheter. Teachers should allow more time for the child during bathroom breaks.

Career Applications

- Students with spina bifida will benefit greatly from transition plans that promote their ability to be as independent as possible in life skills as well as employment skills. Job shadowing, school-to-work programs, and community partnerships may be resources to incorporate into successful transition planning.

Resources with More Detailed Information About Spina Bifida

- KidsHealth. www.kidshealth.org
- Spina Bifida Association. www.sbaa.org

Traumatic Brain Injury

Scott Shaw

Indiana University of Pennsylvania

General Background Information About Traumatic Brain Injury

Acquired brain injury (ABI) includes all brain injuries (for example, stroke, anoxia, chemical poisoning, falls, gunshots, near drowning) that are not congenital in nature or a result of birth trauma. Traumatic brain injuries (TBIs) are ABIs that are the result of an external physical force. A TBI can be caused by something physically impacting the head (for example, falls, vehicle crashes), by something causing the head to rapidly accelerate and decelerate (for example, shaken baby syndrome), or by something penetrating the brain (for example, gunshot, stabbing).[1] The definition used by the Individuals with Disabilities Education Act (IDEA) excludes nontraumatic brain injuries, but children with nontraumatic brain injuries may still qualify for services under the category of Other Health Impairments.[2]

At the time of injury, TBI is classified as being mild, moderate, or severe. Mild TBI involves a brief change in mental status or consciousness, for example, a concussion. Moderate TBI is characterized by a period of unconsciousness (usually less than twenty-four hours). Severe TBI is defined by a prolonged loss of consciousness (coma) that may last for days or weeks. This classification system is misleading, as it is not necessarily predictive of long-term outcomes.[3] Even a mild TBI can result in permanent dysfunction or disability, while some people who experience severe TBI will experience remarkable recovery of function.

TBI is separated into closed-head and open-head injuries. Open-head injuries pose a greater infection risk and tend to be associated with more severe injury. However, closed-head injuries present unique problems as the brain swells and presses against the cranium, which can cause additional injury. Furthermore, closed-head injuries are more likely to be missed by emergency medical personnel. Any delay in treating brain injury can have devastating consequences, as the chemicals released by the destruction of one brain cell are damaging to surrounding cells. This chemical toxicity sets up a domino effect that must be treated immediately.

Because the brain controls all physical, cognitive, behavioral, emotional, and psychological processes, the long-term impact of TBI can take many forms. Some survivors have no mobility, hearing, or cognitive dysfunction, but can speak, though with difficulty (expressive aphasia). Some have no impairment except mobility. Still others experience massive mood swings, severe cognitive dysfunction, sensory issues, seizures, hypersexuality, depression, anxiety, or memory loss. In general, type and severity of dysfunction are dictated by location and severity of injury and tend to be unique to each individual and to change over time. Children specifically may not experience difficulties immediately following a brain injury because the damage may occur in a part of the brain responsible for functions beyond their stage of development at the time of injury.[4] For this reason, it is essential that children continue to be monitored and assessed and that the child's neuropsychological evaluations be current.

What Students and Parents Wish Their Teachers and Counselors Knew About Traumatic Brain Injury

- "I want to be listened to; to do reading, English, science and math [like the other kids do]."

- "Each brain injury is different and unique and comes with its own challenges. A teacher/counselor needs to find the strengths from within each student."

- "It takes patience and persistence. Never assume one has reached a plateau. Never give up HOPE."

Practical Applications

Personal Applications

- A child with a TBI has not only suffered a traumatic event, but may be facing a lifelong disability. Perhaps most significant is the fact that TBI can change who a person is by changing psychological and emotional processes and cognitive function. Frequently survivors remember who they were before their injury. Adapting to these changes as well as specific disabilities is a long and difficult process that may require counseling.[5]

In addition, anxiety and depression are commonly associated with TBI, as is an increased risk for alcohol and substance abuse, all of which may benefit from counseling, in addition to any medical treatment being received. Families can be devastated by the TBI of a child emotionally and financially and may require support or referral.[6]

- Adaptive technology may be required for some children to have access to educational opportunities. Common items include memory aids, communication devices, tape recorders, braces, and mobility aids. While these devices create additional opportunities, they also make the child different and may be a source of conflict for the child, particularly as he or she enters adolescence.

Social Applications

- Social problems are common, including the loss of friends, and may be the result of stigma and isolation, inappropriate behaviors, lack of initiative or motivation, or the inability of the child to properly interpret social cues. Studies have shown that social isolation and loss of friends are positively correlated with the severity of the injury.[7] It must be understood that TBI may have a severe impact on the child's social awareness, abilities, and behaviors. Problematic behaviors may include inappropriate comments, touching of self or others, decreased awareness of personal space, and inappropriate emotional responses, to name a few. Some children may benefit from functional behavior assessment, and the resulting plan of treatment.[8] TBI awareness programs for staff and students may help to mitigate the impact of these behaviors. Some states have statewide or regional consulting teams that conduct trainings or seminars, and in some cases consult on school reentry.[9] State affiliates of the Brain Injury Association of America can usually provide contact information.

Academic Applications

- Children with TBI may experience neurological impairments, cognitive dysfunction, and emotional and behavior problems that interfere with their ability to function academically. Neurological impairments may include seizures (posttraumatic epilepsy), sleep disorders, headaches, sensory issues, and impaired motor function. Cognitive dysfunction may be characterized by problems with thinking, reasoning or problem solving, short-term memory loss, or poor attention and concentration. Emotional and behavioral problems include emotional instability, impulsivity, poor initiation, inappropriate behaviors, and a lack of awareness of deficits known as anosognosia.[10] Any of these may confound the learning process and may require intervention or accommodation.

- Accommodations for sensory issues may include minimizing distractions of noise, light, and movement and may require seating near the front of the classroom. A consistent, predictable classroom routine will minimize distractions and can be organized to moderate behavioral and mobility issues as well as fatigue. Functional assessments can be used to help develop appropriate routines that minimize problem behaviors. Teaching methods (auditory, visual, tactile/kinesthetic) should be geared toward the child's relative strength.[11] In addition, adaptive or assistive technology devices can be used to accommodate visual, auditory, or speech deficits; impaired mobility; or short-term memory loss. Finally, children may require extended or untimed testing, note-taking assistance, learning support, or special education placement.

Career Applications

- Career planning for a student with a TBI should take into account specific disabilities, endurance levels, ability to cope with change in routine, mobility impairments, anxiety, and depression. While many people with TBI have fulfilling careers with little or no impact from their injury, others need modified work schedules, workplace accommodations, or supported employment services. Every effort should be made to engage the student in a conversation about awareness of deficits, as a lack of awareness can lead to significant behavior problems in the workplace.

Resources with More Detailed Information About TBI

- Brain Injury Association of America: A national nonprofit organization geared toward providing information, education, resources, and national advocacy. FAQs, and fact sheets are available on its Web site. http://www.biausa.org/

- National Institute of Neurological Disorders and Stroke: One of the National Institutes of Health. Provides information on treatment and research related to TBI. http://www.ninds.nih.gov/disorders/tbi/tbi.htm

- NDRN (National Disability Rights Network): A nonprofit organization providing legal advocacy services to people with disabilities as part of the federally mandated Protection and Advocacy and Client Assistance Programs. The NDRN works to create equal opportunity and freedom of choice for people with disabilities by providing legal advocacy, legislative advocacy, technical assistance, and training. Areas of focus include "health care, education, employment, housing, transportation, and within the juvenile and criminal justice systems." http://www.napas.org/

- National Dissemination Center for Children with Disabilities (NICHCY): A project of the Academy for Educational Development that is funded by the U.S. Department of Education. NICHCY provides a wealth of information on specific disabilities and disability issues, including the Individuals with Disabilities Act and No Child Left Behind. Disability fact sheets may be printed from the Web site. http://www.nichcy.org/index.html

Visual Impairments

Nadene A. L'Amoreaux and Shanna Rovida
Indiana University of Pennsylvania

General Background Information About Visual Impairments

Approximately twenty-five thousand children in the United States are considered blind or visually impaired. *Partial sight* and *low vision* mean that even if a child is wearing glasses, contacts, or has had surgery, he or she still has significant visual limitations that require the use of assistive technology or devices. Partial sight and low vision impairments include amblyopia, cataracts, diabetic retinopathy, glaucoma, macular degeneration, and trachoma. Blindness is generally considered to be 20/200 or less in the better eye after best correction. While some students with blindness cannot see anything, others may have significantly limited or functional vision even with correction. There are many causes of blindness, many stemming from partial blindness that continued to get worse without treatment. Other causes of blindness include accidents (chemical burns or sports injuries), illnesses (diabetes), congenital conditions, and vitamin A deficiencies.

Vision is the primary sense through which infants and children acquire information about their world, and it is the primary sense relied on in educational settings. When a child has a visual impairment, his accessibility to the world becomes limited to what is available in his immediate environment. As a consequence, students with visual impairments may experience delayed concept development that affects their social, emotional, academic, and career development. This is particularly salient for children who have never been sighted versus children who lost sight later in their development. It is important for educators to understand the nature of an individual's visual impairment in order to identify appropriate supports and assistive technology so as to promote independence (independent living skills), mobility (orientation and mobility tools including long canes, guide dogs), and social functioning. Literacy can be promoted through the use of braille, optical devices, and specialized computer hardware and software, screen readers, and electronic books.

Socially, children with visual impairments or blindness may be isolated from peers due to mobility or independence factors. Students in an inclusion classroom need to be oriented to the classroom, and peers need to be aware of the need to keep the room clear of impediments that might cause injury, such as a chair left in a walkway. Peers and teachers need to be informed how to approach a peer and engage with a peer who has a visual impairment (asking if the child requires assistance rather than assuming assistance is needed, specifically addressing the student rather than assuming he knows he is being addressed). Also, these are children who are not able to observe incidental activities in the class and therefore miss opportunities to join in with peers without being drawn in and included.

What Students and Parents Wish Their Teachers and Counselors Knew About Visual Impairments

- "I can get bored in class even with all of my visual equipment."

- "I may not be able to say exactly what I need to feel included in the classroom or I may not know that I am being left out or excluded."

- "It may take a long time for me to recognize you or the people in my class, and I may need you to tell me who you are when you approach me."
  - Even with partial sight, a person with a visual impairment may not be able to recognize faces of people around him or her. Whereas non-impaired children learn where their classroom is, who their teachers and classmates are, and which book is their spelling book quickly, children with visual impairments may take much longer to learn new routines and environments.

- "I may be just as smart as my peers."
  - Many educators underestimate children with visual impairments. Studies have shown, though, that IQ scores of children with visual impairments are within the normal range as a whole. Self-esteem about school is often affected by how teachers respond to their disability. If a teacher does not expect much from the child, the child may continue to do mediocre or poor-quality work. If a teacher or aide takes the time to explain mistakes and continues to expect more of the visually impaired child, he or she will thrive.

- "I can do many things for myself."
  - Many teachers, counselors, and peers want to be helpful with a student who has a disability. Sometimes this can be debilitating and often enabling for the child to do less and expect less from himself or herself. Teachers and counselors should be aware of the child's current capabilities.

- "I want my child to be as independent as possible."
- "I may need your assistance with identifying technology and devices that will help my child to learn, and I need you to take the time to learn to use it."

Practical Applications

Personal Applications

- *Emotional issues:* Children with visual impairments or blindness may experience anxiety or depression in response to their disability or to social isolation and rejection that they can experience from their peers. Recognition of their emotional reactions and appropriate responsive interventions may be necessary with both the child and his or her peers.

- *Acceptance of the use of devices, technology, and equipment to assist the child:* Children with visual impairments or blindness may be rejecting of the technology and equipment that is designed to help them as they perceive the technology as marking them as different from their peers. They may also become frustrated with the learning curve associated with learning to use the equipment.

- *Self-concept and self-efficacy:* Children with visual impairments may struggle with low self-esteem or see themselves as helpless to achieve academically and socially.

Social Applications

- *Social-behavioral issues:* Children with visual impairments may experience social isolation and rejection from peers, may fail to join with peers because they are not aware of their informal activities, or may not be aware of how they are presenting to their peers. Individual, group, or classroom guidance activities can be designed to address specific needs of the individual or the peer group. Teachers can be encouraged to identify specific tasks that the student can to do make positive contributions to the learning environment.

Academic Applications

- *Seating in class:* Attention should be paid to the equipment that children with visual impairments need to use, as well as to their placement in the classroom for optimal learning.

- *Interactive teaching methods:* Instructional techniques that promote classroom interaction with peers as well as with course material are especially beneficial. Using the child's equipment in creative ways will help the child learn important material in user-friendly ways. For instance, if a child has an interactive whiteboard connected to her closed-circuit monitor, the whiteboard can be used to bring the same course material into closer proximity for the student.

- *Note taking:* Written language may be difficult for students with visual impairments. Laptop computers can be used to take notes in class, voice-recording mechanisms can be used to capture teachers' lectures so information can be reviewed later, peer note takers can be assigned, or the teacher's notes can be printed in braille for the student's use.

- *Test taking:* Written language may be a struggle for children who are visually impaired. Teachers may opt to give tests orally or using a computer so that information can be seen more clearly or repeated back to them verbally as assessment for comprehension.

- *Homework assignments:* In reference to homework, some equipment available at school may not be accessible in a child's home. Special time before or after school may need to be given for the child to complete assignments.

- *Specialized equipment and technology:* Students with visual disabilities may need assistance identifying and accessing appropriate assistive or adaptive technology, including computer hardware or software, screen readers, electronic books, and braille printers. School personnel involved with assisting and instructing the student will also need training in using and troubleshooting the equipment and technology. Students may need to have textbooks and written materials available on tape or accessible to readers.

Career Applications

- *Proper environmental and work demand fit:* The goal of education is to promote independence and productivity in society. Advocating for the incorporation of assistive or adaptive technology that can also be transferred to postsecondary education or training is one way to meet this goal.

- *Realistic career exploration:* Although being visually impaired may limit employment opportunities for students, it is still important to explore many options of careers with them, including identifying school-to-work experiences, apprenticeships, postsecondary education, and community partnerships.

- Transition planning should include orientation and mobility skills within the community. as well as independent living skills.

Resources with More Detailed Information About Visual Impairments

- AFB (American Foundation for the Blind): Provides information online for educators, counselors, and parents about different aspects of vision loss. This Web site shows many informational links about vision loss, as well as articles for ways to include students into classrooms. www.afb.org

- NEI (National Eye Institute): A large network of organizations and doctors who specialize in eye diseases and care. This is a good resource for parents. www.nei.nih.gov/health/resourceAlpha.asp

- Recordings for the Blind and Dyslexic (RFB&D): A nonprofit volunteer organization provides an audio book library with titles available for every subject and grade level. Member Services Department: 800-221-4792. http://www.rfbd.org/

- Bookshare.org library: Provides print-disabled people in the United States with legal access to over 42,400 books and 150 periodicals that are converted to braille, large-print, or digital formats for text to speech audio. www.Bookshare.org

Conclusion

The education of students with disabilities has come a long way, but there is still a long way to go. We have presented many stories in this book designed to help readers develop an appreciation and understanding of the past and present experiences of individuals and students with disabilities. One of the first stories was about some children with disabilities before passage of the Americans with Disabilities Act: a New Jersey zookeeper would not permit them into the monkey house because they would upset the chimpanzees. Similarly, recall Johnnie from Chapter Four who was denied an education and was subsequently institutionalized. These are eye-opening stories. It is hard today to imagine that such blatant discrimination and exclusion existed. Many individuals connect with the racial civil rights movements of the 1960s, but are unaware of a progressive civil rights movement for individuals with disabilities that occurred at the same time. Led by parents of children with disabilities, this movement was key in securing the current rights that we often taken for granted.

In a little more than twenty years, great strides and progress have been made. This is clear in the story of Eliza from Chapter One, whose school counselor was creative and proactive in paving the way for social inclusion with her young peers. The school counselor worked in concert with Eliza and her parents to write her story as a book that classmates could read to understand how Eliza communicates in a different way from them and how to communicate with her. It is easy to see how the compassionate efforts of her school counselor had a positive impact on her life story. Yet that progress is not consistent.

Eliza's story stands in contrast to the life story of Teddy Willis, related in Chapter Seven, a fifth grader with autism who wanted to share his experience with autism during the school's autism awareness month. His story included being denied the opportunity to speak by the school board, only to have this denial overturned after a groundswell of community support. So reality for students with disabilities today is quite varied. Some schools fully embrace their inclusion, and others are still challenged with not only how to address these students' needs but also are mired in the past and cling to the mistaken beliefs and stereotypes from the past.

Looking to the Future

Although this book is grounded in the past and aware of today's realities, it is really about the future for students with disabilities. The message that we have tried to convey throughout is that school counselors can and should play a vital role in working with and providing services for children with disabilities and that school counseling programs should be designed with them in mind. Through these efforts, we can help shape a future in which:

- The school and all its citizens acknowledge that all belong and all are valued.

- School counselors' roles include working with students with disabilities.

- Resilience, persistence, and hope are at the core of all student success.

- The school's physical and learning environment is welcoming and barrier free.

- Students with disabilities are a shared responsibility of everyone in the school.

- Students with disabilities are fully involved and integrated into the school, and there is an honest representation of the sentiment, *nothing about me without me.*

- There is an appreciation that sameness is not fairness, that accommodations for students with disabilities are natural, and that different can be just.

- Ableism is not tolerated.

Imagine the life stories that would be created in this future. Envision the impact on the life stories of the 7 million children with disabilities who are in our schools.

Geometric Good

As we close, we introduce the concept of *geometric good*, which refers to positive actions that have expanding and far-reaching impact. The best way to explain this concept is with an example. For the purpose of illustration, we'll use a secondary school counselor, Ms. Nere. Ms. Nere's positive action that starts the process of expanding "good" is the development of a series of three teacher in-service workshops designed to facilitate understanding of the amplified career development needs for students with disabilities. During these workshops, Ms. Nere teaches the concepts of expansive realism and premature foreclosure. In addition, she provides accurate information about accommodations that can be made in the world of work to facilitate the employment of individuals with disabilities and the services that institutions of higher education provide for these students. Finally, she gives the teachers many examples of individuals with disabilities who are working, contributing members of society. She challenges their beliefs about the work and career possibilities for individuals with disabilities.

The in-service workshops are Ms. Nere's initial positive action. This action has an impact on the forty-five teachers who attended. This action stands alone as a positive action to help teachers increase their understanding of students with disabilities. However, this is just the beginning. Ms. Nere's initial positive action expands geometrically. Some of the teachers (say, two-thirds of them, or about thirty teachers) apply the information and insight they gained in the in-service workshops in their classrooms across the six periods of the day. In essence, as a result of the workshop, they interact differently with their students with disabilities and modify their teaching to include these students. An English teacher chooses an autobiography of an individual with a disability as part of her reading assignments. A chemistry teacher exposes his students to Chemists with Disabilities, an interest group with the American Chemical Society, and shows them examples of chemists with disabilities and how they function in their jobs. These are just two examples of how teachers put their learning into action. This action then touches the lives of their students with disabilities who are in their classrooms. So given that there may be two or three students with disabilities in their classes, here's how the geometric good plays out. One school counselor touches 30 teachers. Each teacher has an impact on 3 students with disabilities per class for 6 periods a day, so 30 teachers each have an impact on 18 students. A total of 540 students benefit from these changes (Figure C.1).

It is easy to see how Ms. Nere's initial positive action goes on to influence 540 students with disabilities. If we assume that these students now become more engaged in their education and more connected to school, the impact of Ms. Nere's in-service workshops could then expand to these children's combined 1,080 parents.

The impact of efforts that expand geometrically can have a powerful and profound effect on the life stories of students with disabilities. Moreover, the impact of this geometric good may extend to the classmates of those with disabilities who will grow up not seeing individuals with disabilities as "them." We hope that school counselors seek out ways to do right by their students with disabilities and to act in ways that do geometric good.

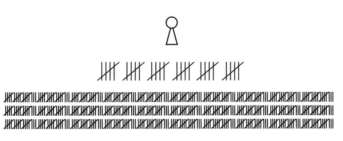

Figure C.1 How the Geometric Good Works

Notes

Chapter One

1. Milsom (2002).
2. National Center for Education Statistics (2006).
3. American School Counselor Association (2008).
4. Virginia Board for People with Disabilities (2004).
5. Weicker (1988, p. 5).
6. "States deny education to children with disabilities" (2000).
7. Associated Press (2008).
8. Rodis, Garrod, & Boscardin (2001, p. 168).
9. Middleton (1999).
10. Snow (2005).
11. Snow (2005, p. 273).
12. American School Counselor Association (2004, para. 1).
13. American School Counselor Association (2004, para. 3).
14. Murray (2006, p. 36).
15. Goodley & Lawthom (2006, p. 40).
16. Parette & Hourcade (1995).
17. Milson (2006).
18. Rutter (1985, cited in Brooks, 1994, p. 607).
19. Deck, Scarborough, Sferrazza, & Estill (1999, p. 151).
20. Werner (1993, cited in Brooks, 1994, p. 546).
21. Segal (1988, cited in Brooks, 1994, p. 546, italics added).
22. Rodis, Garrod, & Boscardin (2001, p. 197).
23. Werner (1993, p. 2).
24. Neill (2006).
25. Blum (2005, p. 344).

Chapter Two

1. Brightman (1984, p. 145).
2. Cited in Goodley & Lathom (2006 p. 39).
3. Bowen (1998 p. 5).
4. Wright (1983a).

5. Sutherland (1981, pp. 6–7)

6. Olkin (1999, p. 70).

7. Gilbert (2005); Marshak & Seligman (1993).

8. Gilbert (2005, p. 115).

9. Marshak (1993).

10. Haller (2000, para. 24).

11. Hawthorne (n.d.).

12. King (2007).

13. Smart (2001).

14. Prockner (2000, para. 3).

15. Lewis (1990, para, 18).

16. Bennetts (1993).

17. Smart (2001).

18. Smart (2001, p. 17).

19. Goffman (1963).

20. Miller & Sammons (1999, p. 249).

21. Miller & Sammons (1999).

22. Miller & Sammons (1999, p. 200).

23. Schmitt (1994, as cited in Miller & Sammons, 1999, p. 223).

24. Assouline, Nicpon, & Huber (2006, p. 5).

25. Smart (2001, p. 5).

26. Rodis, Garrod, & Boscardin (2001, p. 18).

27. Snow (2007, p. 1).

28. Snow (2007, p. 3).

29. Snow (2007, p. 2).

30. Gold (1980).

31. Cohen (2007, para. 2).

32. Gold (1980).

33. Gold (1980).

34. Hallowell (n.d., para. 7).

35. Lewin (1935).

36. Olkin (1999).

37. Middleton (1999).

38. Smart (2001); Sobsey (1994).

39. Snow (2007, p. 2).

40. Olkin (1999, p. 27).

41. Hershey (1997, para. 24).

42. Nathanson (1979, pp. 233–237).

43. Middleton (1999, p. 29).

44. Siller (1976).

45. Davis (1972).
46. Middleton (1999, p. 20).
47. Silver (2006, para. 14).

Chapter Three

1. American School Counselor Association (n.d.-b).
2. Ontario Canada Peel District School Board (2008).
3. Hehir (2003).
4. Hehir (2007, p. 11).
5. American School Counselor Association (n.d.-a, p. 2).
6. Brown & Trusty (2005).
7. Deck, Scarborough, Sferrazza, & Estill (1999, paras. 12–14).

Chapter Four

1. Golfus & Simpson (1994).
2. Stecker, Fuchs, & Fuchs (2008, p. 10).
3. Steedly (2008, para. 3).
4. American School Counselor Association (2008, para. 1).
5. Individuals with Disabilities Education Act, Public Law 105–17 C.F.R. § 300.346 (1997a).
6. Individuals with Disabilities Education Act, Public Law 105–17 C.F.R. § 300.320 (1997b).
7. Individuals with Disabilities Education Act, Public Law 105–17 C.F.R. § 300.320 (1997b).
8. Individuals with Disabilities Education Act, Public Law 105–17 C.F.R. § 300.320 (1997b).
9. Jordan (2006).
10. Weidenthal & Kochhar–Bryant (2007).
11. National Education Association (2004).

Chapter Five

1. American School Counselor Association (2004).
2. American School Counselor Association (2004).
3. Kübler-Ross (1969).
4. Duncan (1977).
5. Marshak, Seligman, & Prezant (1999, p. 71).
6. Taub (2006).
7. Marshak, Seligman, & Prezant (1999, p. 73).
8. Naseef (1999, para. 7).
9. Seligman & Darling (2007, p. 108).
10. Seligman (2000).
11. American School Counselor Association (2004).
12. Mahoney, Boyce, Fewell, Spiker, & Wheeden (1998); Kobe & Hammer (1994).
13. Crosse (1992).

14. Sullivan & Knutson (2000).

15. Feinberg, Beyer, & Moses (2002, as cited in Blue-Banning, Summers, & Frankland, 2004).

16. Quigney & Studer (1998).

17. Carpenter, King-Sears, & Keys (1998); Quigney & Studer (1998).

18. Carpenter, King-Sears, & Keys (1998)

19. Taub (2006); Marshak, Prezant, & Hulings-Shirley (2006).

20. Prezant & Marshak (2006).

21. Prezant & Marshak (2006).

22. Thompson (1997, para. 15).

Chapter Six

1. Hechinger & Golden (2007).

2. Hechinger & Golden (2007).

3. Hechinger & Golden (2007).

4. Stensrud (2006).

5. Stensrud (2006).

6. Stensrud (2006); Mainzer, Deshler, Coleman, Kozleski, & Rodriguez-Walling (2003).

7. McGrady, Lerner, & Boscardin (2001).

8. Hampton & Hess-Rice (2003).

9. Kemp (2006).

10. Stensrud (2006). Hampton & Hess-Rice (2003) report similar findings.

11. Wenz-Gross & Siperstein (1998).

12. Elbaum & Vaughn (2001).

13. L'Amoreaux (2000).

14. Hampton & Hess-Rice (2003).

15. Nitkin (2007); Assouline, Nicpon, & Huber (2006).

16. Hertog (2007).

17. Assouline, Nicpon, & Huber (2006).

18. Assouline, Nicpon, & Huber (2006); McEachern & Bornot (2001)

19. Calabro (2008).

20. Neihart (2004).

21. Gradel, Jabot, Magiera, & Maheady (2005).

22. Assouline, Nicpon, & Huber (2006); McEachern & Bornot (2001).

23. Elbaum & Vaughn (2001).

24. Nitkin (2007).

25. Neihart (2004).

26. Baum, Olenchak, & Owen (2004).

27. McEachern & Bornot (2001); Neihart (2004).

28. Wenz-Gross & Siperstein (1998).

29. Covey (1997).

30. McGrath (2007).
31. McGrady, Lerner, & Boscardin (2001).
32. McGrath (2007).
33. McGrath (2007).
34. McGrath (2007).
35. Hehir (2005).
36. Schwarz (2006).
37. McGrath (2007).
38. Individuals with Disabilities Education Act (IDEA), Public Law 105–17 C.F.R. § 300.5 (1997c).
39. McGrath (2007).
40. Palmer, Fuller, Arora, & Nelson (2001).
41. Frederickson, Dunsmuir, Lang, & Monsen (2004).
42. Hehir (2005).
43. L'Amoreaux (2000).
44. Medina & Luna (2004).
45. Wenz-Gross & Siperstein (1998).
46. Medina & Luna (2004).
47. "Risk, resilience and futurists" (n.d.).
48. Wenz-Gross & Siperstein (1998).
49. McGrady, Lerner, & Boscardin (2001).
50. Hehir (2005).
51. House & Martin (1998).
52. Stensrud (2006, p. 105).
53. McGrath (2007, p. 6).

Chapter Seven

1. Frye (2005).
2. Margalit (1992); Barton & Fuhrmann (1994); Omizo & Omizo (1994); Kottman, Robert, & Baker (1995); Baker (2000); Garcia, Krankowski, & Jones (1998).
3. Wright (1983b).
4. Baker & Donelly (2001).
5. Cook (2003).
6. Diamond (1996).
7. Swaim & Morgan (2001).
8. Nowicki (2006).
9. Terpstra & Temura (2008, p. 35).
10. Terpstra & Temura (2008).
11. Kemple (2004).
12. Diamond (2001).
13. Gladwell (2000); Milgram (1967).

14. Baker & Donelly (2001).
15. Staub (1998).
16. Muscular Dystrophy Association (2005, p. 17).
17. Sowell (1997, para. 5).
18. Sowell (1997).
19. Swaim & Morgan (2001, p. 203, citing Bell & Morgan, 2000); Potter & Roberts (1984); Siperstein & Bak (1980).
20. Siperstein & Bak (1980).
21. Swaim & Morgan (2001).
22. Campbell (2006).
23. Ochs, Kremer-Sadlik, Solomon, & Sirota (2001). Several good resources provide approaches to disclosure of autism, including *Autism: Being friends* (1991).
24. Circle of Inclusion (2002).
25. Snow (2005, p. 280).
26. Wrigglesworth (2005, p. 8).
27. Gleeson (2006).
28. Muscular Dystrophy Association (2005, p. 17).
29. Gleeson (2006, p. 1).
30. Circle of Inclusion (2002).
31. Goodwin (2001).
32. Middleton (1999, p. 131).
33. Van der Klift & Kunc (1994, p. 153).
34. Staub (1998, p. 155).
35. Brooks (1994, p. 549).
36. Brooks (1994, p. 550).
37. Brooks (1994).
38. Gentry (2007, para. 3).

Chapter Eight

1. Blum (2005, p. 333).
2. David (2007, para. 4).
3. Rodis, Garrod, & Boscardin (2001).
4. Miyahara & Piek (2006); Altshuler, Mackelprang, & Baker (2008); Wright (1983a); Marshak & Seligman (1993).
5. Wright (1983a, p. 152).
6. Arnold & Chapman (1992); Altshuler, Mackelprang, & Baker (2008).
7. Wright (1983).
8. Wisniewski (1981, p. 210).
9. Rapp (2007, p. 77).
10. Kellerman, Zeltzer, Ellenberg, Dash, & Rigler (1980); Blum (2005).
11. Blum (2005, p. 336).

12. Calabro (2007, paras. 11, 16).
13. Jackson (2003 p. 36).
14. Ferreyra (2001, para. 1).
15. Rodis, Garrod, & Boscardin (2001).
16. Rodis, Garrod, & Boscardin (2001, pp. 215, 216).
17. Rodis, Garrod, & Boscardin (2001, p. 216).
18. Rodis, Garrod, & Boscardin (2001, p. 218).
19. Rodis, Garrod, & Boscardin (2001, p. 220).
20. Wright (1983a); DeLoach & Greer (1981); Vash (1981); Olkin (1999).
21. Rapp (2007, p. 205).
22. Greydanus (2002, p. 224).
23. Cheng & Udry (2002, 2003).
24. Greydanus, Rimsza, & Newhouse (2002).
25. Greydanus, Rimsza, & Newhouse (2002, p. 235).
26. Falvo (2005)
27. Greydanus, Rimsza, & Newhouse (2002, p. 235).
28. Grealy (1994, p. 206).
29. Siddiqi, Van Dyke, Donohoue, & McBrien (1999).
30. Levey (2007).
31. Blum (2007, p. 337).
32. Matheson, Olsen, & Weisner (2007).
33. Field, Martin, Miller, Ward, and Wehmeyer (1998, as cited in Wehmeyer, 2002).
34. Field, Martin, Miller, Ward, and Wehmeyer (1998, as cited in Wehmeyer, 2002).
35. Chambers et al. (2007).
36. Jackson (2003, p. 153).
37. Moloney, Whitney-Thomas, & Dreilinger (2002, pp. 2, 3).
38. Kriegsman, Zaslow, & D'Zmura-Rechsteiner (1992, pp. 121, 123).
39. Myles (2007, para. 4).
40. Myles & Southwick (1999).
41. Morrissey (2008).
42. Myles & Southwick (1999).
43. Goldberg, Higgins, Raskind, & Herman (2003, pp. 232, 233).
44. American School Counselor Association (2008).
45. DeLoach & Greer (1981); Davis (1972).
46. Davis (1972).
47. McCarthy, Light, & McNaughton (2002, cited in Lilienfeld & Alant, 2005, p. 279).
48. Lilienfeld & Alant (2005).
49. Kriegsman, Zaslow, & D'Zmura-Rechsteiner (1992, p. 124).
50. Calabro (2005).
51. U.S. Department of Health and Human Services, Office of Disability (n.d., para. 3, 5).

Notes

52. Hollar (2005); Hollar & Moore (2004).

53. McCombs & Moore (2002).

54. Jones, Woolcock-Henry, & Domenico (2005, p. 93), note that "an information void exists regarding the population of pregnant & parenting teens with disabilities."

55. Carter (1999).

56. Gordon, Tschopp, & Feldman (2004, p. 514).

57. Casteel, Martin, Smith, Gurka, & Kupper (2008); Kelley & Moore (2000).

58. Sullivan & Knutson (2000). See also Brodwin & Siu (2007).

59. Mears & Aron (2003, p. v).

60. Mears & Aron (2003, pp. 27–28).

61. Wagner (1993).

62. Wagner (1991).

63. Rumberger (1995). Lehr et al. (2004) is an excellent resource for school counselors with respect to dropout prevention and intervention for students with disabilities.

64. Blum (2005).

65. Blatt (1987).

66. Schloss, Alper, & Jayne (1993, p. 216).

67. Calabro (2007, para. 20).

68. Ferro (2006, para. 3).

69. Henderson (1998, p. 15).

70. Morin & Linares (2004, as cited in Burnham, 2009, p. 32).

71. Excellent resources for school counselors are Henderson, Bernard, & Sharp-Light (2000, 2002, 2006) and Henderson & Milstein (2003).

72. Post by Katrina Gossett, retrieved May 1, 2009, http://mda.org/publications/Quest/extra/qe12_3_selfimage.html.

Chapter Nine

1. Erickson & Bjelland (2007).

2. Vaughan (2007).

3. Erickson & Bjelland (2007).

4. Marshak, Seligman, & Prezant (1999, p. 133).

5. Mpofu & Harley (2006).

6. "New career paths for students with disabilities: Opportunities in science, technology, engineering, and mathematics" (2002); Stern & Wood (2001).

7. Marshak, Prezant, & Hulings-Shirley (2006).

8. Clowes (2008).

9. Wehmeyer (1992, p. 305).

10. Osgood, Foster, Flanagan, & Ruth (2005).

11. U.S. Department of Education (2001).

12. Edgar (1990); Frank & Sitlington (1997); Neel, Meadows, Levine, & Edgar (1988).

13. Kregel (1999); Muller, Schuler, Burton, & Yates (2003).

14. Capo (2001); Garcia-Villamisar, Ross, & Wehman (2000); Garcia-Villamisar, Wehman, & Diaz Navarro (2002); Hagner & Cooney (2005); Howlin, Alcock, & Burkin (2005); Mawwood & Howlin (1999); Muller, Schuler, Burton, & Yates (2003); Petty & Fussell (1997); Wehman & Revell (1996).

15. Henn & Henn (2005).

Part Three

Asthma and Allergies

1. "Asthma: Facts and figures" (2005).

2. "Asthma overview: What causes asthma?" (2005).

3. "Asthma overview: What causes asthma?" (2005).

4. "Asthma: Tests and diagnosis" (2008).

5. "Asthma: Treatments and drugs" (2008).

6. "Asthma overview: Prevention" (2005).

7. "Nut allergies" (2006).

8. "Latex allergy: Symptoms" (2007).

9. "Latex allergy: Causes" (2007).

10. "Latex allergy: Causes" (2007).

11. "Latex allergy: Causes" (2007).

12. "Latex allergy: Risk factors" (2007).

13. "Latex allergy: Definition" (2007).

14. "Asthma: Facts and figures" (2005)

Autism

1. *Autism spectrum disorders* (2008).

2. *Autism spectrum disorders* (2008).

3. *Autism spectrum disorders* (2008); American Psychiatric Association (2008).

4. *Autism spectrum disorders* (2008).

5. "Pervasive developmental disorders" (2000).

6. "Pervasive developmental disorders" (2000).

7. "Pervasive developmental disorders" (2000).

8. *Autism spectrum disorders* (2008).

9. *Autism spectrum disorders* (2008).

10. American Psychiatric Association (2008).

11. *Autism spectrum disorders* (2008).

12. Dettmer, Simpson, Myles, & Ganz (2000).

13. Lord & McGee (2001).

14. Steege, Mace, Perry, & Longenecker (2007).

15. Chamberlain, Kasari, & Rotheram-Fuller, 2007; Schwartz, Sandall, McBride, & Boulware (2004).

16. Schwartz et al. (2004).

17. Preis (2007).

Bipolar Disorder and Depression

1. "About mental illness: Bipolar disorder" (2008).

2. Comer (2005).

3. "Bipolar community" (2006).

4. "About mental illness: Bipolar disorder" (2008).

5. Comer (2005).

6. "About mental illness: Bipolar disorder" (2008).

7. "About pediatric bipolar disorder" (2002).

Cerebral Palsy

1. Schenker, Coster, & Parush (2006).

2. "What is cerebral palsy?" (n.d.).

3. Krigger (2006); Sandstrom (2007).

4. "Dysarthria" (2008).

5. "Cerebral palsy" (2008); Krigger (2006).

6. Krigger (2006).

7. Wiegerink, Roebroeck, Donkervoort, Stam, & Cohen-Kettenis (2006).

8. Wiegerink et al. 2006).

9. Cunningham, Dixon-Thomas, & Warschausky (2007).

10. "Dysarthria" (2008).

11. Sandstrom (2007).

12. Wiegerink et al. (2006).

13. Sandstrom (2007).

14. Schenker et al. (2006).

15. "Cerebral palsy" (2008); "Dysarthria" (2008).

16. Whidden (2008).

Diabetes

1. Klingensmith, Kaufman, Schatz, & Clarke (2003).

2. Klingensmith et al. (2003).

Cystic Fibrosis

1. Cfvoice (2009).

2. Cline & Greene (2007, p. 291).

3. About.com, Special Needs Children (2008a).

4. Post from a parent, retrieved Nov. 1, 2008, http://dailystrength.org/c/Cystic_Fibrosis/forum/4129227–504-plan.

5. "Cystic fibrosis in school" (2008).

Deafness and Hearing Disorders

1. Nichcy (2004).
2. Ldonline (2008).
3. American Speech-Language-Hearing Association (2008).
4. Nichcy (2004).
5. American Speech-Language-Hearing Association (2008).
6. World Health Organization (n.d.).
7. National Institute on Deafness and Other Communication Disorders (2008).
8. American Speech-Language-Hearing Association (2008).
9. Schick, De Villiers, De Villiers, & Hoffmeister (2007).
10. Nichcy (2004).
11. American Speech-Language-Hearing Association (2008).
12. Nichcy (2004).
13. American Speech-Language-Hearing Association (2008).
14. Nichcy (2004).
15. Ldonline (2008).

Degenerative Orthopedic Diseases (Muscular Dystrophy)

1. "About Duchenne" (2008); "Diseases: Duchenne muscular dystrophy" (2006).
2. "MDA publications: Facts about Duchenne" (2006).
3. "What is Duchenne/Becker Muscular Dystrophy (DBMD)?" (2006).
4. "Muscular dystrophy: Symptoms" (2007).
5. "MDA publications: Facts about Duchenne" (2006).
6. "Muscular dystrophy: Symptoms" (2007).
7. "MDA publications: Facts about Duchenne" (2006); "Muscular dystrophy: Treatments and drugs" (2007).
8. "Seeking treatment" (2008, para. 2).
9. Parent Project Muscular Dystrophy (2006).
10. Parent Project Muscular Dystrophy (2006).
11. Parent Project Muscular Dystrophy (2006).

Fetal Alcohol Syndrome

1. "Fetal alcohol spectrum disorders" (2008).
2. Burgess & Streissguth (2008).
3. Burgess & Streissguth (2008).
4. Burgess & Streissguth (2008, p. 3).
5. "Personality/learning traits of FAS/FAE children" (2008).
6. Adapted from Kellerman (2008).
7. Adapted from Kellerman (2008).
8. Adapted from Kellerman (2008).
9. Adapted from "Parenting children affected by fetal alcohol syndrome" (2008).

10. Adapted from "Parenting children affected by fetal alcohol syndrome" (2008).
11. Adapted from "Parenting children affected by fetal alcohol syndrome" (2008).
12. Burgess & Streissguth (2008) .
13. "Fetal alcohol syndrome" (2008).
14. "Strategies for daily living: FAS/FASD through the lifespan" (2004).
15. "Strategies for daily living: FAS/FASD through the lifespan" (2004).
16. Streissguth (1997).
17. "Parenting children affected by fetal alcohol syndrome" (2008).
18. "Parenting children affected by fetal alcohol syndrome" (2008).
19. "Parenting children affected by fetal alcohol syndrome" (2008).
20. Burgess & Streissguth (2008).
21. Burgess & Streissguth (2008).
22. "Fetal alcohol syndrome" (2008).
23. Streissguth (1997).
24. Burgess & Streissguth (2008).
25. "Parenting children affected by fetal alcohol syndrome" (2008).
26. Streissguth (1997).
27. "Parenting children affected by fetal alcohol syndrome" (2008).
28. Streissguth (1997, p. 219).
29. Burgess & Streissguth (2008)
30. "Fetal alcohol spectrum disorders" (2008).
31. "Parenting children affected by fetal alcohol syndrome" (2008).
32. "Parenting children affected by fetal alcohol syndrome" (2008).
33. Burgess & Streissguth (2008).

Learning Disabilities

1. "What is a learning disability?" (2008).
2. Milsom & Hartley (2005).
3. "What is a learning disability?" (2008).
4. Learning Disabilities Association of America (2008).
5. "What is a learning disability?" (2008).
6. Learning Disabilities Association of America (2008).
7. Great Schools Parent Community (2008).
8. "What is a learning disability?" (2008).
9. Milsom & Hartley (2005).

Mental Retardation

1. U.S. Department of Education (2002).
2. Reynolds & Dombeck (2008).
3. Reynolds & Dombeck (2008).

4. About.com, Special Needs Children (2008b).

5. The three quotations are from About.com, Special Needs Children (2008b).

Other Orthopedic Impairments

1. "Orthopedic impairments" (2006).

2. Judd (2001).

3. "Orthopedic impairments" (2006).

4. Judd (2001).

5. "Strategies for teaching students with motor/orthopedic impairments" (2005).

6. Livneh, Wilson, & Pullo (2004).

7. "Strategies for teaching students with motor/orthopedic impairments" (2005).

8. Burstein, Bryant, & Chao (2005).

9. Livneh et al. (2004).

10. Hutzler, Fliess, Chacham, & Van den Aweele (2002).

11. "Strategies for teaching students with motor/orthopedic impairments" (2005).

Seizures

1. Sachs & Barrett (1995).

2. Disability Info: Epilepsy (FS6) (2008); "Epilepsy Foundation—Types, triggers, causes and syndromes" (2008); Sachs & Barrett (1995).

3. Sachs & Barrett (1995); "Epilepsy Foundation—Types, triggers, causes and syndromes" (2008).

4. Sachs & Barrett (1995).

5. Caplan, Siddarth, Gurbani, Hanson, Sankar, & Shields (2005); "Epilepsy Foundation—Epilepsy and seizure statistics" (2008); McManus (2002); Sachs & Barrett (1995); Sanchez-Carpintero & Neville (2003).

6. Fastenau, Shen, Dunn, Perkins, Hermann, & Austin (2004).

7. Sachs & Barrett (1995).

8. Sachs & Barrett (1995).

9. Frueh (2007).

10. "Epilepsy Foundation—First aid" (2008); Sachs & Barrett (1995)

11. Caplan et al. (2005).

12. Caplan et al. (2005); Fastenau et al. (2004); Sachs & Barrett (1995)

13. Caplan et al. (2005).

14. Fastenau et al. (2004).

15. Sanchez-Carpintero & Neville (2003).

16. "Epilepsy Foundation—Education and employment" (2008).

Speech and Language Disorders

1. Nichcy (2008).

2. Ziegler, Pech-Georgel, George, Alario, & Lorenzi (2005); Nichcy (2008).

3. KidsHealth (2008).

4. National Institute on Deafness and Other Communication Disorders (2008).

5. Nichcy (2008).

6. Ldonline (2008).

7. Ziegler, Pech-Georgel, Alario, & Lorenzi (2005); Ldonline (2008); Nichcy (2008).

8. National Institute on Deafness and Other Communication Disorders (2008).

9. National Library of Medicine (2009).

10. left.org (2008).

11. American Psychiatric Association (2008).

12. American Speech-Language-Hearing Association (2008).

13. National Library of Medicine (2009).

14. American Speech-Language-Hearing Association (2008).

15. National Institute on Deafness and Other Communication Disorders (2008).

16. American Speech-Language-Hearing Association (2008).

17. Nichcy (2008).

18. Ldonline (2008)

19. National Library of Medicine (2009).

20. American Speech-Language-Hearing Association (2008).

21. Ldonline (2008).

Spina Bifida

1. Brislin (2008).

2. Spina Bifida Association (2008a).

3. Spina Bifida Association (2008d).

4. Spina Bifida Association (2008c).

5. Spina Bifida Association (2008b).

6. Burmeister et al. (2005).

Traumatic Brain Injury

1. Antoinette & McMorrow (2004).

2. Savage & Tyler (2007).

3. Savage (2004).

4. Savage & Tyler (2007).

5. Anson & Ponsford (2006).

6. Rotondi, Sinkule, Balzer, Harris, & Moldovan (2007); Russell (2004).

7. Prigatano & Gupta (2006).

8. Bowen (2005).

9. Glang, Tyler, Peterson, Todis, & Morvant (2004).

10. Jantz & Coulter (2007); Mayfield & Homack (2005).

11. Bowen (2005).

References

About.com, Special Needs Children. (2008a). Preparing the school for your child with cystic fibrosis. Retrieved October 31, 2008, from http://specialchildren.about.com/od/cysticfibrosis/a/CFschool.htm.

About.com, Special Needs Children. (2008b). Preparing the school for your child with intellectual disabilities. Retrieved July 2009 from http://specialchildren.about.com/od/mentalretardation/a/MRschool.htm.

About Duchenne. (2008). Retrieved November 12, 2008, from http://www.parentprojectmd.org/site/PageServer?pagename=understanding_about.

About mental illness: Bipolar disorder. (2008). Retrieved November 3, 2008, from www.nami.org.

About pediatric bipolar disorder. (2002). Retrieved November 5, 2008, from www.bpkids.org.

Altshuler, S. J., Mackelprang, R. W., & Baker, R. L. (2008). Youth with disabilities: A standardized self-portrait of how they are faring. *Journal of Social Work in Disability and Rehabilitation, 7*(1), 1–18.

American Psychiatric Association. (2008). DSM IV-TR diagnostic criteria for the pervasive developmental disorders. Retrieved November 12, 2008, from http://www.cdc.gov/ncbddd/autism/overview_diagnostic_criteria.htm#Autistic.

American School Counselor Association. (2004). The professional school counselor and students with special needs. Retrieved June 4, 2009, from http://www.schoolcounselor.org.

American School Counselor Association. (2008). Student-to-counselor ratios. Retrieved December 30, 2008, from http://www.schoolcounselor.org.

American School Counselor Association. (n.d.-a). The ASCA national model: A framework for school counseling programs. Retrieved December 30, 2008, from http://www.schoolcounselor.org.

American School Counselor Association. (n.d.-b). School counselors: Partners in student achievement. Retrieved December 30, 2008, from http://www.schoolcounselor.org/files/partners%20in%20achievement.ppt.

American Speech-Language-Hearing Association. (2008). American Speech-Language-Hearing Association, ASHA. Retrieved September 2008 from http://www.asha.org/.

Anson, K., & Ponsford, J. (2006). Coping and emotional adjustment following traumatic brain injury. *Journal of Head Trauma Rehabilitation, 21*(3), 248–259.

Antoinette, T., & McMorrow, D. B. (2004). Overview of brain injury. In M. Lash, D. B. McMorrow, J. Tyler, & T. Antoinette (Eds.), *Training manual for certified brain injury specialists* (3rd ed., pp. 1–18). Vienna, VA: American Academy for the Certification of Brain Injury Specialists.

Apel, M. A. *Cystic fibrosis: The ultimate teen guide.* Lanham, MD: Scarecrow Press.

Arnold, P., & Chapman, M. (1992). Self-esteem, aspirations and expectations of adolescents with physical disability. *Developmental Medicine and Child Neurology, 34*(2), 97–102.

Associated Press. (2008, November 19). Elementary school teacher suspended after autistic child voted out of class. Retrieved December 25, 2008, from http://www.gainesville.com/article/20081119/NEWS.

Assouline, S. G., Nicpon, M. F., & Huber, D. H. (2006). The impact of vulnerabilities and strengths on the academic experiences of twice-exceptional students: a message to school counselors. *Professional School Counseling, 10*(1), 14–24.

Asthma: Facts and figures. (2005). Retrieved November 3, 2008, from http://www .aafa.org/display.cfm?id=8&sub=42.

Asthma overview: Prevention. (2005). Retrieved November 3, 2008, from http://www.aafa.org/ display.cfm?id=8&cont=9.

Asthma overview: What causes asthma? (2005). Retrieved November 3, 2008, from http://www.aafa.org/display.cfm?id=8&cont=6.

Asthma: Tests and diagnosis. (2008). Retrieved November 3, 2008, from http://www.mayoclinic .com/health/asthma/DS00021/DSECTION=tests-and-diagnosis.

Asthma: Treatments and drugs. (2008). Retrieved November 3, 2008, from http://www .mayoclinic.com/health/asthma/DS00021/DSECTION=treatments-and-drugs.

Autism: Being friends. (1991). Bloomington, IN: Indiana Resource Center for Autism and WTIU.

Autism spectrum disorders. (2008). Bethesda, MD: National Institute of Mental Health.

Baker, K., & Donelly, M. (2001). The social experiences of children with disability and the influence of environment: A framework for intervention. *Disability and Society, 16*(1), 71–85.

Baker, S. B. (2000). *School counseling for the 21st century.* Upper Saddle River, NJ: Merrill.

Barton, S., & Fuhrmann, B. (1994). Counseling and psychotherapy for adults with learning disabilities. In P. Gerber & H. Reiff (Eds.), *Learning disabilities in adulthood: Persisting problems and evolving issues* (pp. 82–92). Boston: Andover Medical.

Baum, S., Olenchak, R., & Owen, S. (2004). Gifted students with attention deficits: Fact and/ or fiction? Or, can we see the forest for trees? In S. Baum (Ed.), *Twice-exceptional and special populations of gifted students* (pp. 35–50). Thousand Oaks: Corwin Press.

Bell, S. K., & Morgan, S. B. (2000). Children's attitudes and behavioral intentions toward a peer presented as obese: Does a medical explanation for the obesity make a difference? *Journal of Pediatric Psychology, 25,* 137–145.

Bennetts, L. (1993, September). Jerry v. the kids. *Vanity Fair.* Retrieved October 15, 2008, from http://www.cripcommentary.com/jlquotes.html.

Bipolar community. (2006). Retrieved November 4, 2008, from www.healthyplace.com.

Blatt, B. (1987). The community imperative and human values. In R. F. Antonak & J. A. Mulick (Eds.), *Transition in mental retardation: The community imperative revisited* (pp. 236–247). Norwood, NJ: Ablex.

Blue-Banning, M., Summers, J. A., & Frankland, H. C. (2004). Dimensions of family and professional partnerships: Constructive guidelines for collaboration. *Exceptional Children, 70*(2), 167–184.

Blum, R. W. (2005). Adolescents with disabilities in transition to adulthood. In D. W. Osgood, E. M. Foster, C. Flanagan, & G. R. Ruth (Eds.), *On your own without a net* (pp. 323–348). Chicago: University of Chicago Press.

Bowen, J. M. (2005). Classroom interventions for students with traumatic brain injuries. *Preventing School Failure, 49*(4), 34–41.

Bowen, M. L. (1998). Counseling interventions for students who have mild disabilities. *Professional School Counseling, 2*(1), 16–26.

Brightman, A. (1984). *Ordinary moments: The disabled experience.* Baltimore, MD: University Park Press.

Brislin, D. C. (2008). Reaching for independence: Counseling implications for youth with spina bifida. *Journal of Counseling and Development, 86,* 34–38.

Brodwin, M. G., & Siu, F. W. (2007). Domestic violence against women who have disabilities: What educators need to know. *Domestic Violence Education, 127*(4), 548–551.

Brooks, R. B. (1994). Children at risk: Fostering resilience and hope. *American Journal of Orthopsychiatry, 64*(4), 545–553.

Brooks, R. B., & Goldstein, S. (2009). Risk, resilience and futurists: Changing the lives of our children. Retrieved June 5, 2009, from http://www.raisingresilientkids.com/resources/articles/futurists.html.

Brown, D., & Trusty, J. G. (2005). *Designing and leading comprehensive school counseling programs: Promoting student competence and meeting student needs.* Belmont, CA: Thomson Brooks/Cole.

Burgess, D. M., & Streissguth, A. P. (2008). Educating students with fetal alcohol syndrome or fetal alcohol effects. Retrieved June 2, 2008, from http://www.faslink.org/n.htm.

Burmeister, R., Hannay, J. H., Copeland, K., Fletcher, J. M., Boudousquie, A., & Dennis, M. (2005). Attention problems and executive functions in children with spina bifida and hydrocephalus. *Child Neuropsychology, 11.* Retrieved June, 5, 2008, from http://web.ebscohost.com/ehost/detail?vid=4&hid=3&sid=f1845245-41e7-4e60-8af1-077c408adfa6%40sessionmgr2.

Burnham, J. J. (2009). Contemporary fears of children and adolescents: Coping and resiliency in the 21st century. *Journal of Counseling and Development, 87*(1), 28–35.

Burstein, K., Bryant, T., & Chao, P. C. (2005). Promoting self-determination skills among youth with special health needs using participatory action research. *Journal of Developmental and Physical Disabilities, 17*(2), 185–201.

Calabro, T. (2005, September 28). Disabilities complicate adolescence: Social issues loom large as children with disabilities enter their teens. *Pittsburgh Post Gazette.* http://www.post-gazette.com/pg/pp/05271/578693.stm.

Calabro, T. (2007, July 25). Power for disabled comes with accepting themselves. *Pittsburgh Post-Gazette* from http://www.post-gazette.com.

Calabro, T. (2008, November 20). Much-honored Penn Hills senior overcomes disabilities to become National Merit semifinalist. *Pittsburgh Post-Gazette.* Retrieved December 1, 2008, from http://www.post-gazette.com.

Campbell, J. M. (2006). Changing children's attitudes toward autism: A process of persuasive communication. *Journal of Developmental and Physical Disabilities, 18*(3), 251–272.

Caplan, R., Siddarth, P., Gurbani, S., Hanson, R., Sankar, R., & Shields, W. D. (2005). Depression and anxiety disorders in pediatric epilepsy. *Epilepsia, 46*(5), 720–730.

Capo, L. C. (2001). Autism, employment, and the role of occupational therapy. *Work, 16*(3), 201–207.

Carpenter, S., King-Sears, M., & Keys, S. (1998). Counselors + educators + families as a transdisciplinary team = More effective inclusion for students with disabilities. *Professional School Counseling, 2*(1), 1–9.

Carter, J. K. (1999). Sexuality education for students with specific learning disabilities. *Intervention in School and Clinic, 34,* 220–223.

Casteel, C., Martin, S. L., Smith, J. B., Gurka, K. K., & Kupper, L. L. (2008). National study of physical and sexual assault among women with disabilities. *Injury Prevention, 14*(2), 87–90.

CDC Epilepsy. (2008, June 13). CDC—epilepsy. Retrieved June 13, 2008, from http://www.cdc.gov/epilepsy/index.htm.

Cerebral palsy. (2008). Cerebral palsy treatment—Mayo Clinic. Retrieved October 27, 2008, from http://www.mayoclinic.org/cerebral-palsy/treatment.html.

CFvoice, Cystic Fibrosis Community. (2009). *There's no place like hope.* Video. http://www.cfvoice.com/info/caregivers/features/hopes.jsp, Oct, 31, 2008.

Chamberlain, B., Kasari, C., & Rotheram-Fuller, E. (2007). Involvement in isolation? The social networks of children with autism in regular classrooms. *Journal of Autism and Developmental Disorders, 37,* 230–242.

Chambers, C. R., Wehmeyer, M. L., Saito, Y., Lida, K. M., Lee, Y., & Singh, V. (2007). Self-determination: What do we know? Where do we go? *Exceptionality, 15*(1), 3–15.

Cheng, M. M., & Udry, J. R. (2002). Sexual behaviors of physically disabled adolescents in the United States. *Journal of Adolescent Health, 31*(1), 48–58.

Cheng, M. M., & Udry, J. R. (2003). How much do mentally disabled adolescents know about sex and birth control? *Journal of Adolescent and Family Health, 3*(1), 28–38.

Circle of Inclusion. (2002). Circle of Inclusion home page. Retrieved December 21, 2007, from http://www.circleofinclusion.org.

Cline, F. W., & Greene, L. C. (2007). *Parenting children with health issues.* Golden, CO: Love and Logic Press.

Clowes, G. (2008). *One of the gang: Nurturing the souls of children with food allergies.* Bloomington, IN: AuthorHouse.

Cohen, R. A. (2007, Winter). The erosion of developmental services. *RAP Sheet, 8.* Retrieved from http://www.drcnh.org/Rapquality107.pdf.

Comer, R. J. (2005). *Fundamentals of abnormal psychology.* New York: Worth Publishers.

Cook, M. N. (2003). Social skills training in schools. Retrieved December 20, 2008, from http://findarticles.com/p/articles/mi_qa3934/is_200310/ai_n9322569.

Covey, S. (1997). *The seven habits of highly effective people.* New York: Free Press.

Crosse, S. B. (1992). *A report on the maltreatment of children with disabilities.* Rockville, MD: Westat, and Arlington, VA: James Bell Associates. (ED 365 089)

Cunningham, S., Dixon-Thomas, P., & Warschausky, S. (2007). Gender differences in peer relations of children with neurodevelopmental conditions. *Rehabilitation Psychology, 52,* 334–337.

Cystic fibrosis in school. (2008). Retrieved December 10, 2008, from http://www.uams.edu/pediatrics/cf/CF_in_school.asp.

David. (2007, March 8). Disability and gender stereotypes. Message posted to http://growingupwithadisability.blogspot.com.

Davis, F. (1972). Deviance disavowal: The management of strained interaction by the visibly handicapped. In F. Davis (Ed.), *Illness, interaction and the self* (pp. 133–149). Belmont, CA: Wadsworth.

Dawkins, J. L. (1996). Bullying, physical disability and the paediatric patient. *Developmental Medicine and Child Neurology, 38,* 603–612.

Deck, M., Scarborough, J. L., Sferrazza, M. S., & Estill, D. M. (1999). Serving students with disabilities: Perspectives of three school counselors. *Intervention in School and Clinic, 34*(3), 150–155.

DeLoach, C., & Greer, B. G. (1981). *Adjustment to severe disability.* New York: McGraw-Hill.

Dettmer, S., Simpson, R. L., Myles, B. S., & Ganz, J. B. (2000). The use of visual supports to facilitate transitions of students with autism. *Focus on Autism and Other Developmental Disabilities, 15*(3), 163–169.

Diamond, K. E. (1996). Preschool children's conceptions of disabilities: The salience of disability in children's ideas about others. *Topics in Early Childhood Special Education, 16*(4), 458–475.

Diamond, K. E. (2001). Relationships among young children's ideas, emotional understanding, and social contact with classmates with disabilities. *Topics in Early Childhood Special Education, 21*(2), 104–114.

Disability Info: Epilepsy (FS6). (2008, May 4). Retrieved June 1, 2008, from http://www .nichcy.org/pubs/factshe/fs6txt.htm.

Diseases: Duchenne muscular dystrophy. (2006). Retrieved November 13, 2008, from http://www.mda.org/disease/dmd.html.

Duncan, D. (1977). The impact of handicapped child upon family. In L. Marshak, M. Seligman & F. Prezant (Eds.), *Disability in the family life cycle.* New York: Basic Books.

Dysarthria. (2008). Retrieved October 27, 2008, from http://www.asha.org/public/speech/ disorders/dysarthria.htm.

Edgar, E. (1990, Winter). Education's role in improving our quality of life: Is it time to change our view of the world? *Beyond Behavior, 9*–13.

Education for All Handicapped Children Act, P.L. 94-142 C.F.R. (1975).

Elbaum, B., & Vaughn, S. (2001). School-based interventions to enhance the self-concept of students with learning disabilities: A meta-analysis. *Elementary School Journal, 101*(3), 303–329.

Epilepsy Foundation—Education and employment. (2008, June 14). Retrieved June 14, 2008, from http://www.epilepsyfoundation.org/about/quickstart/newlydiagnosed/qsliving/ idveducationjobs.cfm.

Epilepsy Foundation—Epilepsy and seizure statistics. (2008, June 4). Retrieved June 4, 2008, from http://www.epilepsyfoundation.org/about/statistics.cfm.

Epilepsy Foundation—First aid. (2008, June 4). Retrieved June 4, 2008, from http://www.epilepsyfoundation.org/about/firstaid/.

Epilepsy Foundation—Status epilepticus. (2008, June 15). Retrieved June 15, 2008, from http://www.epilepsyfoundation.org/about/types/types/statusepilepticus.cfm.

Epilepsy Foundation—Types, triggers, causes and syndromes. (2008, June 7). Retrieved June 7, 2008, from http://www.epilepsyfoundation.org/about/types/index.cfm.

Erickson, W., & Bjelland, M. (2007). *The 2006 annual disability status report.* Ithaca, NY: Cornell University.

Falvo, D. R. (2005). *Medical and psychosocial aspects of chronic illness and disability.* Sudbury, MA: Jones & Bartlett Publishers.

Fastenau, P. S., Shen, J., Dunn, D. W., Perkins, S. M., Hermann, B. P., & Austin, J. K. (2004). Neuropsychological predictors of academic underachievement in pediatric epilepsy: Moderating roles of demographic, seizure, and psychosocial variables. *Epilepsia, 45* (10), 1261–1272.

Ferreyra, N. (2001). Living out loud: Building resiliency in adolescent girls with disabilities. *International Disability News and Views.* Retrieved October 28, 2008, from http://www .disabilityworld.org/03-04_01/women/lol.shtml.

Ferro, J. (2006). Self-image disability: Who do I think I am? Retrieved July 14, 2007, from http://www.mda.org/publications/Quest/q123self_image.html.

Fetal alcohol spectrum disorders. (2008). Retrieved June 5, 2008, from http://www.cdc.gov/ ncbddd/fas/fasask.htm.

Fetal alcohol syndrome. (2008). Retrieved June 6, 2008, from http://www.kidshealth.org/parent/ medical/brain/fas.html.

Field, S., Martin, J., Miller, R., Ward, M., & Wehmeyer, M. L. (1998). A practical guide for teaching self-determination. Reston, VA: Council for Exceptional Children.

Flexer, R. W., Simmons, T. J., Luft, P., & Baer, R. M. (2000). *Transition planning for secondary students with disabilities.* Upper Saddle River, NJ: Prentice Hall.

Frank, A. R., & Sitlington, P. L. (1997). Young adults with behavioral disorders—before and after IDEA. *Behavioral Disorders, 23,* 40–56.

Frederickson, N., Dunsmuir, S., Lang, J., & Monsen, J. J. (2004). Mainstream-special school inclusion partnerships: Pupil, parent and teacher perspectives. *International Journal of Inclusive Education, 8*(1), 37–57.

Frueh, E. (2007). Seizure management for school-age children. *Education Management, 73,* 38–40.

Frye, H. (2005). How elementary school counselors can meet the needs of students with disabilities. *Professional School Counseling, 8*(5), 442–450.

Garcia, J. G., Krankowski, T., & Jones, L. L. (1998). Collaborative interventions for assisting students with acquired brain injuries in school. *Professional School Counseling, 2,* 33–39.

Garcia-Villamisar, D., Ross, D., & Wehman, P. (2000). Clinical differential analysis of persons with autism in a work setting: A follow-up study. *Journal of Vocational Rehabilitation, 14,* 183–185.

Garcia-Villamisar, D., Wehman, P., & Diaz Navarro, M. (2002). Changes in the quality of autistic people's lives that worked in supported and sheltered employment: A 5-year follow-up study. *Journal of Vocational Rehabilitation, 17,* 309–312.

Gentry, K. (2007, April 20). CR student takes mike, tells story. *Bucks County Courier Times.* Retrieved December 18, 2008, from http://www.couriertimesonline.com.

Gilbert, D. (2005). *Stumbling on happiness.* New York: Random House.

Gladwell, M. (2000). *The tipping point: How little things can make a big difference.* New York: Little, Brown.

Glang, A., Tyler, J., Peterson, S., Todis, B., & Morvant, M. (2004). Improving educational services for students with TBI through statewide consulting teams. *NeuroRehabilitation, 19,* 219–231.

Gleeson, C. (2006). Young people with health problems—their views on how schools can help. *Education and Health, 24*(2).

Goffman, E. (1963). *Stigma.* Upper Saddle River, NJ: Prentice Hall.

Gold, M. (1980). Try another way. Retrieved October 15, 2008, from http://www.mnddc.org/extra/marc-gold1.html.

Goldberg, R. J., Higgins, E. L., Raskind, M. H., & Herman, K. L. (2003). Predictors of success in individuals with learning disabilities: A qualitative analysis of a 20-year longitudinal study. *Learning Disabilities Research & Practice, 18*(4), 222–236.

Golfus, B., & Simpson, D. E. (1994). When Billy broke his head . . . and other tales of wonder [VHS Tape]. (Available from Fanlight Productions, 4196 Washington Street, Boston, MA 02131.)

Goodley, D., & Lawthom, R. (Eds.). (2006). *Disability and psychology: Critical introductions and reflections.* New York: Palgrave Macmillan.

Goodwin, D. L. (2001). The meaning of help in PE: Perceptions of students with physical disabilities. *Adapted Physical Activity Quarterly, 18,* 289–303.

Gordon, P. A., Tschopp, M. K., & Feldman, D. (2004). Addressing issues of sexuality with adolescents with disabilities. *Child and Adolescent Social Work Journal, 21*(5), 513–527.

Gradel, K., Jabot, M., Magiera, K., & Maheady, L. (2005). Special education teaching strategies. In E. Fletcher-Janzen & C. R. Reynolds (Eds.), *The special education almanac* (pp. 1–17). Hoboken, NJ: Wiley.

Grealy, L. (1994). *Autobiography of a face.* Boston: Houghton Mifflin.

Great Schools Parent Community. (2008). Advice from parents about schools, education and community. Retrieved 2008 from http://community.greatschools.net.

Greydanus, D. E., Rimsza, M. E., & Newhouse, P. A. (2002). Adolescent sexuality and disability. *Adolescent Medicine: State of the Art Reviews, 13*(2), 223–247.

Hagner, D., & Cooney, B. F. (2005). "I do that for everybody": Supervising employees with autism. *Focus on Autism and Other Developmental Disabilities, 20*(2), 91–97.

Haller, B. (2000, January–February). False positive. *Ragged Edge, 5.*

Hallowell, E. (n.d.). *What's it like to have ADD?* Retrieved December 31, 2007, from http://www.faslink.org/ADHDLIKE.HTM.

Hampton, S. S., & Hess-Rice, E. K. (2003). Restructuring service delivery for students with emotional and behavioral disorders. In F. E. Obiakor, C. A. Utley, & A. F. Rotatori (Eds.), *Effective education for learners with exceptionalities* (pp. 119–138). Stamford, CT: JAI.

Hawthorne, N. (n.d.). Measured admiration: When not to over-praise an employee with a disability. Retrieved July 14, 2007, from http://www.esight.org/View.cfm?x=1379.

Hechinger, J., & Golden, D. (2007, August 21). Extra help: When special education goes too easy on students. *Wall Street Journal,* p. A1. http://online.wsj.com/public/article_print/SB118763976794303235.html.

Hehir, T. (2003). Beyond inclusion: Educators' "ableist" assumptions about students with disabilities compromise the quality of instruction. *School Administrator, 60*(3), 36–39.

Hehir, T. (2005). The changing role of intervention for children with disabilities. *Principal, 85*(2), 22–25.

Hehir, T. (2007). Confronting ableism. *Education Leadership, 64*(5), 8–14.

Henderson, N. (1998). Make resiliency happen. *Education Digest, 63*(5), 15–18.

Henderson, N., Bernard, B., & Sharp-Light, N. (2000). *Schoolwide approaches for fostering resiliency.* Ojai, CA: Resiliency in Action.

Henderson, N., Bernard, B., & Sharp-Light, N. (Eds.). (2002). *Mentoring for resiliency: Setting up programs for moving youth from "stressed to success."* Ojai, CA: Resiliency in Action.

Henderson, N., Bernard, B., & Sharp-Light, N. (Eds.). (2006). *Resiliency in action: Practical ideas for overcoming risks and building strengths in youth, families, and communities.* Ojai, CA: Resiliency In Action.

Henderson, N., & Milstein, M. M. (2003). *Resiliency in Schools: Making it happen for students and educators.* Thousand Oaks, CA: Corwin Press.

Henn, J., & Henn, M. (2005). Defying the odds: You can't put a square peg in a round hole no matter how hard you try. *Journal of Vocational Rehabilitation, 22,* 129–130.

Hershey, L. (1997). From poster child to protester. Retrieved July 11, 2007, from http://www.independentliving.org/docs4/hershey93.html.

Hertog, A. (2007). Twice exceptional children: Gifted and disabled. Retrieved December 20, 2007, from http://www.iser.com/resources/ld-gifted.html.

Hollar, D. (2005). Risk behaviors for varying categories of disability in NELS:88. *Journal of School Health, 75*(9), 350–358.

Hollar, D., & Moore, D. (2004). Relationship of substance use by students with disabilities to long-term educational, employment, and social outcomes. *Substance Use and Misuse, 39*(6), 931–962.

Hopson, K. (2003). Finding new ways to help kids with disabilities make friends. Retrieved December 20, 2007, from http://www.ur.umich.edu/0203/Mar24_03/19.shtml.

House, R. M., & Martin, P. J. (1998). Advocating for better futures for all students: A new vision for school counselors. *Education, 119*(2), 284–292.

Howlin, P., Alcock, J., & Burkin, C. (2005). An 8 year follow-up of a specialist supported employment service for high-ability adults with autism or Asperger syndrome. *Autism: International Journal of Research & Practice, 9*(5), 533–549.

Hugh-Jones, S., & Smith, P. K. (1999). Self-reports of short and long term effects of bullying on children who stammer. *British Journal of Educational Psychology, 69,* 141–158.

Hutzler, Y., Fliess, O., Chacham, A., & Van den Aweele, Y. (2002). Perspectives of children with physical disabilities on inclusion and empowerment: Supporting and limiting factors. *Adapted Physical Activity Quarterly, 19,* 300–317.

Individuals with Disabilities Education Act, Public Law 105–17 C.F.R. § 300.346 (1997a).

Individuals with Disabilities Education Act, Public Law 105–17 C.F.R. § 300.320 (1997b).

Individuals with Disabilities Education Act (IDEA), Public Law 105–17 C.F.R. § 300.5 (1997c).

Jackson, L. (2003). *Freaks, geeks and Asperger syndrome: A user guide to adolescence.* London: Jessica Kingsley.

Jantz, P. B., & Coulter, G. A. (2007). Child and adolescent traumatic brain injury: Academic, behavioural, and social consequences in the classroom. *Support for Learning, 22*(2), 84–89.

Jones, K. H., Woolcock-Henry, C. O., & Domenico, D. M. (2005). Wake up call: Pregnant and parenting teens with disabilities. *International Journal of Special Education, 20*(1), 92–104.

Jordan, D. (2006). Functional behavioral assessment and positive interventions: What parents need to know. In Pacer Center (Ed.), *ACTion Sheet: PHP-c79.* Bloomington, MN: Pacer Center.

Judd, D. (2001). "To walk the last bit on my own": Narcissistic independence or identification with good objects: Issues of loss for a 13-year-old who had an amputation. *Journal of Child Psychotherapy, 27*(1), 47–67.

Kellerman, J. (2008). Living with FAS. Retrieved November 2, 2008, from http://www.fasarizona .com/ihavefas.htm.

Kellerman, J., Zeltzer, L., Ellenberg, L., Dash, J., & Rigler, D. (1980). Psychological effects of illness in adolescence. I. Anxiety, self-esteem, and perception of control. *Journal of Pediatrics, 97*(1), 126–131.

Kelley, S.D.M., & Moore, J. E. (2000). Abuse and violence in the lives of people with low vision: A national survey. *View, 31*(4), 155–164.

Kemp, S. E. (2006). Dropout policies and trends for students with and without disabilities. *Adolescence, 41*(162), 235–250.

Kemple, K. M. (2004). *Let's be friends: Peer competence and social inclusion in early childhood programs.* New York: Teachers College Press.

Kerr, N. (1984). Help that is helpful. *Rehabilitation Psychology,* 151–159.

KidsHealth. (2009). Retrieved July 2009, from http://www.kidshealth.org.

King, B. (2007). Senco-forum posters. Retrieved September 23, 2008, from http://lists.becta.org .uk/pipermail/senco-forum/2007-February/054411.html.

Klingensmith, G., Kaufman, F., Schatz, D., & Clarke, W. (2003). Care of children with diabetes in the school and day care setting. *Diabetes Care, 26,* 131–135.

Kobe, F. H., & Hammer, D. (1994). Parenting stress and depression in children with mental retardation and developmental disabilities. *Research in Developmental Disabilities, 15,* 209–221.

Kottman, T., Robert, R., & Baker, D. (1995). Parental perspectives on attention-deficit/ hyperactivity disorder: How school counselors can help. *School Counselor, 43,* 142–150.

Kregel, J. (1999). Why it pays to hire workers with developmental disabilities. *Focus on Autism and Other Developmental Disabilities, 14*(3), 130–132.

Kriegsman, K. H., Zaslow, E., & D'Zmura-Rechsteiner, J. (1992). *Taking charge: Teenagers talk about life and physical disabilities.* Bethesda, MD: Woodbine House.

Krigger, K. W. (2006). Cerebral palsy: An overview. *American Family Physician, 73,* 91–100.

Kübler-Ross, E. (1969). *On death and dying.* New York: Macmillan.

L'Amoreaux, N. A. (2000). *Children diagnosed with attention-deficit/hyperactivity disorder(ADHD) and their perceptions of parental helpfulness with homework: A q-methodological study.* Unpublished doctoral dissertation, Kent State University.

Latex allergy: Causes. (2007). Retrieved November 3, 2008, from http://www.mayoclinic.com/health/latex-allergy/DS00621/DSECTION=causes.

Latex allergy: Definition. (2007). Retrieved November 3, 2008, from http://www.mayoclinic.com/health/latex-allergy/DS00621/DSECTION%20=7.

Latex allergy: Risk factors. (2007). Retrieved November 3, 2008, from http://www.mayoclinic.com/health/latex-allergy/DS00621/DSECTION=risk-factors.

Latex allergy: Symptoms. (2007). Retrieved November 3, 2008, from http://www.mayoclinic.com/health/latex-allergy/DS00621/DSECTION=symptoms.

Ldonline. (2008). Auditory processing disorders in children. Retrieved September 2008 from http://www.ldonline.org/article/Auditory_Processing_Disorder_in_Children.

Learning Disabilities Association of America. (2008). ADD/ADHD. Retrieved July 2009 from http://www.ldaamerica.org/aboutld/teachers/understanding/adhd.asp.

Lehr, C. A., Johnson, D. R., Bremer, C. D., Cosio, A., Thompson, M., & National Center on Secondary Education Transition. (2004). *Increasing rates of school completion: Moving from policy and research to practice. A manual for policymakers, administrators, and educators. Essential tools.* Minneapolis: National Center on Secondary Education and Transition, University of Minnesota.

Levey, E. (2007). Addressing sexuality in spina bifida. Retrieved December 29, 2008, from www.articlearchives.com/medicine-health/diseases-disorders-neurological.

Levinson, E. M., & Palmer, E. J. (2005). Preparing students with disabilities for school-to-work transition and postschool life. *Principal Leadership: Middle Level Edition, 5*(8), 11–15.

Lewin, K. (1935). *Dynamic theory of personality: Selected papers.* New York: McGraw-Hill.

Lewis, J. (1990, September 2). If I had muscular dystrophy. *Parade.*

Lewis, J. (1992). Other obnoxious comments made by Jerry Lewis. Retrieved September 23, 2008, from http://www.cripcommentary.com/jlquotes.html.

Lilienfeld, M., & Alant, E. (2005). The social interaction of an adolescent who uses ACC: The evaluation of a peer-training program. *Augmentative and Alternative Communication, 21*(4), 278–294.

Livneh, H., Wilson, L. M., & Pullo, R. E. (2004). Group counseling for people with physical disabilities. *Focus on Exceptional Children, 36*(6), 1–19.

Lord, C., & McGee, J. P. (Eds.). (2001). *Educating children with autism. Committee on educational interventions for children with autism.* Washington, DC: Academy Press.

Mahoney, G., Boyce, G., Fewell, R. R., Spiker, D., & Wheeden, C. A. (1998). The relationship of parent-child interaction to the effectiveness of early intervention services for at-risk children and children with disabilities. *Topics in Early Childhood Special Education, 18,* 5–16.

Mainzer, R. W., Deshler, D., Coleman, M. R., Kozleski, E., & Rodriguez-Walling, M. (2003). To ensure the learning of every child with a disability. *Focus on Exceptional Children, 35*(5), 1–12.

Margalit, M. (1992). Sense of coherence and families with a learning-disabled child. In B. Wong (Ed.), *Contemporary intervention research in learning disabilities.* New York: Springer-Verlag.

References

Marshak, L., & Prezant, F. (2002). *Infusing awareness about assistive technology and its role in employment success: A case study approach for pre-professional rehabilitation professionals.* Albertson, NY: National Center for Disability Services.

Marshak, L., Prezant, F., & Hulings-Shirley, H. (April, 2006). *Facilitating vocational self-concepts in children with disabilities: Books and beyond.* Session presented at the annual conference of the Council for Exceptional Children. Salt Lake City, UT.

Marshak, L. E., & Seligman, M. (1993). *Counseling persons with physical disabilities: Theoretical and clinical perspectives.* Austin, TX: Pro-Ed.

Marshak, L., Seligman, M., & Prezant, F. (1999). *Disability and the family lifecycle.* New York: Basic Books.

Martlew, M., & Hodson, J. (1991). Children with mild learning difficulties in an integrated and in a special school: Comparisons of behaviour, teasing and teachers' attitudes. *British Journal of Educational Psychology, 61,* 355–372.

Matheson, C., Olsen, R. J., & Weisner, T. (2007). A good friend is hard to find: Friendship among adolescents with disabilities. *American Journal on Mental Retardation, 112*(5), 319–329.

Mawwood, L., & Howlin, P. (1999). The outcome of a supported employment scheme for high-functioning adults with autism or Asperger syndrome. *Autism, 3,* 229–254.

Mayfield, J., & Homack, S. (2005). Behavioral considerations associated with traumatic brain injury. *Preventing School Failure, 49*(4), 17–22.

McCarthy, H. (2003). The disability rights movement: Experience and perspectives of senior leaders in the disability community. *Rehabilitation Counseling Bulletin, 50,* 14–23.

McCarthy, J., Light, J., & McNaughton, D. (2002). *Consumer perspectives on social relationships: Lessons for professionals.* Paper presented at the 10th biennial conference of the International Society for Augmentative and Alternative Communication, Odense, Denmark.

McCombs, K., & Moore, D. (2002). *Substance abuse prevention and intervention for students with disabilities: A call to educators.* Arlington, VA: Council for Exceptional Children.

McEachern, A. G., & Bornot, J. (2001). Gifted students with learning disabilities: Implications and strategies for school counselors. *Professional School Counseling, 5*(1), 34–41.

McGrady, H., Lerner, J., & Boscardin, M. L. (2001). The educational lives of students with learning disabilities. In P. Rodis, A. Garrod, & M. L. Boscardin (Eds.), *Learning disabilities and life stories* (pp. 177–193). Needham Heights, MA: Allyn and Bacon.

McGrath, C. (2007). *The inclusion-classroom problem solver: Structures and supports to serve all learners.* Portsmouth, NH: Heinemann.

McManus, R. (2002, August 20). NIH Record—8/20/2002—Epidemiologist Hauser traces roots of epilepsy. Retrieved June 15, 2008, from http://nihrecord.od.nih.gov/newsletters/08_20_2002/story01.htm.

MDA publications: Facts about Duchenne and Becker muscular dystrophies (DMD and BMD). (2006). Retrieved November 13, 2008, from http://www.mda.org/publications/fa-dmdbmd-what.html#whathappens.

Mears, D. P., & Aron, L. Y. (2003). *Addressing the needs of youth with disabilities in the juvenile justice system: The current state of knowledge.* Washington, DC: Urban Institute Justice Policy Center.

Medina, C., & Luna, G. (2004). Learning at the margins. *Rural Special Education, 23*(4), 10–16.

Middleton, L. (1999). *Disabled children: Challenging social exclusion.* Cambridge, MA: Blackwell Science.

Milgram, S. (1967). The small world problem. *Psychology Today, 1,* 60–67.

Miller, N., & Sammons, C. (1999). *Everybody's different.* Baltimore: Paul H. Brookes.

Milsom, A. (2002). Students with disabilities: School counselor involvement and preparation. *Professional School Counseling, 5*(5), 331–339.

Milsom, A. (2006). Creating positive school experiences for students with disabilities. *Professional School Counseling 10*(1), 66–72.

Milsom, A., & Hartley, M. T. (2005). Assisting students with learning disabilities transitioning to college: What school counselors should know. *Professional School Counseling, 8*(5), 436–441.

Mishna, F. (2003). Learning disabilities and bullying: Double jeopardy. *Journal of Learning Disabilities, 36,* 1–15.

Miyahara, M., & Piek, J. (2006). Self-esteem of children and adolescents with physical disabilities: Quantitative evidence from meta-analysis. *Journal of Developmental and Physical Disabilities, 18*(3), 219–234.

Moloney, M., Whitney-Thomas, J., & Dreilinger, D. (2002). Self-determination and struggle in the lives of adolescents. Boston: Institute for Community Inclusion.

Morin, N. A., & Linares, L. O. (2004). Children's resilience in the face of trauma. *Child Study Center Letter, 8,* 1–6.

Morrissey, P. A. (2008, April 15). *Life's transition points.* Paper presented at the Pac Rim 2008 Info, Maui, HI.

Mpofu, E., & Harley, D. (2006). Racial and disability identity: Implications for the career counseling of African Americans with disabilities. *Rehabilitation Counseling Bulletin, 50,* 14–23.

Muller, E., Schuler, A., Burton, B. A., & Yates, G. B. (2003). Meeting the vocational support needs of individuals with Asperger syndrome and other autism spectrum disabilities. *Journal of Vocational Rehabilitation, 18,* 163–175.

Murray, P. (2006). Being in school? Exclusion and the denial of psychological reality. In D. Goodley & R. Lawthom (Eds.), *Disability and psychology: Critical introductions and reflections.* (pp. 34–41). London: Palgrave Macmillan.

Muscular dystrophy: Symptoms. (2007, December 8). Retrieved November 13, 2008, from http://www.mayoclinic.com/health/muscular-dystrophy/DS00200/DSECTION=symptoms.

Muscular dystrophy: Treatments and drugs. (2007, December 8). Retrieved November 13, 2008, from http://www.mayoclinic.com/ health/ muscular-dystrophy/ DS00200/ DSECTION=treatments-and-drugs.

Muscular Dystrophy Association. (2005). A teacher's guide to neuromuscular disease. Retrieved October 6, 2009, http://www.mda.org/publications/tchrdmd/affect_on_child_family.html.

Myles, B. (2007). The hidden curriculum: Unwritten rules that students with disabilities often miss. Retrieved December 30, 2008, from http://www.cec.sped.org.

Myles, B. S., & Southwick, J. (1999). *Asperger syndrome and difficult moments: Practical solutions for tantrums, rage, and meltdowns.* Shawnee Mission, KS: Autism Asperger Publishing Company.

Nabuzoka, D., & Smith, P. K. (1993). Sociometric status and social behaviour of children with and without learning difficulties. *Journal of Child Psychology and Psychiatry, 34,* 1435–1448.

Naseef, R. A. (1999). Big boys don't cry: At least on the outside. Retrieved December 30, 2008, from http://www.fsma.org/FSMACommunity/GriefLoss/griefandlossfiles/index.cfm?ID=2433&TYPE=1312.

Nathanson, R. (1979). Counseling persons with disabilities: Are the feelings, thoughts, and behaviors of helping professionals helpful? *Personnel and Guidance Journal, 58*(4), 233–237.

National Center for Education Statistics. (2006). *Digest of education statistics.* (NCES 2006–030). Washington DC: U.S. Department of Education.

National Education Association. (2004). *The intersection of IDEA and NCLB.* Washington, DC: National Education Association.

References

National Institute on Deafness and Other Communication Disorders. (2008). What to do if your baby's screening reveals a possible hearing problem. Retrieved July 2009 from http://www.nidcd.nih.gov/health/hearing/baby_screening.asp.

National Library of Medicine. (2009). Speech and communication disorders: MedLinePlus. Retrieved October 6, 2009, http://nlm.nih.gov/medlineplus/speechandcommunicationdisorders.html#cat8.

Neel, R. S., Meadows, N., Levine, P., & Edgar, E. (1988). What happens after special education: A statewide follow-up study of secondary students who have behavior disorders. *Behavioral Disorders, 13,* 209–216.

Neihart, M. (2004). Gifted children with Asperger's syndrome. In S. Baum (Ed.), *Twice-exceptional and special populations of gifted students* (pp. 51–64). Thousand Oaks, CA: Corwin Press.

Neill, J. (2006). *What is psychological resilience?* Retrieved July 16, 2008, from http://wilderdom.com/psychology/resilience/PsychologicalResilience.html.

New career paths for students with disabilities: Opportunities in science, technology, engineering, and mathematics. (2002). Retrieved October 15, 2008, from http://ehrweb.aas.org.

New Jersey cares about bullying. Office of bias crime community relations. Retrieved December 8, 2008, from http://www.ebasedprevention.org/toolbox/bullying/chart.

NICHCY. (2004). *Deafness/hearing loss fact sheet.* Retrieved from http://www.nichcy.org/InformationResources/Pages/NICHCYPublications.aspx.

NICHCY. (2008). Intellectual disability. Retrieved 2008 from http://www.nichcy.org/Disabilities/Specific/Pages/IntellectualDisability.aspx.

Nitkin, K. (2007). Kids who don't fit the mold: Nonprofit group wants schools to recognize, better educate "twice-exceptional" children. Retrieved October 1, 2007, from http://www.baltimoresun.com/news/local/howard/bal-ho.learning28sep28,0,7925646,print.story.

Noonan, B. M., Gallor, S. M., Hensler-McGinnis, N. F., Fassinger, R. E., Wang, S., & Goodman, J. (2004). Challenge and success: A qualitative study of the career development of highly achieving women with physical and sensory disabilities. *Journal of Counseling Psychology, 51,* 68–80.

Nowicki, E. A. (2006). A cross-sectional multivariate analysis of children's attitudes towards disabilities. *Journal of Intellectual Disability Research, 50*(5), 335–348.

Nut allergies. (2006). Retrieved June 13, 2008, from http://my.clevelandclinic.org/disorders/nut_allergies/hic_nut_allergies.aspx.

Objectives for behavior plans (n.d.). Retrieved December 30, 2008, from http://www.about.com.

Ochs, E., Kremer-Sadlik, T., Solomon, O., & Sirota, K. G. (2001). Inclusion as a social practice: Views of children with autism. *Social Development, 10,* 399–419.

Olkin, R. (1999). *What psychotherapists should know about disability.* New York: Guilford Press.

Omizo, M. M., & Omizo, S. A. (1994). Group counseling's effects on self-concept and social behavior among children with learning disabilities. *Journal of Humanistic Education and Development, 26,* 109–117.

Ontario Canada Peel District School Board. (2008). *The future we want.* Retrieved July 2008 from http://www.gobeyondwords.org/The_Future_We_Want.html.

Oregon Resiliency Project (2003). All about social and emotional resilience: A guide for educators. Retrieved December 20, 2008, from http://orp.uoregon.edu.

Orr, L. (2007). *Kyle's first playdate.* Bloomington, IN: Authorhouse.

Orthopedic impairments. (2006). Retrieved June 1, 2008, from http://aasep.org/professional-resources/exceptionalstudents/orthopedicimpairment/index.html.

References

Osgood, D. W., Foster, E. M., Flanagan, C., & Ruth, G. R. (2005). Introduction: Why focus on the transition to adulthood for vulnerable populations? In D. W. Osgood, E. M. Foster, C. Flanagan, & G. R. Ruth (Eds.), *On your own without a net: The transition to adulthood for vulnerable populations* (pp. 1–25). Chicago: University of Chicago Press.

Palmer, D., Fuller, K., Arora, T., & Nelson, M. (2001). Taking sides: Parent views on inclusion for their children with severe disabilities. *Exceptional Children, 67*(4), 467–484.

Parenting children affected by fetal alcohol syndrome. (2008). Retrieved June 8, 2008, from http://www.dfps.state.tx.us/Adoption_and_Foster_Care/pdf/fas-2.pdf.

Parent Project Muscular Dystrophy. (Summer/Fall, 2006). Education matters: A teacher's guide to Duchenne muscular dystrophy. Retrieved from http://www.parentprojectmd.org/site/DocServer/EdMatters-TeachersGuide.pdf?docID=2403.

Parette, H. P., & Hourcade, J. J. (1995). Disability etiquette and school counselors: A common sense approach toward compliance with the Americans with Disabilities Act. *School Counselor, 42*(3), 224–233.

Personality/learning traits of FAS/FAE children. (2008). Retrieved June 5, 2008, from http://lcsc.edu/education/fas/traits.html.

Pervasive developmental disorders. (2000). In American Psychiatric Association (Ed.), *Diagnostic and statistical manual of mental disorders* (4th ed., pp. 69–70). Washington, DC: American Psychiatric Association.

Petty, D. M., & Fussell, E. M. (1997). Employer attitudes and satisfaction with supported employment. *Focus on Autism and Other Developmental Disabilities, 12*(1), 15–22.

Potter, P. C., & Roberts, M. C. (1984). Children's perception of chronic illness: The roles of disease symptoms, cognitive development, and information. *Journal of Pediatric Psychology, 9*, 13–27.

Powers, K., Hogansen, J., Geenen, S., Powers, L. E., & Gil-Kashiwabara, E. (2008). Gender matters in transition to adulthood: A survey study of adolescents with disabilities and their families. *Psychology in the Schools, 45*(4), 349–364.

Preis, J. (2007). Strategies to promote adaptive competence for students on the autism spectrum. *Support for Learning, 22*(1), 17–23.

Prezant, F. P., & Marshak, L. (2006). Helpful actions seen through the eyes of parents of children with disabilities. *Disability and Society, 21*(1), 31–45.

Prigatano, G., & Gupta, S. (2006). Friends after traumatic brain injury in children. *Journal of Head Trauma Rehabilitation, 21*(6), 505–513.

Prockner, D. (2000). I (hope to) NEVER! Retrieved July 11, 2007, from http://www.tell-us-your-story.com/disc108r/00000008.htm.

Quigney, T., & Studer, R. (1998). Touching strands of the educational web: The professional school. *Professional School Counseling, 2*(1), 77–82.

Rapp, E. (2007). *Poster child: A memoir.* New York: Bloomsbury.

Rehabilitation Act, PL 93–112 C.F.R. § 504 (1973).

Reynolds, T., & Dombeck, M. (2008). Mental Retardation: IEPs and Choice of School Venue. Retrieved 2008 from http://www.mhmrcv.org/poc/view_doc.php?type=doc&id=10361&cn=208.

Risk, resilience and futurists: Changing the lives of our children. (n.d.). Retrieved October 16, 2008, from http://www.raisingresilientkids.com/resources/articles/futurists.html.

Rodis, P., Garrod, A., & Boscardin, M. L. (2001). *Learning disabilities and life stories.* Needham Heights, MA: Allyn & Bacon.

Rohrer Durham, M. (2007, April 19). Managing cognitive problems. Retrieved November 19, 2008, from http://www.anapsid.org/cnd/coping/managecognitive.html.

Rotondi, A. J., Sinkule, J., Balzer, K., Harris, J., & Moldovan, R. (2007). A qualitative needs assessment of persons who have experienced traumatic brain injury and their primary family caregivers. *Journal of Head Trauma Rehabilitation, 22*(1), 14–25.

Rumberger, R. W. (1995). Dropping out of middle school: A multilevel analysis of students and schools. *American Educational Research, 32*(3), 583–625.

Russell, D. M. (2004). Brain injury: A family perspective. In M. Lash, D. B. McMorrow, J. Tyler, & T. Antoinette (Eds.), *Training manual for certified brain injury specialists* (3rd ed., pp. 143–154). American Academy for the Certification of Brain Injury Specialists.

Rutter, M. (1985). Resilience in the face of adversity: Protective factors and resistance to psychiatric disorder. *British Journal of Psychiatry, 147,* 598–611.

Sachs, H., & Barrett, R. P. (1995). Seizure disorders: A review for school psychologists. *School Psychology Review, 24*(2), 131–145.

Sanchez-Carpintero, R., & Neville, B. G. (2003). Attentional ability in children with epilepsy. *Epilepsia, 44*(10), 1340–1349.

Sandstrom, K. (2007). The lived body—experiences from adults with cerebral palsy. *Clinical Rehabilitation, 21,* 432–441.

Savage, R. C. (2004). Understanding the brain and brain injury. In M. Lash, D. B. McMorrow, J. Tyler & T. Antoinette (Eds.), *Training manual for certified brain injury specialists* (3rd ed., pp. 35–56). Vienna, VA: American Academy of Brain Injury Specialists.

Savage, R. C., & Tyler, J. (2007). Children and adolescents with brain injuries. In T. Antoinette et al. (Eds.), *The essential brain injury guide* (4th ed., pp. 107–122). Vienna, VA: Brain Injury Association of America.

Schenker, R., Coster, W., & Parush, S. (2006). Personal assistance, adaptations and participation in students with cerebral palsy mainstreamed in elementary schools. *Disability and Rehabilitation, 28,* 1061–1069.

Schick, B., De Villiers, P., De Villiers, J., & Hoffmeister, R. (2007). Language and theory of mind: A study of deaf children. *Child Development, 78,* 376–396.

Schlachter, G. A., & Weber, D. (2006). *Financial aid for the disabled and their families, 2006–2008.* El Dorado Hills, CA: Reference Service Press.

Schloss, P., Alper, S., & Jayne, D. (1993). Self-determination for persons with disabilities: Choice, risk and dignity. *Exceptional Children, 60*(3), 215–225.

Schur, L., Shields, T., & Schriner, K. (2003). Can I make a difference? Efficacy, employment and disability. *Political Psychology, 24,* 119–149.

Schwartz, I. S., Sandall, S. R., McBride, B. J., & Boulware, G. L. (2004). Project data (developmentally appropriate treatment for autism): An inclusive school-based approach to educating young children with autism. *Topics in Early Childhood Special Education, 24*(3), 156–168.

Schwarz, P. (2006). *From disability to possibility: The power of inclusive classrooms.* Portsmouth, NH: Heinemann.

Seeking treatment. (2008). Retrieved November 17, 2008, from http://www.parentprojectmd.org/site/PageServer?pagename=caring_care_treatment.

Segal, J. (1988). Teachers have enormous power in affecting a child's self-esteem. *Brown University Child Behavior and Development Newsletter, 4,* 1–3.

Seligman, M. (2000). *Conducting effective conferences with parents of children with disabilities: A guide for teachers.* New York: Guilford Press.

Seligman, M., & Darling, R. B. (2007). *Ordinary families, special children: A systems approach to childhood disability* (3rd ed.). New York: Guilford Press.

Siddiqi, S. U., Van Dyke, D. C., Donohoue, P., & McBrien, D. M. (1999). Premature sexual development in individuals with neurodevelopmental disabilities. *Developmental Medicine and Child Neurology, 41,* 392–395.

Siller, J. (1976). Attitudes towards disability. In H. Rusalem & D. Malikin (Eds.), *Contemporary vocational rehabilitation* (pp. 67–68). New York: University Park Press.

Silver, K. (2006). Q&A: Senior with disabilities speaks out. Retrieved July 11, 2007, from http://www.cas.muohio.edu/compass/2006/QandA.htm.

Siperstein, G. N., & Bak, J. (1980). Improving children's attitudes toward blind peers. *Journal of Visual Impairment and Blindness,* 132–135.

Smart, J. (2001). *Disability, society, and the individual.* Gaithersburg, MD: Aspen.

Snow, K. (2005). *Disability is natural: Revolutionary common sense for raising successful children with disabilities* (2nd ed.). Woodland Park, CO: BraveHeart Press.

Snow, K. (2007). *101 reproducible articles: Revolutionary common sense for a new disability paradigm.* Woodland Park, CO: BraveHeart Press, 2.

Sobsey, D. (1994). *Violence and abuse in the lives of people with disabilities: The end of silent acceptance.* Baltimore: Brookes.

Sowell, C. (1997). First day of school. *MDA Publications, 4(4),* 1–5. Retrieved from http://www.mdausa.org/publications/Quest/q44first.html.

Spina Bifida Association. (2008a). Real stories: Debbie's story. Retrieved 2008 from http://www.spinabifidaassociation.org/site/c.liKWL7PLLrF/b.2644699/k.92F4/Debbies_Story.htm.

Spina Bifida Association. (2008b). Real stories: Jennifer's story. Retrieved 2008 from http://www.spinabifidaassociation.org/site/c.liKWL7PLLrF/b.2644711/k.93AE/Jennifers_Story.htm.

Spina Bifida Association. (2008c). Real stories: Lavonda's Story. Retrieved 2008 from http://www.spinabifidaassociation.org/site/c.liKWL7PLLrF/b.2644715/k.93F1/Lavondas_Story.htm.

Spina Bifida Association. (2008d). Real stories: Livvie's Story. Retrieved 2008 from http://www.spinabifidaassociation.org/site/c.liKWL7PLLrF/b.2644717/k.99C0/Livvies_Story.htm.

States deny education to children with disabilities. (2000, September/October). *The long and sorry history of discrimination against people with disabilities in the United States—and its likely causes.* Retrieved December 16, 2008, from http://www.ragged-edge-mag.com.

Staub, D. (1998). *Delicate threads: Friendships between children with and without special needs in inclusive settings.* Bethesda, MD: Woodbine House.

Stecker, P. M., Fuchs, D., & Fuchs, L. S. (2008). Progress monitoring as essential practice within response to intervention. *Rural Special Education Quarterly, 27(4),* 10–17.

Steedly, K. M. (2008, February 27). Response to intervention. Retrieved December 30, 2008, from http://www.nichcy.org/Pages/RTI.aspx.

Steege, M. W., Mace, F. C., Perry, L., & Longenecker, H. (2007). Applied behavior analysis: Beyond discrete trial teaching. *Psychology in the Schools, 44(1),* 91–99.

Stensrud, R. (2006). Moral hazards and disenfranchisement: Why do so many kids with disabilities end up going nowhere? *Guidance and Counseling, 21(2),* 97–106.

Stern, V. W., & Wood, M. (2001). *Roadmaps and rampways: Profiles of students with disabilities in science, mathematics, engineering, and technology.* Washington, DC: American Association for the Advancement of Science.

Storch, E. A., Lewin, A. B., Silverstein, J. H., Heldgerken, A. D., Strawser, M. S., Baumeister, A., et al. (2004). Peer victimization and psychosocial adjustment in children with type 1 diabetes. *Journal of Pediatrics, 145,* 784.

Strategies for daily living: FAS/FASD through the lifespan. (2004). Retrieved June 8, 2008, from http://www.nofas.org/living/strategy.aspx.

Strategies for teaching students with motor/orthopedic impairments. (2005). Retrieved June 11, 2008, from http://www.as.wvu.edu/~scidis/motor.html.

Streissguth, A. P. (1997). *Fetal alcohol syndrome: A guide for families and communities.* Baltimore, MD: Paul H. Brookes Publishing Company.

Sullivan, P. M., & Knutson, J. F. (2000). Maltreatment and disabilities: A population-based epidemiological study. *Child Abuse and Neglect, 24*(10), 1257–1273.

Sutherland, A. T. (1981). *Disabled we stand* (pp. 6–16). London: Souvenir Press.

Swaim, K. F., & Morgan, S. B. (2001). Children's attitudes and behavioral intentions toward a peer with autistic behaviors: Does a brief educational intervention have an effect? *Journal of Autism and Developmental Disorders, 31*(2), 195–205.

Taub, D. J. (2006). Understanding the concerns of parents of students with disabilities: Challenges and roles for school counselors. *Professional School Counseling, 10*(1), 52–57.

A teacher's guide to neuromuscular disease. (2005). Tucson, AZ: Muscular Dystrophy Association.

Terpstra, J. E., & Tamura, R. (2008). Effective social interaction strategies for inclusive settings. *Early Childhood Education, 35,* 405–411.

Thompson, D., Whitney, I., & Smith, P. (1994). Bullying of children with special needs in mainstream schools. *Support for Learning, 9,* 103–106.

Thompson, M. (1997). Parent support groups. Retrieved December 31, 2008, from http://www.tsbvi.edu/Outreach/seehear/summer97/parent.html.

U.S. Department of Education. (2001). *Twenty-third annual report to Congress on the implementation of the Individuals with Disabilities Act.* Washington, DC: U.S. Department of Education.

U.S. Department of Education. (2002). *Twenty-fourth annual report to Congress on the implementation of the Individuals with Disabilities Act.* Washington, DC: U.S. Department of Education.

U.S. Department of Health and Human Services, Office of Disability. (n.d.). Substance abuse and disability. Retrieved December 30, 2008, from http://www.hhs.gov.

Unnever, J. D., & Cornell, D. G. (2003). Bullying, self-control, and ADHD. *Journal of Interpersonal Violence, 18,* 129–147.

Van der Klift, E., & Kunc, N. (1994). Beyond benevolence: Friendship and the politics of help. In J. S. Thousand, R. A. Villa & A. Nevin (Eds.), *Creativity and collaborative learning: A practical guide to empowering students and teachers.* Baltimore, MD: Paul H. Brookes.

Vash, C. L. (1981). *The psychology of disability.* New York: Springer Publishing Co.

Vaughn, J. R. (2007). Empowerment for Americans with disabilities: Breaking barriers to careers and full employment. Retrieved October 5, 2008, from http://www.ncd.gov/newsroom/publications/2007/NCDEmployment_20071001.htm.

Virginia Board for People with Disabilities. (2004). *People with disabilities in the United States. 2004 estimates for selected disability categories.* Retrieved December 30, 2008, from http://www.vaboard.org/downloads/USDisabilitiesEstimates.doc.

Vyas, P. (1983). Getting on with it. In A. Turnbull & H. R. Turnbull (Eds.), *Families, professionals and exceptionality.* New York: Macmillan.

Wagner, M. (Ed.). (1993). *The secondary school programs of students with disabilities. A report from the National Longitudinal Transition Study of Special Education Students.* Menlo Park, CA: SRI International.

Wehman, P., & Revell, W. G. (1996). Supported employment from 1986 to 1993: A national program that works. *Focus on Autism and Other Developmental Disabilities, 11*(4), 235–243.

Wehmeyer, M. L. (1992). Self-determination and the education of students with mental retardation. *Education and Training in Mental Retardation and Developmental Disabilities, 27,* 302–314.

Wehmeyer, M. L. (2002). Self-determination and the education of students with disabilities. *ERIC Digest.* Retrieved November 30, 2008, from http://eric.ed.gov/ERICDocs/data/ericdocs2sql/content_storage_01/0000019b/80/1a/84/8a.pdf.

Weicker, L. (1988, July–August). Scaring the monkeys. *Disability Rag, 5.*

Weidenthal, C., & Kochhar-Bryant, C. (2007). An investigation of transition practices for middle school youth. *Career Development for Exceptional Individuals, 30*(3), 147–157.

Wells, T., Sandefur, G. D., & Hogan, D. P. (2003). What happens after the high school years among young persons with disabilities? *Social Forces, 82*(2), 803–832.

Wenz-Gross, M., & Siperstein, G. N. (1998). Students with learning problems at risk in middle school: Stress, social support, and adjustment. *Exceptional Children, 65*(1), 91–100.

Werner, E. E. (1993). Risk, resilience, and recovery: Perspectives from the Kauai longitudinal study. *Development and Psychopathology, 5,* 503–515.

What is a learning disability? (2008). Retrieved July 2009 from http://www.ldonline.org/ldbasics/whatisld.

What is cerebral palsy? (n.d.). Retrieved October 27, 2008, from http://www.ofcp.on.ca/aboutcp.html.

Whidden, E. (2008). Accommodation and compliance series: Employees with cerebral palsy. Retrieved October 27, 2008, from www.jan.wvu.edu/media/CP.html.

Wiegerink, D., Roebroeck, M., Donkervoort, M., Stam, H., & Cohen-Kettenis, P. (2006). Social and sexual relationships of adolescents and young adults with cerebral palsy: A review. *Clinical Rehabilitation, 20,* 1023–1031.

Wisniewski, G. (1981). Interview. In M. D. Orlansky & W. L. Heward (Eds.), *Voices: Interviews with handicapped persons* (pp. 206–210). Columbus, OH: Merrill.

World Health Organization. (n.d.). Prevention of deafness and hearing impairment. Retrieved July 2009, from http://www.who.int/pbd/deafness/en/index.html.

Wright, B. A. (1983a). *Physical disability: A psychosocial approach.* New York: HarperCollins.

Wright, B. A. (1983b). Value changes in acceptance of disability. *Physical disability: A psychosocial approach* (2nd ed., pp. 157–192). New York: HarperCollins.

Yude, C., Goodman, R., & McConachie, H. (1998). Peer problems of children with hemiplegia in mainstream primary schools. *Journal of Child Psychology and Psychiatry, 39,* 533–541.

Ziegler, J. C., Pech-Georgel, C., George, F., Alario, F.-X. & Lorenzi, C. (2005). Deficits in speech perception predict language learning impairment. *Proceedings of the National Academy of Sciences of the United States of America, 102*(39), 14110–14115.

Index

Boscardin, M. I., 123

Boscardin, M. L., 114, 137, 169, 172, 173

Boudousquie, A., 301

Boulware, G. L., 232

Bowen, 305, 306

Boyce, G., 90

Braces, 244; and collaborative relationships, 285–286

Brain Injury Association of America, 306

Bremer, C. D., 185

Brislin, D. C., 301

Brooks, R. B., 156, 157

Brown, D., 53

Brown v. Board of Education of Topeka (1954), 60

Bryant, T., 286

Bullying: Antibullying Oath, 151; and Asperger's syndrome, 168; and disability, reality of (table), 148; Kids Against Bullying Web site, 148, 161; levels/types/examples (table), 149; and middle school/junior high school transition, 103; National Center for Bullying Prevention, 148; New Jersey Cares About Bullying program, 147; Olweus Bullying Prevention Program (OBPP), 147; PACER Center, 148; and social rejection, 147–150; Stop Bullying Now Web site, 147

Burgess, D. M., 266, 268, 269, 270

Burkin, C., 206

Burmeister, R., 301

Burstein, K., 286

Burton, B. A., 205, 206

Bush, G. H. W., 58, 80

C

CABF (Child and Adolescent Bipolar Foundation), 238

Calabro, T., 118, 171, 182, 185

Campbell, J. M., 146

Canadian Society of Allergy and Clinical Immunology, 223

Cancer, 239–242; academic applications, 241; American Cancer Society, 242; Association of Cancer Online Resources, 242; career applications, 241; chemotherapy, effects of, 239; general background information about, 239; Oncology Nurse's Patient Guide, 242; Outlook: Life Beyond Childhood Cancer, 242; personal applications, 240; resources, 242; social applications, 240–241; student/parental wishes about teacher/counselor knowledge about, 239–240; treatment, 239

Canes, 44

Caplan, R., 290, 291

Capo, L. C., 206

Career assessment instruments, 198–199

Career development, 190–200, *See also* Students' career planning needs

Career planning needs of students, 189–209, 205–206, *See also* Postsecondary education, transition to; career development, 190–200; Centers for Independent Living (CILs), 202–203; Connecting-to-Success program, 198; Disability Employment Mentoring Day (DMD), 198; expansive realism, 195–196; mentoring, 197–198; role models, 197–198; students with disabilities and the ADA, 204–205; supported employment, 205–206; transition planning, 200–203; transition to postsecondary education, 206–209; transition to work after high school ends, 204–206; vocational rehabilitation services (VRS), 201–203; work, intangible benefits of, 209

Caregivers, partnering with, 92–98

Carpenter, S., 93

Carter, J. K., 183

Casteel, C., 183

Centers for Disease Control and Prevention, on intellectual disability, 279

National Diabetes Education Program, 251

National Dissemination Center for Children with Disabilities (NICHY), 194, 233, 251, 252, 253, 254, 288, 292–293, 294, 295, 298, 307

National Education Association, 76

National Institute of Arthritis and Musculoskeletal and Skin Diseases, 288

National Institute of Mental Health, 233

National Institute of Neurological Disorders and Stroke, 306

National Institute on Deafness and Other Communication Disorders, 252

National Model for School Counseling programs, 48

National Organization on Fetal Alcohol Syndrome, 270

Natural supports, encouraging, 135

NDRN (National Disability Rights Network), 288, 292–293, 307

Needs, amplified, 14–15

Neel, R. S., 204

Negative academic self-concepts, 116–118; development of skills for improving learning, 116–117; relevance of school/school activities to life, 117; school personnel's perception of students' future success, 116

NEI (National Eye Institute), 312

Neihart, M., 119, 120, 121

Nelson, M., 134

Neville, B. G., 290, 292

New Jersey Cares About Bullying program, 147

Newhouse, P. A., 174

NICHCY, See National Dissemination Center for Children with Disabilities (NICHY)

Nicpon, M. F., 118, 119

NIDCD Directory, 260

NIDCD (National Institute on Deafness and Other Communication Disorders), 298

nidcd.nih.gov, 294, 295, 296

nidch.nih.gov, 297

Nitkin, K., 118, 120

nlm.nih.gov, 297, 298

No Child Left Behind Act (NCLB), 60; and IDEA, 80

Nonverbal, 296–297

Nonverbal learning disabilities, 273

Nowicki, E. A., 142

O

Obsessive compulsive disorder (OCD), 225

Ochs, E., 146

ODD/CD, See Oppositional defiant disorder/conduct disorder (ODD/CD)

Olenchak, R., 121

Olkin, 38

Olkin, R., 173

Olsen, R. J., 176

Olweus Bullying Prevention Program (OBPP), 147

Omizo, M. M., 140

Omizo, S. A., 140

Oncology Nurse's Patient Guide, 242

One of the Gang, 197

Ontario Canada Peel District School Board, 49

Open-head injuries, 303–304

Opening Doors to Postsecondary Education and Training: Planning for Life After High School (George Washington Heath Resource Center), 209

Oppositional defiant disorder/conduct disorder (ODD/CD): AACAP (American Academy of Child and Adolescent Psychiatry), 283; academic applications, 282–283; Behavioral Neurotherapy Clinic, 283; career applications, 283; defined, 280; general background information about, 280–281; personal applications, 282; resources, 283; social applications, 282; student/parental wishes about

Sanchez-Carpintero, R., 290, 292
Sandall, S. R., 232
Sandstrom, K., 243, 245, 246
Sankar, R., 290, 291
Savage, R. C., 303, 304
"Saving" the student, 40
Scarborough, J. L., 10, 56
Schatz, D., 261, 262
Schenker, R., 243, 246
Schick, B., 252
Schloss, P., 185
School bus: bullying on, 161; and social integration, 160–161
School counseling advisory council, 53
School counseling programs, 47–56; ableism, 50–52; accountability, 53; delivery system, 52; foundational beliefs, 48–49; inclusion, 49–50; management, 52–53; sameness compared to fairness, 50; systemic advocacy, 55–56; targeted advocacy, 54–55; from theory to practice, 53–54
School counselor: addressing the needs of parents/teachers/students, 13–14; advocating for genuine inclusion, role in, 9; amplified needs, 14–15; changes in role of, 59; developmental needs of students with disabilities, 7; establishing trust with parents, 98; natural supports, encouraging, 135; negative attitude in counselor-parent relationship, 98; power dynamic with parents, 98; professional distance, 98; resilience, fostering, 13–14; responsibilities, and legislation, 63–73; role of, 6–15; serving as a liaison between school and home, 135
School disengagement/dropping out, and high school transition, 104
School transitions, See Critical school transitions
Schuler, A., 205, 206
Schwartz, I. S., 232
Schwarz, P., 125, 139

Scooters, 244; and school environment, 262
Section 504 and 504 plans, 59, 78–79, 95, 207–208, 213, 225, 235; IEP and 504 plan comparison, 78–79
Seizures, 289–293; academic applications, 291–292; career applications, 292; controlling, 290; defined, 289; Epilepsy Foundation, 292–293; general background information about, 289; National Dissemination Center for Children with Disabilities (NICHY), 292–293; NDRN (National Disability Rights Network), 292–293; personal applications, 291; resources, 292–293; social applications, 291; student/parental wishes about teacher/counselor knowledge about, 290–291
Selective mutism, 296
Self-acceptance, 168
Self-advocacy, 176–178; modeling, 122
Self-concept, and resiliency, 156–157
Self-determination, 176–178, 199
Self-esteem: and elementary school transition, 100; and identity, 169
Self-fulfilling prophecies about, 33–34
Seligman, M., 87, 88, 89, 169, 192
Sensorineural hearing loss, 256
Separation anxiety, 224
Seven Habits of Highly Effective People, The (Covey), 122
Sexual abuse, 183
Sexuality issues, 174–176
Seybold, R. A., 234, 247
Sferrazza, M. S., 10, 56
Shaw, S., 229, 284
Shen, J., 290, 291
Shields, W. D., 290, 291
Siddarth, P., 290, 291
Siddiqi, S. U., 174
Siller, J., 42
Simpson, D. E., 58
Simpson, R. L., 229
Singh, V., 176